Machine Learning Approach for Cloud Data Analytics in IoT

Scrivener Publishing
100 Cummings Center, Suite 541J
Beverly, MA 01915-6106

Publishers at Scrivener
Martin Scrivener (martin@scrivenerpublishing.com)
Phillip Carmical (pcarmical@scrivenerpublishing.com)

Machine Learning Approach for Cloud Data Analytics in IoT

Edited by

Sachi Nandan Mohanty
Jyotir Moy Chatterjee
Monika Mangla
Suneeta Satpathy
Sirisha Potluri

Scrivener
Publishing

This edition first published 2021 by John Wiley & Sons, Inc., 111 River Street, Hoboken, NJ 07030, USA and Scrivener Publishing LLC, 100 Cummings Center, Suite 541J, Beverly, MA 01915, USA
© 2021 Scrivener Publishing LLC
For more information about Scrivener publications please visit www.scrivenerpublishing.com.

Wiley Global Headquarters
111 River Street, Hoboken, NJ 07030, USA

For details of our global editorial offices, customer services, and more information about Wiley products visit us at www.wiley.com.

Limit of Liability/Disclaimer of Warranty
While the publisher and authors have used their best efforts in preparing this work, they make no representations or warranties with respect to the accuracy or completeness of the contents of this work and specifically disclaim all warranties, including without limitation any implied warranties of merchantability or fitness for a particular purpose. No warranty may be created or extended by sales representatives, written sales materials, or promotional statements for this work. The fact that an organization, website, or product is referred to in this work as a citation and/or potential source of further information does not mean that the publisher and authors endorse the information or services the organization, website, or product may provide or recommendations it may make. This work is sold with the understanding that the publisher is not engaged in rendering professional services. The advice and strategies contained herein may not be suitable for your situation. You should consult with a specialist where appropriate. Neither the publisher nor authors shall be liable for any loss of profit or any other commercial damages, including but not limited to special, incidental, consequential, or other damages. Further, readers should be aware that websites listed in this work may have changed or disappeared between when this work was written and when it is read.

Library of Congress Cataloging-in-Publication Data

ISBN 978-1-119-78580-4

Cover image: Pixabay.Com
Cover design by Russell Richardson

Contents

Preface   xix

Acknowledgment   xxiii

1   Machine Learning–Based Data Analysis   1
    M. Deepika and K. Kalaiselvi
    1.1   Introduction   1
    1.2   Machine Learning for the Internet of Things Using Data Analysis   4
          1.2.1   Computing Framework   6
          1.2.2   Fog Computing   6
          1.2.3   Edge Computing   6
          1.2.4   Cloud Computing   7
          1.2.5   Distributed Computing   7
    1.3   Machine Learning Applied to Data Analysis   7
          1.3.1   Supervised Learning Systems   8
          1.3.2   Decision Trees   9
          1.3.3   Decision Tree Types   9
          1.3.4   Unsupervised Machine Learning   10
          1.3.5   Association Rule Learning   10
          1.3.6   Reinforcement Learning   10
    1.4   Practical Issues in Machine Learning   11
    1.5   Data Acquisition   12
    1.6   Understanding the Data Formats Used in Data Analysis
          Applications   13
    1.7   Data Cleaning   14
    1.8   Data Visualization   15
    1.9   Understanding the Data Analysis
          Problem-Solving Approach   15
    1.10 Visualizing Data to Enhance Understanding and Using
          Neural Networks in Data Analysis   16
    1.11 Statistical Data Analysis Techniques   17

	1.11.1	Hypothesis Testing	18
	1.11.2	Regression Analysis	18
1.12		Text Analysis and Visual and Audio Analysis	18
1.13		Mathematical and Parallel Techniques for Data Analysis	19
	1.13.1	Using Map-Reduce	20
	1.13.2	Leaning Analysis	20
	1.13.3	Market Basket Analysis	21
1.14		Conclusion	21
		References	22
2		**Machine Learning for Cyber-Immune IoT Applications**	**25**
		Suchismita Sahoo and Sushree Sangita Sahoo	
2.1		Introduction	25
2.2		Some Associated Impactful Terms	27
	2.2.1	IoT	27
	2.2.2	IoT Device	28
	2.2.3	IoT Service	29
	2.2.4	Internet Security	29
	2.2.5	Data Security	30
	2.2.6	Cyberthreats	31
	2.2.7	Cyber Attack	31
	2.2.8	Malware	32
	2.2.9	Phishing	32
	2.2.10	Ransomware	33
	2.2.11	Spear-Phishing	33
	2.2.12	Spyware	34
	2.2.13	Cybercrime	34
	2.2.14	IoT Cyber Security	35
	2.2.15	IP Address	36
2.3		Cloud Rationality Representation	36
	2.3.1	Cloud	36
	2.3.2	Cloud Data	37
	2.3.3	Cloud Security	38
	2.3.4	Cloud Computing	38
2.4		Integration of IoT With Cloud	40
2.5		The Concepts That Rules Over	41
	2.5.1	Artificial Intelligent	41
	2.5.2	Overview of Machine Learning	41
		2.5.2.1 Supervised Learning	41
		2.5.2.2 Unsupervised Learning	42
	2.5.3	Applications of Machine Learning in Cyber Security	43

2.5.4 Applications of Machine Learning in Cybercrime 43
2.5.5 Adherence of Machine Learning With Cyber
Security in Relevance to IoT 43
2.5.6 Distributed Denial-of-Service 44
2.6 Related Work 45
2.7 Methodology 46
2.8 Discussions and Implications 48
2.9 Conclusion 49
References 49

3 **Employing Machine Learning Approaches for Predictive Data Analytics in Retail Industry** 53
Rakhi Akhare, Sanjivani Deokar, Monika Mangla
and Hardik Deshmukh
3.1 Introduction 53
3.2 Related Work 55
3.3 Predictive Data Analytics in Retail 56
3.3.1 ML for Predictive Data Analytics 58
3.3.2 Use Cases 59
3.3.3 Limitations and Challenges 61
3.4 Proposed Model 61
3.4.1 Case Study 63
3.5 Conclusion and Future Scope 68
References 69

4 **Emerging Cloud Computing Trends for Business Transformation** 71
Prasanta Kumar Mahapatra, Alok Ranjan Tripathy
and Alakananda Tripathy
4.1 Introduction 71
4.1.1 Computing Definition Cloud 72
4.1.2 Advantages of Cloud Computing Over On-Premises
IT Operation 73
4.1.3 Limitations of Cloud Computing 74
4.2 History of Cloud Computing 74
4.3 Core Attributes of Cloud Computing 75
4.4 Cloud Computing Models 77
4.4.1 Cloud Deployment Model 77
4.4.2 Cloud Service Model 79
4.5 Core Components of Cloud Computing Architecture:
Hardware and Software 83
4.6 Factors Need to Consider for Cloud Adoption 84

	4.6.1	Evaluating Cloud Infrastructure	84
	4.6.2	Evaluating Cloud Provider	85
	4.6.3	Evaluating Cloud Security	86
	4.6.4	Evaluating Cloud Services	86
	4.6.5	Evaluating Cloud Service Level Agreements (SLA)	87
	4.6.6	Limitations to Cloud Adoption	87
4.7	Transforming Business Through Cloud		88
4.8	Key Emerging Trends in Cloud Computing		89
	4.8.1	Technology Trends	90
	4.8.2	Business Models	92
	4.8.3	Product Transformation	92
	4.8.4	Customer Engagement	92
	4.8.5	Employee Empowerment	93
	4.8.6	Data Management and Assurance	93
	4.8.7	Digitalization	93
	4.8.8	Building Intelligence Cloud System	93
	4.8.9	Creating Hyper-Converged Infrastructure	94
4.9	Case Study: Moving Data Warehouse to Cloud Boosts Performance for Johnson & Johnson		94
4.10	Conclusion		95
	References		96

5 Security of Sensitive Data in Cloud Computing 99

Kirti Wanjale, Monika Mangla and Paritosh Marathe

5.1	Introduction		100
	5.1.1	Characteristics of Cloud Computing	100
	5.1.2	Deployment Models for Cloud Services	101
	5.1.3	Types of Cloud Delivery Models	102
5.2	Data in Cloud		102
	5.2.1	Data Life Cycle	103
5.3	Security Challenges in Cloud Computing for Data		105
	5.3.1	Security Challenges Related to Data at Rest	106
	5.3.2	Security Challenges Related to Data in Use	107
	5.3.3	Security Challenges Related to Data in Transit	107
5.4	Cross-Cutting Issues Related to Network in Cloud		108
5.5	Protection of Data		109
5.6	Tighter IAM Controls		114
5.7	Conclusion and Future Scope		117
	References		117

6   Cloud Cryptography for Cloud Data Analytics in IoT   **119**
N. Jayashri and K. Kalaiselvi

6.1   Introduction   120
6.2   Cloud Computing Software Security Fundamentals   120
6.3   Security Management   122
6.4   Cryptography Algorithms   123
    6.4.1   Types of Cryptography   123
6.5   Secure Communications   127
6.6   Identity Management and Access Control   133
6.7   Autonomic Security   137
6.8   Conclusion   139
    References   139

**7   Issues and Challenges of Classical Cryptography in Cloud
    Computing**   **143**
Amrutanshu Panigrahi, Ajit Kumar Nayak and Rourab Paul

7.1   Introduction   144
    7.1.1   Problem Statement and Motivation   145
    7.1.2   Contribution   146
7.2   Cryptography   146
    7.2.1   Cryptography Classification   147
        7.2.1.1   Classical Cryptography   147
        7.2.1.2   Homomorphic Encryption   149
7.3   Security in Cloud Computing   150
    7.3.1   The Need for Security in Cloud Computing   151
    7.3.2   Challenges in Cloud Computing Security   152
    7.3.3   Benefits of Cloud Computing Security   153
    7.3.4   Literature Survey   154
7.4   Classical Cryptography for Cloud Computing   157
    7.4.1   RSA   157
    7.4.2   AES   157
    7.4.3   DES   158
    7.4.4   Blowfish   158
7.5   Homomorphic Cryptosystem   158
    7.5.1   Paillier Cryptosystem   159
        7.5.1.1   Additive Homomorphic Property   159
    7.5.2   RSA Homomorphic Cryptosystem   160
        7.5.2.1   Multiplicative Homomorphic Property   160

7.6	Implementation	160
7.7	Conclusion and Future Scope	162
	References	162

8 Cloud-Based Data Analytics for Monitoring Smart Environments 167
D. Karthika

8.1	Introduction	167
8.2	Environmental Monitoring for Smart Buildings	169
	8.2.1　Smart Environments	169
8.3	Smart Health	171
	8.3.1　Description of Solutions in General	171
	8.3.2　Detection of Distress	172
	8.3.3　Green Protection	173
	8.3.4　Medical Preventive/Help	174
8.4	Digital Network 5G and Broadband Networks	174
	8.4.1　IoT-Based Smart Grid Technologies	174
8.5	Emergent Smart Cities Communication Networks	175
	8.5.1　RFID Technologies	177
	8.5.2　Identifier Schemes	177
8.6	Smart City IoT Platforms Analysis System	177
8.7	Smart Management of Car Parking in Smart Cities	178
8.8	Smart City Systems and Services Securing: A Risk-Based Analytical Approach	178
8.9	Virtual Integrated Storage System	179
8.10	Convolutional Neural Network (CNN)	181
	8.10.1　IEEE 802.15.4	182
	8.10.2　BLE	182
	8.10.3　ITU-T G.9959 (Z-Wave)	183
	8.10.4　NFC	183
	8.10.5　LoRaWAN	184
	8.10.6　Sigfox	184
	8.10.7　NB-IoT	184
	8.10.8　PLC	184
	8.10.9　MS/TP	184
8.11	Challenges and Issues	185
	8.11.1　Interoperability and Standardization	185
	8.11.2　Customization and Adaptation	186
	8.11.3　Entity Identification and Virtualization	187
	8.11.4　Big Data Issue in Smart Environments	187
8.12	Future Trends and Research Directions in Big Data Platforms for the Internet of Things	188

8.13   Case Study   189
8.14   Conclusion   191
         References   191

**9   Performance Metrics for Comparison of Heuristics Task
     Scheduling Algorithms in Cloud Computing Platform   195**
     Nidhi Rajak and Ranjit Rajak
9.1   Introduction   195
9.2   Workflow Model   197
9.3   System Computing Model   198
9.4   Major Objective of Scheduling   198
9.5   Task Computational Attributes for Scheduling   198
9.6   Performance Metrics   200
9.7   Heuristic Task Scheduling Algorithms   201
         9.7.1   Heterogeneous Earliest Finish Time (HEFT) Algorithm   202
         9.7.2   Critical-Path-on-a-Processor (CPOP) Algorithm   208
         9.7.3   As Late As Possible (ALAP) Algorithm   213
         9.7.4   Performance Effective Task Scheduling (PETS)
                   Algorithm   217
9.8   Performance Analysis and Results   220
9.9   Conclusion   224
         References   224

**10 Smart Environment Monitoring Models Using Cloud-Based
     Data Analytics: A Comprehensive Study   227**
     Pradnya S. Borkar and Reena Thakur
10.1   Introduction   228
         10.1.1   Internet of Things   229
         10.1.2   Cloud Computing   230
         10.1.3   Environmental Monitoring   232
10.2   Background and Motivation   234
         10.2.1   Challenges and Issues   234
         10.2.2   Technologies Used for Designing Cloud-Based
                   Data Analytics   240
                   10.2.2.1   Communication Technologies   241
         10.2.3   Cloud-Based Data Analysis Techniques and Models   243
                   10.2.3.1   MapReduce for Data Analysis   243
                   10.2.3.2   Data Analysis Workflows   246
                   10.2.3.3   NoSQL Models   247
         10.2.4   Data Mining Techniques   248
         10.2.5   Machine Learning   251

          10.2.5.1   Significant Importance of Machine
                        Learning and Its Algorithms   253

     10.2.6 Applications   253

10.3   Conclusion   261

     References   262

11 Advancement of Machine Learning and Cloud Computing in the Field of Smart Health Care   273

Aradhana Behura, Shibani Sahu and Manas Ranjan Kabat

11.1   Introduction   274

11.2   Survey on Architectural WBAN   278

11.3   Suggested Strategies   280

     11.3.1 System Overview   280

     11.3.2 Motivation   281

     11.3.3 DSCB Protocol   281

          11.3.3.1   Network Topology   282

          11.3.3.2   Starting Stage   282

          11.3.3.3   Cluster Evolution   282

          11.3.3.4   Sensed Information Stage   283

          11.3.3.5   Choice of Forwarder Stage   283

          11.3.3.6   Energy Consumption as Well as
                        Routing Stage   285

11.4   CNN-Based Image Segmentation (UNet Model)   287

11.5   Emerging Trends in IoT Healthcare   290

11.6   Tier Health IoT Model   294

11.7   Role of IoT in Big Data Analytics   294

11.8   Tier Wireless Body Area Network Architecture   296

11.9   Conclusion   303

     References   303

12 Study on Green Cloud Computing—A Review   307

Meenal Agrawal and Ankita Jain

12.1   Introduction   307

12.2   Cloud Computing   308

     12.2.1 Cloud Computing: On-Request
                Outsourcing-Pay-as-You-Go   308

12.3   Features of Cloud Computing   309

12.4   Green Computing   309

12.5   Green Cloud Computing   309

12.6   Models of Cloud Computing   310

12.7	Models of Cloud Services	310
12.8	Cloud Deployment Models	311
12.9	Green Cloud Architecture	312
12.10	Cloud Service Providers	312
12.11	Features of Green Cloud Computing	313
12.12	Advantages of Green Cloud Computing	313
12.13	Limitations of Green Cloud Computing	314
12.14	Cloud and Sustainability Environmental	315
12.15	Statistics Related to Cloud Data Centers	315
12.16	The Impact of Data Centers on Environment	315
12.17	Virtualization Technologies	316
12.18	Literature Review	316
12.19	The Main Objective	318
12.20	Research Gap	319
12.21	Research Methodology	319
12.22	Conclusion and Suggestions	320
12.23	Scope for Further Research	320
	References	321

13 Intelligent Reclamation of Plantae Affliction Disease   **323**
Reshma Banu, G.F Ali Ahammed and Ayesha Taranum

13.1	Introduction	324
13.2	Existing System	327
13.3	Proposed System	327
13.4	Objectives of the Concept	328
13.5	Operational Requirements	328
13.6	Non-Operational Requirements	329
13.7	Depiction Design Description	330
13.8	System Architecture	330
	13.8.1 Module Characteristics	331
	13.8.2 Convolutional Neural System	332
	13.8.3 User Application	332
13.9	Design Diagrams	333
	13.9.1 High-Level Design	333
	13.9.2 Low-Level Design	333
	13.9.3 Test Cases	335
13.10	Comparison and Screenshot	335
13.11	Conclusion	342
	References	342

14 Prediction of Stock Market Using Machine Learning–Based Data Analytics 347

Maheswari P. and Jaya A.

14.1 Introduction of Stock Market 348
    14.1.1 Impact of Stock Prices 349
14.2 Related Works 350
14.3 Financial Prediction Systems Framework 352
    14.3.1 Conceptual Financial Prediction Systems 352
    14.3.2 Framework of Financial Prediction Systems Using Machine Learning 353
        14.3.2.1 Algorithm to Predicting the Closing Price of the Given Stock Data Using Linear Regression 355
    14.3.3 Framework of Financial Prediction Systems Using Deep Learning 355
        14.3.3.1 Algorithm to Predict the Closing Price of the Given Stock Using Long Short-Term Memory 356
14.4 Implementation and Discussion of Result 357
    14.4.1 Pharmaceutical Sector 357
        14.4.1.1 Cipla Limited 357
        14.4.1.2 Torrent Pharmaceuticals Limited 359
    14.4.2 Banking Sector 359
        14.4.2.1 ICICI Bank 359
        14.4.2.2 State Bank of India 359
    14.4.3 Fast-Moving Consumer Goods Sector 362
        14.4.3.1 ITC 363
        14.4.3.2 Hindustan Unilever Limited 363
    14.4.4 Power Sector 363
        14.4.4.1 Adani Power Limited 363
        14.4.4.2 Power Grid Corporation of India Limited 364
    14.4.5 Automobiles Sector 368
        14.4.5.1 Mahindra & Mahindra Limited 368
        14.4.5.2 Maruti Suzuki India Limited 368
    14.4.6 Comparison of Prediction Using Linear Regression Model and Long-Short-Term Memory Model 368
14.5 Conclusion 371
    14.5.1 Future Enhancement 372
    References 372
    Web Citations 373

15 Pehchaan: Analysis of the 'Aadhar Dataset' to Facilitate
   a Smooth and Efficient Conduct of the Upcoming NPR   375
   Soumyadev Mukherjee, Harshit Anand, Nishan Acharya,
   Subham Char, Pritam Ghosh and Minakhi Rout
   15.1   Introduction   376
   15.2   Basic Concepts   377
   15.3   Study of Literature Survey and Technology   380
   15.4   Proposed Model   381
   15.5   Implementation and Results   383
   15.6   Conclusion   389
          References   389

16 Deep Learning Approach for Resource Optimization in
   Blockchain, Cellular Networks, and IoT: Open Challenges
   and Current Solutions   391
   Upinder Kaur and Shalu
   16.1   Introduction   392
          16.1.1   Aim   393
          16.1.2   Research Contribution   395
          16.1.3   Organization   396
   16.2   Background   396
          16.2.1   Blockchain   397
          16.2.2   Internet of Things (IoT)   398
          16.2.3   5G Future Generation Cellular Networks   398
          16.2.4   Machine Learning and Deep Learning Techniques   399
          16.2.5   Deep Reinforcement Learning   399
   16.3   Deep Learning for Resource Management in Blockchain,
          Cellular, and IoT Networks   401
          16.3.1   Resource Management in Blockchain for 5G
                   Cellular Networks   402
          16.3.2   Deep Learning Blockchain Application
                   for Resource Management in IoT Networks   402
   16.4   Future Research Challenges   413
          16.4.1   Blockchain Technology   413
                   16.4.1.1   Scalability   414
                   16.4.1.2   Efficient Consensus Protocols   415
                   16.4.1.3   Lack of Skills and Experts   415
          16.4.2   IoT Networks   416
                   16.4.2.1   Heterogeneity of IoT and 5G Data   416
                   16.4.2.2   Scalability Issues   416
                   16.4.2.3   Security and Privacy Issues   416

16.4.3   5G Future Generation Networks   416
    16.4.3.1   Heterogeneity   416
    16.4.3.2   Security and Privacy   417
    16.4.3.3   Resource Utilization   417
16.4.4   Machine Learning and Deep Learning   417
    16.4.4.1   Interpretability   418
    16.4.4.2   Training Cost for ML and DRL
                Techniques   418
    16.4.4.3   Lack of Availability of Data Sets   418
    16.4.4.4   Avalanche Effect for DRL Approach   419
16.4.5   General Issues   419
    16.4.5.1   Security and Privacy Issues   419
    16.4.5.2   Storage   419
    16.4.5.3   Reliability   420
    16.4.5.4   Multitasking Approach   420
16.5   Conclusion and Discussion   420
        References   422

17 Unsupervised Learning in Accordance With New Aspects
    of Artificial Intelligence   429
    Riya Sharma, Komal Saxena and Ajay Rana
    17.1   Introduction   430
    17.2   Applications of Machine Learning in Data Management
            Possibilities   431
        17.2.1   Terminology of Basic Machine Learning   432
        17.2.2   Rules Based on Machine Learning   434
        17.2.3   Unsupervised vs. Supervised Methodology   434
    17.3   Solutions to Improve Unsupervised Learning Using
            Machine Learning   436
        17.3.1   Insufficiency of Labeled Data   436
        17.3.2   Overfitting   437
        17.3.3   A Closer Look Into Unsupervised Algorithms   437
            17.3.3.1   Reducing Dimensionally   437
            17.3.3.2   Principal Component Analysis   438
        17.3.4   Singular Value Decomposition (SVD)   439
            17.3.4.1   Random Projection   439
            17.3.4.2   Isomax   439
        17.3.5   Dictionary Learning   439
        17.3.6   The Latent Dirichlet Allocation   440
    17.4   Open Source Platform for Cutting Edge Unsupervised
            Machine Learning   440

17.4.1   TensorFlow   441
17.4.2   Keras   441
17.4.3   Scikit-Learn   441
17.4.4   Microsoft Cognitive Toolkit   442
17.4.5   Theano   442
17.4.6   Caffe   442
17.4.7   Torch   442
17.5   Applications of Unsupervised Learning   443
17.5.1   Regulation of Digital Data   443
17.5.2   Machine Learning in Voice Assistance   443
17.5.3   For Effective Marketing   444
17.5.4   Advancement of Cyber Security   444
17.5.5   Faster Computing Power   444
17.5.6   The Endnote   445
17.6   Applications Using Machine Learning Algos   445
17.6.1   Linear Regression   445
17.6.2   Logistic Regression   446
17.6.3   Decision Tree   446
17.6.4   Support Vector Machine (SVM)   446
17.6.5   Naive Bayes   446
17.6.6   K-Nearest Neighbors   447
17.6.7   K-Means   447
17.6.8   Random Forest   447
17.6.9   Dimensionality Reduction Algorithms   448
17.6.10 Gradient Boosting Algorithms   448
References   449

18   **Predictive Modeling of Anthropomorphic Gamifying
     Blockchain-Enabled Transitional Healthcare System**   **461**
     *Deepa Kumari, B.S.A.S. Rajita, Medindrao Raja Sekhar,
     Ritika Garg and Subhrakanta Panda*
18.1   Introduction   462
18.1.1   Transitional Healthcare Services and
         Their Challenges   462
18.2   Gamification in Transitional Healthcare: A New Model 463
18.2.1   Anthropomorphic Interface With Gamification   464
18.2.2   Gamification in Blockchain   465
18.2.3   Anthropomorphic Gamification in Blockchain:
         Motivational Factors   466
18.3   Existing Related Work   468
18.4   The Framework   478

18.4.1 Health Player 479
18.4.2 Data Collection 480
18.4.3 Anthropomorphic Gamification Layers 480
18.4.4 Ethereum 480
18.4.4.1 Ethereum-Based Smart Contracts for Healthcare 481
18.4.4.2 Installation of Ethereum Smart Contract 481
18.4.5 Reward Model 482
18.4.6 Predictive Models 482
18.5 Implementation 483
18.5.1 Methodology 483
18.5.2 Result Analysis 484
18.5.3 Threats to the Validity 486
18.6 Conclusion 487
References 487

Index **491**

Preface

Sustainable computing paradigms like cloud and fog are capable of handling issues related to performance, storage and processing, maintenance, security, efficiency, integration, cost, energy and latency in an expeditious manner. According to statistics, billions of connected IoT devices will be producing enormous amounts of real-time data in the coming days. In order to expedite decision-making involved in the complex computation and processing of collected data, these devices are connected to the cloud or fog environment. Since machine learning as a service provides the best support in business intelligence, organizations have been making significant investments in the creation of the first artificial intelligence services. The abundant research occurring all around the world has resulted in a wide range of advancements being reported on computing platforms. This book elucidates some of the best practices and their respective outcomes in cloud and fog computing environments. The practices, technologies and innovations of business intelligence employed to make expeditious decisions are encouraged as a part of this area of research.

This book focuses on various research issues related to big data storage and analysis, large-scale data processing, knowledge discovery and knowledge management, computational intelligence, data security and privacy, data representation and visualization and data analytics. The featured technology presented herein optimizes various industry processes using business intelligence in engineering and technology. Light is also shed on cloud-based embedded software development practices to integrate complex machines so as to increase productivity and reduce operational cost. The various practices of data science and analytics which are used in all sectors to understand big data and analyze massive data patterns are also essential sections of this book.

Chapter 1 focuses on the use of large amounts of information that enable a computer to carry out a non-definitive analysis based on project understanding. Chapter 2 explains an approach to establish an interactive network of cognitively intervening domains of cyber security services to the computational specifications of the Internet of Things (IoT). Various approaches for predictive data analytics are briefly introduced in Chapter 3; and Chapter 4 covers details of cloud evolution, adaptability and key emerging trends of cloud computing. Chapter 5 discusses the security challenges as well as methods used for tackling those challenges along with their respective advantages and disadvantages for protecting data when using cloud storage. Chapter 6 methodically audits the security needs, the assault vectors and the current security responses for IoT systems and also addresses insights into current machine learning solutions for solving various security issues in IoT systems and a few future cryptographic cloud analysis headlines. In Chapter 7, the RSA algorithm is implemented as homomorphic encryption and the authors attempt to reduce its time complexity by implementing the homomorphism RSA. Chapter 8 discusses the challenges of using smart city technology and IoT networks via CR and EH technologies. In Chapter 9, a study of the four well-known heuristic task scheduling algorithms of HEFT, CPOP, ALAP and PETS is presented along with their comparative study based on performance metrics such as schedule length, speedup, efficiency, resource utilization and cost. Chapter 10 overviews the potential applications of cloud computing in smart working systems and case studies; and a study is presented in Chapter 11 on the dual sink approach using clustering in body area network (DSCB). Chapter 12 reviews the comprehensive literature on green cloud computing and exposes the research gaps in this field that have a lot of research potential for future exploration. In Chapter 13, a system is proposed which identifies the disease, classifies it, and responds according to the type of disease identified and also describes the preventive measures using deep learning. Chapter 14 aims to predict the five sectors—the pharmaceutical, banking, fast-moving consumer goods, power and automobile sectors—using linear regression, recurrent neural network (RNN) and long short-term memory (LSTM) units. Chapter 15 analyzes the Aadhaar dataset and draws meaningful insights from the same that will surely ensure a fruitful result and facilitate smoother conduct of the upcoming NPR. Chapter 16 first outlines the current block chain techniques and consortium block chain framework, and after that considers the application of blockchain with cellular 5G network, Big Data, IoT, and mobile edge computing. Chapter 17 shows how various advanced machine learning methods are used for different application in real life scenario. Chapter 18 explores the anthropomorphic gamifying elements, mostly on how it can be implemented in a blockchain-enabled transitional healthcare system in a more lucrative manner.

Sachi Nandan Mohanty, India
Jyotir Moy Chatterjee, Nepal
Monika Mangla, India
SuneetaSatpathy, India
Sirisha Potluri, India
May 2021

Acknowledgment

The editors would like to pass on our good wishes and express our appreciation to all the authors who contributed chapters to this book. We would also like to thank the subject matter experts who found time to review the chapters and deliver their comments in a timely manner. Special thanks also go to those who took the time to give advice and make suggestions that helped refine our thoughts and approaches accordingly to produce richer contributions. We are particularly grateful to Scrivener Publishing for their amazing crew who supported us with their encouragement, engagement, support, cooperation and contributions in publishing this book.

1

Machine Learning–Based Data Analysis

M. Deepika[1]* and K. Kalaiselvi[2]

*[1]Department of Computer Science, School of Computing Sciences, Vels Institute
of Science, Technology and Advanced Studies (Formerly Vels University),
Chennai, Tamil Nadu, India
[2]Department of Computer Applications, School of Computing Sciences, Vels
Institute of Science, Technology and Advanced Studies (Formerly Vels University),
Chennai, Tamil Nadu, India*

Abstract

Artificial intelligence (AI) is a technical mix, and machine learning (ML) is one of
the most important techniques in highly personalized marketing. AI ML presup-
poses that the system is re-assessed and the data is reassessed without human intervention. It is all about shifting. Just as AI means, for every possible action/reaction,
that a human programmer does not have to code, AI machine programming can
evaluate and test data to replicate every customer product with the speed and capacity that no one can attain. The technology we have been using has been around for a
long time, but the influence of machines, cloud-based services, and the applicability
of AI on our position as marketers have changed in recent years. Different information and data orientation contribute to a variety of technical improvements. This
chapter focuses on the use of large amounts of information that enables a computer to carry out a non-definitive analysis based on project understanding. It also
focuses on data collection and helps to ensure that data analysis is prepared. It also
defines such data analytics processes for prediction and analysis using ML algorithms. Questions related to ML data mining are also clearly explained.

Keywords: Big data, data analysis, machine learning, machine learning algorithms,
neural networks

*Corresponding author: deepika.rbp@gmail.com

Sachi Nandan Mohanty, Jyotir Moy Chatterjee, Monika Mangla, Suneeta Satpathy and Sirisha Potluri
(eds.) Machine Learning Approach for Cloud Data Analytics in IoT, (1–24) © 2021 Scrivener
Publishing LLC

1.1   Introduction

Machine taking into consideration is an immense topic with different extra ordinary serving calculations [1]. It is classically associated with constructing techniques that connect ideas to explore away from being altered to fix a problem. Commonly, a system is trying to repair a sort of problem and later exposed the consumption of system actual factors from the difficult space. In this area, it will deal with two or three general problems and methods used in record analysis. A massive number of these techniques use planned information to demonstrate a model. The data contains an extension of influence factors of the difficult space. At the point when the model is prepared, it tried and reviewed the use of testing data. The model is then used to input information to make requirements.

Machine receiving information is a function of the false cerebrum [artificial intelligence (AI)] that allows structures to these lines take in and improvement from leaving over an except for being customized. Machine leading workplaces on the development of PC functions that can get to assessments and use it study for themselves. The approach of study starts with recognitions of data such as traces and support incorporation in the plan to practice structures in facts and makes a superior decision within the prospect of the cases that offer. The essential factor is to allow the PCs to separate generally other than individual involvement or assist and modify performs appropriately [2]. In any case, utilizing the common assessments of AI, content is measured as a public occasion of sayings. A policy subject to semantic assessment reflects the individual capability to get it the techniques for a material. Figure 1.1 clarifies the data analysis procedure in the machine learning (ML) approach where all the information are collected, developed, stored, and achieved with ML algorithms.

Massive data exists in different spots in recent days. Apparent causes of online databases are those made by strategy for agents to follow customer buys. Resulting dissimilar non-clear bits of information sources and most of the time these non-clear sources give immense forces to achieve something remarkable. Considering turning out as origins of massive records builds PC considering results in which a PC can disconnect in a demonstrated way and nimbly longed for the outcome. By receiving huge actual features together with bits of facts, it can make a figuring machine getting gradually more recognizable with natural aspects in which the work region considers the possibility of some uneven circumstances. All effects measured, articulating that opinions are the in a way PC leading approach is mixed up.

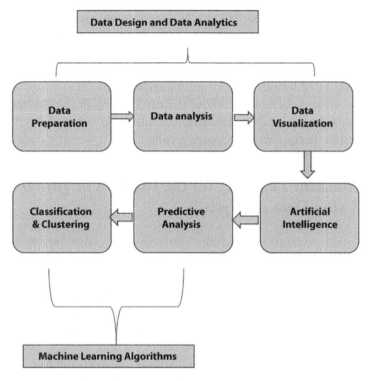

Figure 1.1 Data analysis process.

Because of expanding authentic burden, the credit of excellent things continues succeeding as an essential dominant factor to guarantee about the drawn-out achievement of an organization. Moreover, in creating a personalization view, the amount of diversity and therefore the strange of assessment organizing and deed widen enormously. Business four connects the model toward AI and information varies in gathering growths and techniques including Cyber-Physical Systems, Internet of Things (IoT), and AI. CPS tackles several other methods with composed computational and physical capability that allows the association with persons through new modalities. The IoT is a key facilitate impact for the following time of front line creating, defining the functional examinations of a general concern that reward to achieve physical and essential things by techniques for data and conversation applied analysis.

Distributed processing is consuming the existing forms as it permits on-demand and important to get the region into an enormous group of flexible and configurable registered resources. PC-based facts have severe restrictions in gathering such as, sensible assessment, remarkable evaluation, intense mechanization, and sensors which are in a common intelligence recognized on excessive AI headways. A person of the supreme relevant AI propels is ML, which gives remarkably practicable for the improvement and association of techniques for modernizing things and assembling constitutions. Applying a scientific approach to create formless databases authorized to leave under the careful look of dark systems and rules to distribute new data. This connects the progression of desire structures for data-based and PC-assisted estimation of upcoming results.

1.2   Machine Learning for the Internet of Things Using Data Analysis

Quick enhancements in hardware, programming, and correspondence applied analysis have empowered the ascent of Internet-related unmistakable devices that grant recognitions and records estimations from this present reality. This year, it is assessed that the aggregate sum of Internet-related contraptions being used will be someplace in the scope of 25 and 50 billion. As these numbers create and applied analysis end up progressively significant create, the measure of records being dispersed will increase. The development of Internet-related devices, implied as to the IoTs, continues extending the current Internet with the guide of presenting system and interchanges between the genuine and advanced universes. Despite a copied volume, the IoT makes huge information portrayed by techniques for its pace in articulations of time and zone dependence, with an extent of a few modalities and various estimations quality. Quick getting ready and appraisal of these gigantic truths are the best approach to creating splendid IoT applications.

This part reviews a collection of PCs getting data on procedures that deal with the challenges by strategies for IoT data by considering clever urban networks in the central use case. The key duty of this get some answers concerning is the presentation of a logical arrangement of work region considering computations explaining how different methodologies are utilized to the data to expel higher stage information [3].

Since IoT will be among the most immense wellsprings of new data, estimations analysis will surrender a gigantic responsibility for making IoT applications additional insightful. Data analysis is the mix of exceptional coherent fields that uses records mining, PC learning, and different techniques to find structures and new bits of information from data. These techniques fuse a wide extent of figuring's significant specifically zones. The methodology for using real factors examination techniques to regions joins describing information sorts, for instance, volume, arrangement, and speed; information models, for instance, neural frameworks, request, and clustering methodologies, and using capable computations that strong with the real factor's characteristics [4]. Based on the reviews, first, since records are created from obvious sources with uncommon bits of knowledge types, it is basic to endeavor or lift counts that can manage the characteristics of the real factors. Second, the sensational collection of sources that produce information persistently is no longer without the trouble of scale and speed. Finally, finding the eminent data model that fits the information is the fundamental issue for test thought and higher assessment of IoT data.

The explanation behind this is to develop progressively splendid ecological elements and a smoothed-out lifestyle by saving time, essentialness, and money. Through this development, costs in select organizations can be lessened. The sizeable hypotheses and numerous investigations running on IoT have made IoT a making design of late. IoT includes an associated unit that can move records among one another to update their introduction [5]; these improvements show precisely and besides human thought or information. IoT involves four key parts:

- Sensors,
- Dealing with frameworks,
- Information evaluation data, and
- Machine detecting.

The most recent advances made in IoT began when RFID marks have been put into use even more, as a rule, lower regard sensors got increasingly imperative open, web mechanical aptitude made, and verbal exchange shows balanced. The IoT is worked in with a collection of advances, and the system is an objective and satisfactory condition for it to work. Thus, verbal exchange shows are portions of this mechanical skill that must be updated. Planning and getting ready estimations for these correspondences is a fundamental test. To respond to this test, wonderful sorts of records getting ready, for instance, assessment at the edge, circle examination, and IoT appraisal at the database must be applied. The decision to follow any of the referred to systems depends upon the application and its wants. Murkiness and cloud taking care of our two indicative techniques got for getting ready and planning records before moving it to various things. The entire task of IoT is summarized as follows. First, sensors and IoT units' aggregate records from the earth. Next, data is isolated from the uncooked data. By then, records are set ready for moving to different things, devices, or servers by methods for the Internet [6].

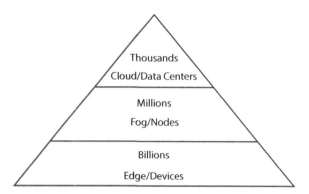

Figure 1.2 Fog computing and edge computing.

1.2.1   Computing Framework

Another imperative portion of IoT is the computing system of handling information, the foremost celebrated of which fog and cloud are computing. IoT applications utilize both systems depending on the application and handle area. In a few applications, information ought to be handled upon the era, whereas in other applications, it is not essential to prepare informatio n quickly. In Figure 1.2, the moment preparing of information and the organization and design that underpins it is known as fog computing. Collectively, these are connected to edge computing.

1.2.2   Fog Computing

The engineering of this computing is associated with relocating data from an information center assignment to the frame of the servers. This is constructed based on the frame servers. Fog computing gives restricted computing, capacity, and organize administrations, moreover giving coherent insights and sifting of information for information centers. This engineering has been and is being executed in imperative ranges like e-health and military applications.

1.2.3   Edge Computing

In this design, handling is run at a separate from the center, toward the edging of the association [6]. This sort of preparing empowers information to be at first handled at edge gadgets. Gadgets at the edge may not be associated with the arranging ceaselessly, and so, they require a duplicate of the ace data/reference information for offline handling. Edge gadgets have diverse highlights such as

- Improving security,
- Examining and cleaning information, and
- Putting away nearby information for region utilization.

1.2.4   Cloud Computing

Here, information for handling is sent to information centers, and after being analyzed and prepared, they ended up accessible. This design has tall idleness and tall stack adjusting, demonstrating that this design is not adequate for handling IoT information since most preparation ought to run at tall speeds. The volume of this information is tall, and enormous information handling will increment the CPU utilization of the cloud servers.

1.2.5   Distributed Computing

This building is gotten ready for planning tall volumes of data. In IoT applications, since the sensors badly produce data, enormous data challenges are experienced [7]. To defeat this wonder, dispersed figuring is intended to seclude data into packs and give out the groups to differing PCs for dealing with. This scattered processing has assorted frameworks like Hadoop and Start. While moving from cloud to fog and passed on registering, the taking after wonders occurs:

1. A decrease in organizing stacking,
2. In addition to data planning speed,
3. A diminishment in CPU usage,
4. A diminishment in imperativeness use, and
5. An ability to set up the following volume of data.

Since the adroit city is one of the essential utilization of IoT, the preeminent basic use instances of the keen city and their data attributes are discussed inside the taking after regions.

1.3   Machine Learning Applied to Data Analysis

AI has wrapped up constantly fundamental for information analysis evaluation since it has been for a giant number of various locales. A depicting typical for AI is the restriction of a reveal to be a huge contract of representative facts and after that later used to see for complete goals and determinations indistinguishable issues. There is no must unequivocally program

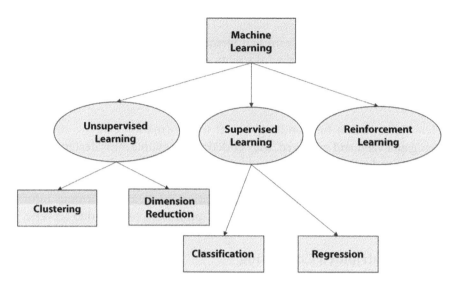

Figure 1.3 Machine learning algorithms.

an application to illuminate the issue. A show could be a depiction of this current reality battle. For depiction, a client buys can be utilized to set up an outline. Accordingly, guesses can be made around such buys a client may thusly make. This allows a relationship to modify notification and coupons for a client and possibly giving evacuated client experience. In Figure 1.3, arranging can be acted in one of the different explicit methods.

- Supervised Learning: The model is set up with commented on, stepped, information displaying seeing right outcomes.
- Unsupervised Learning: The information does not contain results; in any case, the model is required to discover the relationship in isolation.
- Semi-Coordinated: An obliged measure of stepped information is gotten along with a more prominent extent of unlabeled information.
- Reinforcement learning: This looks like managed learning; at any rate, a prize is obliged sufficient outcomes.

1.3.1   Supervised Learning Systems

Many controlled work zones are getting progressively familiar with counts available. They are decision trees, direct vector machines, and Bayesian frameworks. They all use explained datasets that fuse attributes and the right response. Regularly, preparing and a testing dataset is used.

1.3.2   Decision Trees

A figuring contraption getting data on a choice tree is a model used to make gauges. It maps certain recognitions to choices about a goal. The interval of time tree begins from the branches that reflect select states or characteristics. The leaves of a tree speak to results and the branches suggest parts that lead to the results. In evaluation mining, the decision tree is a representation of data used for gathering [8]. Such as, it can use a decision tree to choose if a man is conceivable to buy a thing primarily subject to positive characteristics, for instance, pay degree and postal code. Right when the target variable takes on tenacious characteristics, for instance, real numbers, the tree is known as a backslide tree.

A tree contains internal center points and leaves. Each inside center point addresses a component of the mannequin, for instance, the wide arrangement of significant lots of planning or whether an advanced book is a delicate spread or hardcover. The edges key out of an inward center depicts the estimations of these features. Each leaf is known as a representation and has a related chance course. Decision thistles are useful and advantageous to understand. Preparing records for a mannequin is basic regardless, of immense datasets.

1.3.3   Decision Tree Types

A tree can be taught by strategy for isolating an enter dataset by using the features. This is routinely developed in a recursive structure and is suggested as recursive allotting or top-down induction of decision trees. The recursion is restricted when the center point's characteristics are the sum of a comparative kind as the target or the recursion no longer incorporates regard. The leaf has a real sum addressing a segment during the method of examination; various bushes can in like manner be made. There are a couple of methods used to make trees. The methods are insinuated as outfit techniques: With a given course of action of data, it is down to earth that more imperative than one tree models the data. Such as, the establishment of a tree may similarly decide if a bank has an ATM PC and a following interior center point may moreover demonstrate the measure of tellers. The tree ought to be made to detect the number of tellers is at the root, and the nearness of an ATM is an inside center point [7, 8]. The separation in the structure of the tree can choose how conditions very much arranged the tree is. There are different strategies of comprehending the solicitation for the center points of a tree. One procedure is to pick a property that gives the most estimations gain; that is, select a quality that higher weakens the commonsense decisions fastest.

1.3.4   Unsupervised Machine Learning

Independent PC considering does not use remark on data; that is, the dataset does to combine foreseen results. While there are different independent getting familiar with figuring's, it will show the usage of affiliation rule acing to portray this getting familiar with the approach.

1.3.5   Association Rule Learning

Association rule is very successful is a procedure that perceives associations between information things. It is a bit of what is called exhibit compartment assessment. Exactly when a client makes purchases, these purchases are most likely going to involve more important than a certain something, and when it does, certain things will in general be sold together. Connection rule perusing is one approach for understanding these related things.

1.3.6   Reinforcement Learning

Reinforcement learning is getting familiar with is such a sensitive at the lessening some portion of present-day inquiry into neural frameworks and PC learning. As opposed to independent and oversaw learning, bolster learning chooses choices subject to the consequences of a movement [9]. It is a goal organized by getting data on process, like that used by strategies for some mother and father and educators over the world. Teach children to find a few solutions concerning and function admirably on tests with the objective that they gain extreme assessments as a prize. In like way, stronghold acing can be used to teach machines to make picks that will realize the perfect prize. There are two or three strategies that help AI. Man-made intelligence will show three strategies:

- Decision Trees: A tree is made utilizing highlights of the difficulty as inner focus focuses and the outcomes as leaves.
- Support Vector Machines: This is utilized for demand with the guide of making a hyperplane that divides the dataset and sometime later makes wants.
- Bayesian Structures: This is utilized to portray the probabilistic relationship between events.

1.4   Practical Issues in Machine Learning

It is basic to appreciate the nature of the confinements and conceivably sub-optimal conditions one may stand up to when overseeing issues requiring ML. An understanding of the nature of these issues, the impact of their closeness, and the techniques to deal with them will be tended to all through the talks inside the coming chapters. Here, Figure 1.4 shows a brief introduction to the down to soil issues that go up against us: data quality and commotion: misplaced values, duplicate values, off base values due to human or instrument recording bumble, and off base organizing are a couple of the basic issues to be considered though building ML models. Not tending to data quality can result in inaccurate or fragmented models. Inside the taking after chapter highlights many of these issues and several procedures to overcome them through data cleansing [10].

Imbalanced Datasets: In numerous real-world datasets, there is an imbalance among names within the preparing information. This lopsidedness in dataset influences the choice of learning, the method of selecting calculations, show assessment, and confirmation. If the correct procedures are not utilized, the models can endure expansive predispositions, and the learning is not successful.

Data Volume, Velocity, and Scalability: Frequently, an expansive volume of information exists in a crude frame or as real-time gushing information at a high speed. Learning from the complete information gets to be infeasible either due to limitations characteristic to the calculations or equipment

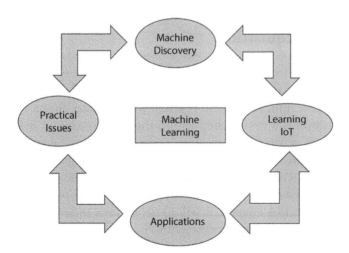

Figure 1.4 Issues of machine learning over IoT applications.

confinements, or combinations there from. In arranging to decrease the measure of the dataset to fit the assets accessible, information examining must be done. Testing can be drained in numerous ways, and each frame of testing presents a predisposition. Approving the models against test predisposition must be performed by utilizing different strategies, such as stratified testing, shifting test sizes, and expanding the estimate of tests on diverse sets. Utilizing enormous information ML can moreover overcome the volume and testing predispositions.

Overfitting: The central issue in prescient models is that the demonstrate is not generalized sufficient and is made to fit the given preparing information as well. This comes about in destitute execution of the demonstration when connected to inconspicuous information. There are different procedures depicted in afterward chapters to overcome these issues.

Curse of Dimensionality: When managing with high-dimensional information, that is, data sets with numerous highlights, adaptability of ML calculations gets to be a genuine concern. One of the issues with including more highlights of the information is that it introduces scarcity, that is, there is presently less information focuses on normal per unit volume of feature space unless an increment within the number of highlights is going with by an exponential increment within the number of preparing cases. This could obstruct execution in many strategies, such as distance-based calculations. Including more highlights can moreover break down the prescient control of learners, as outlined within the taking after the figure. In such cases, a more appropriate calculation is required, or the dimensions of the information must be decreased [11].

1.5   Data Acquisition

It is never much fun to work with code that is not designed legitimately or employments variable names that do not pass on their aiming reason. But that terrible information can result in wrong comes about. In this way, data acquisition is a critical step within the investigation of information. Information is accessible from a few sources but must be recovered and eventually handled some time recently it can be valuable. It is accessible from an assortment of sources. It can discover it in various open information sources as basic records, or it may be found in more complex shapes over the web. In this chapter, it will illustrate how to secure information from a few of these, counting different web locales and a few social media sites [12].

It can get information from the downloading records or through a handle known as web scratching, which includes extricating the substance of a web page. It moreover investigates a related point known as web slithering, which includes applications that look at a web location to decide whether it is of intrigued and after that takes after inserted joins to recognize other possibly significant pages. It can extricate data from social media destinations. It will illustrate how to extricate information from a few locales, including:

- Twitter
- Wikipedia
- Flicker
- YouTube

When extricating information from a site, many distinctive information groups may be experienced. At first, diverse information designs are taken after by an examination of conceivable information sources. Require this information to illustrate how to get information utilizing distinctive information procurement techniques.

1.6 Understanding the Data Formats Used in Data Analysis Applications

When examining information designs, they are alluding to substance organize, as contradicted to the basic record organize, which may not indeed be obvious to most designers. It cannot look at all accessible groups due to the endless number of groups accessible. Instep, handle a few of the more common groups, giving satisfactory models to address the foremost common information recovery needs. Particularly, it will illustrate how to recover information put away within the taking after designs [13]:

- HTML
- PDF
- CSV/TSV
- Spreadsheets
- Databases
- JSON
- XML

A few of these designs are well upheld and archived somewhere else. XML has been in utilizing for a long time and there are well-established procedures for getting to XML information. For these sorts of information, diagram the major techniques accessible and show a couple of illustrations to demonstrate how they work. This will give those peruses who are not commonplace with the innovation a little understanding of their nature. The foremost common information arranges is parallel records. In case, Word, Excel, and PDF records are all put away in double. These require an extraordinary program to extricate data from them. Content information is additionally exceptionally common.

1.7   Data Cleaning

Real-world information is habitually messy and unstructured and must be revamped sometime recently it is usable [14]. The information may contain blunders, have copy passages, exist within the off-base format, or be conflicting. The method of tending to these sorts of issues is called information cleaning. Information cleaning is additionally alluded to as information wrangling, rubbing, reshaping, or managing. Information combining, where information from numerous sources is combined, is regularly considered to be an information cleaning movement. Must be clean information since any investigation based on wrong information can create deluding comes about. This wants to guarantee that the information network is quality information. Information quality involves:

- Validity: Guaranteeing that the information has the right shape or structure.
- Accuracy: The values inside the information are representative of the dataset.
- Completeness: There are no lost elements.
- Consistency: Changes to information are in sync.
- Uniformity: The same units of estimation are used.

There are frequently numerous ways to achieve the same cleaning errand. This apparatus permits a client to examine in a dataset and clean it employing an assortment of procedures. In any case, it requires a client to interact with the application for each dataset that should be cleaned. It is not conducive to computerization. This will center on how to clean data utilizing method code. Even then, there may be distinctive strategies to clean the information. It appears different approaches to supply the user with experiences on how it can be done.

1.8   Data Visualization

The human intellect is frequently great at seeing designs, patterns, and exceptions in visual representations. The expansive sum of information display in numerous information analysis issues can be analyzed utilizing visualization strategies [12–15]. Visualization is suitable for a wide extend of groups of onlookers, extending from examiners to upper-level administration, to custom. Visualization is a vital step in information investigation since it permits us to conceive of huge datasets in viable and significant ways. It can see at little datasets of values and maybe conclude the designs, but this can be an overpowering and questionable handle. Utilizing visualization instruments makes a difference us recognize potential issues or startling information that comes about, as well as develop important translations of great information. One illustration of the convenience of information visualization comes with the nearness of exceptions. Visualizing information permits us to rapidly see information comes about essentially exterior of our desires and can select how to adjust the information to construct a clean and usable dataset. This preparation permits us to see mistakes rapidly and bargain with them sometime recently they have gotten to be an issue afterward. Also, visualization permits us to effortlessly classify data and help examiners organize their requests in a way best suited to their dataset.

1.9   Understanding the Data Analysis Problem-Solving Approach

Information analysis is engaged with the taking care of and assessment of extensive amounts of records to shape molds that are used to frame desires or something different restored a target. This plan normally incorporates developing and getting ready for models. The technique to light up trouble is subordinate to the idea of the issue. Regardless, all in all, the taking after are the significant level tasks that are used inside the assessment plan [11]:

Acquiring the Data: The records are single occasionally set aside in a combination of organizations and will start from a wide extent of data sources.

Cleaning the Data: Once the actuality is secured, it is often altered over to substitute and set up before it could be used for analyzing. In like manner, the measurements should be arranged or cleaned, to oust botches, get to the base of anomalies, and regardless put it in a shape sorted out for assessment [12–17].

Analyzing the Data: This can be done utilizing a lot of techniques including Statistical assessment: This uses numerous authentic ways to deal with manage give understanding into data. It fuses basic procedures and likewise created systems.

AI Valuation: These can be assembled as AI, neural frameworks, and significant examining strategies. Machine considering methods are depicted through bundles that can break down other than being unequivocally redone to complete a specific task; neural frameworks are worked round models structured after the neural association of the psyche; deep contemplating tries to see increasingly duplicated degrees of reflection inside a great deal of data [18].

Text Examination: This is a customary kind of assessment, which works with visit vernaculars to recognize features, for instance, the names of people and spots, the association between parts of the substance, and the forewarned estimation of substance [19].

Data Representation: This is an across the board examination device. By showing the information in a noticeable structure, a hard-to-understand set of numbers can be even more without a moment's delay measured.

Video, Image, and Complete Production With and Inspection: This is an increasingly more exact kind of assessment, which is getting logically ordinarily as higher examination methods are seen and quicker processors develop as available [20–23]. This is as threatening to the more noteworthy run of the mill content material adapting to and assessment tasks.

1.10   Visualizing Data to Enhance Understanding and Using Neural Networks in Data Analysis

The assessment of information now and again comes to fruition in a plan of numbers conversing with them comes to fruition of the examination [24–26]. In any case, for most people, along these lines of imparting comes about is not in every case consistently natural. A significantly higher approach to get it comes about is to make diagrams and outlines to depict it comes to fruition and the connection between the parts of the outcome. The human acumen is regularly awe-inspiring at seeing plans, models, and special cases in the noticeable portrayal. The enormous aggregate of records show in various insights analysis inconveniences can be investigated utilizing perception methodologies. Representation is suitable for an enormous run of social affairs of people reaching out from specialists to the upper-level organization to business.

The Artificial Neural Network, which is going to call a neural sort out, depends on the neuron found inside the cerebrum. A neuron may furthermore be a cell phone that has dendrites interfacing it to enter sources and different neurons. Contingent upon the enter source, a weight indicated to a source, the neuron is authorized and, after that, fires a banner down a dendrite to another neuron. A progression of neurons can be set up to answer to a lot of entering signals [27]. A produced neuron may likewise be a center point that has one or more prominent information sources and a private yield. Each enter incorporates a weight given out to it that can adjust after some time. A neural orchestrate can learn by methods for supporting a contribution to an organization, conjuring an activation work, and assessing occurs.

1.11   Statistical Data Analysis Techniques

These techniques connect from the generally basic coldblooded estimation to the front line apostatize evaluation models. Certifiable evaluation can be a genuinely jumbled handle and requires essential assessment to be driven really [28]. It will begin with a prologue to major quantifiable assessment techniques, counting learning the savage, focus, mode, and standard deviation of a dataset. Lose faith evaluation is a fundamental methodology for looking at information. The framework makes a line that endeavors to encourage the datasets. The condition tending to the line can be utilized to envision future lead. There are two or three sorts of break faith assessment. Test size affirmation incorporates perceiving the measure of data required to coordinate exact verifiable assessment. When working with gigantic datasets, it is not commonly imperative to use the entire set. The use test size verification to guarantee that it picks a model adequately little to control and separate successfully, anyway tremendous enough to address our masses of data decisively. It is not exceptional to use a subset of data to set up a model and another subset is used to test the model. This can help check the precision and constancy of data. Some essential consequences for an insufficiently chosen model size consolidate counterfeit positive results, fake negative results, recognizing quantifiable criticalness where none exists [29].

1.11.1   Hypothesis Testing

Hypothesis testing is used to test whether certain doubts or premises, about a dataset, could not happen by some happenstance. Assuming this is the case, by then, the eventual outcomes of the test are quantifiably significant. Performing hypothesis testing is unquestionably not a direct task. In the past, a part will achieve a result that they accept is typical. In the onlooker sway, in like manner called the Hawthorne sway, the results are inclined considering the way that the individuals acknowledge they are being seen. Because of the amazing idea of human direct assessment, a couple of kinds of quantifiable examinations are particularly obligated to inclining or degradation.

1.11.2   Regression Analysis

Regression analysis is important for choosing designs in data. It exhibits the association between dependent and free factors [30]. The free factors choose the estimation of a dependent variable. Each independent variable can have either a strong or a fragile effect on the assessment of the reliant variable. Straight backslide uses a line in a scatter plot to show the model. Non-straight backslide uses a kind of curve to depict the associations. The circulatory strain can be treated as the dependent variable and various components as self-sufficient elements.

1.12   Text Analysis and Visual and Audio Analysis

The content assessment would perhaps be a widespread concern and is diligently implied as Normal Language Preparing [31, 32]. It is utilized for a scope of one of a kind errands, checking content looking, language interpretation, assumption assessment, talk affirmation, and gathering, to decide a couple. The methodology for separating can be hazardous because of the reality of the particularities and irregularity decided in like way vernaculars.

These involve working with:

Tokenization: The route toward separating the text into solitary tokens or words.

Stop words: These are phrases that are standard and may moreover now not be basic for planning. They fuse such words as the, an, and to.

Name Entity Recognition: This is the path toward recognizing parts of a text, for instance, people's names, territories, or things.

Syntactic assortments: This recognizes the etymological bits of a sentence, for instance, thing, movement word, enlightening word, and so forth.

Associations: Here, it is worried about perceiving how parts of the literary substance are perceived with each other, for instance, the worry and object of a sentence.

The thoughts of words, sentences, and entries are outstanding. In any case, separating and separating these fragments is not typically that direct. The timespan corpus every single now and again suggests a combination of text. The utilization of sound, pictures, and accounts is persuading the hazard to be an inexorably essential perspective of regular day to day existence [33]. Telephone discussions and machines problem to voice orders are eternally typical. Persons direct video conversations with others around the planet. There is a smart duplication of photograph and video sharing objectives. Applications that utilize pictures, video, and sound from a progression of sources are finding the opportunity to be progressively increasing.

1.13   Mathematical and Parallel Techniques for Data Analysis

The synchronous execution of an application can achieve titanic execution updates. In this area, it will address the more than two or three strategies that can be used in estimations analysis applications. These can go from low-level logical tallies to progressively raise level API unequivocal other options [34].

Constantly keep in felt that introduction overhaul begins with ensuring that the right game plan of utilization execution is completed. If the utility does no longer do what a buyer expects, by then the overhauls are futile. The plan of the utility and the figuring used are moreover more unmistakable essential than code upgrades. Consistently use the most condition very much arranged to figure. Code update should then be thought of. It cannot deal with the enormous level of smoothing out issues in this part; rather, it will focus on code enhancements [35].

Various information analysis works and helping APIs use structure exercises to accomplish their tasks. Much of the time these errands are secured inside an API, anyway, there are times when it may also need to use these honestly. Regardless, it might be recommended to see how these exercises are reinforced. To this end, it will explain how system increment is overseen using a couple of remarkable strategies. Synchronous getting ready can be applied using method strings. A planner can use strings and string pools to improve an application's response time. Various APIs will use strings when a few CPUs or GPUs are not, now available, like the case with patriotism. It will not depict the usage of strings here. Regardless, the user is acknowledged to have significant data on strings and string pools. The guide decline figuring is used broadly for information analysis applications. It will exist as a procedure for achieving such an equivalent setting up the use of Apache's Hadoop. Hadoop is a structure helping the control of monstrous datasets and can colossally lessen the fundamental taking care of time for tremendous real factors analysis adventures. It will show a method for calculating a typical cost for a model arrangement of data [36].

1.13.1   Using Map-Reduce

Guide reduction is a model for dealing with tremendous game plans of real factors in an equivalent, allocated way [37]. This model contains a guide system for isolating and organizing data and a reduction strategy for summarizing data. The guide decline framework is incredible since it flows through the getting ready of a dataset across more than one server, performing arranging and markdown all the while on smaller portions of the data. Guide decrease offers broad execution refreshes when applied in a multi-hung way. In this portion, it will show a procedure for the utilization of Apache's Hadoop execution. Hadoop is an item program natural framework helping for equivalent enlisting. Guide decrease occupations can be run on Hadoop servers, generally set up as gatherings, to altogether improve dealing with speeds. Hadoop has trackers that run map-decrease strategy on center points inside a Hadoop gathering. Each center point works self-governing and the trackers screen the development and arrange the yield of every center to make a complete yield [38].

1.13.2   Leaning Analysis

Leaning assessment is the coronary heart of market bushel evaluation. It can discover co-occasion associations among practices did by strategy for standout customers or social affairs. In retail, affection evaluation can assist you with fathoming the buying conduct of customers [39].

These encounters can oblige pay through wise deliberately pitching and upselling systems and can help you in creating trustworthiness programs, bargains progressions, and cut worth plans. It will adjust the inside affiliation rule getting increasingly familiar with guidelines and counts, for instance, support, lift, apriorism computation, and FP-advancement figuring. Next, let us use Weka to work our first loving evaluation on the market dataset and find a few solutions concerning how to unravel the resulting standards. It will wrap up the area by dismembering how connection rule learning can be utilized in various spaces, for instance, IT operations analytics, drugs, and others.

1.13.3   Market Basket Analysis

Since the introduction of a modernized retail store, shops have been totaling a lot of data [36–40]. To utilize this real factor to convey business regard, they at first developed a way to deal with join and mix the data to understand the basics of the business. At this degree of detail, the retailers have direct detectable quality into the market bushel of each client who shopped at their store, seeing not, now simply the level of the purchased dissents in that carton, in any case also how these gadgets were offered identified with each other. This can be used to drive choices about how to isolate shop gatherings and items, similarly as adequately solidify bears of a few things, inside and every single through class, to drive progressively significant arrangements and advantages. These choices can be finished over an entire retail chain, by techniques for the channel, at the close by keep level, and regardless, for an intriguing client with implied modified publicizing, they recognize an uncommon thing giving is made for every customer.

1.14   Conclusion

In its core, information processing requires the capability to give chase and break down vast quantities of mathematical data. The choice and decrease of unassisted knowledge, detailed estimates, grouping assessment strategies, and discovery of utilizing empirical, isolation, and circulation procedures are analyzed. Each segment concentrates on a clear and objective analysis of knowledge and thoughts related to guided and inaccurate learning. This is likewise conversant with different kinds of AI currently in office. Thinking critically how a machine manages large quantities of data. The method employed by AI determines the result of the learning phase and the results develop in this direction. Lots may be accomplished in the AI system before a computation. This determines how AI tests and analysis of different kinds of evidence effectively completes the knowledge discovery process.

References

1. Pandit, A. and Radstake, T.R., Machine learning in rheumatology approaches the clinic. *Nat. Rev. Rheumatol.*, 2, 69–70, 2020.
2. Kulin, M., Kazaz, T., De Poorter, E., Moerman, I., A survey on machine learning-based performance improvement of wireless networks: PHY, MAC and network layer. *Electronics*, 3, 318, 2021.
3. Alsharif, M.H., Kelechi, A.H., Yahya, K., Chaudhry, S.A., Machine Learning Algorithms for Smart Data Analysis in the Internet of Things Environment: Taxonomies and Research Trends. *Symmetry*, 12, 1, 88, 2020.
4. Liu, C., Feng, Y., Lin, D., Wu, L., Guo, M., Iot based laundry services: an application of big data analytics, intelligent logistics management, and machine learning techniques. *Int. J. Prod. Res.*, 58, 17, 5113–5131, 2020.
5. Roccetti, M., Delnevo, G., Casini, L. and Salomoni, P., A Cautionary Tale for Machine Learning Design: why we Still Need Human-Assisted Big Data Analysis. *Mobile Networks Appl.*, 25, 1–9, 2020.
6. https://learning.oreilly.com/library/view/machine-learning-end-toend/9781788622219/index.html
7. https://learning.oreilly.com/library/view/machine-learning/9780128015223/Cover.xhtml
8. Zolanvari, M., Teixei ra, M.A., Gupta, L., Khan, K.M., Jain, R., Machine learning-based network vulnerability analysis of industrial Internet of Things. *IEEE Internet Things J.*, 6, 4, 6822–6834, 2019.
9. da Costa, K.A.P., Papa, J.P., Lisboa, C.O., Munoz, R., de Albuquerque, V.H.C., Internet of Things: A survey on machine learning-based intrusion detection approaches. *Comput. Networks*, 151, 147–157, 2019.
10. Tuli, S., Basumatary, N., Gill, S.S., Kahani, M., Arya, R.C., Wander, G.S., Buyya, R., Healthfog: An ensemble deep learning based smart healthcare system for automatic diagnosis of heart diseases in integrated iot and fog computing environments. *Future Gener. Comput. Syst.*, 104, 187–200, 2020.
11. Liang, F., Hatcher, W.G., Xu, G., Nguyen, J., Liao, W., Yu, W., Towards online deep learning-based energy forecasting. *2019 28th International Conference on Computer Communication and Networks (ICCCN)*, IEEE, pp. 1–9, 2019.
12. Ren, J., Wang, H., Hou, T., Zheng, S., Tang, C., Federated learning-based computation offloading optimization in edge computing-supported internet of things. *IEEE Access*, 7, 69194–69201, 2019.

13. Verma, A. and Ranga, V., Machine learning based intrusion detection systems for IoT applications. *Wireless Pers. Commun.*, 111, 4, 2287–2310, 2020.

14. Msadek, N., Soua, R., Engel, T., Iot device fingerprinting: Machine learning based encrypted traffic analysis. *2019 IEEE Wireless Communications and Networking Conference (WCNC)*, IEEE, pp. 1–8, 2019.

15. Tuli, S., Basumatary, N., Buyya, R., Edgelens: Deep learning-based object detection in integrated iot, fog and cloud computing environments. *2019 4th International Conference on Information Systems and Computer Networks (ISCON)*, IEEE, pp. 496–502, 2019.

16. Luo, X.J., Oyedele, L.O., Ajayi, A.O., Monyei, C.G., Akinade, O.O., Akanbi, L.A., Development of an IoT-based big data platform for day-ahead prediction of building heating and cooling demands. *Adv. Eng. Inf.*, 41, 100926, 2019.

17. Zafar, S., Jangsher, S., Bouachir, O., Aloqaily, M., Othman, J.B., QoS enhancement with deep learning-based interference prediction in mobile IoT. *Comput. Commun.*, 148, 86–97, 2019.

18. Min, Q., Lu, Y., Liu, Z., Su, C., Wang, B., Machine learning based digital twin framework for production optimization in petrochemical industry. *Int. J. Inf. Manage.*, 49, 502–519, 2019.

19. Garg, S., Kaur, K., Kumar, N., Kaddoum, G., Zomaya, A.Y., Ranjan, R., A hybrid deep learning-based model for anomaly detection in cloud datacenter networks. *IEEE Trans. Netw. Serv. Manage.*, 16, 3, 924–935, 2019.

20. Tiwari, R., Sharma, N., Kaushik, I., Tiwari, A., Bhushan, B., Evolution of IoT & Data Analytics using Deep Learning. *2019 International Conference on Computing, Communication, and Intelligent Systems (ICCCIS)*, IEEE, pp. 418–423, 2019.

21. Sujatha, R., Nathiya, S., Chatterjee, J.M., Clinical Data Analysis Using IoT Data Analytics Platforms, in: *Internet of Things Use Cases for the Healthcare Industry*, pp. 271–293, Springer, Cham, 2020.

22. Potluri, S., Health record data analysis using wireless wearable technology device. *JARDCS*, 10, 9, 696–701, 2018.

23. Mangla, M., Akhare, R., Ambarkar, S., Context-Aware Automation Based Energy Conservation Techniques for IoT Ecosystem, in: *Energy Conservation for IoT Devices*, pp. 129–153, Springer, Singapore, 2019.

24. Akhare, R., Mangla, M., Deokar, S., Wadhwa, V., Proposed Framework for Fog Computing to Improve Quality-of-Service in IoT Applications, in: *Fog Data Analytics for IoT Applications*, pp. 123–143, Springer, Singapore, 2020.

25. Potluri, S., IOT Enabled Cloud Based Healthcare System Using Fog Computing: A Case Study. *J. Crit. Rev.*, 7, 6, 1068–1072, 2020.

26. Chatterjee, J., IoT with Big Data Framework using Machine Learning Approach. *Int. J. Mach. Learn. Networked Collab. Eng.*, 2, 02, 75–85, 2018.

27. Chatterjee, J.M., Priyadarshini, I., Le, D.N., Fog Computing and Its security issues, in: *Security Designs for the Cloud, Iot, and Social Networking*, pp. 59–76, 2019.

28. Shri, M.L., Devi, E.G., Balusamy, B., Chatterjee, J.M., Ontology-Based Information Retrieval and Matching in IoT Applications, in: *Natural Language Processing in Artificial Intelligence*, pp. 113–130, Apple Academic Press, India, 2020.

29. Kumar, A., Payal, M., Dixit, P., Chatterjee, J.M., Framework for Realization of Green Smart Cities Through the Internet of Things (IoT), in: *Trends in Cloud-based IoT*, pp. 85–111, Springer, Cham, 2020.

30. Sujatha, R., Nathiya, S., Chatterjee, J.M., Clinical Data Analysis Using IoT Data Analytics Platforms, in: *Internet of Things Use Cases for the Healthcare Industry*, pp. 271–293, Springer, Cham, 2020.

31. Priya, G., Shri, M.L., GangaDevi, E., Chatterjee, J.M., IoT Use Cases and Applications, in: *Internet of Things Use Cases for the Healthcare Industry*, pp. 205–220, Springer, Cham, 2020.

32. Raj, P., Chatterjee, J.M., Kumar, A., Balamurugan, B., *Internet of Things Use Cases for the Healthcare Industry*, Springer International Publishing, India, 2020.

33. Garg, S., Chatterjee, J.M., Le, D.N., *Implementation of Rest Architecure-Based Energy-Efficient Home Automation System*, Security Designs for the Cloud, Iot, and Social Networking, 143–152, 2019.

34. Almusaylim, Z.A. and Zaman, N., A review on smart home present state and challenges: linked to context-awareness internet of things (IoT). *Wireless networks*, 25, 6, 3193–3204, 2019.

35. Almulhim, M. and Zaman, N., Proposing secure and lightweight authentication scheme for IoT based E-health applications. *2018 20th International Conference on Advanced Communication Technology (ICACT)*, IEEE, pp. 481–487, 2018, February.

36. Almulhim, M., Islam, N., Zaman, N., A Lightweight and Secure Authentication Scheme for IoT Based E-Health Applications. *Int. J. Comput. Sci. Netw. Secur.*, 19, 1, 107–120, 2019.

37. Alshammari, M.O., Almulhem, A.A., Zaman, N., Internet of Things (IoT): Charity Automation. *Int. J. Adv. Comput. Sci. Appl. (IJACSA)*, 8, 2, 166–170, 2017.

38. Mangla, M. and Sharma, N., Fuzzy Modelling of Clinical and Epidemiological Factors for COVID-19, *Research Square*, 1, 1–15, 2020.

39. Potluri, S., An IoT based solution for health monitoring using a body-worn sensor enabled device. *JARDCS*, 10, 9, 646–651, 2018.

40. Potluri, S., Health record data analysis using wireless wearable technology device. *JARDCS*, 10, 9, 696–701, 2018.

2

Machine Learning for Cyber-Immune IoT Applications

Suchismita Sahoo[1]* and Sushree Sangita Sahoo[2]

[1]Biju Patnaik University of Technology, Rourkela, India
[2]Department of Computer, St. Paul's School (ICSE), Rourkela, India

Abstract

Today's era, which is being ruled by Internet of Things (IoT) or the reformation; being the Internet of Everything, has combined various technological affirmations with it. But along with its deployment, it is also undergoing malicious threats to compromise on the security issues of the IoT devices with high priority over the cloud, hence proving to be the weakest link of today's computational intelligence infrastructure. Digital network security issue has become the desperate need of the hour to combat cyber attack. Although there have been various learning methods which have made break through, this chapter focuses on machine learning being used in cyber security to deal with spear phishing and corrosive malwares detection and classification. It also looks for the ways to exploit vulnerabilities in this domain which is invading the training data sets with power of artificial intelligence. Cloud being an inherent evolution, so as to deal with these issues, this chapter will be an approach to establish an interactive network, cognitively intervening the domains of cyber security services to the computational specifications of IoT.

Keywords: Cyber security, machine learning, malware detection, classification

2.1 Introduction

This chapter is structured with an overview that "It's only when they go wrong that machines remind you how powerful they are" by Clive James.

*Corresponding author: suchismita.sahoo86@gmail.com

Sachi Nandan Mohanty, Jyotir Moy Chatterjee, Monika Mangla, Suneeta Satpathy and Sirisha Potluri (eds.) Machine Learning Approach for Cloud Data Analytics in IoT, (25–52) © 2021 Scrivener Publishing LLC

The major concern of these days is digital security, which is at its heights; this is because the era is becoming digitech uninterrupted exponentially. At the same time, our customizable environment becoming dynamic and scalable with its inevitable warehouse differentiated as cloud computing is one of the major concerns. Cyber security can be applied upon to attain the grip over this digital surface, whereby the veritable exposure of various machines on the web provides an area for hackers in committing frauds, which we name it as cybercrime with an internet intervention being globally at 3.9 million users across the world as per the recent news of 2020 in BBC, has aired up the opportunity for cybercrime exponentially. It is a multi-disciplinary prevention where it spans IoT through it by constantly evolving some active processes like minimizing or preventing its impact by cyber security. There exist a large number of serious issues related to the frightening situations in the growth of IoT, specifically in ground of security, privacy, and, furthermore, in all the aspects in technical environment to relocate the concerned areas which have started to move on with a rapid pace. As of need of the hour, our study also focuses on forming it as a basic entity of every design attribute for each of the related database of the electronic data transfer, so that the world could rely upon the technology as a potential of enriched dimension to take over the world with the striding facts of accessing IoT with relevance to secured encryption routes over the cloud and its associated tech facts. This secure revolution may be tough in its approach but will definitely be a renaissance.

It is a matter of great concern that, as we are progressively moving ahead with highly advanced computing technologies being deduced over internet, at the same time, the perception that is being provoked upon the security risks hovering over World Wide Web is a matter to be explored. Several encryption technologies are fuelling the online gambling and fraudulence, which is hampering the transformation of secret messages over internet.

Hence, to fine-tune the exploitation and get a makeover, the concept of cyber security needs to be embedded into the interoperability of the impaction presumption in such a way that security is restored at proactive way. Cyber security demonstrates the coaxial control over the offending activity congruency supporting the formal anticipation of stronger IT skills, suggesting the vulnerable access to the World Wide Web in increasingly analyzing the threats, and significantly making an attempt to secure usage and integration of digital information. With this being the most debated, recently, machine learning is able to resolve the conflict and can enormously bypass the network structure and work over the latest digital infrastructure.

2.2   Some Associated Impactful Terms

2.2.1   IoT

It can be enumerated in a sense of a sensible system of interrelated computing mediums along w ith association of electronic, mechanical, and digital machines that were built up with unique identifiers and its capability to get on over the network for transferring data without the intervention among the human beings as well as in between the users and computer.

It also can be noted as a perfect definition of a large range of globally connected devices of many forms starting from a sensor to that of smart phones and even beyond these.

The IoT has come up as the next revolutionary ideology [1], which enables billions of devices all over the world over a distributed network to be networked completely for transformation of data and its exchange, which would enhance the quality of our day-to-day lives. At the same time, cloud computing paves demand for convenient and stupendous network accessibility to enable sharing computing of resources possible in all aspects which would, in turn, make data integration dynamically from all the relative data sources in an adherent way. There exist various issues while implementing cloud and IoT, and the defragmentation of cloud computing with IoT is the one of the most purposeful ways, in which it needs to come over such issues. The wide range of resources available over the cloud can be effectively beneficial toward the cause of IoT, while the cloud can be profitable in gaining publicity to enhance its efficiency by coming over its shortcomings with the real-world objects in a versatile and distributed way. This study of ours provides an overview of integrating cloud and IoT over basing each other for a generous dealing with cybercrimes, thereby implementing the machine learning methodological algorithms over it in a procuring way.

IoT presents ubiquitous connectivity for a wide range of devices, services, and applications. These include intelligent computers, smart phones, office equipment, wireless-enabled cars, lighting systems, heating, ventilation, and air condition (HVAC), household appliances, and many others. To be IoT-enabled, a device ("thing") ought to be on a network and connected to a communicating node. Various communication network technologies and their architectural infrastructures in a fully connected network such as 3G, LTE, Wi-Fi, Bluetooth, ZigBee, Z-wave, and Sigfox provide reinforced connectivity services for IoT deployment on many services platforms [2].

Over the past decade, internet technologies have revolutionized the interconnection among people at an unprecedented scale and pace. The next revolution is expected to craft the interconnection among diverse objects leading to what experts termed as the smart environment.

As we move from World Wide Web (static pages web) to web2 (social networking web) to web3 (ubiquitous computing or web of things), the need for data-on-demand using sophisticated intuitive queries continues to increase significantly. This era could be consequently termed as the post-PC era where smart phones and related devices are changing our environment and the way "thing" (including humans) interacts. Things in the new environment are becoming more interactive as well as informative in an operative manner.

2.2.2 IoT Device

An IoT device comprises of sensors, actuators, working frameworks, operating systems, framework programming, preloaded applications, and lightweight administrations conglomerating internet technology with featuristic devices.

Examples are PC, laptops, tablets, and smart phones.

IoT devices are usually of the sensible architectural gadgets integrated with software connected with each other over the web for communication, so that they help programmers for simple defragmentation of the scientific world [3].

In today's era, the devices are in utility of internet and its related devices are rising rapidly. It basically includes all the gadgets which are well equipped digitally.

It usually depends upon the capability of getting in connection with the web in all aspects.

The device is integrated with all the latest technical entities like sensors and actuators to all the functional software devices.

When both of such functionalities are merged on, an IoT device is created. The strategy of market is increasing rapidly, and they are gaining popularity at a higher strand where the users are also increasing rapidly.

Advantages

- It facilitates the interaction among gadgets called as machine-to-machine interaction.
- It embarks upon proper automation and control.

- Defragmentation which would be generous for operating.
- Possession of strong feature of guarding IoT.
- Time saving.
- Reduction of manually carrying out task, and time is taken over by IoT as a cost saving approach.

2.2.3   IoT Service

For the most part, IoT services are facilitated on cloud with the goal that clients can get to IoT objects whenever and wherever [4]. The dynamic duties of these administrations incorporate IoT process computerization, gadget the executives, dynamic, signal processing, and so on.

It includes proper strategic consultation, along with development and analysis of data and the management of applications with an objective of sharing the organization's issue to solve the challenges of business which would tap into the various channels of IoT technologies [5].

2.2.4   Internet Security

An overall term alluding to the security of web, which is also a branch of computer security, is not only operationally related technologies, such as web browsers and the World Wide Web, but also applies to that of the highlighted operating system or networks over it as a whole too.

It is nothing less than a requirement to protect our digital way of life.

It assigned to a lot of strategies used to ensure the integrity of systems, devices, and data from attack, harm, or unapproved access, thereby deploying the array of tactics to get over information exchange globally.

The control and practice of forestalling and moderating attacks on PC frameworks and systems can also catch over the broader issue of security transactions over it.

It is the defragmentation of a form correlating to the basic technological advances in information technology, the network of networks, and virtual reality along with the computations over the clouds.

It can be perforated as being the descriptive structure of technologies, and the associated design methodologies to safeguard the networks, the system establishments, and its programming approaches are associated to information, thereby protecting the information from cyber attacks that would purely damage all the usable structures, hence being accessed in unauthorized way.

Digital security is a kind of assortment of advancements, and the various practices are intended to ensure the systems, the PC frameworks, and the different projects and information from the digital assaults, thereby with its unapproved accessibility.

Some advantages of cyber security:

- Improvised guarding of cyberspace.
- A credible growth in cyber speed and defense.
- Safeguarding organization's data.
- Safeguarding computer systems against malwares, spywares, etc.
- Safeguarding networks and its available resources.
- Safeguarding personal information of people.
- Proactive approach against hackers and identity thefts.
- Reducing freezing and crashing of computer systems.
- Provides private space to users [6].

There are some cyber security issues:

i) Phishing attacks.
ii) IoT ransomware.
iii) Increased data privacy regulation.
iv) Cyber attacks on mobile devices.
v) Increased investment in automation.

Cyber security demonstrates the following strategies:

- Firstly, adopting proper measures to safeguard the software information and its relative devices, which contain the information.
- Secondly, emphasizing on the qualitative status of being proactively protecting from various threats.
- Thirdly, deducing scripting of the above related data contents, its implementation, and the required digital transformation [7].

2.2.5 Data Security

Data security apropos the way toward shielding data from unapproved access and data defilement eventually all through its lifecycle, thereby ensuring the applications with no possibility of deciphering the informative codes. Data security incorporates data encryption, tokenization, hashing, and key administration rehearses that ensure information over all applications and stages.

Besides, it could be enumerated as of being a procedure of ensuring documents, databases, and records on a system by receiving a lot of controls, applications, and strategies that recognize the overall significance of various data sets, their affectability, and administrative consistence prerequisites and, afterward, by applying suitable assurances to make sure about those assets.

2.2.6   Cyberthreats

It takes numerous structures, for example, social designing, ransomware, and malware. Late mechanical progressions have opened up additional opportunities for cyber security. In any case, sadly, enemies have profited by these advances too.

A brief note to this conceptual term could be a potential negative action or event which is usually facilitated by vulnerability of the PC frameworks and innovation, regularly from the web and its associated applications.

Business leaders must design a security strategy to secure their organization. The best system is one that can give steady, avoidance-based insurance for endpoints, server farms, systems, and cloud environment, and the sky is the limit from there.

2.2.7   Cyber Attack

This spatial term refers to an attempt to offensive act to expose, alter, disable, destroy, and gain unauthorized access against computer systems, networks, or infrastructure.

This is an unauthorized access which is usually launched from one or more systems over another system or several systems or the networks.

It could be classified into two broader aspects, one being the goal to disable the target computer by knocking it over out of web and another being the target to have accessibility to specifically aim at computer's data and to gain admin's privacy [8].

Hence, an attack can be enumerated as the attempt to alter and to get over to have an access in unauthorized way of using any assets.

This offensive maneuver which is the so called cyber attack attempts to facilitate itself as anonymously originating from sources renamed as cyberweapon which have increasingly become highly dangerous [9].

2.2.8   Malware

It is an obligative term which is used for the programs which are very harmful, and at the same time, it erodes the system servers as well as the system-based malwares for their intended usage which can creep into the technical walls which interchangeably infects the target computers [10].

This stand-alone piece can force the programs to replicate and spread itself unanimously, which gets accessibility by attackers themselves.

It could get all terms to allude to a program or a file of malevolent programming, normally utilized regarding viruses, ransomware, spyware, and comparative.

2.2.9   Phishing

This disguised weapon keeps the objective of getting on to the emails and the links and even the attachments while being downloaded. Usually, a phishing attempt goes over to do two broad areas of work which are as enumerated below [11]:

- ✓ Sensitive information handover: It has the objective of getting on to reveal the important data which an attacker can get to breach an account, thereby the classic version of this particular scam spans the emails provoked by the attackers to get the enthralling recipients who hopefully enter their user ids and passwords but resemble the fake attacker's web page which hopefully enters the victim's webpage to take over a malicious attempt.
- ✓ Download malware: This being another approach of phishing that aims at getting the victim to infect his own system with malware. Usually, the messages are found to be softly and generously targeted in such an apprehensive way, so that they creep over the attachments unanimously, usually catching over the zip files, documents, etc.

This performative term being a form of social engineering refers to the beguiling endeavor, as a rule over email, to fool clients into giving over actually recognizable or basic data (for example, passwords, or card numbers).

2.2.10   Ransomware

It is otherwise known to be cryptoware which associates malware used to hold over an individual or association to recover, normally by surmounting encoding records or a whole hard drive and requesting installment to "open" the information.

This is a kind of malware which has its feasibility over just like creeping into the files of a victim. Then, the attacker gets on to demand as the most common way of access through the vectors which masquaders to take over the victim's system usually those built with social engineering tools. Once they are downloaded, they creep into the system files.

Among all, some of the aggressive ones are NotPetva which explodes the security holes while infecting without the rarest even need to track the users.

Preventing ransomware grooves over the course of security practices which would improve the defensive attack from all sorts of attacks to keep the operating system safeguard from several vulnerable attacks.

Usually, the operating system needs to be patched up and made up to date, thereby ensuring the rarest exploits.

The software should not be installed with administrative privileges to deduce it exactly and insignificantly over the white listing software and take a proper back up.

Ransonwares are existing since 90s but its effect has been taken off within these past few years because of some alarming methodologies like that of Bitcoins which is the worst among offences. Some more includes crypto locker, teslacrypt, locky, wannacry, BadRabbit, and so on the list continues [12].

2.2.11   Spear-Phishing

It is a rigorously targeted form of phishing which directs its instincts evitably toward an individual or business, regularly utilizing social building strategies to seem, by all accounts, to be from a confided in source.

It is the one where the attacker tries to craft over the appealing messages through specific individual, so that the targets would hook upon the informative sites which would bind upon the targets, so that it would pretend the victim managers to request, for example, large bank transfers with short notice.

2.2.12 Spyware

An infi ltrating software program intended to take information or screen individuals and structures for cybercriminals, associations, or kingdom states invading devices for sensitive information relying on the behavioral properties of the associated applicable applications on and over the respective devices.

Spyware does not really spread similarly as a worm in light of the fact that contaminated frameworks for the most part do not endeavor to communicate or duplicate the product to different PCs [13]. Rather, spyware introduces itself on a system by deceiving the client or by misusing programming weaknesses.

Most spyware is introduced without information or by utilizing misleading strategies. Spyware may attempt to deceive clients by packaging itself with attractive programming. Other basic strategies are utilizing a Trojan horse, that is, spy devices that resemble ordinary gadgets however end up being something different, for example, a USB Keylogger. These gadgets really are associated with the gadget as memory units yet are equipped for recording each stroke made on the keyboard. Some spyware creators contaminate a system through security openings in the Web browser or in other software. At the point when the client explores to a Web page constrained by the spyware creator, the page contains code which attacks the browser and powers the download and installation of spyware.

2.2.13 Cybercrime

With the expanding number of PC proprietors associated with web, the possibility for cybercrime is growing [14].

A notable explanation to this concept can be those encrypted PCs that encouraged violations however, as often as possible, can be accustomed to discuss with all kinds of innovation-empowered wrongdoings.

Cybercriminals are additionally utilizing an assortment of other assault vectors to fool their planned victims into surrendering individual data, login credentials, or, in any event, sending cash. We have seen assailants acquire certifications to email accounts, study the casualty for quite a long time, and, when all is good and well, create a focusing on assault against accomplices and clients to take cash [15].

Regardless of threat of viruses and malware nearly since the beginning of computing, awareness of the protection and holiness of information with PC frameworks did not pick up foothold until the touchy development of the web, whereby the presentation of such huge numbers of machines on the web gave a genuine play area to programmers to test their abilities, conveyance down websites, taking information, or submitting misrepresentation. It is one thing that we tend to currently decision cybercrime.

Types of cybercrime:

   i) Virus attack
  ii) Cyber pornography
 iii) Online gambling
 iv) E-mail frauds
  v) Cyber terrorism, etc.

2.2.14   IoT Cyber Security

As indicated by Roman *et al.*, one key test which must be defeated so as to push IoT into this present reality is security. Security challenges with reference to IoT line up with the normal information systems (IS) and security objectives (SO) which are secrecy, respectability, and information accessibility.

The IoT has emerged as a catchall word for the expression for the developing pattern of interfacing numerous varieties of devices to the web among producers and integrators. At times, web network is a beneficial function to include in new hardware. For instance, a wellness tool that that gathers well-being facts can ship it instantly to the cloud or a stand-alone domestic digital camera can stream ongoing pictures and the proprietor can access from the workplace [16].

Sometimes, be that as it may, providers are able to interface devices without including the necessary safety efforts, a fantasy situation for programmers or hackers and different aggressors. Having direct access to all ways of the system permits cybercriminals to assume control over these web-empowered machines substantially more without any problem. When the device is pwned, a programmer can take the information it holds or maybe utilize the device as an assaulting stage against different casualties.

Frequently, a powerless security setup is the thing that permits an aggressor a path into the device. For example, online cameras that utilize an anticipated secret key or have no verification at all are generally normal, and certain devices are discovered online at alternative times when they should not be. This is obviously ludicrous when it happens to mechanical hardware in an assembling or healthcare atmosphere, for example, industrial facilities and hospitals. These mechanical machines ought to rather use a virtual private system (VPN) association in the event that they should be gotten distantly. Aside from the utilization of VPN, there are varieties of secure configurations that may not need these devices to be straight-forwardly presented to the web at massive. It is suggested that integrators invariably follow their industry's prescribed procedures with regard to the IoT.

Furthermore, pedestrian applications of the IoT will experience the similar issue. Let us say, web-associated home or workplace printers do not build a great deal of sense, as these sorts of machines ought not to be accidentally presented to the web. On the off chance that a client requires distance printing, there are various safer alternatives, for example, Cloud Printing Services or a protected VPN. At the point when utilized for asso-ciated devices, switches can likewise be considered as IoT devices. Home and office switches have been predominant for a long time, and from our experience, they are as yet the most every now and again assaulted IoT device along these lines, if this pattern was to stay unaltered, switches are the most inclined to future assaults. Assailants consider switches as IoT devices since they are conceivable passage focuses for an assault. For this reason, in this chapter, we will consider those IoT devices too.

2.2.15   IP Address

IP (Internet Protocol) is a numerical name which is given to the devices taking part in and over a network which fills in as an identifier for the spe-cific machine; e.g., 152.16.0.140.

2.3   Cloud Rationality Representation

2.3.1   Cloud

The expression "cloud" begins from the broadcast communications uni-verse of the 1990s, when suppliers started utilizing virtual private network (VPN) services for data communication [17].

The cloud refers to servers which can be accessed over the web and the software and databases that run on the ones servers, that is architecturally explained in Figure 2.1. It is self-defined to rule over the World Wide Web, in which the warehouse remains an apathetic topic of applications being run over the medium which not only transforms the resources but also vulnerably defines the concept in a performed program which happens to be its access medium, i.e., internet, thereby creating an interface between the user device and application and database over the server.

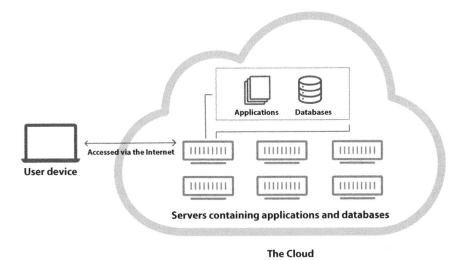

Figure 2.1 The cloud.

This term is itself a collaborated term of literal technology associated with fugitive conglomeration of aspiring trends of technical aspects where it mends the database over its storage aspect of learnt theories for a safer access.

2.3.2   Cloud Data

Cloud storage is an architectural model representing the potential transformation of an informative digitalized database that is encrypted over being a model of computer data storage in and over the logical feasibilities and implemented over distributed network. The architectural storage spans several servers (occasionally in various locations), and the physical surroundings are typically taken over and controlled by a hosting company.

Cloud storage is not the simplest one as it allows us to save the records and files in an offshore sites that we need to have an entry through the public and for personal community connection in which data transfer for transferring the responsibility over the cloud. The provider hosts, secures, manages, and continues the servers and associated infrastructure and ensures that you got entry to the information every time you want it [18].

Cloud storage can provide a price-effective and versatile option for keeping files on premise hard drives or storage networks. PC hard drives can just store a limited measure of data. At the point when clients come up short on capacity, they have to move documents to an outer stockpiling device.

Generally, companies constructed and maintained storage area networks to archive data and files. Storage area networks are costly to keep up but, due to the fact that saved data grows, organizations should put resources on including servers and infrastructure to accommodate accelerated demand.

Cloud storage services give versatility, which implies that you can scale limit as your information volumes increment or dial down limit if necessary. By storing records in a cloud, your association spare by paying for capacity innovation and limit as a help, instead of putting resources into the capital expenses of building and keeping up in-house stockpiling systems. You pay for just precisely the limit you use. While your expenses would possibly increase after some time to represent higher data volumes, you do not need to overprovision stockpiling systems fully expecting expanded data volume.

2.3.3   Cloud Security

Cloud computing security or, truly great, cloud security alludes to a wide arrangement of approaches, advanced techniques, applications, and controls applied to ensure virtualized IP, applications, data, programs, and the related framework of cloud computing. It is a sub-area of PC security, network security, and, all the more extensively, data security [19].

2.3.4   Cloud Computing

It is the proliferative implied system resources of computer, and it is on demand availability over the cloud storage when refers to the basic data storage and the power of computation not being the proper involvement of specific active management of the recognized users.

It can be described as a model for tuning the ubiquitous, improvised, on a focused credibility network accessibility to a varying contempt which lies within a group of configurable resources of computing, which includes networks, storage, and servers, applying rules and its respective services which can provide a platform for proper interaction. This is described as interactive organized modules in Figure 2.2.

It can also be put up as a disruptive budding technology with various profound implications for the corporate sector that includes IT as of being a complete whole of an ensembling area.

"Going green" and saving costs are key focus points for organizations.

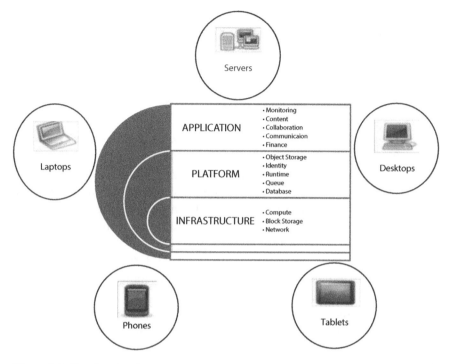

Figure 2.2 Cloud computing.

Cloud computing compels over in providing stupendous savings in IT-correlated costs that include a very low implementation and maintenance cost; very low requirement of hardware to purchase, reducing of the cost of power, cooling, and the space for storage of the resources, and shifting to the service provider; a drop in the operational cost and giving up the value for only those which being used as a part of the reduced measurable service [20].

It also enriches the organizations in becoming more and more competitive due to a much flexible and nimble computing platform, thereby with provisions for scaling up with high performance resources and with that of the available data sources and information being reliable.

Cloud computing helps organizations to reduce power and proper usage of space which would facilitate the sustainable and eco-friendly data centers.

Cost efficiency is the vital regulator for cloud computing adoption.

Besides, the other primarily beneficial includes the scalability and flexibility in agility for a better IT resource management and lighting over the business management with a greater efficiency in a greater reliability and high speed development and change deployment and its managerial activity for a high profile mobilization and performance.

2.4   Integration of IoT With Cloud

IoT and cloud computing have evolved to be two highly advanced technologies although they differ from each other, which have become part and parcel of our lives. Their acceptance and usage are expected to be represented in a pervasive way, thereby making its components the important constituent of the internet of future. A performative paradigm where there is merging of IoT and cloud is marked as disruptive and as capable as of a greater number of application's environment [21].

When there is integration of IoT with cloud, it is termed as the CloudIoT paradigm. A perfomative paradigm where IoT and cloud are conglomerated and are henceforth coercively profounded to be the issue of involvement of research, challenges, and wide range of applications. The architecture and organization of the above concepts is relatively enumerated in Figure 2.3.

The IoT generates profusely a large amount of data and cloud computing paves a pathway for the respective data to transfer. By making the developers to keep and have an access to the remote data, it can be made to work on the project without being late in responding the theme-based project work which can be taken up as one of the prioritized task featured jobs.

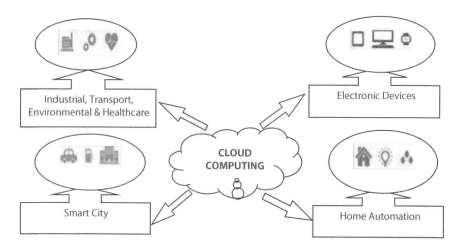

Figure 2.3 Integration of cloud computing and IoT.

2.5   The Concepts That Rules Over

2.5.1   Artificial Intelligent

This unifying theme is the idea of thought processes and reasoning addressing the behavior which measures the success in terms of fidelity to human performance with an ideal concept of rationality referring to the study of computation that perceives reasons and act. This study of ours cognitively works with the basics of our latest technological artifacts of this artificial intelligence in a relative approach to machine learning theories and algorithms being play backed upon with reasons. It is a formal analysis of propositional logic [22]. This is what we have put up in our study.

2.5.2   Overview of Machine Learning

Machine learning which is deduced as a structural study in presenting the theme as a substantial field of artificial intelligence which has an objective of empowering the systems with the capability of using data to learn and develop without the process of being programmed explicitly.

Machine learning algorithms can be categorized as follows.

2.5.2.1   Supervised Learning

It is one of those learning methods, which makes over the models which are being trained using marked data. The goal of this learning technique is to train the model in such a way that we can predict the output when it is being applied upon with given new data over it. Here, both input and

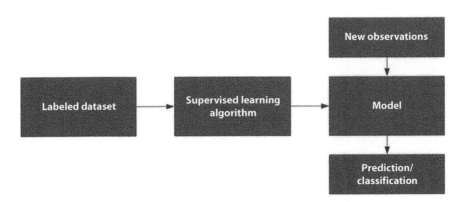

Figure 2.4 Supervised learning.

desired output data pave path for future events predictions [23]. For accurate predictions, the fed data is labeled or tagged as the perfect presumption. The schematic representation of output prediction or classification represented in Figure 2.4.

2.5.2.2 Unsupervised Learning

Unsupervised learning is one those finest learning techniques being a diversified part of machine learning methods in which the unlabeled input data infers the patterns desired [24]. There is no provision of providing training data, and hence, the machine is made to learn by its own. But at the same time, it is also taken care of that the machine must be able to do the data classification without any information about the data is being given beforehand.

The objective of unsupervised learning is to find out the structural prospective and patterns from the data which given as input. It does not require any kind of supervision for training the model. Rather, it makes out the patterns from the data on its own. The structure of this learning process can be referred from Figure 2.5. The basic ideology behind this is to expose the machines to a greater volume of different data and allow it to learn from the provided insights which happened to be unrecognizable previously to recognize the hidden patterns.

Like that, there are no necessarily defined outcomes as deduced from unsupervised learning algorithms. Instead, it reciprocates what is the indifference feature from the provided data set.

The machine requires to be programmed in such a way that it learns on its own. The machine needs to understand and get on with distinctive insights from both structured as well as unstructured data.

It may also so happen that the unsupervised learning model may provide less accurate results as in comparison to supervised learning technique.

It includes various algorithms such as Clustering, K-Nearest Neighbor (KNN), and Apriori algorithm.

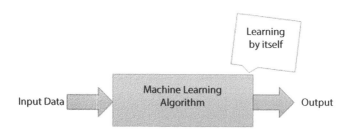

Figure 2.5 Unsupervised learning.

2.5.3   Applications of Machine Learning in Cyber Security

- Threats upcoming and classification
- Scheduled security task, automations, and user analysis optimization
- Network risk scoring

2.5.4   Applications of Machine Learning in Cybercrime

- Unauthorized access
- Evasive malware
- Spear phishing

2.5.5   Adherence of Machine Learning With Cyber Security in Relevance to IoT

Along with machine learning, cyber security systems perform a proper analysis of patterns and learn the ways to help associate the ways of prevention of liked attacks and reciprocate to the changing behavior. At the same time, it can help the cyber security teams to be proactively involved in prevention of threats and reactively responding to the real-time active attacks. It can also lessen the amount of time spent on scheduled tasks and enable the users and the related organizations in any similar aspects for resource utilization more strategically. Machine learning can take over cyber security in a simpler and effective way which seems to be more proactive but less expensive. But it can only perform if the underlying data supporting machine learning gives a clear image of the environment. As they say, garbage in, garbage out [25]. As of the concerned study, the explicit description is much flexible with respect to the changes carried out in the conditional algorithm in the utility functions that can be reflected by the identical data nodes in evaluating the decision network strong enough to accommodate the observational reflections in cyber metric network zones, which when applied will definitely go on for a substantial proliferation of safety and security in going at par with IoT devices in excellence.

As of a debated verse, these days that internet is hardly a secure environment itself that makes IoT devices even less so, but with technical knowhow and implementing those technical aspects, we can make a turnover to make it a differentiable in its context. There have been several high-profile events, involving the use of IoT devices as nodes in wider botnet attacks that highlight IoT's vulnerability. With one of the finest examples being the Mirai malware which runs over the largest DDoS attack that targeted French cloud computing site OVH and even lighter in the particular year. Besides, along with the advent of maturity, security will tend to be a market differentiator.

A company selling web cameras which provides lifelong security upgrades may accumulate greater sales than a rivalry company which never does [26]. Further, many risks are enliven with both home and enterprise. IoT makes up the following non-exhaustive list:

- Secured data issues
- Risk of being safe personally and publicly physical safety
- Privacy issues like home devices being hacked
- Growth of IoT devices being followed by data storage management

2.5.6 Distributed Denial-of-Service

A distributed denial-of-service (DDoS) attack can be enumerated as a malevolent attempt to disrupt the congestion within target server, amenity, or network by profusing the target and its neighboring architectural infrastructure with a rush of internet traffic.

A DDoS attack can be enumerated as an initiative toward attacked traffic.

From the greater level, a DDoS attack is just like a congestion, which can prohibit the regular accessibility within the desired destination that seeks an attacker to have authority of the network of the machines over the web to perform an attack.

Computer systems and various other machines (like IoT devices) are thrushed with malwares, making over each one into a zombie or bot. The attacking host has the overall control over the group of zombies or bots, which is termed as botnet. Once a botnet has been set up, the attacking agent is capable of directing the machines by passing the latest instruction to each bot directed by a method similar to that of a remote control. At the same time, if the IP address of a victim is on target reflected by the botnet, each bot will reciprocate by prolifering the requests to the targets, thereby causing the target server to potentially overflow requests to the targets, leading denial of service to normal traffic. This is all because each particular bot is a legitimate internet instrument in which disintegrating attack traffic from normal traffic becomes difficult approach [27].

2.6   Related Work

Here, we present the analytic report which logically protects the mind front of every individual interest related to be it government, business, and industry or academic with IoT in their own prospective. As a part of this opportunity, the threat issues around cyber security are manipulated and controlled with concepts of machine learning. This guide also looks at warnings which consist of data manipulations, theft identification, and cyber warfare. It also focuses upon the current issues correlating data autonomy, digital succession, and leveraging technical talent. It also looks upon for the need of the hour, i.e., the challenging issues of collaboration for mitigating the treats with education and awareness of artificial intelligence to maintain a balance between the nomenclature of privacy and security where cyber security is encountered with sanctity of data in computer system.

Cybercrime overhauls in versatility approaches like denial-of-service attacks over the web to theft, exaction, and manipulative annihilations.

It is also found from the study that in various fiber optic routers and networks which constantly fend off the queries and with virtual address being played as the medium of data communication, that allows the software to delve into over predictions and emerge as the sensor encompassing it. Here, we can think of the latest developments from 2018 to 2019 in terms of Botnets. This is because be it a personal computer, laptop, tab, webcam, or even a Wi-Fi router which are very common these days in our homes, this is where a moderate security design visualizes devices that have come up with designs that can easily bypass and foster into installation of malware and control the device remotely and this is where the Zombies can be trained like trained data sets using the learning methodologies that could go forward to a nautical DDOS attack. This was first seen over when Australian Bureau of Statistics & Census website that was publicly hacked and later on when French Internet service provider OVH suffered an attack. The above concept implemented here can be topped up by exponentially increasing the botnets capacities, thereby making the source code being hardcoded range of shell scripts applied over to scan the IP ranges and attempt to remotely sense and test the data sets eventually before the technology gets integrated upon cyber infrastructure in a secured transformation. Hence, the above implementation could potentially give terrific results.

As machine learning is at its pace fastened up as a leverage tool against malicious attackers, at the same time, cybercriminals are also on the tip of their toes for getting into new artificial intelligent (AI) techniques for a better data analysis and pattern recognition. Hence, the machine learning algorithms, such like neural networks, can also be thought of as an attempt to research upon to train and speed up the automation process of the algorithms which can enhance the possibility of combating over cybercrimes.

Various studies have also been performed in showcasing the intelligent studies which can be revived upon AI-powered leaning algorithms which not only can record the malware signature but also can replace the generation of codes with human intervention. A burning illustration is in a recent operational research at Microsoft to create AI system that can generate code even without human intervention.

The analytic algorithms will enable the IoT device manufacturers to ensure the recognition of the requirement to order and re-organize the materials and its associated products being technically enabled to reduce the interaction between users as well as intervention for an enterprising replenishment which will make sure that the information reports a huge percentage (around 92%) of total cyber incidents.

This is because the various IOT-enabled sectors are getting hitched over protecting the sensitive data as estimated. The study is a mechanism which can allow the harmless constituents to be seamlessly desegregated into the IoT structure and hence has implemented "immune automated security response mechanism".

2.7   Methodology

In order to integrate the technology approach, we can enumerate the equational approaches which are limited to opportunity by using them as defense against threat as there is no silver bullet. Be it any among the world's leading business conducts that have their fortune counterparts, being crowned with cybercrime slows down the resource allocation process within the CPU for being a vulnerable threat.

Considering the next phase of work being threat detection and classification where machine learning algorithms play the major role of identifying with the model-based approach, the data sets are trained with patterns of malicious activities. When the data sets are put over the equations and tested within the axis, this presents recorded indicators that reciprocate to the real-time treats. This is where the unsupervised learning algorithm methodology of machine learning would find the interesting patterns in data sets, thereby identifying computer programs suggesting malwares and its associative crimes over cloud in terms of patterns using clustering and association algorithm. These derived learned patterns can be applied over IP bottleneck categorization, thereby further automating the procedural equation of deleting the trespassing of the system. It can also navigate throughout the cloud for identifying the behavioral patterns in DDOS attack.

The huge proliferation of machine learning techniques which highlights the analysis of multiple machine detection system hovering over the contextual topic is so called the cybercrime. Our studies have been put forth over to prioritize the cyber security resources with the co-relative approach of machine learning algorithm to determine which are linking networks involved in these certain types of attacks. It is really pros as it has been for the implementation of such algorithms that give rise to results based on network domain knowledge with the resultant values being data specific. Studies are based upon the use of anticipated usage of KNN algorithm for clustering the similar data to foster the enriched study with respect to IoT devices connected over the cloud. It is would definitely decipher to determine the cognitive analysis and reinforcement alerts over the network to subsidize the risk pondering over the association of smart thefts over various network attributes.

The resultant throughput of such a model can be referred to the pioneering act of intrusion detection, and protection of IoT devices can be carried out by machine learning models which aim at detection and segregation of similar ones into clusters and situations, preventing alterations of data during the testing phase. The algorithm used here can also get on to a regular system operation as of when applied over some data sets like (wine and viscos) which have proved to have made significant contributions in speech recognition, biometric systems, and so on. It automates complex cyber offences as well as defenses, powered by the learning models and their data sets, which act as a weapon to deal with the vulnerability of continuous intrusions, to stay forceful in combating the related issues as well as managing the network resource to balance the cloud content preferred with adversial use of cognitive artificial intelligence.

The synchronization of the spatial and temporal data from both ends and distribution of the power and bandwidth at both ends, i.e., of the IoT devices and there at the threshold of data server, is itself a high performance intelligent computation which desires to be providing the best of time complexity and space complexity. Each and every relationship established between the various components in IoT conglomeration has interchange of information which could be termed as best approach of cyber vulnerability as in reference to the context of being free from risk and secured in association to that of workforce inhabitants of the on possession of its access and its service.

The efficiency of cloud to receive and process it to get the information is virtually beyond limit. As it is more readily scalable intelligent algorithm, it has driven the authentication process in an enforcement of modality-based cyber metric captures and its facts of the cyber specification and just in time sharing mode; it is useful in automatically updating the information to identity authentication.

2.8   Discussions and Implications

It is definitely difficult to automate the security task hundred percent but our application of KNN can intervene with its data-based design model which can identify similar kinds of attacks and can combat over it eventually. It can be automated to gain authorized access to the networks communicating with the IOT devices, thereby the collision of human intelligence and artificial intelligence together would produce much of generic outputs accomplished with greater efficiency. Besides, to enrich the content of security analysis activity, studies have been further elongated upon the visualized parameters of defending cognitive infrastructures compelling over the security vector machines which can deduce the clusters with maximized efficiency to create AI products of making it imprecate for us to get on to IoT devices.

In our study of computational intelligence which has raised its impactable approach over cyber intelligence in getting on to analyzing and identifying the digital safety threats to deal with the intruders over the clouds for various application tools has embarked upon the security design and security architecture with hostile alterations to data which is nothing but intellectual property secrets. As IoT enriched cyber-based existing systems are coming across vulnerabilities, the intruder over the cloud from the web have compelled our introspective technical ideas to do the makeover of the secured thread caused by the generously malicious systems.

It is approximately calculated that the number of connected devices will increase to 40 billion by end of 2020. But the latest research says that it may further exceed 60 billion because of this pandemic situation that we are undergoing. Hence, it becomes the call of the hour to put up our keen study and implementation ideas to provide a real-time response to do the diagnose data processing and analysis to have been applied with the machine learning techniques with data retrieval to make the decision accurate and timely which is the goal of this data-based work.

2.9   Conclusion

In this strategic study, the surveyed paradigm includes the security aspect of IoT and what is being carried out over it as a thoughtful concern of today's era and as well as the prospective which need further concern. It renders over the architectural infrastructure IOT-enabled devices and the design model of the computational intelligent approach which is applied over with machine learning algorithms. It also looks upon the perfect analysis of the vulnerabilities of the related devices over the cloud which limits the failure ratio by the use of cognitive intelligence techfacts and forms. It also overhauls the cryptographic protocols which would enable IOT devices to process the computational data signals without the interventions of intruding threats. It gives us a dynamic efficacy for a secured communication, thereby developing schemes to address the security in context. Besides, it clearly reflects the security in context to both defense as well as attack.

The machine learning algorithm acts as a cyberweapon and an automated tool for automating the correlated cyber activities, with use of which this leverages the sophisticated power of adversarial machine learning. This study can be better basis for future resources dynamically analyzing the existing security solutions and develop a scalable cyber security system. It is also observed the extracted high-order implicable technology can further be modified where single malicious node can give signals to multiple identities and thus reducing the effectiveness of their faults schemes.

Hence, we may brief up as follows: Whenever a contravention occurs, the earlier it is detected and responded to the maximum is the opportunity of reducing loss vividly in a dynamic and vulnerable incidental operation.

References

1. Atlam, H.F., Alenezi, A., Alharthi, A., Walters, R.J., Wills, G.B., Internet of Things (iThings) and IEEE Green Computing and Communications (GreenCom) and IEEE Cyber, Physical and Social Computing (CPSCom) and IEEE Smart Data (SmartData). *IEEE International Conferenece*, Exeter, UK, 2017, https://ieeexplore.ieee.org/document/8276823.

2. Tweneboah-Koduah, S., Skouby, K.E., Tadayoni, R., Cyber Security Threats to IoT Applications and Service Domains, Wireless Personal Communications. *Int. J.*, 94, 4, June 2017. Springer.
3. https://www.softwaretestinghelp.com/iot-devices/
4. Hossain, Md. M., Fotouhi, M., Hasan, R., Towards an Analysis of Security Issues, Challenges, and Open Problems in the Internet of Things. *IEEE 11th World Congress on Services*, New York, NY, USA, June 2015, https://www.researchgate.net/publication/279801184_Towards_an_Analysis_of_Security_Issues_Challenges_and_Open_Problems_in_the_Internet_of_Things.
5. https://www.scnsoft.com/services/iot
6. Buch, R., Borad, N., Kalola, P., World of Cyber Security and Cybercrime. *STM J.*, August 2018. https://www.researchgate.net/publication/327110771.
7. Saravanan, A. and Sathya Bama, S., A Review on Cyber Security and the Fifth Generation Cyberattacks. *Orien. J. Comput. Sci. Technol.*, 12, 2, 50–56, 2019.
8. Fruhlinger, J., What is a cyber attack? Recent examples show disturbing trends, CSO |, 27 February 2020. https://www.csoonline.com/article/3237324/what-is-a-cyber-attack-recent-examples-show-disturbing-trends.html.
9. Wikipedia, https://en.wikipedia.org/wiki/Cyberattack.
10. Fruhlinger, J., Malware explained: How to prevent, detect and recover from it CSO |, 17 May 2019. https://www.csoonline.com/article/3295877/what-is-malware-viruses-worms-trojans-and-beyond.html.
11. Fruhlinger, J., What is phishing? How this cyber attack works and how to prevent it CSO|, 4 September 2020. https://www.csoonline.com/article/2117843/what-is-phishing-how-this-cyber-attack-works-and-how-to-prevent-it.html.
12. Fruhlinger, J., Ransomware explained: How it works and how to remove it, CSO |, 19 June 2020. https://www.csoonline.com/article/3236183/what-is-ransomware-how-it-works-and-how-to-remove-it.html.
13. Wikipedia, https://en.wikipedia.org/wiki/Spyware
14. Gunjan, V.K., Kumar, A., Avdhanam, S., A Survey of Cyber Crime in India. *Conference: ICACT*, 2013.
15. https://www.ntsc.org/assets/pdfs/cyber-security-report-2020.pdf
16. Hilt, S., Kropotov, V., Mercês, F., Rosario, M., Sancho, D., The Internet of Things in the Cybercrime Underground, Trend Micro Research, For Raimund Genes, 1963–2017.
17. Kaufman, L.M., BAE Systems, Data Security in the World of Cloud Computing, Security & Privacy IEEE, ieeexplore.ieee.org, 2009.
18. IBM cloud education, in: *Cloud Storage 24th*, June 2019, https://www.ibm.com/cloud/learn/cloud-storage.
19. Wikipedia, https://en.wikipedia.org/wiki/Cloud_computing_security.
20. Carroll, M., van der Merwe, A., Kotzé, P., Secure Cloud Computing: Benefits, Risks and Controls. *Conference: Information Security South Africa (ISSA)*, IEEE Xplore, 2011.

21. Survey, A., Integration of cloud computing and Internet of Things. *Future Gener. Comput. Syst.*, 56, 2015. https://www.researchgate.net/publication/283236612_Integration_of_Cloud_computing and_Internet_of_Things_A_survey.

22. Russel, S.J. and Norvig, P., *Artificial Intelligence: A modern Approach*, 2nd Edition, Pearson Education, Inc., Dorling Kindersley (India) Pvt. Ltd, 2007.

23. Sethi, A., Supervised Learning vs. Unsupervised Learning, 2020. https://www.analyticsvidhya.com/blog/2020/04/supervised-learning-unsupervised-learning/.

24. https://www.javatpoint.com/difference-between-supervised-and-unsupervised-learning

25. Perlman, A., The Growing Role of Machine Learning in Cybersecurity, June 18, 2019.

26. Katz, H., IoT Cybersecurity Challenges and Solutions, 2019.

27. https://www.cloudflare.com/learning/ddos/what-is-a-ddos-attack/

3

Employing Machine Learning Approaches for Predictive Data Analytics in Retail Industry

Rakhi Akhare*, Sanjivani Deokar, Monika Mangla and Hardik Deshmukh

CSED, Lokmanya Tilak College of Engineering, Navi Mumbai, India

Abstract

The retail industry is experiencing a drastic transformation during the past few decades. The technological revolution has further revolutionized the face of the retail industry. As a result, each industry is aiming to obtain a better understanding of its customers in order to formulate business strategies. Formulation of efficient business strategies enables an organization to lure maximum customers and thus obtain a largest portion of market share. In this chapter, authors aim to provide the importance of predictive data analytics in the retail industry. Various approaches for predictive data analytics have been briefly introduced to maintain completeness of the chapter. Finally, authors discuss the employment of machine learning (ML) approaches for predictive data analytics in the retail industry. Various models and techniques have also been presented with pros and cons of each. Authors also present some promising use cases of utilizing ML in retail industry. Finally, authors propose a framework that aims to address the limitations of the existing system. The proposed model attempts to outperform traditional methods of predictive data analytics.

Keywords: Predictive data analytics, retail industry, machine learning, e-business

3.1 Introduction

In this modern world, it is observed that the face of each business is experiencing a drastic transformation owing to huge technological advancements.

Corresponding author: rakhiakhare@gmail.com

Sachi Nandan Mohanty, Jyotir Moy Chatterjee, Monika Mangla, Suneeta Satpathy and Sirisha Potluri (eds.) Machine Learning Approach for Cloud Data Analytics in IoT, (53–70) © 2021 Scrivener Publishing LLC

Also, this technological revolution has influenced the mode of operation of the retail industry due to the change in the shopping behavior of customers. As a result, customers have shifted from conventional in-store shopping to shopping through online platforms, mobile channels, or even through machine-to-machine (M2M) commerce during the past few decades. The prime technologies which have propelled this business transformation are recent emergence in artificial intelligence (AI), big data, blockchain technologies, and the Internet of Things (IoT) [1, 2]. For instance, big business groups like Amazon and Flipkart have established a cut-throat competition to lure customers in the retail industry employing advancements in data analytics. Retail organizations have also been formulating different business and marketing strategies to garner the largest share of customers. Retail industries have been employing data analytics capabilities to better understand their customers in terms of choice, budget, and demand, which enables them to provide efficient and dynamic customer service. The retail industries obtain this competence of providing dynamic and user-specific service by gaining detailed information about purchase, location, and social media data of its customers. Here, social media data refers to the opinions and feedback about a product, service, or organization posted by customers, helpful to other prospective customers to make an informed purchase decision. Handling such huge data consisting of purchase, location, and social media is achievable as a result of advancements in big data technology [3, 4].

Big data is an efficient technology to handle complex, unstructured, varying, and voluminous data in comparison to traditional data-processing technologies. Basically, big data is characterized by four V's, *viz.*, velocity, volume, variety, and veracity. Big data facilitates efficient analysis of such complex data to reveal patterns, associations, and hidden patterns. Advancement in the big data has enhanced its employment in the retail industry as it significantly aids them to frame future policies and business strategies [3]. The process of discovering meaningful and useful information in big data is referred to as big data analytics (BDA). BDA enables industries to collect and process the big data to discover insights for fact-based and informed decision-making [5]. BDA has proved its potential and capability in diverse domains including retail industry. In the retail industry, BDA aims to deliver an enhanced shopping experience through recommendations, optimized operational system, and improved supply chain management (through demand forecasting). BDA can be broadly classified into three categories as shown in Figure 3.1.

Here, descriptive analytics is used to obtain summarized sales along various (region, product, etc.) dimensions [6]. Prescriptive analytics enables

Figure 3.1 Classification of big data analytics.

retailers to devise best strategies like market price in order to maximize business performance. Predictive analytics uses the historical data from past years to create empirical predictions [7]. There is sufficient number of techniques and technologies in existence to perform BDA. Some of the prominent technologies are data mining, optimization method, and machine learning (ML) [8]. The authors in this chapter primarily focus on the ML approaches employed for *predictive data analytics* in the retail industry. The chapter is organized as follows.

Section 3.1 of the chapter briefly introduces the concept of predictive data analytics and its requirements in the retail industry. Various approaches of predictive data analytics have also been mentioned in this section. Background and related work has been elaborated in Section 3.2. The predictive data analytics in the retail industry has been discussed in Section 3.3. It also presents various models for predictive data analytics using ML. Associated challenges and use cases have also been discussed in this section. Authors attempt to propose a framework for predictive data analytics in Section 3.4. Finally, conclusion and future direction for research has been presented in Section 3.5.

3.2   Related Work

This section presents the background and related work of ML in the context of retail industries. The employment of ML in retail industries has started since its inception [9]. However, the emergence in ML has further boosted its employment in this domain during the past decade. The major employment of ML approaches is for prediction of sales, revenue and stock requirement in the retail industry. Authors in [4] established that the predictive model is generally suitable for estimating and predicting future observations and assessing their predictability levels.

Authors in [10] determined the possibilities of integrating big data in the retail industry. Authors discussed the usage of Bayesian approach and predictive analytics in the context of the retail industry. Authors also mentioned the concern for data privacy in retail industry. This research was taken one step ahead by authors in [11] who have used different ML techniques to predict the sales. In [11], it is observed that the normal regression techniques when integrated with boosting techniques have observed better results in comparison to mere regression algorithms. Using the same principle, authors in [12] also used ML approaches to predict future sales using the historical sales data. Authors discussed various approaches for the sales prediction and finally concluded that gradient boost algorithm is the best fit model for this scenario as it achieves highest accuracy and efficiency. The authors in [13] also implemented a stacking approach for regression ensemble to further improve prediction for sales. Authors in [14] proposed a model using ML techniques to optimize pricing on a daily basis. All these predictive models can be employed to predict demand and sales of products in future. Authors in [15] presented a regression model using regression trees for each department to predict future demand. The proposed model is authenticated in terms of its efficiency using least squares regression, principal components regression, and other similar regressions. Similarly, authors in [15] used historical data and Rue La La's expertise for building size curves for each product p which represents the percentage of product demand for each size of p. Here, authors also attempted a price optimization problem with an object to set a prime for each product so as to maximize the revenue.

Authors in [16] proposed a framework to perform requirement analysis in the retail industry. The proposed framework consists of three modeling views: business view, analytics design view, and data preparation view. These views collectively perform data preparation activities. The authors in [17] employed descriptive analytics in relation to data mining for decision-making. Here, it is worth mentioning that predictive data analytics employs deterministic optimization techniques such as the decision tree method.

3.3   Predictive Data Analytics in Retail

Each retail industry aims to devise attractive and efficient business strategies to lure the largest portion of customers. For the past few years, retail industries had been using historical data to frame business strategies [18]. Focusing on mere historical transaction data fails to give promising results in this rapidly evolving and competing business world involving huge ocean of data [19]. This inability is addressed using predictive data analytics, an efficient approach to use big data to predict the activity, behavior, and future trends for any enterprise. Further, predictive data analytics is required owing to exponential rise in data and cut-throat competition. Predictive data analytics also helps to obtain a thorough understanding of customers, budget, and stock. As a result, predictive data analytics has gained wide acceptance and attracted several researchers and academicians. Predictive data analytics fails to achieve the desired results using simple regression type methods as it is not suitable in this multidimensional environment. Hence, it employs ML to enhance its capability [20]. The following are the most prevailing models for predictive data analytics [14]:

- Classification Model
- Clustering Model
- Outliers Model
- Time Series Model

The readers may refer to [14] for the explanation of these models. All these models use common predictive algorithms. The various predictive algorithms can be broadly categorized into two groups, *viz.*, ML and deep learning. ML primarily works for tabular data which may be linear or nonlinear. Basically, deep learning is also a subset of ML but it has better optimization when dealing with audio, text, and images. ML-based predictive modeling uses various algorithms. Some common algorithms are discussed below in brief [21].

Random Forest: It is the most popular classification and regression algorithm of ML capable of handling huge volumes of data. Random forest implements bagging where a subset of training data is used to train the network. Training process may be repeated with another subset in parallel thus achieving a strong learner.

Generalized Linear Model (GLM): This model narrows down the list of variables and thus performs better than the general linear model. As a result of narrowing down the variables, it gets trained quickly. The limitation of this model is that it requires relatively huge training data sets.

Gradient Boosted Model (GBM): it generates a model that uses decision trees for classification. In this approach, each tree rectifies errors present in previously trained tree. As it builds one tree at a time, it takes longer but gives better generalizations. Hence, it is used in ML-based ranking in Yahoo, among others.

K-Means: It is a popular and fast algorithm to classify data points in various groups so that all points in the same group are highly similar. The aim of this classification is that intragroup similarity is maximized and intergroup similarity is minimized.

Owing to abovementioned algorithms, ML has been widely accepted and recognized as an efficient choice for handling huge volumes of data in the retail industry. It enables sophisticated algorithms for customers' understanding and thus provides customer-oriented shopping experience. The subsequent subsection discusses the employment of ML for predictive data analytics in the retail industry.

3.3.1   ML for Predictive Data Analytics

As mentioned earlier, ML has been accepted as an efficient and effective choice for predictive data analytics in the retail industry. ML algorithms aid in identification of valued customers for a retail industry. These valued customers need to be retained by devising exciting and attractive strategies for success of any business entity. ML also enjoys the facility of customizing personalized customer's view based on his likings and history [22]. Ability to provide user-oriented customer view further escalates its popularity in the retail industry. Similarly, it can also be utilized for predicting required stock so as to minimize involved risks and uncertainties [23]. The basic model of ML for predictive data analytics in the retail industry performs several functions. A sample description for same is as follows:

1. It initially gathers the data from diverse sources related to products for training purposes.
2. Thereafter, an algorithm is chosen to analyze the features of training data. Algorithms also precisely predict the product price.
3. It is followed by prediction of the right price in comparison to real price of the product.
4. ML algorithm continuously adjusts the prediction mechanism in order to minimize the gap between predicted price and actual price.
5. This pre-training is followed by prediction of price of numerous products and a feedback loop is also considered to further enhance the accuracy of the model.
6. To further refine the model, new product data is added to the system.

The abovementioned steps are the basic steps to employ predictive data analytics in the retail industry. Few such examples of its applications are as follows [16]:

ML for Demand Prediction: ML uses high computations power to handle highly volatile data to predict the demand in future. For the same prediction, ML uses external and internal sources (structured, semi-structured, and unstructured data) of information so as to make informed decisions. This data may involve historical data, social media data, etc. Here, ML applies complicated mathematical algorithms to uncover hidden patterns in complicated and large datasets and thus provide reliable and accurate forecasts [24].

ML for Predictive Sales Analytics: Another common application of predictive data analytics is to understand the driving motive behind customer's purchase and their behavior under particular circumstances. Similarly, data from different sources is aggregated. The aggregated data is cleansed to determine the best forecasting algorithm for the current scenario. It then builds a predictive model to identify relationships among various factors. This is followed by monitoring the model to measure its accuracy with an objective to maximize its prediction accuracy.

ML for Customer's Customization: Using ML, recommendation engines are developed which give a customized view to each individual customer based on his likes and requirements. Provision of customized view ensures retention of customers to the same platform. Amazon has got the best recommendation engine which has significantly helped it to ace the competition.

ML for Supply Chain Planning: As ML can be employed for predicting the future sales, it can also be utilized for maintaining hassle-free supply chain management despite involvement of several uncertain features. Moreover, it can also be used for optimized route planning for delivery of goods or warehouse maintenance. A route suggested by ML algorithms ensures to efficiently optimize cost, time, and carbon emission in comparison to humans.

ML for price Optimization: ML algorithms can be employed for predicting the optimized price of products considering several factors like amount of discount, product type, competing retailers, and time dimension. Usage of ML in price optimization yields accurate predictions over traditional methods of price optimization. It can also be used for revenue forecasting during a particular month, quarter, or financial year [25].

3.3.2   Use Cases

As discussed earlier, ML has been employed in several leading retail industries to sustain and excel in this cut-throat competing business world. Traditionally, managers would have predicted sales based on various factors like brand quality, promotion, and discount. Managers used to implement a series of regressions to predict the sales volume. The efficiency of such an approach heavily relied on the capability of the human brain. Traditional methods even led to inefficient forecasting. This inefficiency has been completely handled by incorporating ML approaches. In this subsection, authors discuss few popular use cases of ML employment in retail industries.

According to [26], a ML model is devised to predict sales in response to promotion by a multinational retailer. An efficient model would enable to garner a huge leap in sales. Here, the retail company wanted to have an idea about the strongly and weakly performing products in the store. In the model, the company used several variables like discount, promotion duration, size of promotional advertisement, placement of products, and seasonality, among others. It was observed in [26] that a traditional method which involved several data analysts and a series of linear regression models predicted the results with 30% to 35% error rate. This error rate was brought down in the first attempt to 24% using ML model, and the error rate is expected to further reduce over time. Thus, integration of ML approaches in prediction models provided exciting and attractive results. It helped to curb the cost involved in generous promotions and maintaining inventory in the warehouse. Using the similar predictive model, Target Corp. also observed the growth of 15%–30% in revenue.

A renowned retailer *Walmart* has also incorporated technologies to understand customers' needs and act accordingly. The company employed facial recognition software to understand the experience level (frustration, happiness, and satisfaction) during checkout. It also triggers an alert for customer representatives to approach frustrated customers in order to provide better customer service. Usage of this facial recognition model eliminates the need of maintaining expensive and appropriate staff for providing enhanced customer service.

Amazon has been proudly employing ML for predictive data analytics to enhance its sales. Amazon has garnered its outstanding benefit for demand prediction in business management [27]. It has also filed a patent for the process of its anticipatory shipping that predicts sales of a product in a particular region or city. Amazon uses this information to store the targeted products in nearest warehouses. It is also planning to deliver the product to the customers using drones in minimum time thus excelling the experience of shopping.

Authors in [28] have presented the implementation of predictive analytics in the *retail banking sector*. Here, authors claim that predictive analytics through traditional tools necessitates a specialized skill in statistics and mathematics. However, the same can be performed much easily in R, a language that includes around 4,000 algorithms of ML ranging from basic regression model to advanced model. In the banking sector, predictive analytics can be used to estimate churning rate and product propensity.

3.3.3   Limitations and Challenges

ML has observed widespread deployment in various domains including retail industry. In the retail industry also, it has been implemented for numerous purposes as discussed earlier. Despite its widespread deployment, it has some limitations and challenges. The major challenge is handling an ocean of data from diverse sources involving structured, semi-structured, and even unstructured data. This huge data collected from various sources is generally of poor quality, and therefore, efficient data cleaning methods need to be used to infer meaningful data [17]. Thereafter, it also has the challenge of maintaining stringent privacy and security policies for this huge data. It also has a challenge of acquiring trained and competent professionals who have vision of the future data requirement so as companies are able to draw useful insights from historical data.

3.4   Proposed Model

In this section, authors propose a model for predictive data analytics in retail industries using ML approaches. Ahead of proposing the model, authors attempt to thoroughly understand the requirements of retailers. It is understood that retailers have various queries in mind which need to be addressed by an efficient model. Some of these queries are as follows:

- What is the probability of a person who is predicted to have online purchase behavior truly purchases online?
- Which segment of customers the retailer should focus on?
- Which are the geographical regions for online and offline channels?

A detailed understanding of the various queries of retailers enables devising an efficient predictive model. Here, authors aim to devise a model that provides various functions. Some of these functions are illustrated in Figure 3.2.

For instance, the proposed model can be used to estimate and forecast the sales of a particular product for a particular region. It can be performed

Figure 3.2 Illustration of major functions of predictive data analytics.

at various levels of abstraction as per retailer's choice and requirement. The proposed model aims to find the prospective buyers for a product even with very little probability of purchase. As it is observed, if a model targets more customers, then it may involve some additional costs but will not miss any probable buyer. Authors aim to not miss any probable customer as it may result in loss of some potential customers. The proposed model also attempts to predict the likelihood of a customer purchasing a particular product. This helps in targeting the prospective customers thus yielding an increase in revenue.

The proposed model collects data from various sources like social media, history data, and transaction details. This data from diverse sources is in disparate forms and thus needs to be cleaned during preprocessing. Thus, cleaned data from various sources is integrated, which is used for training the predictive model. The accuracy of model is largely dependent upon the size of training dataset. The basic structure of proposed model is represented in Figure 3.3.

As represented in Figure 3.3, the data integration is followed by algorithm selection for predictive model. There are several related algorithms like regression, boosting, or bagging, to name a few. Regression algorithms

Figure 3.3 General framework of proposed model for predictive data analytics.

are basic algorithms for any predictive model. Boosting algorithms trains a model in a sequential and gradual manner. These algorithms perform both classification and regression. Boosting algorithms basically aim to identify weak learners which further can be improvised so as it turns to be a strong learner. Gradient boosting and AdaBoost are the two popularly used boosting algorithms. These two boosting algorithms basically differ in identification of weak learners. Weak learners are identified based on error rate. Error rate depends on the parameters to be optimized. For instance, if a model tries to predict sales, then error rate will be difference in predicted sale and actual sale.

Random forest regression may also be employed for prediction problems as it performs classification and regression. Random forest regression employs some classification criteria to classify data. Thereafter, qualities of this split are measured using mean squared error or mean absolute error. It employs the concept of averaging to improve accuracy of prediction.

Authors in the chapter propose usage of bootstrap aggregating ML algorithm also referred to as bagging algorithm. Bagging algorithm aims to improve efficiency and accuracy of ML algorithms by reducing the variance. Usage of bagging algorithm advocates achievement of efficient and accurate predictive model. The accuracy of proposed model increases rapidly over time.

3.4.1   Case Study

For the sake of illustration of implementation of AI in retail industry, authors in the chapter consider a case study. Similarly, authors have taken a dataset pertaining to a retail store. This dataset comprises of observation for duration of 4 years from 2011 to 2015. This dataset has been taken from kaggle (https://www.kaggle.com/jr2ngb/superstore-datausername: jr2ngb). The considered dataset has 16 variables. Out of these 16 features, 10 are categorical features, 5 are numerical features, and 1 is date feature as follows.

#	Feature Name	Non-Null	Dtype
0	Order Date	51290	datetime64[ns]
1	Customer_Name	51290	object
2	Segment	51290	object
3	City	51290	object
4	State	51290	object
5	Country	51290	object
6	Category	51290	object
7	Sub-Category	51290	object
8	Product Name	51290	object
9	Sales	51290	float64
10	Quantity	51290	int64
11	Discount	51290	float64
12	Profit	51290	float64
13	year	51290	int64
14	month	51290	int64
15	Day	51290	object

The number of observations in the considered dataset is 51,290. The considered retail store broadly deals in three types of products, *viz.*, office supplies, technology, and furniture.

First of all, authors attempt to understand the correlation among various features of the dataset. Similarly, authors employ Pearson's correlation that signifies the measure of correlation between two variables. The value lies between −1 and +1. Here, negative value indicates negative linear correlation; 0 signifies no correlation and +1 indicates the positive linear correlation. The Pearson's correlation among various attributes of the dataset is shown in Figure 3.4.

Further, authors would like to demonstrate how this dataset can be used to understand its chunk of customers across the country. This helps retailer to understand that its largest market share lies in the country and thus enables it to focus in the weaker market section. It can be performed by region-wise analysis as shown in Figure 3.5. The figure shows the histogram plot for frequency of customers across various states in India. From Figure 3.5, it is evident that Maharashtra has the highest number of customers in the country followed by the Uttar Pradesh. On the contrary, places like Manipur, Tripura, Chandigarh, and Pondicherry have the lowest number of customers.

The analysis can further be drilled down to find best and worst performing city in a state so as to exactly identify the specific region or branch.

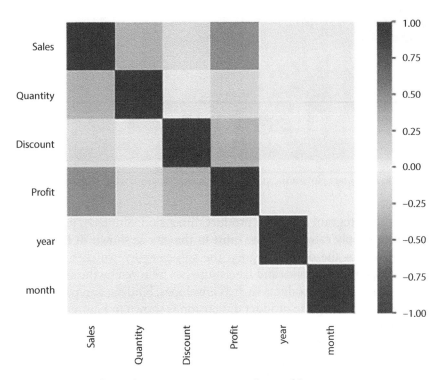

Figure 3.4 Pearson's correlation among various attributes of dataset.

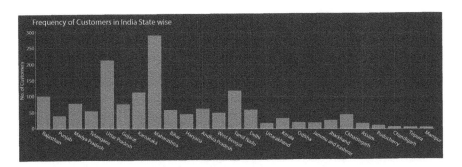

Figure 3.5 Histogram plot for the frequency of customers in country level (India).

Such drilled down histogram is shown in Figure 3.6. For Maharashtra, it shows that the top performing cities in the state are Mumbai, Pune, Thane, and Nagpur.

Further, it is evident from above two graphs that Mumbai has the highest number of customers. Hence, further the retailer is interested to find which the best performing product in the city is. Therefore, retailer is interested

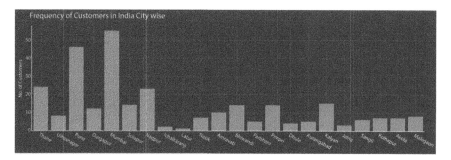

Figure 3.6 Histogram plot for the customers' frequency at city level in Maharashtra.

to find the histogram along the product dimension. Similarly, it is evident that office supply category is the most in the city as shown in Figure 3.7. Further, within the office category, the sub-category which has highest demand is storage supplies and labels supplies followed by the art supplies and other stationary products such as envelopes, binders, and papers. This histogram plot along the product dimension is shown in Figure 3.7.

Additionally, box plot represents minimum, maximum, and median of sales in each category of every segment. The highest median for technology category is from consumer segment as shown in Figure 3.8. Similarly, the highest median for furniture category is from the corporate segment.

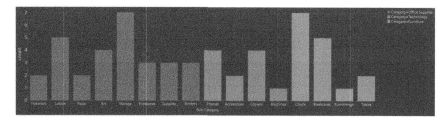

Figure 3.7 Histogram plot for Mumbai along the product dimension.

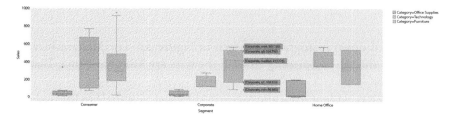

Figure 3.8 Box plot for products across consumer segment.

Home office segment has the maximum sales in office supplies, and the highest median for the office supplies is from consumer segment.

In order to analyze the day that observes highest and minimum sale, authors suggest usage of pivot table as shown in Figure 3.9. From Figure 3.9, it is evident that every Saturday of August from 2011 to 2015 experiences maximum sale. However, the minimum sale is recorded on every Monday of November from 2011 to 2015. This gives an idea to retail to have an idea of its sales forecast.

Finally, the heatmap in Figure 3.10 shows the sales of various countries across the globe. From Figure 3.10, it is clear that United States records maximum sale in comparison to any other country. It is followed by sales of France and Australia. This analysis helps the retail industry to understand that there is a huge potential for increasing in sales in Southeast Asian Region and also in Oceania.

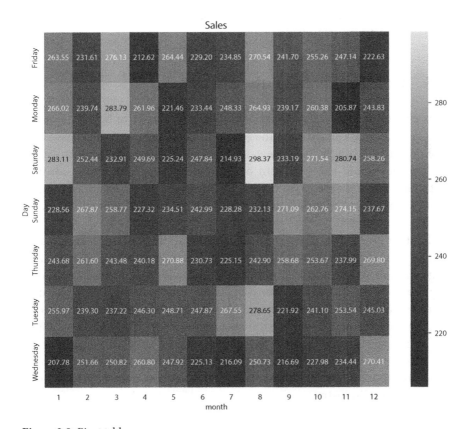

Figure 3.9 Pivot table.

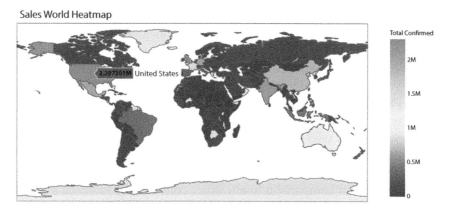

Figure 3.10   Heatmap of the world.

Thus, from the above case study, it is clear that data analytics can be quite helpful for a retail industry, and thus, it has a huge potential in retail apart from various promising fields.

3.5   Conclusion and Future Scope

This chapter has discussed the potential and capability of ML approaches for predictive data analytics in the retail industry. Various models have also been discussed briefly. Few use cases have been presented to give readers a clear idea about the spectrum of its application in the retail industry. Although it has observed widespread applications, it still bears some challenges. These challenges as discussed above must be addressed by taking the research ahead.

First and foremost, researchers must work in the direction of maintaining security and privacy of data as data is the most precious asset for any organization. Work should also be done in the direction of conceptualizing usage of big data so as to benefit retailers and customers. The research must be taken ahead in the direction of efficient customized promotions that basically sends promotional messages for a specific product to a specific customer at specific time. Implementation of customized promotion will further enhance the revenue generation. Additionally, it must also be ready to develop new operational models in response to the future need and growth of industry.

References

1. Grewal, D., Motyka, S., Levy, M., The Evolution and Future of Retailing and Retailing Education. *J. Mark. Educ.*, 40, 1, 85–93, 2018.
2. Mangla, M., Akhare, R., Ambarkar, S., Context-Aware Automation Based Energy Conservation Techniques for IoT Ecosystem, in: *Energy Conservation for IoT Devices*, pp. 129–153, Springer, Singapore, 2019.
3. Avinash, B.M. and Babu, S.H., Big Data Analytics – Its Impact on Changing Trends in Retail Industry. *Int. J. Adv. Res. Comput. Eng. Technol.*, 7, 4, 379–382, 2018.
4. Souza, T.T.P., Kolchyna, O., Treleaven, P.C., Aste , T., Twitter sentiment analysis applied to finance: A case study in the retail industry. arXiv preprint arXiv:1507.00784, 2015.
5. Akhare, R., Mangla, M., Deokar, S., Wadhwa, V., Proposed Framework for Fog Computing to Improve Quality-of-Service in IoT Applications, in: *Fog Data Analytics for IoT Applications*, pp. 123–143, Springer, Singapore, 2020.
6. Potluri, S., IOT Enabled Cloud Based Healthcare System Using Fog Computing: A Case Study. *J. Crit. Rev.*, 7, 6, 1068–1072, 2020.
7. Deokar, S., Mangla, M., Akhare, R., A Secure Fog Computing Architecture for Continuous Health Monitoring. In *Fog Computing for Healthcare 4.0 Environments*, pp. 269-290. Springer, Cham, 2021.
8. Mangla, M., & Sharma, N., Fuzzy Modelling of Clinical and Epidemiological Factors for COVID-19, 2020.
9. Chatterjee, J.M., Bioinformatics using machine learning. *Global Journal of Internet Interventions and IT Fusion*, 1, no. 1, 2018.
10. Bradlow, E.T., Gangwar, M., Kopalle, P., Voleti, S., The Role of Big Data and Predictive Analytics in Retailing. *J. Retail.*, 93, 1, 79–95, 2017, doi: 10.1016/j.jretai.2016.12.004.
11. Krishna, A., Akhilesh, V., Aich, A., Hegde, C., Sales-forecasting of Retail Stores using Machine Learning Techniques. *Proc. 2018 3rd Int. Conf. Comput. Syst. Inf. Technol. Sustain. Solut. CSITSS 2018*, pp. 160–166, 2018, doi: 10.1109/CSITSS.2018.8768765.
12. Cheriyan, S., Ibrahim, S., Mohanan, S., Treesa, S., Intelligent Sales Prediction Using Machine Learning Techniques. *Proc. - 2018 Int. Conf. Comput. Electron. Commun. Eng. iCCECE 2018*, August 2018, 53–58, 2019, doi: 10.1109/iCCECOME.2018.8659115.
13. Pavlyshenko, B.M., Machine-learning models for sales time series forecasting. *Data*, 4, 1, 1–11, 2019, doi: 10.3390/data4010015.
14. Aktas, E. and Meng, Y., An Exploration of Big Data Practices in Retail Sector. *Logistics*, 1, 2, 12, 2017, doi: 10.3390/logistics1020012.
15. Ferreira, K.J., Lee, B.H.A., Simchi-Levi, D., Analytics for an online retailer: Demand forecasting and price optimization. *Manuf. Serv. Oper. Manag.*, 18, 1, 69–88, 2016, doi: 10.1287/msom.2015.0561.

16. Nalchigar, S. and Yu, E., Business-driven data analytics: A conceptual modeling framework. *Data Knowl. Eng.*, 117, 2017, 359–372, 2018, doi: 10.1016/j.datak.2018.04.006.

17. Lam, D. A Survey of Predictive Analytics in Data Mining with Big Data. Athabasca University, 2014.

18. Shankar, V., Big Data and Analytics in Retailing. *NIM Mark. Intell. Rev.*, 11, 1, 36–40, 2019, doi: 10.2478/nimmir-2019-0006.

19. Chatterjee, J.M., Kumar, R., Khari, M., Hung, D.T., & Le, D.N., Internet of Things based system for Smart Kitchen. *Int. J. Eng. Manuf.*, 8, 4, 29, 2018.

20. Chatterjee, J., IoT with Big Data Framework using Machine Learning Approach. *Int. J. Mach. Lear. Networked Collab. Eng.*, 2, 02, 75–85, 2018.

21. Belarbi, H., Tajmouati, A., Bennis, H., Mohammed, E.H.T., Predictive Analysis of Big Data in Retail Industry. *1st Int. Conf. Comput. Wirel. Commun. Syst.*, December, 560–562, 2016.

22. Chatterjee, J.M., Kumar, R., Pattnaik, P.K., Solanki, V.K., Zaman, N., Privacy preservation in data intensive environment. *Tourism & Management Studies,* 14, 2, 72–79, 2018.

23. Farid, M., Latip, R., Hussin, M., Hamid, N.A.W.A., A survey on QoS requirements based on particle swarm optimization scheduling techniques for workflow scheduling in cloud computing. *Symmetry,* 12, 4, 551, 2020.

24. Potluri, S., An IoT based solution for health monitoring using a body-worn sensor enabled device. *JARDCS*, 10, 9, 646–651, 2018.

25. Potluri, S., A study on technologies in cloud-based design and manufacturing. *IJMPERD*, 8, 6, 187–192, 2018.

26. Chandramana, S., (PDF) Retail Analytics: Driving Success in Retail Industry with Business Analytics. *Int. J. Res. Publ.*, 7, 4, 159–166, 2017.

27. Fuggetta, R., Brand advocates: Turning enthusiastic customers into a powerful marketing force. John Wiley & Sons, 2012.

28. Budale, D. and Mane, D., Predictive Analytics in Retail Banking. *International Journal of Engineering and Advanced Technology,* 2, 5, 508–510, 2013.

4

Emerging Cloud Computing Trends for Business Transformation

Prasanta Kumar Mahapatra¹, Alok Ranjan Tripathy¹* and Alakananda Tripathy²

¹Department of Computer Science, Ravenshaw University, Cuttack, Odisha, India
²Department of Computer Science and Engineering, ITER,
S'O'A Deemed to be University, Bhubaneswar, Odisha, India

Abstract

Concept of cloud computing emerges to address traditional on-premise infrastructure issue and its resolution. Cloud computing is primarily formed to solve the storage and computing problems due to enormous data generated with the popularity of digitalization. But due to technological advancement, both business and technology are integrated. This forced cloud to evolve and incorporate all technology and business processes and become a vital part of business operations. Cloud is widely accepted due to its flexibility and platform independence nature. Operating business fully on cloud provides many benefits to business organizations, such as easier and instant installation, high availability, lightning fast performance, quicker application development, high security and easy disaster recovery, platform independence services, and more focus on business processes rather application maintenance. This paper covers detail about cloud evolution, adoptability, and key emerging trends of cloud computing.

Keywords: Digitalization, business, data center, computing

4.1 Introduction

In a layman's view, cloud computing is an abstract view of a single system which has unlimited pool of resources in terms of hardware, software, and other services available over the internet required to operate the business

---
**Corresponding author*: tripathyalok@gmail.com

Sachi Nandan Mohanty, Jyotir Moy Chatterjee, Monika Mangla, Suneeta Satpathy and Sirisha Potluri (eds.) Machine Learning Approach for Cloud Data Analytics in IoT, (71–98) © 2021 Scrivener Publishing LLC

in the digital world. Internet has developed itself into tremendous fast pace since its origin around 90s and become a necessary part of daily life and every business operations by connected through all kind of digital assets. With the evolvement of 5G technology and IoT (Internet of Things), every digital device varying from computers, tables, mobile phones, vehicles, and home appliances is now connected and seems all are part of a single system connected over internet. Distributed computing is gaining its popularity due to its diversity of operation to gain high performance and scaling without compromising its integrity, fault tolerance, and security [1]. So, cloud computing was born making footprint over distributed computing and internet connectivity.

Traditional IT industries are discrete in operations, which means they have their own setup operating under individual premises with their own rules and regulations with a limited scope of visibility to outside of their organizational [2]. They have their own pros and limitations.

Pros of on-Premises IT Operation [3]

- Complete control over infrastructure: customized setup can be done.
- Complete data visibility and control
- Highly secure
- Independent on internet and is operating on own intranet connectivity.

Limitations of on-Premises IT Operation [2]

- Large Capital Expenditure: To setup any IT infrastructure, organization has to purchase all hardware, licensed software, and necessary legal permission of the local authorities.
- Regular Maintenance: Not only setup requires capital expenditure, maintaining them over period of time requires a lot of capital expenditure in terms of license renewal, dedicated IT team operation, backups, storage, and disaster recovery process.
- Larger Implementation Time: It takes a lot of time for the installation of servers, software while upgrading the IT infrastructure.

4.1.1   Computing Definition Cloud

Many definitions have been given by various organizations, looking into properties and scope of cloud computing over time. But cloud is getting refined and changing the definition over time and technology advancement.

NIST	Gartner	Forrester
• A model for enabling convenient, on-demand network access to a shared pool of configurable computing resources, such as networks, servers, storage, applications and services, that can be rapidly provisioned and released with minimal management effort or service provider interaction.	• It is a style of computing in which massively scalable and elastic IT-enabled capabilities and delivered as a service using internet technologies.	• A standardized IT capability, such as software, application platform, or infrastructure, delivered via internet technologies in a pay-per-use and self-service way.

4.1.2   Advantages of Cloud Computing Over On-Premises IT Operation

To overcome the limitations of on-premises IT operation, adopting cloud computing is the best approach [5]. The following are the properties of cloud computing over on-premises IT operation to overcome the above limitations for smooth business operation.

- Plug and Use: Without worrying the physical location and infrastructure setup, it can be accessed from any system and any place just by connecting to the web browser.
- Affordable: As there is no big investment in initial setup, anyone can set up a start-up operation just by subscribing the necessary commodity from cloud provider.
- Predictable Cost: As all the available assets and their maintenance have a defined fee structure, it is very easier to define the budget for any organization
- Free From Dedicated IT Operation: As all the services are self-maintainable, so user has nothing to worry about the upgradation of hardware and software. Cloud service provider takes care of all these upgradation and maintenance.
- Highly Scalable: The more attractive benefit of cloud computing is its amazing scalability properties. Any type or size of the organization may it be, all cloud users can easily achieve the benefit of scalability property of the cloud. User has just to pay only for what they use.
- Quick Deployment: As virtualization is the basic properties of cloud computing, cloud-based applications can easily hosted on the virtual server in a matter of hours which on-premises deployment could take a much more time than cloud.
- Highly Standardize and Compliance: Many standards and compliance have been defined by different reputed

Government policy organization. It varies to some extend based on different country's Government policies and local laws [2].

- Lower Space and Energy Cost: As no separate infrastructure setup required, it reduces the energy consumption cost for the organization and helps the earth to be greener environment.

4.1.3 Limitations of Cloud Computing

- Connectivity: Internet connectivity is a mandate for cloud computing.
- Long-Term Cost: For larger organization, in a long-term plan cloud computing cost might be more than on-premises setup.
- Less Control Over Own Data Storage: As everything will remain out of premises, and under the control of cloud provider, data owner will have less control over data.

4.2 History of Cloud Computing

- Modern cloud computing evolves from 50 years old technology mainframe. The cloud computing evolution as shown in Figure 4.1.
- In 1960s, standalone mainframes are built keeping in the purpose of doing all calculations and storages in mainframes and client terminals are the dumb terminals sending client requests and getting responses just by connecting to the mainframes without doing any processing.
- In 1970s, virtualization concept was developed where one system can operated within another system. To make the virtualization concept into reality, collections of hardware components are tightly coupled on which multiple installations of operating systems or software's became feasible [4].
- In 1980s, client-server architecture became popular, where servers did not take all workloads. Though servers had major workload, clients systems also had the capacity to do independent small portions of work to reduce the workload from the server as well as the overall response time.

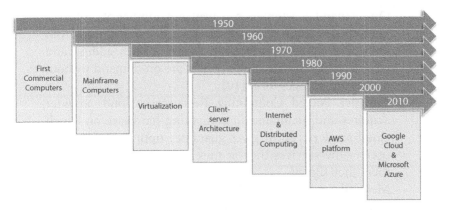

Figure 4.1 Technology evolution related to cloud computing [3].

- In 1990s, distributed system concept had developed where centralized servers workloads are distributed among multiple systems reducing the bottleneck of centralized system to gain high availability and throughput. Due to evolve of internet software application need not to mandatorily run on the client system rather on distributed systems across the network. This made applications modular where it can be controlled by the owner or vendor and can be available as a service to other clients over the internet. Similarly, hardware virtualization could become feasible over the internet.
- In 2000s, mass adoption of internet has been done and Amazon starts its initial version of cloud computing platform known as AWS.
- In 2010s, other cloud providers are comes into picture such as Microsoft's Azure and Google cloud and adoption of cloud computing has started by major IT vendors.

4.3   Core Attributes of Cloud Computing

- Elasticity: With the varying and increasing of data, evolution of technology, and business, organization has to provisioning and de-provisioning resources and software services in a faster pace without hampering business. Cloud has the ability to achieve elasticity in a multitenant model [7].

- On-Demand: Customers can avail any number of resources and services required on-demand at any point of time from anywhere connecting through internet. Both adding and removing of resources and services are on-demand without paying any charges for it [10].
- Provider Pooled Computing Resources: Cloud provider acquires and maintains all computing hardware on which cloud services run. It gives guarantee uptime to the cloud user of the services they acquire mentioned in the agreement they signed.
- Metered Service Usage: Cloud provides a flexibility subscription method to the customer for the services they consume. Cloud provides a metered service method where it provides transparency to the users to the consumption of resources and the billing amount at any point of time with a well-designed representative model. This model helps user to track the proper utilization of their money on cloud services. The following are the benefits of metered service
  - Automatic work load ensures no fee has to pay during idle time without releasing the services.
  - It creates alerts and notifies users if service consumption exceeds the limit set by user. This helps user no to track the consumption every time and focus on business.
  - This service also provides suggestions to redesign the resource allocation in case of improper usage of resources and unused storage spaces.
- Broad Network Access: Cloud services can be accessed from any type of devices such as desktops, laptops, mobile phones, and tablets just connecting through internet regardless of geographical location of use [11].
- Easy Maintenance: Servers are auto maintained means maintained by cloud provider not impacting the uptime for the users. Also, the upgrades are auto updates and make services more efficient.
- Multi-Business: Due to distributed networking and virtualization properties, cloud computing is efficient in parallel processing and resource sharing. This enables cloud to operate effortlessly across multiple-business lines without duplicating environments. Figure 4.2 shows the characteristics of cloud computing.

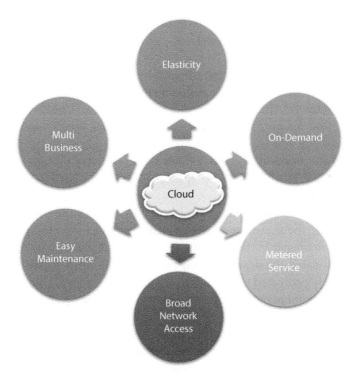

Figure 4.2 Cloud characteristics.

4.4   Cloud Computing Models

To understand cloud computing in better way, different models have been defined based on resource physical distribution and service principles. There are two major models defined [6].

- Cloud Deployment Model
- Cloud Service Model

4.4.1   Cloud Deployment Model

Based on cloud infrastructure setup, NIST has broadly defined the deployment model into four sub-categories such as public cloud, private cloud, hybrid cloud, and community cloud. These models are defined keep into consideration of the ownership of the cloud infrastructure between cloud provider and the user. Before moving the business process into the cloud, organizations have to evaluate different parameters such as existing infrastructure, ownership of the infrastructure, cost involvement during the transition, and future continuity with cloud computing. Figure 4.3 elaborates the cloud deployment model.

- Public Cloud: This kind of cloud service is an open service and available to public and all organizations for use. Cloud provider is the sole ownership of the cloud and mostly preferred for generic non-critical applications, email services, and file sharing applications. The actual physical location of the infrastructure is hidden from all users though user can select different geographical location for their services to operate [13].
- Private Cloud: Private cloud is deployment in the premises or off the premises of the organization and the cloud will be managed by the various teams in the organization or a dedicated third-party cloud provider. The infrastructure is solely dedicated to the owner organization and will fulfill the requirement of the same organization. Setting up and maintaining private cloud requires huge investment and time. Private cloud is best suited when privacy and security in the most concern. It generally preferred for organization working for critical applications and government agencies such as defense and intelligence department.
- Hybrid Cloud: As all the operations of an organization are not critical, so organization can set up hybrid cloud by deploying both the private cloud and public cloud. Hybrid

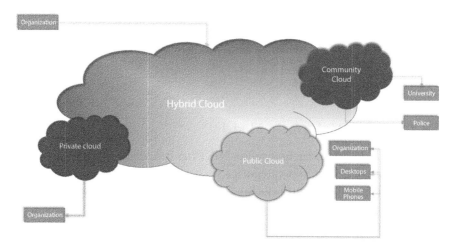

Figure 4.3 Cloud deployment model.

cloud reduces the cost of the infrastructure. Also, organization can get benefit of both the clouds, getting security and privacy through private cloud for critical operations and flexibility from public cloud for non-critical applications [9].

- Community Cloud: This model supports computer resources sharing among a community over the cloud; for example, universities co-operating with each other for certain fields of research and police departments within a country sharing information over the community cloud. The access to cloud is restricted within the members of the community [21].

4.4.2   Cloud Service Model

There are there basically three types of cloud service models, IaaS, PaaS, and SaaS, available in the cloud based on the types of service available. Refer to Figure 4.4 for the cloud service model architecture.

- IaaS (Infrastructure as a Service): In this model, cloud provider sets up and manages all the IT infrastructures and creates an abstract layer for the users to use all the underlying hardware without impacting the performance and hiding their physical presence [9].
  - It basically includes the hardware services provided by the vendors who already configured all the required hardware such as virtual machines, storage, and network components. User has to subscribe and use only required

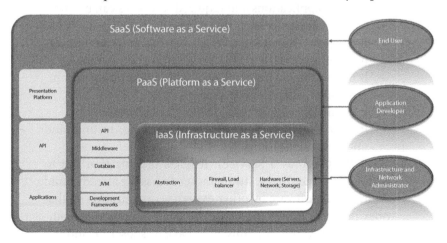

Figure 4.4 Cloud service model.

or allocated hardware components over the network without bothering its underlying setups.

- It makes the IT manager's task easier.
- It is available to any device on the network
- Rapidly provision and de-provisioning new computer resources can be done without impacting the other IT services.
- Computing infrastructure is not required locally as user has to work above the abstraction layer.
- Less local square footage for IT resources required for the organization that set up the infrastructure on IaaS.
- Less local energy consumption as infrastructure setup has to set by cloud provider.
- Offers the most complex services for easy use.

- PaaS (Platform as a Service): It is basically accessing system where all the required application are running and forming an environment where software developments can be done without bothering the compatibility of underlying installed application. Platform application are includes web servers, database servers, application servers along with development software that helps users to build their own applications over the available platform framework [13].
  - It basically reduces IT developer's workload.
  - It enables to design custom applications.
  - It can be available to any device on the network.
  - Rapidly provisioning and de-provisioning of new and existing applications and required resources can be done.
  - Server Infrastructure is not required
  - It has faster time to market as user has to focus on business rather underlying platform setup and upgrade.
  - It is available on demand basis and can be easily decommissioned when not required.
  - It eliminates wasted time due to IT acquisition.
  - It also simplifies the process of creating, testing, and updating applications.

- SaaS (Software as a Service): It helps organization not to build all the required software rather access the already build or available software by other expertise organization so that they need not have to purchase or install or update or maintain the software [15]. Only they have to subscribe and use it over the internet.

- It helps end users or application developers to be more focused on business rather application programs.
- Let users leverage existing application
- Rapidly provision or de-provision of users can be done.
- It can be available to any device on the network.
- Application licensing, monitoring management done by provider themselves.
- XaaS (Anything as a Service): Along with these three basic cloud computing services, there are other specializations of cloud services present and it is growing with time to fulfill the business need. It is called XaaS (Everything as a service or Anything as a Service). These services helped the enterprises to get benefit of such services which they could not able to access without cloud integration [10]. The following are few XaaS services evolved over time.
  - DaaS (Data as a Service): DaaS is a data management strategy that provides data, storage, processing, and integration along with analytics services. The following are the advantage of DaaS.
    - Data is available on-demand and with encrypted format.
    - Data storage and process can be done with greater speed.
    - Physical location of data is independent of user.
    - It is compatible with any type of physical storage device.
  - STaaS (Storage as a Service): Cloud provider provides storage space for the vendors who are willing to host their data over the network. Public cloud storage method includes back up and disaster recovery, block storage, SSD storage, and also block data transfer. Advantage of using STaaS includes the following:
    - Reduced storage cost
    - Disaster recovery
    - Scalability: resources can be added to any degree without degrading performance
    - Automatic sync: files will be synced automatically across devices
  - SECsaS (Security as a Service): In this model, cloud provider integrates security services into organization's infrastructure over the internet. It includes services to protect

the organization against antivirus or malware, intruder attack and other security management events. Cloud provider also gives services to protect individual system or whole network system of the subscribed vendors.

- DRaaS (Disaster Recovery as a Service): DRaaS is a backup service model in cloud to protect applications and data during any unpredicted disaster. DRaaS is associate with business continuity plan (BCP) and disaster recovery plan (DRP), which allows organization to continue their business as usual from any location over the cloud. It allows the application to run on virtual machines enabling continuous replication and backups. Benefit of DRaaS are as follows:
  - Multisite copy: It assures 100% availability even-if disaster happens in multiple geographical locations
  - Transparency: Data protection does not limits to one platform or vendor
  - Granularity: Cloud users have the flexibility to select the data protection requirement to save the cost of unnecessary backups.
- CaaS (Communication as a Service): It is a part of SaaS service. All communication infrastructures such as connections, uploading the contents, and managing communication platforms are managed by cloud provider assuring fault tolerance of the communication system [11].
  - Example of CaaS is VoIP (Voice over Internet Protocol) or Internet telephonic solution, Video conferencing via internet.
- BPaaS (Business Process as a Service): Companies are giving efforts to make their business process automated in their own way. But cloud BPaaS provides a generic package solution that includes business logic, data, and processes that can be used in many different application environment. This process is uniform across the organization. For example, payroll, email service, shipping a package or managing a customer credit. This service is designed over IaaS, PaaS, and SaaS. Cloud provides an interface for BPaaS to business hiding all business complexity and all the regulatory compliance are handled by cloud provider.

- AIaaS (AI as a Service): To analyze big data and making the business more efficient artificial intelligence and machine learning now becoming integral part of the most of the business. But infusing AI into business is very challenging task and need expertize, so many organizations are unable to do so though they need them. So, to avoid this difficulties cloud provides AI services called as AIaaS. Some common types of AIaaS are as follows:
  - Bots and digital assistance: It includes chat bots.
  - Cognitive computing APIs: It helps to infuse specific technology or services into application without writing the code from scratch. Inclusion of NPL, computer speech or vision, translation, search, mapping, and emotion detection are few examples.
  - ML frameworks services: These services enable companies to infuse machine learning capability without big data environment using ML templates, pre-build models, and drag-drop tools.
- POCaaS (Proof of Concept as a Service): Validating a POC in a traditional way is mostly time and resource consuming. As POC is initial trial version of business idea implementation, there is always a chance of unsuccessfully. So, to avoid such initial cost and time cloud provides POCaaS service which enables business stake holders validate the feasibility of their idea in the real world.
  - Example of cloud POCaaS is CloudShare.

4.5   Core Components of Cloud Computing Architecture: Hardware and Software

- Cloud Datacenter: Cloud datacenter is different from traditional datacenter. The infrastructure is spread across different geographical locations. Data is fragmented and replicated across different geographical locations to make it fault tolerant [27].
  - It provides high scalability and reliability system.
  - Data centers are strategically located in cost-effective areas to reduce the cost of infrastructure.
  - It is designed to form a modular database framework.

- Virtualization: It is the most important technological driver. It allows cloud to perform basic operation such as resource management, optimization, load balance, and isolation. Multiple virtual operating systems are running on a single physical computer. Resources are designed to be optimized and efficiently accessed irrespective of their physical presence. Resources are also available on demand or on pay-as-you-go pricing mode [8].
- Cloud APIs: It serves as a layer between users and cloud services and resources. API layer provides an interface to access, control and manage the provisioned resources. REST (Representational State Transfer) model is commonly used for cloud API design.
- Cloud Storage: Cloud storage is designed with high security, reliability, availability, and efficiency as it has to be accessed by large group of users concurrently using a web-based HTTP interface offered by cloud service provider.
- Cloud Database: Traditional database are best suited for relational DBMS due to its limited data volume. But cloud computing is well suited for non-relational databases such as key-value, object-oriented which can easily be scalable, and have the capacity to any volume of data without hampering the performance of accessibility [4].

4.6   Factors Need to Consider for Cloud Adoption

As cloud services are covering a lot of area of IT operation with a pay-as-you-use strategy, many organizations are considering to move their IT set-ups from on-premises to cloud. As agile methodology is widely accepted by many organizations due longer project life cycle is divided into multiple small cycles and deployment life cycle is reduced greatly as well [16]. This forced many organizations to rethink for setting up large time consuming IT infrastructure toward rapid deployment model available through cloud for smooth business operation.

4.6.1   Evaluating Cloud Infrastructure

The following scenarios are best suited for considering cloud infrastructure over traditional setup [27].

- Initiate With a Minimal Budget: As business needs a continuous process, improvement and the continuity depends on initial success so investing a lot of money on infrastructure in the beginning of the project is not a good decision. So, adopting cloud helps business
  - To setup the process with minimal budget
  - To provision and de-provision of resources and processes quickly giving more time to focus on business
    - Not adding extra cost for any infrastructure failure
- Handle Fluctuating or Unpredicted Load Pattern of Business: In traditional model of IT setup, infrastructure is required to cope with the highest level of load of the business. So, most of the times resources remain underutilized or unutilized due to unpredictable load, but IT cost remains high always. But cloud computing has the flexibility only to pay the value of resource actually consumed not for the resource acquired [12].
- Generic Communized System Resource or Services: Generic applications or services which are not relevant to business core functionality such as storage infrastructure, backups, and emails can be serviceable through external system such as cloud at a very cheaper price.
- High Infrastructure Management or Operation Cost: Cloud allows to manage both infrastructure and services separately. Cloud automatically recovers the application or resource from failure at any point of time with no impact on business with a minimal downtime.

4.6.2   Evaluating Cloud Provider

Depending on business and technology standards, organization has to choose the cloud provider as there are multiple cloud providers who are best in different services and standards. The following are the parameters which are to be looked into to choose a best suite cloud service provider [15].

- Platform Maturity: Richness of platform should be available for better application development
- Technology Alignment: Technology provider by cloud provider should be aligned with the technology expertize organization posses

- Operational Alignment: Proper service level agreements and compliances should be in place to ensure data security and accessibility
- Geographic Alignment: Though cloud service is free from geographical constraints, business has to consider the number of regions where cloud server provider its service to ease data protection compliance and standard with the permitted standards of the local authorities.

4.6.3   Evaluating Cloud Security

It is important to consider data security when evaluating cloud computing solutions as data are stored off-site, in the cloud infrastructure. Organization has less control over own data. So, there will be always concern of data security. Data may be vulnerable to third-party control as data transfer is always done over internet [14]. To overcome the security concerns, cloud computing solutions offer the following data security majors

- Encryption: Data will always be in encrypted format while accessing from cloud or storing in cloud.
- Password Authentication: There will always be layers of authentication for the user to save the data from any kind of attack whether passive or active.
- Basic Identity Management: Identity management is basically managing personal unique identity required to access data, resources, and services over cloud. It prevents unauthorized access and reduces security risk while accessing data in cloud.
- Data Regulatory Compliance: It refers the defined rules and regulations for using data in cloud. These compliance are the defined rules formed with a mutual agreement between customer and cloud provider.
- Handling of Sensitive Data: As organization has no control of the data, cloud provider should ensure that, in any means, this information will not be exposed to unauthorized party.

4.6.4   Evaluating Cloud Services

Enterprises have to evaluate the services [9] available by cloud provider whether they match their required services or not keeping the following properties.

- Scalability: Capacity resources should easily expandable on service provider's infrastructure and should be based on subscription.
- Network Connectivity: Services should be internet hosted services and flexible depending on business needs.
- Speed of Implementation: As cloud services are inbuilt and flexible, it should be deployed instantly with immediate resource availability.
- Greenness: As cloud architecture is based on shared resources it reduces power consumption to a large extent.
- Control: Enterprise has less direct control over own data and services than in-house server setup model but protection should be guaranteed.
- Interoperability: As cloud services are used by multiple vendors, it should be ease of service interoperability.
- Compliance: Regulatory compliance requirements with the security and privacy of personal data should be thoroughly reviewed before choosing cloud services.

4.6.5   Evaluating Cloud Service Level Agreements (SLA)

A SLA outlines [8] the following:

- Service Scope: It defines expected level of cloud provider technical support.
- Service availability: It defines service uptime expectations.
- Customer Requirements: SLAs are different for type of organization who uses the cloud such as private and government organization.
- Payment Methods: It should be clearly defined all payment frequency and subscription fees for kind of service used.

4.6.6   Limitations to Cloud Adoption

Though cloud service provider assures of unlimited scalability, technology diversity through a highly secure network, still, few organizations are still reluctant to move all their infrastructure and services to cloud or only moved non-critical business to cloud. The following are few limitations for cloud adoption [16].

- Fully Guaranteed Reliable, High-Quality Services: Though cloud provider guaranteed of reliability and high-quality, still cloud is solely dependent on internet latency and commodity hardware. Internet speed and infrastructure are not in the control of cloud provider and it varies from country to country and quality of service provided by ISPs of that country. Similarly, fully scalability of cloud computing is still not being tested as lot of business operations are yet to move into the cloud.
- Pay-Per-Use Model Add-Ons: Enterprises have to thoroughly compare the on-premises vs. cloud adoption cost keeping in mind the extra cost for needed to support, disaster recovery, application modifications, and data loss insurance in both the cases in long run.
- Effort Cost of Adoption: As cloud technology adoption needs a different set of skill set for both the enterprise and its customer, time and money required to train users to use the technology need to be evaluated with the profit margin gained from cloud adoption.
- Business Data Security and Privacy: As control is lost under third-party management, organizations have to think of their business policies applied in different continents of their operation while moving to cloud [17].
- Compliance: Necessary logging and auditing and legal procedures have to in place in the SLAs before adoption of cloud.
- Geographical Location of Stored Data: As cloud is mainly depend on internet, so a huge amount of data has to move through internet during business operation and it can impact performance of business process. For better performance, data should reside in the cloud data center which is closest to the business operation though actual physical location is abstract.

4.7   Transforming Business Through Cloud

- Nowadays, every business industries are transforming their business models and integrating software as an important dimension of their business models, to cope with the ever changing business world and customer perception.

- Traditional organizational structure is mostly based on business functionality and importance of process transformation that have limited scope. But with the inclusion of digitalization, business process becomes that much of importance as business functionality.
- For example, CAR lease companies like OLA and UBER are now moved from manual structure of execution to fully automated software system, from booking to payment to tracking vehicle information through multiple concurrent devices. These companies are investing a major portion of their money on setting up IT infrastructures and processes.
- Similarly, manufacturing industries are also investing a bigger chunk of their budget on system automation, which provides them higher output and error free system operation with a stipulated budget and time. Software is now become the integral part of every corporation business from a start-up to large enterprises.
- As digitalization becomes inseparable part of business, with the increase in business and industrial growth data becomes enormous so also complexity of managing the data increases. Data is increasing rapidly not only in volume but also in other dimensions as well such as variety and speed. Detailed business data growth is clearly represented in Figure 4.5.
- As data becomes big data, organizations put lot of efforts to manage and utilize the data for betterment of business profitability and future growth [18].
- Data needs to analyze and convert into meaningful business knowledge by applying intelligence. To do so, various techniques/algorithms/tools have to apply and make the data useful [13]. So, digital transformation is necessary keeping in mind the following aspects.
  - Gaining efficiencies
  - Increasing profitability
  - To remain in pace with competitor
  - Future survival

4.8   Key Emerging Trends in Cloud Computing

Cloud is no longer just a resource and service provider. It is changing itself to cope with all challenges that come across during business process

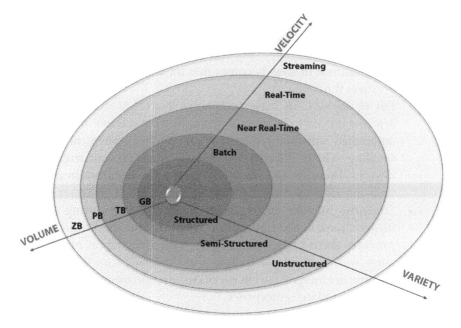

Figure 4.5 Business data growth over dimension.

deployment. The following are some major key trends that enable cloud from service provider to business transformation gateway.

- Technologies
- Business models
- Product transformation
- Customer engagement
- Employee empowerment
- Data management and assurance
- Making everything digital
- Building intelligence cloud system by infusing AI and ML
- Creating hyper-converged infrastructure

4.8.1 Technology Trends

Various latest technologies are added to cloud to provide wide range of technological options to choose for application development within cloud. Figure 4.6 shows the key emergence trends in cloud computing.

- Edge Computing: It is a distributed computing mechanism where data storage and computation are to be done nearer

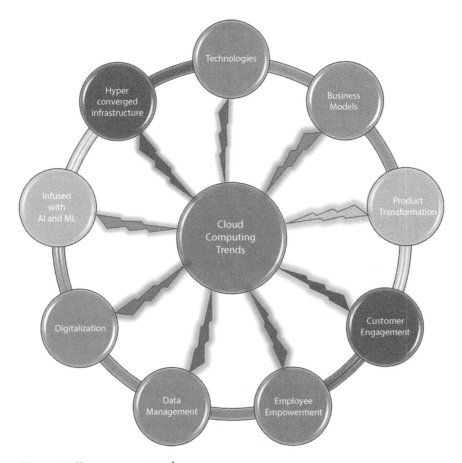

Figure 4.6 Key emergence trends.

to the location of request. Including edge computing into the cloud improves response time and minimizes network load in cloud. It helps to reduce network congestion during peak hour of use of cloud services [19].

- Serverless Computing: User will always work on virtual servers, i.e., underlying resources are dynamically allocated based on the availability. It enhances the elasticity and scalability properties of cloud. It is cost-effective and produces high productivity.

- Distributed Computing: Distributed computing is the technique of dividing bigger tasks into smaller ones and executing them in multiple nodes simultaneously and reassembling the result without impacting the integrity. As cloud runs on distributed node architecture, implementing distributed computing enhances performance of the computed process [24].

- Real-Time Analysis: While dealing with huge volume of data analysis like streaming data analysis and vehicle tracking system, cloud will be good choice to be used due to high processing capacity [11].
- High Speed Connectivity: 5G technology helps to deliver low latency high bandwidth network. Hence, cloud performance will definitely enhanced by adopting the latest connectivity network service.

4.8.2   Business Models

Business models are the key trends defined looking into the cloud on business perspective rather technology [20]. Three major benefits of using business models in cloud.

- Flexible Utilization: Ease provision and de-provision of resources can be done. Seasonal high demand of resource can be handled efficiently. Hence, save business cost.
- Driving Business Agility: XaaS such as DaaS, CaaS, and SECaaS allows business to use variety of services on-demand to fulfill their need.
- Faster Innovation: Due to ease of implementation and maintenance, new applications can be developed and tested in an agile mode.

4.8.3   Product Transformation

Cloud avails variety of services to build highly integrated, scalable, and tensile products to keep the business ahead of current market. Products developed are built in with AI-enabled and capable of analytics solutions [22].

4.8.4   Customer Engagement

Customer-centric products can be developed due to diversity of technologies available.

- High Visual Experience: Interactive visual contents such as AR (augmented reality) and VR (visual reality) gain more customer attraction toward business products. Adding this type of content requires high processing capabilities and cloud computing can provide such facilities.

- IoT-Based Solution: Cloud services and internet are complementary to each other. So, cloud can well manage IoT solutions such as home automation, manufacturing automation, and enrich customer experience [26].
- Independent of Location and Device: Customer can use the product from anywhere and from any device just by logging through proper authentication mechanism.

4.8.5 Employee Empowerment

During the pandemic situation like covid-19, employees are forced to start work from home instead of office premises where no in-house infrastructure is available. Cloud is helping people productive remotely from home. All the required application and services can easily available through cloud network. Application developers can build their code offline and integrated into the business through cloud.

4.8.6 Data Management and Assurance

Cloud has well-designed frameworks to manage organizations data. Cloud provides robust security and well defined compliances to secure data. Cloud can solve the problem of data growth and scale of operation [24].

4.8.7 Digitalization

Moving all business processes into the boundary of information technology makes business more meaningful. Integrating data from multiple business units helps organization to take proactive futuristic decision and make the business upfront of the competitor [21].

4.8.8 Building Intelligence Cloud System

Infusing AI and ML into business processes cloud can be integrate with more functionalities [25].

- Systems will be closely integration with cloud
- Enhancing scalability
- Making development agile ready
- Analytic solutions will be integral part of the business

- Artificial intelligence inclusion into every part of the cloud boosts better decision making capabilities
- Will proactively identify and define security risks and its solution approaches
- Make cloud more robust and trustworthiness

4.8.9   Creating Hyper-Converged Infrastructure

It is an IT framework model where storage, network, and services are integrated and working as a single platform without compromising the scalability. The key benefits of this infrastructure are as follows.

- Lower Cost: Data storage has to done on commodity low cost hardware instead of costly data center setup to reduce the infrastructure cost.
- Smaller and Efficient IT Team: All the infrastructures can be managed on the virtual servers by the organizations and complex operations are managed by cloud providers. So, business organizations do not need large technical expertise team to manage the infrastructure.
- Simple Policies and Easier Support: Enterprises does not have to manage the infrastructure and get support from the service provider.
- Robust Data Protection: Hyper-converged software is designed to handle all types of data losses or failure. Backup, recovery, and replications are inbuilt properties.

4.9   Case Study: Moving Data Warehouse to Cloud Boosts Performance for Johnson & Johnson

Teradata is an established and well-known EDW (Enterprise Data Warehouse) solution provider by setting up its reputation from last 40 years for providing on premise EDW hardware and software solutions to many of the major business vendors like P&G, eBay, General Motors, and Boeing. Reputed pharmaceutical and healthcare company Johnson & Johnson (J&J) also adopted EDW data storage system supplied by Teradata which is the most adopted data-warehouse solution.

In early 2017, J&J's data analytics team face many challenges even with on premises EDW system to cope with 300 TB of storage, which includes 50 business applications and 2,500 analytics users, handling more than

200 million queries per month. So, Irfan Siddiqui, senior manager for data and analytics team, J&J, decided to migrate the EDW system from on premises to the cloud. But at that time, cloud was not popular and Teradata system was not ready to adopt the cloud computing services.

So, Siddiqui decided to make J&J be the first company to adopt cloud among the major stakeholders using Teradata as their data warehouse solution and agreed to make POC (proof of concept) for Teradata in the cloud. They started the POC with lot of questions which was to be answered such as *"How to migrate?"*, *"How the application will perform?"*, *"What will be the uptime?"*, *"What about data security and system stability?"*, and the most import one is *"How it will benefit to J&J?"*. To their surprise, scaling for 80 TB of space took only 20 minutes in AWS which an on-premises setup could take at least 6 months to scale up. This is "a-ha moments" for them and was the driving force to move further to adopt cloud transformation.

To a precautionary move, initially, J&J moved all their data warehouse workloads into clouds keeping analytics applications and visualization tools (like Informatia, Talend, TiBco, and Qlik) on premise. Also, they have moved many of their applications into cloud within a short span of time. By the end of 2019, they moved most of their applications into cloud removing almost all on-premises data warehouse hardware systems. Transforming business and application into cloud not only helps them reduce the cost and maintenance headache but also increases the performance of the application by 60%.

Despite all the challenges and questions regarding cloud migration, the percentage of cloud adaptation increases year by year, expecting 44% of the market share by 2022.

4.10   Conclusion

Cloud is gaining popularity due to its versatile nature and extraordinary power of collaboration in terms of technology and business adoption. But still cloud is in its infant state. Cloud adoption is still below 20% of the total infrastructure. Different cloud services are adopted by enterprises due to platform independence, richness of features, and ease of integration into business. Starting up business in cloud minimizes initial IT infrastructure cost and deployment time with increase in performance. This paper covered key trends adopted by cloud describing its pros and limitations. Looking into current trends it seems cloud computing has a bright future not only in business world but also it will be necessary part of everyday life.

References

1. Maggiani, R., Communication Consultant, Solari Communication (2009), "*Cloud Computing is Changing How we Communicate*". *IEEE International Professional Conference, IPCC*, Waikiki, HI, USA, pp. 1–4, 22, 2009.

2. Zhao, F. and Kirche, E., Continuing On-Premise or Adopt On-Demand? An Empirical Study of ERP Adoption in SMEs, in: *Human-Computer Interaction. Users and Contexts of Use. HCI 2013. Lecture Notes in Computer Science*, vol. 8006, M. Kurosu (Ed.), Springer, Berlin, Heidelberg, 2013, https://doi.org/10.1007/978-3-642-39265-8_55.

3. Fisher, C., *Cloud versus On-Premise Computing. American Journal of Industrial and Business Management*, Scientific Research Publishing, China, vol. 8, pp. 1991–2006, 2018.

4. Nikhil, D., Dhanalaxmi, B., Reddy, K.S., The Evolution of Cloud Computing and Its Contribution with Big Data Analytics, in: *Innovative Data Communication Technologies and Application. ICIDCA 2019. Lecture Notes on Data Engineering and Communications Technologies*, vol. 46, J. Raj, A. Bashar, S. Ramson (Eds.), Springer, Cham, 2020, https://doi.org/10.1007/978-3-030-38040-3_38.

5. Abadi, D.J., Data Management in the Cloud: Limitations and Opportunities. *IEEE Data Engineering Bulletin*, 32, 3–12, 2009, March 2009.

6. Prajapati, A.G., Sharma, S.J., Badgujar, V.S., All About Cloud: A Systematic Survey. *IEEE International Conference on Smart City and Emerging Technology (ICSCET), Mumbai, 2018*, pp. 1–6, 2018.

7. Gong, C., Liu, J., Zhang, Q., Chen, H., Gong, Z., The Characteristics of Cloud Computing. *2010 39th IEEE International Conference on Parallel Processing Workshops, San Diego, CA, 2010*, pp. 275–279, 2010.

8. Shawish, A. and Salama, M., Cloud Computing: Paradigms and Technologies, in: *Inter-cooperative Collective Intelligence: Techniques and Applications. Studies in Computational Intelligence*, vol. 495, F. Xhafa and N. Bessis (Eds.), Springer, Berlin, Heidelberg, 2014.

9. Nwobodo, I., Cloud Computing: Models, Services, Utility, Advantages, Security Issues, and Prototype, in: *Wireless Communications, Networking and Applications. Lecture Notes in Electrical Engineering*, vol. 348, Q.A. Zeng (Ed.), Springer, New Delhi, 2016, https://doi.org/10.1007/978-81-322-2580-5_110.

10. Widjajarto, A., Supangkat, S.H., Gondokaryono, Y.S., Prihatmanto, A.S., Cloud computing reference model: The modelling of service availability based on application profile and resource allocation. *2012 International Conference on Cloud Computing and Social Networking (ICCCSN), Bandung, West Java, 2012*, pp. 1–4, 2012.

11. Naseer Qureshi, K., Bashir, F., Iqbal, S., Cloud Computing Model for Vehicular Ad hoc Networks. *IEEE 7th International Conference on Cloud Networking (CloudNet), Tokyo, 2018*, pp. 1–3, 2018.

12. Smith, A., Bhogal, J., Sharma, M., Cloud Computing: Adoption Considerations for Business and Education. *IEEE, International Conference on Future Internet of Things and Cloud, Barcelona, Spain, 2014*, pp. 302–307, 2014.

13. Mahapatra, P.K., Tripathy, A.R., Tripathy, A., Mishra, B., Security Model for Preserving Privacy of Image in Cloud, in: *Advances in Data Science and Management. Lecture Notes on Data Engineering and Communications Technologies*, vol. 37, S. Borah, V. Emilia Balas, Z. Polkowski (Eds.), Springer, Singapore, 2020.

14. El-Gazzar, R.F., A Literature Review on Cloud Computing Adoption Issues in Enterprises, in: *Creating Value for All Through IT. TDIT 2014. IFIP Advances in Information and Communication Technology*, vol. 429, B. Bergvall-Kåreborn and P.A. Nielsen (Eds.), Springer, Berlin, Heidelberg, 2014.

15. Zied Milian, E., Spinola, M.M., Gonçalves, R.F., Leme Fleury, A., An Analysis of the Advantages, Challenges and Obstacles of Cloud Computing Adoption to an Academic Control System, in: *Advances in Production Management Systems. Innovative and Knowledge-Based Production Management in a Global-Local World. APMS 2014. IFIP Advances in Information and Communication Technology*, vol. 439, B. Grabot, B. Vallespir, S. Gomes, A. Bouras, D. Kiritsis (Eds.), Springer, Berlin, Heidelberg, 2014, https://doi.org/10.1007/978-3-662-44736-9_68.

16. Zhao, F., Scheruhn, H.J., von Rosing, M., The Impact of Culture Differences on Cloud Computing Adoption, in: *Human-Computer Interaction. Applications and Services. HCI 2014. Lecture Notes in Computer Science*, vol. 8512, M. Kurosu (Ed.), Springer, Cham, 2014, https://doi.org/10.1007/978-3-319-07227-2_74.

17. Rai, R., Sahoo, G., & Mehfuz, S. *Exploring the factors influencing the cloud computing adoption: a systematic study on cloud migration*. SpringerPlus, Germany, 4(1), 1-12, 2015.

18. Hosseinian-Far, A., Ramachandran, M., Slack, C.L., Emerging Trends in Cloud Computing, Big Data, Fog Computing, IoT and Smart Living, in: *Technology for Smart Futures*, M. Dastbaz, H. Arabnia, B. Akhgar (Eds.), Springer, Cham, First Online, 06 September 2017, 2018, https://doi.org/10.1007/978-3-319-60137-3_2.

19. Rimal, B.P. and Lumb, I., The Rise of Cloud Computing in the Era of Emerging Networked Society, in: *Cloud Computing. Computer Communications and Networks*, N. Antonopoulos and L. Gillam (Eds.), Springer, Cham, First Online, 03 June 2017, 2017, https://doi.org/10.1007/978-3-319-54645-2_1.

20. Menychtas, A., Kousiouris, G., Kyriazis, D., Varvarigou, T., Minimizing Technical Complexities in Emerging Cloud Computing Platforms, in: *Euro-Par 2010 Parallel Processing Workshops. Euro-Par 2010. Lecture Notes in Computer Science*, vol. 6586, M.R. Guarracino (Eds.), Springer, Berlin, Heidelberg, 2011, https://doi.org/10.1007/978-3-642-21878-1_74.

21. Shi, Y., Yang, H.H., Yang, Z., Wu, D., Trends of Cloud Computing in Education, in: *Hybrid Learning. Theory and Practice. ICHL 2014.*

Lecture Notes in Computer Science, vol. 8595, S.K.S. Cheung, J. Fong, J. Zhang, R. Kwan, L.F. Kwok (Eds.), Springer, Cham, 2014, https://doi. org/10.1007/978-3-319-08961-4_12.

22. Sehgal, N.K. and Bhatt, P.C.P., *Future Trends in Cloud Computing. In: Cloud Computing*, Springer, Cham, First Online, 24 March 2018, 2018, https://doi. org/10.1007/978-3-319-77839-6_12.

23. Garg, D., Sidhu, J., Rani, S., *Emerging trends in cloud computing security: a bibliometric analyses*, vol. 13, pp. 223–231, IEEE, in IET Software, 20196 2019, England, doi: 10.1049/iet-sen.2018.5222.

24. Yadav, P.K., Sharma, S., Singh, A., Big Data and Cloud Computing: An Emerging Perspective and Future Trends. *IEEE, International Conference on Issues and Challenges in Intelligent Computing Techniques (ICICT), Ghaziabad, India, 2019*, pp. 1–4, 2019.

25. More, N.S. and Ingle, R.B., Challenges in green computing for energy saving techniques. *IEEE International Conference on Emerging Trends & Innovation in ICT (ICEI), Pune, 2017*, pp. 73–76, 2017.

26. Jindal, F., Mudgal, S., Choudhari, V., Churi, P.P., Emerging trends in Internet of Things. *IEEE Fifth HCT Information Technology Trends (ITT), Dubai, United Arab Emirates, 2018*, pp. 50–60, 2018.

27. Sunyaev, A. and Sunyaev, A., Cloud Computing. Chapter 7, in: *Internet Computing*, Springer, Cham, First Online, 13 February 2020, 2020, https:// doi.org/10.1007/978-3-030-34957-8_7.

28. https://www.cloudpro.co.uk/it-infrastructure/8290/how-johnson-johnson-boosted-its-performance-by-lifting-teradata-to-aws.

5

Security of Sensitive Data in Cloud Computing

Kirti Wanjale¹*, Monika Mangla² and Paritosh Marathe²

¹Department of Computer Engineering, Vishwakarma Institute of Information Technology, Pune, India
²Department of Computer Engineering, Lokmanya Tilak College of Engineering, Navi Mumbai, India

Abstract

Cloud computing is one of the most important technologies in today's data-driven world. It allows scaling of large computing resources and data storage facilities for industries, without a compulsory requirement of the underlying hardware. These are provided on a subscription basis with pricing based on provided data storage and compute facilities where the price may vary with up scaling or downscaling of required resources. With large as well as smaller companies gearing toward a data-driven approach for providing better customer service, there is a general trend of moving toward cloud computing for faster, cheaper, and maximally available data and computing resources which also allow faster up scaling and downscaling on demand. It has a high potential of cost reduction while improving functionality and scalability of an application while allowing for the cooperation of multiple entities in the same project. This allows for newer industries to scale up production of new software at a reduced cost and without the requirement of an initial investment in hardware. It may also increase the pace of production and deployment of a software product, due to availability of high performance compute and storage units which may not be conventionally available contain sensitive information such as customer data as well as the company mission-critical data, which is being hosted on an external cloud storage server. The data storage facilities are managed by CSPs (cloud service provider) at various physical locations. Thus, traditional security

---

*Corresponding author: kirti.wanjale@viit.ac.in

Sachi Nandan Mohanty, Jyotir Moy Chatterjee, Monika Mangla, Suneeta Satpathy and Sirisha Potluri (eds.) Machine Learning Approach for Cloud Data Analytics in IoT, (99–118) © 2021 Scrivener Publishing LLC

measures such as firewalls are not sufficient to insure the security of the data, especially in a case where a data breach will cause personal, ethical, and financial harm. Hence, there exists a strong requirement for protection of this sensitive data which is related to company functioning. Multiple security measures must be placed to ensure the security of the said data. This chapter discusses the security challenges as well as the methods used for tackling the said challenges with their respective advantages and disadvantages for protecting data on cloud storage.

Keywords: Cloud computing, data security, privacy, sensitive data

5.1   Introduction

Cloud computing is a ubiquitous, on-demand model for the provision of computer resources, especially data storage and compute unit facilities which are provided to the user in a convenient manner without the direct involvement of the user itself [1, 2]. The aim is to provide a large amount of computing resources and data storage facilities in a fast and reliable manner at a reduced cost and without requirement for purchase of physical hardware.

5.1.1   Characteristics of Cloud Computing

- On-Demand Self-Service Services: This allows users to gain resources as per their requirement through a simple and flexible method. Initially, the user is provided with a set amount of resources which the user may scale up on the basis of requirement. The user gets to choose how much resources he may require and has to pay accordingly.
- Resource Pooling: This refers to a pool of IT resources (storage, memory, and GPUs) maintained by the cloud service provider (CSP) to allow dynamic allocation and reallocation of resources as per the requirement of the users.
- Ubiquitous Network Arrangement: A broad level of network access via which a user may connect to his cloud. The aim is to provide access to cloud services through various interfaces and devices requiring multiple protocols and API services to let the user access to cloud through various technologies.
- Ubiquitous Network Arrangement: A broad level of network access via which a user may connect to his cloud. The aim is to provide access to cloud services through various interfaces and devices requiring multiple protocols and

API services to let the user access to cloud through various technologies.

- Location Independent: This allows users to access cloud services from irrespective of location.
- Low Maintenance and Reliability: The user in not required to perform any maintenance while being assured a stable and reliable service.
- Rapid Scaling (High Scalability): This allows users to increase the amount of resources utilized, on request, and give them up as the requirement reduces.
- Measured Service: Pay-as-you-use service lets the user pay only for what he has used rather than a set subscription.

CSPs deploy the resources in certain models which are defined by the need and requirement of the targeted organization. The cloud resources may be deployed over network and, in some cases, are restricted by network.

5.1.2   Deployment Models for Cloud Services

The following are some of the widely used deployment models for cloud services:

- Private Cloud: It is for the exclusive use of an organization. Hence, all its members may use the cloud data and services, but any outside the organization cannot access the cloud.
- Public Cloud: It is provisioned for open use by the general public. In this, all the cloud services are provided over the internet and the cloud itself is owned by a cloud service providing organization.
- Community Cloud: Community cloud is provisioned for use by a specific set of consumers or organizations which have shared interests, such as security, policies, missions, or compliance considerations, hence require similar resources.
- Hybrid Cloud: It is a combination of the previous types (private, public, and community) that are bound together by some standard protocols to ensure data and resource portability.

These models are used as a guideline to develop a cloud service for the organization. However, the usage of the said model by the user is a different issue. Hence, CSPs provide different models in which way the services can be "delivered" to the user for consumption [1, 4, 5].

5.1.3   Types of Cloud Delivery Models

- Software as a Service (SaaS): This layer gives the ability to a consumer to use applications provided by the vendor. These applications are available through a client interface like a web browser. The provider may charge a subscription fee for a membership based on the user's use of the application (which may be tiered). With the exception of a few user-specific app configurations, everything else from the software application to the underlying hardware is managed by the service provider [1].
- Platform as a Service (PaaS): This layer provides the user with all the necessary libraries, services and tools for use of programming languages for the creation and deployment of an application. The user controls has control over the deployed application and configuration settings of the application. Everything else from the platform (operating system) to underlying hardware such as networking and servers is controlled by the provider [1].
- Infrastructure as a Service (IaaS): This layer provides the user with the ability to choose processing units, storage, and any other fundamental resources which may be required to develop and deploy an application. With the exception of the underlying IT resources and cloud infrastructure, the user has control over operating systems, libraries, storage, and deployed applications with limited control over networking (e.g., host firewall configuration) [1].

5.2   Data in Cloud

The advancement of technology has been pushing the world toward digitization. It has led to massive generation of all kinds of data, be it personal or application related. This has pushed data storage to be one of the most important services provided by cloud. Due to the move toward digitization, users have been moving data on cloud storage for affordable storage with large capacity and ease of access from anywhere in the world. This may include personal data, customer data, and company data.

The data stored on the cloud may be sensitive and have paramount importance in terms of company functioning or user information. This type of data must be protected from unauthorized access, data corruption, or any kind of data leak or damage which further may lead to customer dissatisfaction and damage to company functioning. Hence, there is a rising concern toward security in cloud computing as the user does not control the logical and physical aspects of the data storage. The user has no idea where the given data is physically stored and has no control over the methods used to store the data which has led to distrust over data security issues [6, 8, 9].

The cloud provider is responsible for the security, storage, integrity, and reliable access of the data. The cloud provider must ensure the following.

- Confidentiality: Keeping the data safe from being accessed by unauthorized parties and allowing only authorized parties to access the data.
- Integrity: Keeping data from being altered or modified in any way during data storage or transfer and allowing only authorized parties to copy, delete, or modify the data.
- Authentication: Ensuring the identity of the user before allowing access to the stored data by employing various identification strategies.
- Availability: Allowing users to access the data and services anytime anywhere constantly.
- Authorization: Allowing the user to choose which data the other part can access and whether they can modify, delete the data.

5.2.1   Data Life Cycle

The cloud architecture provides many advantages such as cheaper and more efficient quantitative data storage and faster compute units. Hence, a large amount of data may be created, stored and processed with data varying from different types to data input coming from various sources. Figure 5.1 shows data life cycle. Therefore, we may say that data itself as a unit has a lifecycle. It comprises six stages. Data from its creation to its end goes through a sequence of stages or "phases" which comprise the lifecycle of a data unit. These stages define the tasks that are performed generally on the data and may be subdivided in to multiple stages as per required granularity. Roughly, the six stages are as follows:

- Data Generation: This involves creation of data from the end user or other sources collected from various sources.
- Data Transfer: This involves transfer of data either from an external source or within enterprise boundaries.

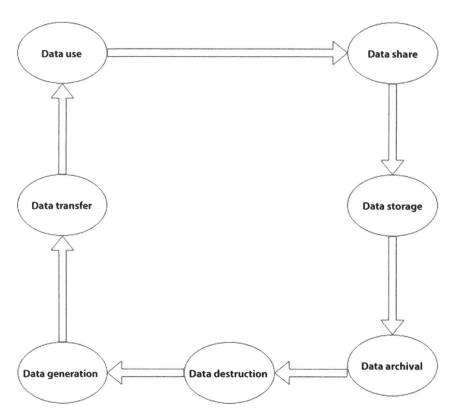

Figure 5.1 Data life cycle.

- Data Use: This involves processing of the data taken in from the source and processed.
- Data Share: This involves data sharing in enterprise or externally based on access control
- Data Storage: This involves storing data on-site or in ready mode for active process usage. In this stage, data may be used or referenced frequently.
- Data Archival: This involves storage of data off site as it is not required for any active process with no actions being performed on it. It is stored in case there may be a future use for the data.
- Data Destruction: This involves destruction of all data when it is no longer of any use. The entire data and its existing copies are deleted from all physical media.

Once data has been created, it may move freely among any stages in the life cycle. However, data security must be ensured during all the stages during a life cycle. Based on the data state during the stages, the stages may be classified in the following three stages.

- Data in use: data generation, data use, data destruction
- Data in transit: data share, data transfer
- Data in rest: data storage, data archival

(Note: Data destruction can be considered as its own stage; however, for convenience, we can put it under data in use.)

5.3   Security Challenges in Cloud Computing for Data

As discussed earlier, the cloud computing has several advantages. On the other hand, it also bears some security challenges that poses a security threat which may lead to data security compromise in the cloud. This section discusses the challenges associated with the security of data. We may divide the presented challenges presented under three groups based on the area they target. The three sections are illustrated in Figure 5.2 as follows:

- Security challenges related to data at rest
- Security challenges related to data in use
- Security challenges related to data in transit

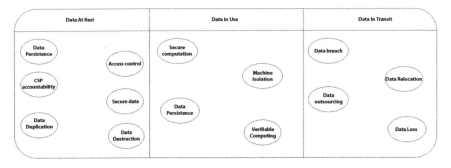

Figure 5.2 Problems related to data in rest, data in use, and data in transit.

5.3.1   Security Challenges Related to Data at Rest

Data at rest refers to the data maintained at persistent storage in cloud. CSPs provide data owners with highly scalable and customizable storage instances where these storages are unreliable and removed in case of non-requirement. Persistent storage gives a reliable storage solution for the long term storage of data. However, in both the types, the data is stored at a location far removed from users. Location gives rise to the security challenges [11, 13, 14].

Data Persistence: The standard model for cloud computing includes allocation and deallocation of resources as per requirement. This means hosting the data required for that business transaction on the cloud servers itself.

After the work has been done, the resources are then de-allocated from the cluster used by the company. It may happen that data that was used during the business process may persist after the storage has been deallocated and maybe accessible in the network. Such a type of security fault is referred to as *data persistence.*

Data Duplication: Data hosted on the cloud is subjective to the hardware provided by the CSP. That includes the network, processors, and storage available. It may have its own set of vulnerabilities. They may be exploited to duplicate the data or the VM (virtual machine itself.

Access Control: Data is an asset. It may be required by multiple parties within the same organization. This requires fine grained access control. Access control refers to the right given to any party regarding the ability to read, write, or manipulate the data in any way based on its role. Irregular access control may lead to unauthorized access to the sensitive data which may be corrupted malicious parties.

Secure Data: Securing the data itself is necessary. Unencrypted data is easy to read and in case of unauthorized access it may really harm the organization as the data can be utilized immediately. Any counter measures may be too slow to prevent the damage caused.

CSP Accountability: Hardware faults may lead to data corruption and loss. Hence, the CSP must have countermeasures in place to avoid such faults. The CSP may utilize facilities like redundant storage, to protect the organization from unwanted data loss. The CSP must establish failsafe strategies in case of failure of the cloud, especially for organizations which store sensitive data on the CSPs cloud with the subscription for it. Another issue with CSP accountability relates to low level trust between the organization and the CSP. One problem related to it is the verification of data manipulation, accidentally or maliciously, by the CSP.

Data Destruction: After the data has served its purpose it has to be deleted. The CSP must be able to securely delete the data. Failure to do so may result in the exposure of data to other users and anyone who may gain access to the drives.

5.3.2   Security Challenges Related to Data in Use

Data in use is also referred to as data in processing. In this stage, the data may be held in primary storage. This stage requires the data to be decrypted for processing and therefore stripped of most of its protections. Hence, it is the most vulnerable stage for the data. In order to address the challenges of data security, the following are some security measures [15, 16].

Secure Computation: Normally, for security reasons, an organization may prefer to compute the data on its own resources. However, it may incur extra data transfer costs to and from the cloud. To avoid this, it is preferable to compute the data on the cloud itself in a secure manner as to avoid exposure to attackers. This is known as secure computing.

Machine Isolation: Virtualization is the most prominent technologies for cloud computing. Virtualization enables multiple VMs to share hardware resources thus allowing a higher level of resource utilization from the CSPs point of view. Additionally, it brings its own share of exploitable flaws. VMs, when running, concurrently utilize the same CPUs, primary and secondary storages on the same network. This may introduce non-malicious fluctuations in the data and allows a new attack for malicious attackers. They may try to co-locate in the same physical resource as the machine they want to attack.

Verifiable Computing: Verifiable computing provides assurance to the organization that the data has been computed as per expectation without any manipulations. This is related to the trust between the CSP and the organization related to computing the data securely and the accounting for the use of the resources.

5.3.3   Security Challenges Related to Data in Transit

Unlike data in rest, data in transit refers to the data in motion. Hence, it refers to the state of data during movement or transfer from one location to another over a network. The data may be moved from the cloud client's local storage to CSPs storage and vice versa. Data may also move among multiple cloud systems.

Data Relocation: A CSP may move the data from one data centre to another for better resource utilization, faster network performance, and lower latency. However, the CSP must follow all local regulations and honour all agreements between the CSP and the organization.

Data Outsourcing: A CSP may choose to delegate data storage and tasks to other CSP owing to cost minimization and lack of resources. The other CSP may not have the necessary level of protection or the same agreements as the primary CSP and the organization. This introduces another attack vector.

Data Loss: Data loss may take place by modification, deletion, loss of encryption key, and other natural reasons such as earthquakes, tsunamis, or fires. Data loss may or may not be malicious.

Data Breach: Data breach may take place due to improper authentication or authorization and unreliable encryptions.

5.4   Cross-Cutting Issues Related to Network in Cloud

Some issues related to data security cut across all the three areas above. Organizations demand access to high speed data transmission rates and low latency. This requires the setup of a complex network to provide the users with their required specifications. Many CSPs also provide the user with a browser based user login platform for GUI (Graphical User Interface) based access to data and its management. This however introduces another attack vector onto the network itself to gain access to the sensitive information stored on the cloud [7]. The following problems deal with the network attacks which may be used to gain malicious access to the data.

SQL Injection Attack: It is common from CSPs to maintain databases in SQL databases. This includes storing the user id and login for an account. In this attack, attacker penetrates malicious code to gain unauthorized access to the databases so as to access the sensitive data [10].

Cross-Site Scripting (XSS) Attack: In this attack, attacker puts nasty script into the web page at user side so as to redirect it to the attacker's website. This allows the attacker to access sensitive data such as login credentials and passwords stored in the browser. It also enables attacker to execute malicious code in the target's computer and gain control of it. It can also be done by using stored XSS (permanent insertion of the code into a source code managed by the web application) or reflected XSS which instantly reflects malicious code to the user computer [12].

Phishing Attacks: In these attacks, the attacker exploits cloud service. Here, the attacker redirects the target to a fake website which is made to look exactly like the original one. The target uses their credentials to access the cloud. These credentials are stolen by the attacker and used to gain access to the cloud.

Man-in-the-Middle Attack (MITM): In such attacks, attacker "taps" in between the user and cloud to listen into the traffic going on in between. The attacker may try to gain access to the communication by decrypting, snooping on the data traffic. It may also redirect the data traffic so as to perform other malicious activities.

Wrapping Attacks: When a user requests a VM through a web browser, a web server generates a SOAP message. This SOAP message contains XML packages containing information that is to be communicated among server and browser. However, the XML packages are signed in order to validate trust between the browser and server. Usually, this is done using digital signature which is placed in the header. In a wrapping attack, the attacker copies the SOAP message by using a man-in-the-middle attack. The header containing the signature is preserved while the contents are changed. This is then sent to the server as an authorized user allowing the attacker to gain access to the cloud.

Domain Name Server (DNS) Attack: Normally, the user accesses a server through its domain name which is further mapped to its IP address. In DNS attack, the attacker wrongly forward to some other malicious site. It may also uses DNS poisoning to insert code into the target computer by gaining access to it.

5.5   Protection of Data

There are always attacks taking place on data. Foreign state actors, hackers, and malicious individuals try to gain sensitive data to either harm the users and clients of the organization or commit corporate espionage against the organization itself. Another type of attack vector may be found in disgruntled employees and may become malicious insiders.

There are newer technologies to be implemented which may have multiple entry points. Even legacy systems may have zero day vulnerabilities which hackers may exploit to gain access to the data. It is not possible to have absolute protection. To implement some features introduces some faults into the system. Hackers will always keep trying to get access to sensitive data. We can however take some measure to slow them down if not to completely thwart them. The following techniques can ensure protection from a lot of attack vectors.

Encryption of Data
Encryption of data refers to the process of encoding the data. The process converts the original data known as plaintext in a different format called cipher text using a "key" as the method to convert the data into cipher text and back.

The authorized entity may use the key to decrypt the ciphertext back into plain text for use. It is possible to decrypt the data without the key but it takes a lot of time and computational resources to decrypt the data encrypted with a good algorithm. Some of the existing algorithms are as follows.

Data Encryption Standard
Data Encryption Standard (DES) was established in 1977 based on the Feistel cipher by Horst Feistel. It applies a 56-bit key to each block of 64 bits [3]. The encryption standard was submitted to the National Bureau of Standards and is the first encryption standard to be approved by NIST and was pushed as a standard security method. This method generally needs 16 rounds and works in various modes. Although, the algorithm is designed using "strong" encryption but it is found to be unfit for use as it can be easily cracked. Hence, it has been replaced by more powerful Advanced Encryption Standard (AES) as presented in Figure 5.3.

Triple Data Encryption System
In Triple Data Encryption System (3DES), it applies the DES algorithm three times to the data block hence the name 3DES. TDES utilizes a block size of 64 bits and operates in 48 processing rounds.

Advanced Encryption Standard
AES is also known as Rijndael cipher and uses a symmetric key encryption approach. AES is a block cipher algorithm that uses key size of variable lengths, viz., 128, 192, or 256 bits. The standard key size is 256 bits [3]. AES is fast, flexible, and effective encryption algorithm in comparison to DES. Like key size, the number of rounds also varies as 10, 12, and 14 for 128, 192, and 256 bits, respectively. The algorithm uses substitutions, permutations and direct changes. Hence, financial organizations and various security frameworks around the world employ AES for the encryption standard owing to its enhanced security and reliability. Figures 5.4 and 5.5 explain AES encryption and AES decryption methods.

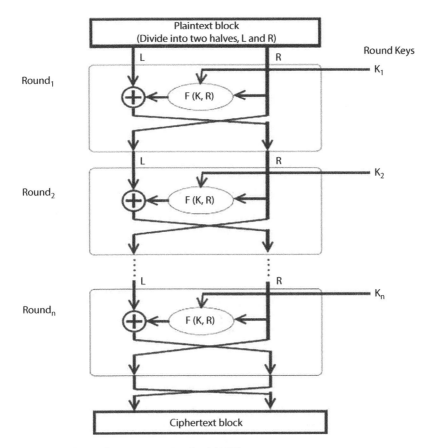

Figure 5.3 Advanced Encryption Standard (AES).

RSA

RSA algorithm is one of the earliest crypto key encryption techniques to be proposed in 1973 that uses two keys related to each other. Here, public key is shared publicly while private key is kept with user only. In this algorithm, public and private key pair is generated using two large prime numbers. In RSA, cipher texts are multiplied to discover the plain text and vice versa [3].

Diffie-Hellman Key Exchange

Diffie-Hellman (D-H) is a method to exchange the keys used for encryption. Firstly, a hidden private key is used to perform communication among two parties. This private key is then utilized to obtain the public key which is shared among two end users which do not have any historical information about each other. Finally, a third key is calculated through shared keys which cannot be found by a hacker.

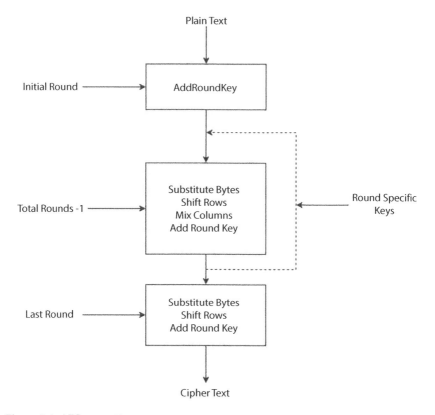

Figure 5.4 AES encryption.

DSA

The DSA is a technique for the exchange of digital signatures which is used for the authentication of messages. It is based on the ELGamal scheme and uses a discrete logarithm problem implementing the properties of algebraic properties of modular exponentiation. DSA was introduced by the NIST (National Institute of Standards and Technology) to detect the unauthorized changes made to the data sent by the source to the receiver. It also has a public and private key required to solve the problem. It also helps avoid non repudiation of message as the transmission must be signed by the public key.

Blowfish

It is a symmetric encryption algorithm. It has a 64 bit block cipher. It was developed by Bruce Schneider in 1993. It is effective for 32-bit mainframes with large data stores. It is comparatively faster than DES. Key lengths can differ from 32 to 448 bits in range. It is based on the Feistel cipher and has

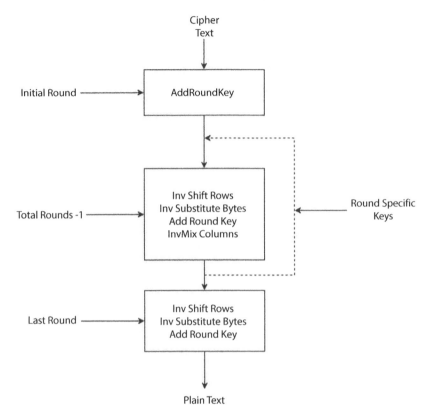

Figure 5.5 AES decryption.

a large S-box and a complex key round scheme which makes the algorithm difficult to crack.

RC5
It is a symmetric encryption algorithm. It has a variable block (32, 64, and 128 bits) size, but usually, it is 128 bit block. Also, it has 12 rounds. The general structure is again that of the feistel cipher. The RC5 algorithm is used for encryption of data in cloud computing. It can also be used in data transmission to ensure the security of the day during transfer. We can then be sure that the transmission of data will be encrypted. Even if the data is stolen during transmission, there is no related key that can be used to crack it easily.

Elliptic Curve Cryptography Algorithms
Elliptic Curve Cryptography (ECC) was introduced in 1985 as a comparative method for public-key cryptography. This method is comparatively

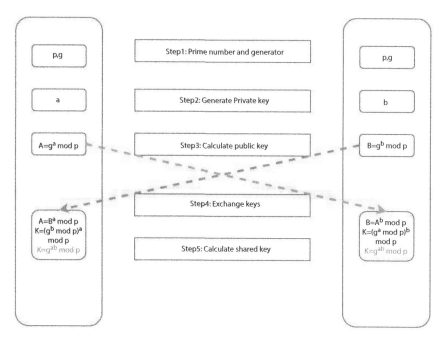

Figure 5.6 Swapping of keys.

secure and efficient in comparison to RSA owing to usage of smaller key sizes to obtain same level of security. Although, public key algorithms provide a method to share keys among several participants in a network. This method is based on discrete logarithms, which is hard to crack and thus obtain enhanced security as shown in Figure 5.6. A comparative analysis of various algorithms is presented in Table 5.1 for enhanced understanding of the reader.

5.6   Tighter IAM Controls

Identity and access management is one of the most important parts of cloud security. It ensures that the authorized entities have the proper access to the data and services provided by the cloud and all other parties are denied access.

IAM typically follows the PARC model. Namely:

P = Principles (users, groups, programs)
A = Actions (create, read, update, delete)
R = Resources (OS, network, files)
C = Conditions (time of the day, date, type of OS, etc.)

Table 5.1 Comparison of algorithms.

Algorithm	DES	3DES	AES	Blowfish	RC5	RSA	DSA	Diffe-Hellman
Developed	IBM in 1975	IBM in 1978	Daeman, Rijmen in 1998	Bruce Schneir in 1998	Ronal Rivest in 1994	Rivest, Shamir, Addlemn in 1977	NIST in 1991	Diffe-Hellman in 1976
Key Size	56	112	128, 192, 256	32–448	128	1,024 – 4,096	--	1,024
Block Size	64	64	128	64	64	--	--	--
Rounds	16	48	10, 12, 14	16	12	1	--	--
Cipher Type	Block	Block	Block	Block	Block	Asymmetric Block	--	
Algorithm type	Feistel Network	Feistel Network	Substitution Permutation	Feistel Network	Feistel Network	--	--	--
Security against attacks	Brute Force	Brute Force, Chosen Plaintext, Known Plaintext	Brute Force	Dictionary Attack	Brute Force	Brute Force, Timing Attack	--	Logjam Attack

The IAMs must be defined properly so that the principals may have authorized resources under the appropriate conditions. The IAMs are defined by the organization. However, the enforcement of these IAMs is done by the CSP. Hence, it becomes a complex problem to define all the IAM policies for all the related parties, especially with every CSP having its own way of enforcing them.

The policy must be properly defined lest unauthorized access may be given to an unrelated party which may or may not be malicious in nature.

Network Security

Attacks on the data will usually take place through the network. Hence, securing the network is one of the primary things to do toward strong data security. Therefore, we must take the appropriate measures toward securing the network toward network-based attacks.

Some of the measures are as follows:

- Sanitizing input data for logins
- Use of proper authentication and authorizations
- Use of proper Secure Socket Layer (SSL) configuration
- Use of proper DNS security measures, e.g., Domain Name System Security Extensions (DNSSEC)
- Use of an Intrusion Detection System (IDS)/Intrusion Prevention System (IPS)
- Using sniffer detection technique based on Address Resolution Protocol (ARP)
- Regular cleaning and purging of cookies (browser data)
- By proper utilization of the browser's security policy
- By creation of dedicative sessions and use of other authentication mechanisms as 2FA
- Implementation of backup policies to avoid issues with data recovery
- Using secure hypervisor and proper hypervisor monitoring
- Implementing proper VM isolation
- Use of active content filtering
- Use of web application vulnerability detection technology
- Use of an anomaly detection system to identify out-of-normal behavior

5.7   Conclusion and Future Scope

Data is one of the most important commodities in today's market. Data dictates how the organization moves and the preferences of the organization and its clients. Data leads to the creation of new technologies and features. It pans out the next move an organization may make in development toward a niche in the market. Data dictates the move of the market and therefore its profit. We can therefore say we are in a data centric world. It is common that organizations are under constant attack by various parties.

Malicious hackers, foreign state actors, corporations, contenders, and many other parties attack an organization for profit or in an act of corporate espionage. There will be bad implications for not only the organization but also its clients and affiliated 3rd parties, the cost of which may not be just limited to financial loss. It then becomes important that the organization protects its data to protect itself and its clients and subsidiaries. Hence, it is necessary for organizations to take the necessary precautions and measures to keep these parties at bay. Efforts must be taken by both the organizations and the CSPs to encrypt the data and proof the network against a data breach to protect itself and its interests.

Cyber warfare is said to be the next form of warfare. Governments, corporations, malicious hackers, and other related parties conduct attacks on each other to gain economic leverage and gauge the progress of each other. Based on the nature of the sensitive data, larger corporations and foreign governments may target the organization and its members to gain access to that data. Attacks targeting the members of the organization are common in order to gain access to the internal network of the organization. It is not easy nowadays to just "hack" into a network due to stronger encryptions, firewalls, and network security practices. The party may have to target an existing employee to reveal his access and logins in the network. This is called a social engineering attack. It remains to be one of the easier ways in as compared to directly hacking into a very secure network. Hence, we may state that a organization is as strong as its weakest link, i.e its members and users. The future scope explores social engineering attacks and their prevention through employee training and it reduces damage through proper access control.

References

1. Amara, N., Zhiqui, H., Ali, A., Cloud Computing Security Threats and Attacks with their Mitigation Techniques. *International Conference on Cyber-Enabled Distributed Computing and Knowledge Discovery*, 2017.

2. Mangla, M., Suneeta, S., Bhagirathi, N., Sachi Nandan, M., eds. *Integration of Cloud Computing with Internet of Things: Foundations, Analytics and Applications.* John Wiley & Sons, 2021.

3. Prakash, G.L., Prateek, Dr. M., Singh, Dr., II, Data Encryption and Decryption Algorithms using, Key Rotations for Data Security in Cloud System. *International Conference on Signal Propagation and Computer Technology*, 2014.

4. Potluri, S., Monika, M., Suneeta, S., Sachi Nandan, M., Detection and Prevention Mechanisms for DDoS Attack in Cloud Computing Environment. In 2020 11th International Conference on Computing, *Communication and Networking Technologies (ICCCNT)*, pp. 1–6. IEEE, 2020.

5. Akhare, R., Mangla, M., Deokar, S., Wadhwa, V., Proposed Framework for Fog Computing to Improve Quality-of-Service in IoT Applications. *Fog Data Analytics for IoT Applications*, pp. 123–143. Springer, Singapore, 2020.

6. Moghaddam F, F., Karimi, O., Alrashdan, M.T., A Comparative Study of Applying Real-Time Encryption in Cloud Computing Environments. *Proceedings IEEE 2nd International Conference on Cloud Networking (CloudNet), San Francisco, USA*, pp. 185–189, 2013.

7. Liu, W., Research on cloud computing security problem and strategy, in: *2012 2nd International Conference on Consumer Electronics Communications and Networks (CECNet)*, pp. 1216–1219, 2012.

8. Behl, A. and Behl, K., An analysis of cloud computing security issues. *IEEE World Congress on Information and Communication Technologies*, 2012.

9. Ko, R.K.L. *et al.*, Trustcloud: a framework for accountability and trust in cloud computing. *IEEE World Congress on Services*, 2011.

10. Cloud Computing-ENISA-Benefits, risks, and recommendations for information security. *ENISA*, 2009.

11. CSA: The Notorious Nine Cloud Computing Top Threats. *Cloud Security Alliance*, 2013.

12. Archana, M. and Shastry, M., A Review on Security Algorithms in Cloud Computing. *Int. J. Sci. Res. Sci. Eng. Technol.*, 4,1, 1490–1495, 2018.

13. Chen, D. and Zhao, H., Data Security and Privacy Protection Issues in Cloud Computing. *International Conference on Computer Science and Electronics Engineering*, 2012.

14. Omotosho, OI., A Review on Cloud Computing Security. *Int. J. Comput. Sci. Mobile Comput.*, 8,9, 245–257, 2019.

15. Y.Y.D.W. Anyi Liu, SQLProb: A Proxy-based Architecture towards Preventing. *Proceedings of the 2009 ACM Symposium on Applied Computing*, 2009.

16. Vogt, P., Nentwich, F., Jovanovic, N., Kirda, E., Kruegel, C., Vigna, G. Cross site scripting prevention with dynamic data tainting and static analysis. *In NDSS*, 2007, 12, 2007.

6

Cloud Cryptography for Cloud Data Analytics in IoT

N. Jayashri[1]* and K. Kalaiselvi[2]†

[1]Department of Computer Applications, Dr. M.G.R. Educational and Research Institute, Chennai, Tamilnadu, India
[2]Department of Computer Applications, School of Computing Sciences, Vels Institute of Science, Technology and Advanced Studies (Formerly Vels University), Chennai, Tamil Nadu, India

Abstract

The potential Internet of Things (IoT) will have a profoundly prudent business and social impact on our lives. A hub of interest in IoT systems is typically an asset obligation, which makes them focus on digital assault baiting. In this way, broad attempts have been devoted to identifying security and safety difficulties in trendy IoT, primarily through conventional cryptographic methodologies. In any case, the remarkable qualities of IoT hubs make it the main objective of the association and collaboration between objects and objects sent through remote systems to satisfy the target set for them as a united element, to achieve a superior domain for the use of big data. What is more, based on the creativity of remote systems, both platforms and IoT may grow quickly and together. In this section, it methodically audits the security needs, the assault vectors, and the current security responses for IoT systems. It also addresses insights into current machine learning solutions for solving various security issues in IoT systems and a few future cryptography cloud analysis headlines.

Keywords: Internet of Things, cloud computing, big data, security, privacy

*Corresponding author: jayashrichandrasekar@yahoo.co.in
†Corresponding author: kalairaghu.scs@velsuniv.ac.in

Sachi Nandan Mohanty, Jyotir Moy Chatterjee, Monika Mangla, Suneeta Satpathy and Sirisha Potluri (eds.) Machine Learning Approach for Cloud Data Analytics in IoT, (119–142) © 2021 Scrivener Publishing LLC

6.1   Introduction

Cloud-based organizations' introduction presents many obstacles for memberships. When a membership moves to use cloud organizations and open cloud organizations, a huge part of the system creation is affected by the cloud provider (CSP) of laughing stock directly. A variety of these disadvantages can and should be resolved by the organization [1]. These organizational exercises require a clear depiction of the CSP (which might be an affiliation)'s ownership and commitments and the affiliation's client work. Security administrators also must be able to ascertain the inspector and insurance checks that exist for the security status of the associate to be adequately defined. Nevertheless, appropriate safety controls should be conducted out subordinating to systems for the asset, danger, and chance screening, and depending on the level of data protection necessary, with a few large-scale modes of the organization paying little notice to think about trade in the organization [2]. That includes the following:

- Security approach execution
- Computer interruption identification and reaction
- Virtualization security the board

The board of directors for cloud security can also develop advanced capabilities and conduct criminal investigations using a quantifiable cloud-based information framework. In this report, swift and thorough clarity is required in the event of the exploitation of modified hazards and the lack of data in the cloud. Also, cloud security managers will make improvements by using robotics in practice and using better server management levels in regions such as interoperable security, operational design, bookkeeping, delivery, and API zones. APIs are meant to control cloud resources that GUI frameworks and remote APIs must figure out how to chronicle and unfiltered [3]. The board can handle information security applications to control huge trade by way of flexibility, invest more because expense models occur, use and supply, on request, and delegate data to the cloud operating activities of the administrator.

6.2   Cloud Computing Software Security Fundamentals

Security is a primary consideration when confiding the basic data of an organization to the cloud stages which are not topographically distributed. Despite regular IT data framework security procedures, the cloud surface will unbelievably be lowered by structuring safety to software programming throughout the invention of life cycle development. Three properties to be safe are as follows [4].

Addiction: Software that typically runs and works effectively under a variety of conditions, even when targeting or working on a dangerous host.

Trust: Program that contains a few baseline bugs or faults that may threaten the reliability of the product. It should also be irrelevant to false reasoning.

Survival: Program that is prone to and oblivious of threats and can rebound as easily as can be imagined, with the least maliciousness that is predicted in the circumstances.

Seven relevant rules for the authentication of data include secrecy, truthfulness, entry, assurance, consent, inspection, and responsibility.

Confidentiality, Integrity, and Availability The anonymity, cleverness, and usability of the data framework are sometimes referred to as the CIA group of three and are essential colons of cloud service security.

Confidentiality
This introduces the possibility of intentional or accidental data disclosure. Cloud protection is related to mental data, incognito networks, behavior analysis, coding, and inference fields [5].

- Intellectual Property (IP) Rights: IP blends innovations, strategies, and creative, melodic, and informative practices. IP patent regulations that guarantee signals of judgment skills and permits that are given to innovative innovations protect mental protection. Mental property rights are guaranteed.
- Covert Channels: A secret channel allows the sharing of information through an illegal and accidental means of communication. Uncovered networks may be accomplished by pacing messages or using power structures in an undeclared manner.
- Traffic Analysis: Intervention test may be a design of a breach of mystery that can beyond question be fulfilled by examining the duration, pace, direction, and intent of the communication action, should it be combined. Extensive correspondence and large action bursts can show that a major event takes place. Countermeasures for action review incorporate the near-constant rate of communication measures to protect the traffic's origin and aim areas.
- Encryption: Encryption involves scrambling notes, on the day of their interception, so that they cannot be searched

by an illegal material. The overall amount of effort needed (work figure) to decode the message may be a process of encryption quality and encoding estimation quality and quality.

- Inference: Derivation is often associated with the efficiency of the sample. The capacity of a product to use and device details obtained to reveal material that consumes remained assured at an advanced level of safety is established.

6.3 Security Management

The application concept includes the practice of cloud computing in effective security management. The appropriate management and administration of cloud security, such as surveillance, review of powerlessness, law adjustment, response to incidents, catastrophe resistance, dyspeptic recovery, and trade union arrangement, may consider problems of management and management. The correct use and analysis of cloud security controls improve these systems and safeguards them. The classification principles indicate those used in the private sector and are appropriate for cloud data. The classification laws are as follows [6].

Public Information: Data that is like unclassified information; the mixture of knowledge from a class incompatible organization, because data are available. While its unapproved liberality will undermine its policy, it must not influence either positively or unfavorably the organization, its members, or its customers.

Sensitive Data: Data on a classification level that is more relevant than normal data. Due to unauthorized modification, this information is protected from inaccurate classification. This is an intelligence course that requires an unparalleled pledge to confidence in protection against unauthorized alteration or eradication. Knowledge needs to be re-examined more correctly and accurately than ever.

Private Data: This function refers to certain information submitted for use by the organization. An unapproved indulgence of the Company and its employees may result from an honest and antagonistic influence.

Confidential Information: This agreement applies to the most important trade information that is intentionally expected for the partnership. It seems real and antagonistic to the accepting of the investor, his speculators, his staff, or perhaps his clients. Although data about the almost unknown production are classified as unidentified, market advantages, and fusion courses.

Controls: Cloud security checks are designed to minimize the consequences of an intrusion and reduce vulnerabilities to a reasonable extent. An organization needs to evaluate the impact of an attack and the risk of failure in this context. Cash stealing, reputation misfortune, and physical destruction are indicators of misfortune in commitments to sensory data. The method for analyzing different risk scenarios and creating a vulnerability of the agent toward the calculated possible disaster is called a hazard analysis (RA). As practicable countermeasures, controls serve [7].

6.4   Cryptography Algorithms

Are we naive to believe that we do not have to provide security with basic safeguards? Security is an important issue in this era of direct communication between tens of millions of people and is increasingly being used as a platform for trade. Security aspects are complex and the basic needs of users include numerous applications for secure business, private communications, and password protection transactions. Consequently, encryption is necessary because it gives an encrypted messaging environment. The main determination of cryptography remains toward stop unauthorized access to secure information [8]. Cryptography involves research and analysis of safe communication methods in the presence of third parties. Hidden research and analysis are hidden in cryptography. It is the craft and sympathetic of the turn into a clear text cipher board. In cryptographic language, the communication is named plaintext. The authentication is called encryption so that the content of the message cannot be exposed by external sources. The authentication process is indeed a number and types used to label the sender's message or sign ID which ensures that the meaning of the initial message or email is modified. Digital signatures that no one else can replicate are easily transmitted and can be synchronized automatically. The original signed message cannot be refused by the ability to ensure that it is authenticated. Use of a digital signature may be allowed with any type of communication, whether concealed or not, indicating an encrypted message or a decrypted text, allowing the receiver to be sure of the sender's identification and demonstrating that the message is consistent and implying that the message is initial or unchanged [9].

6.4.1   Types of Cryptography

Symmetric Key Cryptography: This is also known since main key, secret key, or single key Encryption. The same key for encryption and decryption is used to send and receive in that process [10]. The key symmetric is split into two parts: first, the BLOCK CIPHER data block, which is then separated into bits and used as encryption and decryption. The first is a BLOCK CIPHER data layer. For example, the block chauffer is AES, the most common symmetrical algorithm techniques are three times DES. Secondly, STREAM CIPHER operates on a given part. It is also a threat to breach faith and transfer the secret key to the unsafe network. Symmetrical code offers many benefits, as coding is easier. Single key encryption requires not a lot of computer resources in comparison to public-key encryption. A single secret key is used to communicate with all stakeholders. When a key is compromised, messages between a dispatcher and the beneficiary are only affected. The communication of other people remains secure.

Asymmetric Key Cryptography: Encryption of public key is also known. There are two types of keys, one of them is public encryption main and the other is a private decryption key. Only a consumer/device knows the private key, while the public key is used by everyone who wants to communicate. They are slightly faster and more vulnerable to attack than symmetrical algorithms but make key sharing more convenient. For asymmetric cipher, their pace and defensive strength are the major problems. RSA, elliptic curve, Diffie-Hellman key algorithm, and digital signature are the popular asymmetric chipboard. The advantages of the asymmetric key method are that they overcome the key problem of cryptography. The publishers of public keys and isolated keys are reserved secret [11]. The public key encryption requires the use of digital signatures to ensure that the communication is from a specific source. A digitally signed record cannot be changed deprived of canceling the sign.

Algorithms

DES

In the 1970s, when the US government needed the security of data and sensitive information, DES was established. However, for the NIST's notion, none was acceptable. In 1974, IBM developed an algorithm based on Host-Fiestal which was called Lucifer Cipher in 1973–1974. The machine encoding system (DES) is the symmetrical block cipher used for data encoding. It was based on a Lucifer algorithm proposed by IBM. In the 1970s and later 1975s, DES was developed and it needs a set plaintext length and has been translated by several operations to ciphertext.

Blowfish

Bruce Schneider invented Blowfish in 1993 and was used in multiple encryption products. The variable key length for Blowfish is from 0 to 448 bits ideally from 32 to 448 bits. It has a 64-bit block size and a 16-round Feistel slot, which uses large S-boxes. Blowfish utilize circular keys and several variations of the block chip generate all S-boxes. This improves the safety of the block cipher because of the complex key check and could be known as the safest symmetric algorithm.

3-Way

Joan Daemen developed a block cipher in 1994. In a broad spectrum of hardware platforms, it was very good. The key duration of the algorithm is 96 bits and it uses 32-bit words to measure it, and so, its name is 3-Way. The 3-Way block size is 96 bits and the S-P network is 11-round.

GOST

As a national standardization strategy, a GOST block cipher was created by the Soviet government. GOST operates over 64-bit block size and has a key size of 256 bits. GOST is a 32-round Feistel network with the algorithm of S-box. The new enhanced encryption standard (IPES) was originally referred to as an updated version. As a replacement for DES, the algorithm was developed. It uses 52 subkeys, each 16-bit long. The block size of the definition is 64-bit and it has 8 triangles.

LOKI 97

The original design is LOKI 89 or LOKI 91 as a DES replacement, each using a differentiating from Xbox, an S-Box to an Extension table, respectively.

RC2

RC2 was created by symmetric key block ciphers, which Lotus supported with Lotus Notes' tech. RC2 is a 64-bit, variable key and has 16 rounds of the block size.

RC5

In 1994, RC5 was created as a symmetrical block processor. RC5 is a quick-block cipher and is suitable for the application of hardware. The number of rounds, the text dimensions, and an underground important variable is on RC5. It has extensive utilization of facts in need of revolutions.

RC6
The RC6 was created from the RC5 with an upgraded RC5, providing better protection against attacks than the RC5.

Information Concealment Engine (ICE)
Kwan developed a Knowledge Case Engine (ICE) symmetric block cipher that was introduced at the Quick System Encryption Workshop in January 1997. The Feistel architecture is 64-bit like the DES, except that it incorporates the principle of main-dependent permutation contributing to linear and differentiated attack resistance. The standard version of ICE is usable on a 64-bit block and contains 64-bit keys in 16 rounds plus 16 subkeys. A quick-mounted model called Thin-ICE operates on a 64-bit8-round block with a 64-bit key and open-ended 16n and 64-bit ICE-n models. ICE input is 64-bit, divided into two parts, i.e., 32-bit. The right half of the 32-bit sub-key and the 60-bit sub-key take each round of the F function, and this value is XORed and left, and then swapped. Repeats for all but the final section, the expansion part, main permutation, Xor operation, S-boxes, permutation mechanism, and key schedule where the transformation is left out, the half is concatenated and the ciphertext is formulated [12].

The comparison of algorithms explained in Figure 6.1 with the different modes based on processing and size.

Algorithm	Modes	Processing	Size
DES	Yes CBC,CFB,EC B OFB	No Initial	64 to 56 bit
3-DES	Yes	No	Three times increase then DES
AES	Yes	CTR	No Variable
BlowFish	EBC	CBC	No Variable
GOST	OFB	CFB	NO
B-REA	CBC	Yes	NO
Square	N/A	Yes	Variable
SERPENT	N/A	Yes	Variable
Shark	N/A	Yes	Fixed
IDEA	N/A	Yes	Fixed
CRYPT ON	N/A	Yes	Variable

Figure 6.1 Comparison of algorithms.

KASUMI

A 64-bit cipher block algorithm, a 128-bit hardware knowledge optimization element, is a KASUMI idea originally derived from the MISTY1 algorithm. KASUMI is an eighth round, Feistel-like, network structure with round functions irreversibly and around key composed of 16 sub-keys originally drawn from a 128-bit fixed key program [31] is used for each round function [13]. KASUMI is mainly used in mobile communications systems for universal mobile telecommunications systems (UMTS), GSM, and Global Packet Radio (GPRS).

Threefish

Asymmetrical chip block was produced in 2008 by Bruce Schneier and Jesse Walker, Niels Ferguson, Stefan Lucks, Doug Whiting, and Mihirbellare. Threefish is the same as a blowfish. However, Threefish uses three keys: 256, 512, and 1,024 bits with the same string size. It usually has 72 rounds, but it operates for 80 rounds and 1,024 pieces. In addition to these two, Threefish is a tweakable block cipher, i.e., the key one, the shift value, and the message node are three parameters. The tweak value is used to encrypt a message block. To avoid time assaults, Threefish does not use S-Box or other table searches [14].

6.5   Secure Communications

As the creation of cloud application involves a revaluation of communications security, it is restricted to providing supervised secure communication between storage assets within an enterprise. These signals are essential both to movement information and to rest knowledge. Structures, transmission techniques, transport designs, and security measures that provide confidentiality, astuteness, accessibility, and legitimacy for transmissions through private or accessible communications systems are part of secure cloud communications. Secure cloud computing will ensure the following [15–17]:

Confidentiality: It ensures the retrieval of information by the isolated person. Loss of classification may occur if privately owned business data are intentionally shown or device privileges are misapplied. Part of the media communications elements used to ensure privacy is as follows [18]:

- Conventions on network protection.
- Administrations of network authentication.
- Administrations for data encryption.

Integrity: It makes sure the knowledge is not changed due to maladministration or malignancy. Trust is the assurance that the letter that is sent is accepted and that the response is not modified deliberately or accidentally. The principle of non-repudiation of a message source is also expressed with reverence. A part of the trustworthiness electors shall be as follows:

- Control of firewall.
- Security management of messages.
- Administrators of the location of intrusion.

Availability: It allows accepted clients to access the system or systems when and where they are needed and maintain that functionality is accessible when required. Also, the assurance that security administrations for the security specialist can be used as needed is recalled for this clarification. A few of the elements used to ensure accessibility shall be as follows:

- Fault resistance to access to information, such as refurbishments and excess circle structures.
- Suitable logins and views of work procedure.
- Security procedures and system components secure and interoperable.

APIs

Common vulnerabilities such as powerless antivirus computer program, unattended computing stages, destitute passwords, frail verification components, and lacking interruption discovery that can affect communications must be more stringently analyzed, and appropriate APIs must be utilized [19].

Virtual Private Networks

A virtual private network (VPN) is another key strategy to secure internet communications. A VPN will be generated by establishing safe connections between two hubs, imitating the properties of a private network point-to-point. A VPN can be used for safe, insecure access to the cloud, for protected interfaces between two systems, or a secure information burrow inside a network. The portion of the connection that typifies personal information is known as the burrow. It could be referred to as a safe, coded burrow, although it is defined more specifically as a standard burrow because encryption can or cannot be used. Connecting information was typed or filled with a header that offers to guide details to mimic a point-to-point. The data is most often broken up for privacy. This scrambled

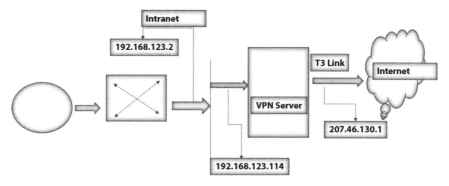

Figure 6.2 VPN configuration.

connecting portion is known to be the true private computer system. Figure 6.2 shows a shared VPN arrangement with instance IP discourses for distant access via the Internet to an organization's intranet. The organization's router names are 192.168.123.2 [20].

Incredible to and from network to network are two common VPNs that are essential for cloud computing. These VPN forms are shown in the following sections.

Remote Access VPNs
A VPN can be designed to provide hidden access to business resources through the open web to maintain privacy and continuity. It allows the farther user, without pushing the client to establish a gap, to use anything accessible via local ISPs to the network and to make 800 calls to a third party. The VPN program makes a virtual private relationship between the customer dial-up and a business VPN server on the network by way of the ISP neighborhood association. A farther VPN client link occurs in Figure 6.2 [21].

Network-to-Network VPNs
Two systems that may be the more company LAN and a far-off office LAN are commonly associated with a VPN via the network. The partnership can use either dedicated lines for the internet or wireless dial-ups. However, if the VPN server is accessible 24 hours a day, the business center switch, which functions as a VPN server, must be linked with a local ISP on a dedicated thread. The VPN computer program utilizes the connection to make a VPN burrow between the office switch and the network switch of the business center. In Figure 6.3, the departmental agency associated with the fundamental corporate office using a network VPN tunnel appears to be inaccessible [22].

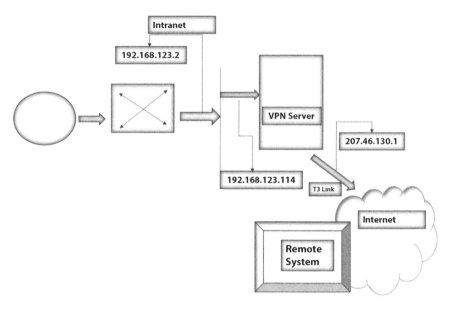

Figure 6.3 Remote access VPN configuration.

VPN Tunneling

Tunneling could be a technique to exchange information in an extra header from one entity to another organization [23]. The additional header provides directional information so that the standard payload can access the intermediate networks, as shown in Figure 6.4. The burrow client and the burrow server must use the same tunneling system to build a burrow. Innovation in tunneling may be based either on a convention on layer 2 or a convention on tunneling layer 3. These layers equate to the interconnection of open systems (OSI). Type for example. As a replacement for

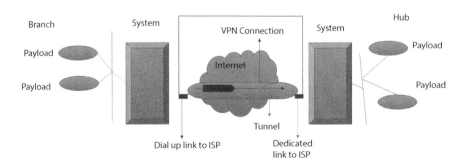

Figure 6.4 A network-to-network VPN configuration.

encryption/decryption tunneling and use of a VPN is not expected. If a high-security standard is necessary, then the most well-founded possible encryption should be used in Figure 6.5 within the VPN and tunneling should be convenient.

IPsec, which in comparison to the IP header characterizes IPsecs, is a well-known network tunneling protocol. IPsec operates on the Assembly Layer OSI Reference Panel which allows multiple simultaneous burrows. IPsec provides the ability to scrape and verify IP information. The IPv6 standard is included and serves as a complement to the current IPv4. You can hack and convert the wireless packages in the IPsec burrow mode via the company Mobile intranet or the free IP internet like the internet into a typewritten IP header [24]. The IPsec Authentication Header (Ah) uses the ESP (ESP) function to authenticate and evaluate the source and the consistency without encryption. The sender and the receiver know the IPsec code.

Public Key Infrastructure and Encryption Key Management

The cloud can exchange information to encrypt communications, track connections to other secret malware networks, and to use it and preserve it. Preparing passwords would be used to connect people to open keys for secure key coding purposes. The Certificate Authority (CA) recognizes a person's identity as a lawyer and issues credentials to make sure that the accepted claimant is publicly available. The credential is checked with its private key by the qualified individual. The receiver is therefore identified when opening the files as the sender. In what is called encryption resources (PKI), computerized logos and licenses, and other e-commerce agencies are being implemented [25]. They make electronic transactions easy to track, secrecy, secrecy, and denial.

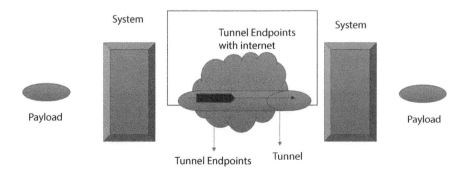

Figure 6.5 A VPN tunnel and payload.

Digital Certificates
Core elements of PKI are the digital certificate and qualification administration. Keep in mind that specialized certificates are designed to show us that an individual's open key—shown on a clear "keyring"— is his own is explained in Figure 6.6. An important third party CA guarantees that the name of the person is the open key and that a certificate to validate this reality is provided. The CA completes the certificate by carefully identifying the person's open key and associated information. Licenses and CRLs between the shop and the CA with agreements should be stored in the warehouse. The shop decides how these tasks can be assigned. At a conference, the shop meets other stores, CAs, and customers. The CA holds the CRLs and their licenses. Customers will at some stage use this stuff [26].

Key Management
The same protections as physical keys are used to protect regions or variations to the safeguards while handling them with encryption keys [27]. The following fields represent the key administration components.

Key Distribution
As the password symmetry keys are a difficulty to convey, asymmetrical crypto-systems will communicate mystery keys. Other means that mystery keys are passed to personal meetings, to stable flag bearers, or some other secured swap network for exchange keys. Another option is to delete the

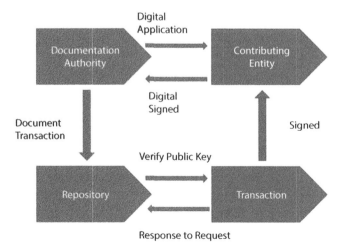

Figure 6.6 A transaction with digital certificates.

mystery key and give the expected recipient a scratched mystery main with another secret, the key-encryption key [28]. These major coding keys can be distributed physically, but need not be scattered constantly. The keys can also be partly divided into different parts and each part can be conveyed through a separate media. Key distribution in costly schemes can lead to a real problem as N(N − 1)/2 is an N-person scheme that is named multiple key firms. To control the main transport issue, the use of open key cryptography or the development and trade of session keys, which are necessary for a session and length. The main could be changed by using the old password to create a modern password. If you are likely to have a mystery key for yourself, Alice and Bounce can use the same change process (a hash algorithm).

Multiple Keys
A private always has more than one match between a public and a remote key. The keys can be of differing sizes for different safety levels. For carefully labeling records a bigger key calculation can be used, while a smaller key indicator can be used for encryption. An individual may additionally be required to sign messages with a distinctive signature in different parts or duties. One essential match can be used for the company, another for individual purposes, and another for a few other actions, for example, as part of a school board [29].

Distributed Versus Centralized Key Management
A CA can be a centralized key power. It can be a key area where certificates are given and CRLs are maintained. Optional key management is distributed to establish a "trust chain" or "esteem network" among familiar clients. They can presume that each open key is essential since they know each other. Some of these customers can recognize other users and thus accept their open key. From the first encounter, the chain extends further [30]. This course takes place in a relaxed system of validation based on people understanding each other and respecting each other.

6.6   Identity Management and Access Control

Recognition and entry are key capabilities for secure cloud assessment [31]. A programming system with a client name and a secret word is the best way to manage the character. In any case, real character management needs better security, identification, and control for cloud computing, as needed. It shall set out the characteristics of products, such as biometric or shrewd cards, which may be entered or used by the user, and decide the illegal content that has been received.

Identity Management

Identification of this security is the foundation of most control frameworks. Identification is the act of a customer when sending a character to a database, usually in the form of a user login ID. Client liability for staggered operations is established by law. User IDs should be of a sort and should not be sold by distinguished individuals. Customer IDs follow similar requirements in several large organizations, such as beginning after the final title. The ID should not represent the user's job title or feature to upgrade and reduce the amount of data accessible to the intruder. Authentication confirms that the stated identity of the individual is true and is usually executed utilizing a hidden login word of the client. Confirmations are based on three types of data. Category1: for example, an individual recognizable number of proofs (PIN) or a secret key. Category 2: It has an ATM card or a smart wallet. Something for contrast [32]. Category 3: Sometimes, the fourth element is used for this repeat (e.g., unique fingerprinting or retina check). Something you did can be classified as a name or various phrases on your phone. Two-factor authentication allows two of the three variables to be used in the verification process.

Passwords

Passwords must be guarded because they can be abused. In the perfect case, a watchword should be used as it once was [33]. This "one-time watchword," or OTP, is very secure because every new connection needs a modern secret word. A secret word is equal to each username, a secret inactive word is named. A dynamic secret word is a secret word that varies with every logon. Passwords can also be modified from one extreme to another. Depending on the criticality of the data that require verification and the recurrence of the password execution, passwords may need to be changed on a weekly, annual, or another basis. Of necessity, the more often a password is used, the more likely it is to break. A character assignment that is often longer than the number given for a secret word may be a passphrase. The passphrase is converted into a secret computer word by the door. An inbound authorization gadget or a back-end evaluation device can perform tests for all these proposals and support different workstations or hosts. Various devices, such as buttons, memory cards, and smart cards, can provide passwords.

Tokens

Tokens are used to provide passwords as tiny, handheld devices. The four basic types of tokens will arrive next:

- Token are standard hidden statement.
- By writing a cryptic secret phrase, owners validate the token.
- The token would prove that the owner has a data framework if the secret phrase is right.

A clock-based token, a synchronous dynamic hidden expression, creates an additional, uncommon, secret word, a fixed time incentive associated with a similar secret word on a validity server (this key is a hidden-stick period). A mysterious secret key is mounted in a workstation alongside the owner's lock. The information search in the working set or frame recognizes the mystery key of the owner and the lock, and the segment verifies that the secret key entered is legitimate and that it is installed in the time window.

Asynchronous Tokens, Challenge-Reaction

- An abnormal test string arrives from a workstation or system and together with the strongest PIN, the proprietor inserts the string into the token.
- The token counts on the string that uses the PIN which produces an answer recognition that is then put in the workstation or the system.
- The authentication method at the workstation or frame provides an evaluation equivalent to a token that utilizes the PIN of the user and contests the performance and validity the owner has entered.

Memory Cards

Memory cards give non-volatile data capacity, but they have no preparedness. Scrolling passwords and other associated information are stowed in a unique recollection card. Memory card images are a cell calling card and an ATM card.

Smart Cards

Smart cards make holding cards more efficient than memory cards. Batteries and chips are stored in the credit card facilities and used for holding computerized numbers, private keys, passwords, and other personal information.

Biometrics

Biometrics is an alternative to use codes to validate in a precise or sophisticated manner. The biometrics emphasis on the search factor Sort 3—you're anything. Biometrics is characterized as a robotic device that indicates the distinction or evaluation of the physiological or behavioral characteristics of a living person. Identity in biometrics could be a one-to-one look at the characteristics of an individual in a series of lost images. Evaluation can be a single attempt to verify an individual's identity assertion [34]. Biometrics are used to identify the evidence in physical checks and to validate them in reliable tests.

- There are three fundamental gages of execution in biometrics: false dismissal rate (FRR) or form I error—the level of valid topics that are falsely dismissed.
- False recognition rate (Extreme) or type II error—the level of invalid objects that are wrongly identified.
- CER—The number at which the FRR increases to the FAR. The bigger the CER, the more efficient the device.

Additional variables, including the enrolment period, throughput rate, and reliability, must be tested to increase the accuracy of the biometric system. The registration period is the time to register with the system first by checking the biometric characteristics. It is about 2 minutes to the point of entry. The true mark is provided with unique fingerprint frames for illustration with needs up to 250 KB per digit for a high-quality photograph. This level of data is sufficient if you are searching for exceptionally large databases under forensic applications. Absolute special labeling shall not be omitted from the innovation of finger scanning, or the highlights derived from that unique fingerprint shall be processed in a small format needing about 500 to 1,000 bytes of space. Enrolment data services may well be required because certain biometric features, such as voice and signature, can change over time. The rate of output is the rate at which the system defines and separates or recognizes individuals [35–38].

Valuable throughput rates are per decrease in the region of 10 subjects. Acceptability refers to protection, evasiveness, and physical and mental reassurance when the framework is used. In some situations, the exchange in body fluids in the oyster may be an issue with the eye filtering system. In the area that implies as a corpus, the biometric assembled photographs are incomplete. The collection is not included in the image database. Potential bumble sources include the confusion and mislabeling of images and other identity issues related to the image database. Similarly, the process and intent of image grouping should be carried out with unrelenting control focus [39]. These images are taken within the context of the admission plan and are essential for the correct movement of the biometric contraction in these areas.

6.7   Autonomic Security

Autonomous computing refers to a self-managing software series in which computer structures are reconfigured and self-cured. It will take several years for automatic computing to be fully realized, but it offers technology that can improve the security of specific data systems and cloud storage. The capacity of autonomous systems to gather and interpret data and to suggest or update protocols can help to improve safety and recovery from dangerous accidents [40].

Autonomic Systems
Autonomous systems focus on an individual, autonomous, and self-managed nervous system that tracks changes in the body and retain internal equalization. Thus, considering the annoyances of the network, an autonomous computer system attempts at self-management to sustain redress operations. Such a system requires the ability to provide direct support, decision-making skills, and therapeutic exercises and to create a harmonious normal operating atmosphere. Illustrations of occasions to be treated separately include the following:

- Outbreaks malignant
- The liability of hardware or software
- Extreme use of CPU
- Deceptions of influence
- Regulations on administration
- Unwanted failures of the staff
- Communication with other structures
- Learning apps

Self-management is the basic definition of autonomous systems by which the programming system guarantees a consistent role in the face of changing conditions both externally and internally, determines the need for revision, performs programs, performs repeat tests, performs medium products, and identifies and overrides the circumstances of problems in general.

Autonomic Protection

Autonomous self-protection includes knowledge of a hurtful condition and actions to alleviate the state. These program structures shall also be established to predict issues with the production of tangible data and to take corrective action. The independent security solution framework is based on organizational knowledge, associated resource capability, data accumulation, scenario complexity, and effect on the program concerned. The decision-making a feature of autonomous computation will act, such as changing the quality of the necessary authentication or updating the encryption keys, considering the current security situation and the safe environment of the system. The security environment is based on data obtained from networking or system management modules and then extracted to provide a higher representation of the safety position of the request. The often-underestimated concept of autonomous systems is that configuration changes, and additionally, independent experiments aimed at resolving other computing fields can generate security vulnerabilities.

Autonomic Self-Healing

The way IT systems are handled and restored, which can be problematic, can be time-consuming, and usually require a lot of effort. Autonomous self-healing systems can provide for differentiating and fixing software issues without manual intervention and identification of system defects. The cloud describes five basic features, three model benefits, and four model combinations. As polling, the five key features are follows:

- Self-service on request
- Admission to the universal network
- Mounting of reserve
- The personality of the position
- Rapid power
- Poor implementation

The kit templates are like the following:

- Service Cloud Applications (SaaS)—Network queries by customers have been completed.
- Cloud as a Service (PaaS) platform—Organize cloud requests from customers.
- Cloud Service Architecture (IaaS)—Delivery of fees, data, net volumes, and other major computing functions.

Independent management will record and track data and evaluate the issue area. This approach is sometimes directed by an independent leader who manages the computing of asset components with well-defined interfaces that support the activities of symptoms and mitigation. Regulated components control their internal conditions and have established performance characteristics and relationships with other computer components. The aim of self-healing therapy is to ensure that the components meet the requirements of their program.

6.8   Conclusion

Cloud computing security can be a key component of the cloud computing system. The reliability of cloud usage depends on reliable computer tools, good character management, and control methods that make for safe execution. This chapter focuses on data authentication for cloud systems that rely on traditional concepts of privacy, connectivity, and knowledge and are implemented geographically, physically, and dynamically. Essentially stable program plan and execution requirements provide minimal benefit, bond exchange, in-depth protection, protection, and open design. The use of computer program requirements for computer design, scheduling parameters, code hones, security execution and decay method, and safe software testing is also important for secure cloud programs. Penetration testing, functional testing, run testing, and vulnerability testing is cost-effective software types. The primary concern with the use of cloud services would be the availability of cloud server applications and information for the enterprise. It provides a reliable source framework for the cloud. Online sources may be an important requirement to set up a Cloud Trust System. Domain building needs reliable self-managed administrators who can handle cloud users' resources efficiently and without any human involvement.

References

1. *Security Guidance for Critical Areas of Focus in Cloud Computing V3.0*, 177 pp, 2011 (http://www.cloudsecurityalliance.org/guidance/csaguide.pdf).
2. *Information Assurance Technology Analysis Center (IATAC)*, Information Assurance Technology Analysis Center Falls Church VA. July 31, 2007.
3. Komaroff, M. and Baldwin, K., DoD Software Assurance Initiative. *Software security assurance: A state-of-art report (sar)*. Information Assurance Technology Analysis Center (IATAC) Herndon VA. September 13, 2005, (https://acc.dau.mil/CommunityBrowser.aspx?id=25749).

4. Goertzel, K., Winograd, T. *et al.*, Enhancing the Development Life Cycle to Produce Secure Software, Draft Version 2.0, United States Department of Defense Data and Analysis Center for Software, Rome, New York, July 2008.

5. Saltzer, J.H. and Schroeder, M.D., The Protection of Information in Computer Systems. *Fourth ACM Symposium on Operating Systems Principles*, October 1974.

6. Davis, J. F., Information systems security engineering: A critical component of the systems engineering lifecycle. *ACM SIGAda Ada Letters*, 24, 4, 13–18, 2004.

7. Goertzel, K., Winograd, T. *et al.*, *Enhancing the development life cycle to produce secure software*, vol. 1, pp. i–iv, U.S. Department of Defense, 2008.

8. van Lamsweerde, A., Brohez, S., De Landtsheer, R., Janssens, D., From System Goals to Intruder Anti-Goals: Attack Generation and Resolution for Security Requirements Engineering, in: *Proceedings of the Requirements for High Assurance Workshop*, Monterey Bay, CA, September 8, 2003, pp. 49–56.

9. American Institute of Certified Public Accountants (AICPA), Accounting for the Costs of Computer Software Developed or Obtained for Internal Use, AICPA Statement of Position (SOP) No. 98-1, The Evolution of Computer Software on Business Practices and Standards. *Academy of Legal, Ethical and Regulatory Issues,* 19., March 1998, www.aicpa.org.

10. ISACA, *IS Auditing Guideline on Due Professional Care*, Information Systems Audit and Control Association, March 1, 2008, Mangla, M., Akhare, R., Ambarkar, S., Context-Aware Automation Based Energy Conservation Techniques for IoT Ecosystem, in: *Energy Conservation for IoT Devices*, pp. 129–153, Springer, Singapore, 2019.

11. Akhare, R., Mangla, M., Deokar, S., Wadhwa, V., Proposed Framework for Fog Computing to Improve Quality-of-Service in IoT Applications, in: *Fog Data Analytics for IoT Applications*, pp. 123–143, Springer, Singapore, 2020.

12. Deokar, S., Mangla, M., Akhare, R., A Secure Fog Computing Architecture for Continuous Health Monitoring, in: *Fog Computing for Healthcare 4.0 Environments*, pp. 269–290, Springer, Cham., 2021.

13. Potluri, S., Quality of Service based Task Scheduling Algorithms in Cloud Computing. *Int. J. Electr. Comput. Eng.*, 7, 2, 1088–1095, April 2017.

14. Potluri, S., Efficient Hybrid QoS Driven Task Scheduling Algorithm in Cloud Computing Using a Toolkit: Clouds. *JARDCS*, 12-Special Issue, 1270–1283, 2017.

15. Potluri, S., A study on technologies in cloud-based design and manufacturing. *IJMPERD*, 8, 6, 187–192, 2018.

16. Potluri, S., Software virtualization using containers in google cloud platform. *IJITEE*, 8, 7, 2430–2432, May 2019.

17. Potluri, S., Simulation of QoS-Based Task Scheduling Policy for Dependent and Independent Tasks in a Cloud Environment, in: *Smart Intelligent Computing and Applications*, vol. 159, pp. 515–525, May 2019.

18. Potluri, S., Quality of Service-Based Cloud Models in Manufacturing Process Automation, in: *Lecture Notes in Networks and Systems*, vol. 32, pp. 231–240, 2019.

19. Potluri, S., Optimization model for QoS based task scheduling in cloud computing environment. *IJEECS*, 18, 2, 1081–1088, 2020.

20. Potluri, S., IOT Enabled Cloud Based Healthcare System Using Fog Computing: A Case Study. *J. Crit. Rev.*, 7, 6, 1068–1072, 2020.

21. Potluri, S., Improved quality of service-based cloud service ranking and recommendation model. *TELKOMNIKA Telecommun. Comput. Electron. Control*, 18, 3, 1252–1258, June 2020, accredited First Grade by Kemenristekdikti, Decree No: 21/E/KPT/2018.

22. Potluri, S., A Hybrid PSO Based Task Selection and Recommended System for Cloud Data. *Test Eng. Manage.*, 83, 10210–10217, March-April 2020.

23. Potluri, S., A Hybrid Self-Adaptive PSO and QoS Based Machine Learning Model for Cloud Service Data. *Test Eng. Manage.*, 83, 23736–23748, May-June 2020.

24. Le, D.N., Kumar, R., Nguyen, G.N., Chatterjee, J.M., *Cloud computing and virtualization*, John Wiley & Sons, India, 2018.

25. Jha, S., Kumar, R., Chatterjee, J.M., Khari, M., Collaborative handshaking approaches between internet of computing and internet of things towards a smart world: a review from 2009–2017. *Telecommun. Syst.*, 70, 4, 617–634, 2019.

26. Chatterjee, J.M., Kumar, R., Khari, M., Hung, D.T., Le, D.N., Internet of Things based system for Smart Kitchen. *Int. J. Eng. Manuf.*, 8, 4, 29, 2018.

27. Sujath, R., Chatterjee, J.M., Hassanien, A.E., A machine learning forecasting model for COVID-19 pandemic in India. *Stochastic Environ. Res. Risk Assess.*, 1, 34, 2020.

28. Chatterjee, J., IoT with Big Data Framework using Machine Learning Approach. *Int. J. Mach. Learn. Networked Collab. Eng.*, 2, 02, 75–85, 2018.

29. Moy Chatterjee, J., Fog computing: beginning of a new era in cloud computing. *Int. Res. J. Eng. Technol. (IRJET)*, 4, 05, 735, 2017.

30. Iwendi, C., Bashir, A.K., Peshkar, A., Sujatha, R., Chatterjee, J.M., Pasupuleti, S., Jo, O., COVID-19 Patient Health Prediction Using Boosted Random Forest Algorithm. *Front. Public Health*, 8, 357, 2020.

31. Kumar, A., Chatterjee, J.M., Díaz, V.G., A novel hybrid approach of SVM combined with NLP and probabilistic neural network for email phishing. *Int. J. Electr. Comput. Eng.*, 10, 1, 486, 2020.

32. Chatterjee, J.M., Priyadarshini, I., Le, D.N., Fog Computing and Its security issues, in: *Security Designs for the Cloud, Iot, and Social Networking*, pp. 59–76, 2019.

33. Choudhuri, A., Chatterjee, J.M., Garg, S., Internet of Things in Healthcare: A Brief Overview, in: *Internet of Things in Biomedical Engineering*, pp. 131–160, Academic Press, India, 2019.

34. Chatterjee, J.M., Bioinformatics Using Machine Learning. *Global J. Internet Interv. Fusion*, 1, 1, 28–35, 2018.

35. Shri, M.L., Devi, E.G., Balusamy, B., Chatterjee, J.M., Ontology-Based Information Retrieval and Matching in IoT Applications, in: *Natural Language Processing in Artificial Intelligence*, pp. 113–130, Apple Academic Press, India, 13, 4, 2020.

36. Radhakrishnan, S., Lakshminarayanan, A.S., Chatterjee, J.M., Hemanth, D.J., Forest data visualization and land mapping using support vector machines and decision trees. *Earth Sci. Inf.*, 1–19, 2020.

37. Jain, V. and Chatterjee, J.M. (Eds.), *Machine Learning with Health Care Perspective: Machine Learning and Healthcare*, vol. 13, Springer Nature, India, 2020.

38. Chatterjee, J.M., COVID-19 Mortality Prediction for India using Statistical Neural Network Models. *Front. Public Health*, 8, 441, 2020.

39. Kumar, A., Payal, M., Dixit, P., Chatterjee, J.M., Framework for Realization of Green Smart Cities Through the Internet of Things (IoT), in: *Trends in Cloud-based IoT*, pp. 85–111, Springer, Cham, 2020.

40. Sujatha, R., Nathiya, S., Chatterjee, J.M., Clinical Data Analysis Using IoT Data Analytics Platforms, in: *Internet of Things Use Cases for the Healthcare Industry*, pp. 271–293, Springer, Cham, 2020.

7

Issues and Challenges of Classical Cryptography in Cloud Computing

Amrutanshu Panigrahi[1]*, Ajit Kumar Nayak[2] and Rourab Paul[1]

[1]Department of CSE, I.T.E.R., S'O'A University, Bhubaneswar, India
[2]Department of CS & IT, I.T.E.R., S'O'A University, Bhubaneswar, India

Abstract

Cloud computing nowadays draws the attention of different users as it gives scalable and on-demand access to the resource. As a large number of users can access various cloud resources simultaneously, there will be a threat to every user present in the cloud environment. With the advent of cloud computing, security plays the primary concern. The cryptography plays a key role in maintaining the basic property such as confidentiality, integrity, and availability (CIA) of the information shared between different users. Traditional cryptography provides a secure exchange of information between the users. The data can be shared by using some key which will be used to encrypt the data at the sender side and to decrypt the data at the receiver side. In traditional cryptography, any operation to be performed in the cloud data need a decryption process that exposes confidential data in the cloud platform. These issues are addressed by the homomorphic encryption (HE) technique. This technique enables the cloud user to operate such as update and sort on the encrypted data itself. The partial HE (PHE) and full HE (FHE) are two available variants of HE to overcome the issues of the traditional cryptography system. This research is based on the different traditional cryptography and HE technique along with issues and challenges faced during the implementation. In this paper, the RSA algorithm is implemented as HE. Moreover, the authors try to reduce the time complexity of the RSA algorithm by implementing the homomorphic RSA.

Keywords: Cryptography, homomorphic encryption, RSA, PHE, FHE

**Corresponding author*: amrutansup89@gmail.com

Sachi Nandan Mohanty, Jyotir Moy Chatterjee, Monika Mangla, Suneeta Satpathy and Sirisha Potluri (eds.) Machine Learning Approach for Cloud Data Analytics in IoT, (143–166) © 2021 Scrivener Publishing LLC

7.1   Introduction

Cloud computing is one of the quickest developing techniques today, as confirmed by the cloud service pro, for example, Amazon's S3 and EC2 [1], Microsoft Azure [2], and Rackspace [3]. This is not unexpected, as distributed computing permits the joining of countless virtual assets (e.g., processing power, and storage) to amplify the viability and utility of the (incorporated) assets. Cloud clients can get to these assets' day in and day out over a Web association (i.e., on-request benefits) on a compensation as-you-use plan of action. Cloud computing nowadays draws the attention of different users as it gives scalable and on-demand access to the resource. A large number of users are interested in cloud computing due to its scalable behavior. It provides the service to the user on-demand basis [4]. The highlights of cloud computing are as follows.

- Enhanced Network Access: Utilizing this characteristic, the cloud service provider achieves the ubiquity property. By this, the user can access and store the data in the cloud regardless of the place. While providing this kind of property to the end-user, the admin maintains the latency, access time for getting the asset from the cloud [1].
- Resource Pooling: The multi-tenant architectural behavior of the cloud enables multiple users at the same time. The load from the user end is extracted from the dedicated hardware and software and submitted to different VMs for balancing the load on each processor. The cloud service provider depends upon the specific hardware for maintaining the security of the cloud assets [5].
- Flexibility and Scalability: Traditional architectures do not support scaling but the resource pooling characteristic cloud has the flexibility to scale up the storage capacity dynamically which helps to avoid the bottleneck problem from the multitenant users [3–5].
- Location Independency and Robustness: Cloud service providers utilize various techniques for avoiding downtime such as optimizing the time of access whiling operating in different regions. The users can store and retrieve the data from the cloud at any time without bothering the place from which it belongs. This characteristic makes the service more efficient. Along with the above-said feature the cloud service

is not pruned to a single point of failure because it utilizes various VMs and processors across different geographical regions for providing the service to different user requests collected from various data centers [5].

- On-Demand Service: The popular cloud service provider such as Amazon AWS and Azure makes the resource available for the end-user at on click. This characteristic of cloud computing enhances the on-demand capacity of the cloud thus making the platform the client's self-service platform. But for this, the admin puts some restrictions on the access for providing some kind of security to cloud assets [6].

- Security: It is the most important feature of cloud computing. As a large number of users are accessing and the assets in the cloud, there is a chance of vulnerability of the information. Hence, the cloud service provider makes the use of cryptography mechanisms for securely storing and operating the data in a public cloud.

7.1.1   Problem Statement and Motivation

Cloud storage has a lot of vulnerability by means which the CIA (Confidentiality, Availability, and Integrity) property is challenging to maintain. Information security of a cloud framework relies intensely upon the cloud service providers, and the applied security mechanism, still there should be a strategy to screen vulnerabilities and to secure the data and assets [7].

Classical cryptography and homomorphic cryptography are the two popular approaches present to maintain information security. In classical cryptography, various methods are available for preserving the CIA of the information. IT is very easy to implement but has several disadvantages which increase the difficulty level for the researcher for implementation. The advantage of classical cryptography includes the less requirement of the dedicated hardware. But the use of secret keys plays a vital role during the communication and string of the data. The size of the key sometimes is very huge which also increases the computational complexity in terms of time. Another disadvantage of this method is every time the user wants to do some modification with the existing data it has to retrieve the data and decrypt the data. After the decryption, only it can apply the modification. Hence, during the modification, an attacker can access the data and can misuse the same which tends to fail in maintaining the CIA property. Due to this biggest disadvantage, the researchers and cloud service provider are paying their attention to homomorphic cryptography. These issues are addressed by the homomorphic encryption (HE) technique. This technique enables the cloud user to operate such as update, sort, etc. on the encrypted data itself. The partial HE (PHE) and full HE (FHE) are two available variants of HE to overcome the issues of the traditional cryptography system.

This research is based on the different traditional cryptography and HE technique along with issues and challenges faced during the implementation. In this paper, the RSA algorithm is implemented as a classical cryptography technique and as a homomorphic technique as well. Moreover, the authors try to reduce the time complexity while performing the encryption and decryption for the RSA algorithm by implementing the homomorphic RSA.

7.1.2   Contribution

- To analyze the available classical security and to analyze the performances when applied in the cloud computing environment considering different parameters and indicating the deficiencies found while implementing those for storing the data in the cloud environment.
- To determine and analyze the present concerns, vulnerabilities, and threats for the cloud computing environment and thereafter to find out the feasible solution to the existing concerns.
- To implement homomorphic RSA and traditional RSA cryptosystem as a solution to the raised problems of cloud computing and also to measure the performance of these protocols.

7.2   Cryptography

In this modern world where technology has immersed society in each part of life, information security becomes an important factor while dealing with the effective storing of the data. Information privacy alludes to have controlled access to the information that is looking for security. There are three significant factors utilized as a security aspect that are vital for making sure about data security which is known as confidentiality, integrity, and availability. Cryptography is the method of hiding data with the end goal that it is available just for the genuine receiver of the data and no other interloper can get to it and cryptosystems are those frameworks that bargain with encryption and decryption of data [7, 8]. In contrast to now, cryptography previously was more connected with encryption which was for the most part for data encryption. Traditional strategies for encryption would secure the information while it is in the transition process to the receiver end, yet not while the data computation is in progress. This strategy incorporates securing the data in the computational cycle which becomes the main disadvantage in taking the traditional methods for securing the data [9]. Homomorphic encryption is one such sort of encryption where the first plaintext or information is not uncovered and subjective calculations can be executed on the ciphertext.

7.2.1 Cryptography Classification

The cryptography mechanism is being classified into two groups, i.e., classical cryptography and homomorphic cryptography. Both of the cryptography mechanism has a different approach to secure the data but does not focus on decreasing the computation complexity of the encryption and decryption process. These strategies fully rely on the key that will be used for encryption and decryption. The computation time depends upon the key size and message size. With the key and message, size increases. Still, these methods are nowadays taken as a solution to the data threat in cloud computing. Figure 7.1 shows the detailed classification of the cryptography mechanism.

7.2.1.1 Classical Cryptography

In the classical cryptography, key is used as a basic parameter. By using this parameter, the sender and receiver interpret the data. In this technique, before sending the data, it has to be converted into an encrypted format employing one or more keys which are known as ciphertext. Then, the

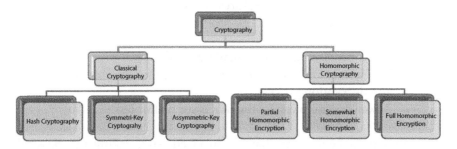

Figure 7.1 Cryptography classification.

sender will decide whether to send the data or to store in the cloud storage. Whenever the receiver receives the ciphertext, it decrypts the message and retrieves the plain text. Otherwise, if the user wants to store the data in cloud storage, then it stores it and for any kind of modification, it retrieves the ciphertext from the storage and decrypts it and then does the modification and again encrypts the modified data into the ciphertext for storing purpose [9].

During the update process, any third-party user can access and modify the data which will deviate from the primary characteristic called integrity. The objective of the cryptography is that it has to maintain the CIA property while storing and communicating the message or plain text. It is further classified into three subgroups such as hash cryptography, symmetric key cryptography, and asymmetric key cryptography.

7.2.1.1.1   Hash Cryptography

In this kind of cryptography, generally, one CHF or cryptographic hash function is being used to generate a message digest which is also known as ciphertext. This message digest is further taken for further communication. Once the message has been converted into digest, then practically, it is not possible to revert the plain text from the digest. Various popular hash techniques such as MD4, MD5, SHA-1, and SHA-2 are available for generating the message digest from the plain text [31].

7.2.1.1.2   Symmetric Key Cryptography

In this cryptography, the plain text is being converted into ciphertext by using a key which will be shared among the sender and receiver for decrypting the ciphertext. For the encryption and decryption process, the same key is being used which will be shared with the intended recipient before sharing the ciphertext. Few popular techniques such as AES, DES, Triple DES, Blowfish, and RC4 are being used as the symmetric key cryptography methods. The main features of this mechanism are as follows [29]:

- Faster process due to the small size of the key.
- Less number of keys have to be generated for the encryption and decryption process.
- Power consumption by the processor will be less.

The main challenges that have been faced while taking the classical cryptography as a solution are described as followed.

- Key exchange: Before starting the communication, the key has to be exchanged between the client and server which will require a secure key agreement policy.
- Trust: AS the same key will be used for encryption and decryption, so both sender and receiver have to believe each other or the communication process is not possible.

7.2.1.1.3 Asymmetric Key Cryptography

Two different keys such as private key and the public key will be used during the communication. The public key will be used for encrypting the data and the secret key is being used for decrypting the data. Before starting the communication process the private key is being exchanged with the receiver only. After encrypting the data the public key is made available in the network so that the attacker can be distracted from accessing the private key which is only responsible for decrypting the message. Various available techniques such as RSA, Paillier, and Elgamal are being used for public-key cryptography. The features of this mechanism are as follows [8]:

- Different keys to be used for encryption and decryption process.
- High power consumption.
- The use of public-key prohibits the attackers from retrieving the plaintext back from the ciphertext.

7.2.1.2 *Homomorphic Encryption*

To overcome the limitation of symmetric key and asymmetric key cryptography, the homomorphic cryptography has been developed. This technique allows the user to operate on the encrypted text after storing the data in the cloud. This HE technique can also be called as the key concept while dealing with the modern-day security mechanism. As per the definition of the HE technique, if the user has the message M, then it just applies the available techniques to obtain the ciphertext C. After generating the C, the user can do the update such as addition multiplication, deletion on the C only. IT can be further classified into three subgroups known as partial HE (PHE), somewhat HE (SWHE), and fully HE (FHE) [31, 32].

7.2.1.2.1 Partial Homomorphic Encryption

This kind of HE technique will allow the user to do only one kind of operation, i.e., either addition or multiplication operation. The existing technique RSA is known as multiplicative PHE whereas the Paillier is known as additive PHE.

7.2.1.2.2   Somewhat Homomorphic Encryption

This homomorphic technique allows one operation unlimited time but there is a limitation in the second operation. If the SWHE allows multiple addition operation, then a limited number of multiplication operations are being supported or vice versa.

7.2.1.2.3   Homomorphic Encryption

FHE differs from PHE and SWHE a way that it supports a large number of multiplication and addition operations. In general, FHE performs multiple numbers of addition and multiplication operation. DGHV and BGV are two well-known FHE techniques available.

7.3   Security in Cloud Computing

Cloud security is also known as cloud computing security includes the methods and techniques to secure the computing assets such as software, hardware, and data from the internal and external security attacks. Due to multi-tenant architecture, multiple clients are acting simultaneously to store or to perform some kind of operation on the stored data. If the assets have not been protected, then the CIA property can be achieved. The security of cloud assets will be dependent on the service provider which takes the cryptography methods as discussed in section 7.2. For organizations making the change to the cloud, vigorous cloud security is basic. The threats are continually advancing and getting more modern, and cloud computing is at risk. Hence, it is basic to work with a cloud supplier that offers top tier security that has been altered for the framework. Cloud computing security depends upon the type of cloud service is being used. Based on the cloud service, there are four different security processes present as follows:

- Security for public cloud controlled by the public cloud service provider.
- Security for the private cloud controlled by a public service provider.
- Security for the private cloud service controlled by the particular admin.
- Security for the hybrid cloud service

7.3.1   The Need for Security in Cloud Computing

With the advent of cloud computing, security plays the primary concern [3]. In cloud computing, simultaneously multiple users are there to access the cloud resources which will indirectly. The cryptography plays a key role in maintaining the basic property such as the CIA of the information shared between different users. CIA stands for confidentiality, integrity, and availability.

- Confidentiality: It refers to the security provided to the information stored by the cloud client on the server side. For confidentiality, the server uses two basic things such as encryption and decryption. The encryption is the process of hiding the original in data into an unreadable format known as ciphertext. Whenever the client wants to do some operation on the stored information, then it has to unhide the information which is called decryption. These two processes will be achieved by the server by using some keys. Based on the keys used, the cryptography process is being divided into two groups: symmetric key and asymmetric key cryptography. In the symmetric method, a single key is being used for both the encryption and decryption process. Whereas in asymmetric key, the public key is being used for the encryption process and the private key is being used for the decryption process. Hence, the service provider will use various available techniques to achieve confidentiality in the public cloud [6].
- Integrity: Integrity is the process of keeping consistency in the stored information. Once the information has been stored at the server side by the client, then it is the whole responsibility of the service provider to provide the correct information at the required time. This can only be achieved by the service provider if and only if the unauthorized attacks have been prevented from the data. This is the most important feature of cloud computing because the information stored by the client has been to remain unchanged during the transit. Some techniques are available to check the originality of the data. The most common process is the use of hashing techniques. By this method, the client will be provided with a hash value initially. After retrieving the data at the required time, the client needs to check the hash value.

If the hash value is being changed, then the data has been altered, otherwise the data is safe and unchanged [6].

- Availability: Availability is the process of getting the right information at the right time. This characteristic allows the cloud clients to store the information and data in the server for accessing at the required time. Once the data has been stored at the server side, the cloud service provider ensures the client in getting the right and unchanged information at the required time. This can be achieved by two different processes known as authorization and authentication. Authentication is the process of validating a user and the authorization is the process of giving proper access to the client. Authentication can be further be classified into two different groups such as one-way authentication and two-way authentication. In one way, the client has to give the credentials based on which the service provider will recognize and the two-way authentication gives a two-way communication between the client and the service provider. After the successful submission of client credentials, the server will send an OTP to confirm the actual client who wants to access the stored resource [6].

7.3.2   Challenges in Cloud Computing Security

Since the data is being stored in the cloud by a third party, there is a chance of threat in handling the cloud assets. The multi-tenant architecture of cloud computing has lots of challenges as discussed below.

- Data Visibility: The client can access the data from anywhere and from any kind of device. So, this is most challenging to monitor the traffic with the presence of a large variety of devices in the computing environment.
- Data Control: When an organization stores its data in the cloud, then it takes the help of a third-party cloud service provider. So, the admin of the organization has less control over the data that is being stored in the cloud server.
- Data Breach: While dealing with the public cloud, there is always a chance of data theft. The native breach is a series of actions taken by the third party for attacking the stored data.

The data breach leads to misconfiguration which prevents the cloud service provider in maintaining the CIA property of information security.

- Data Recovery: If the stored data are lost, then the service provider Ha to maintain a perfect recovery policy to keep the organization safe in operating the normal activities.

7.3.3   Benefits of Cloud Computing Security

Cloud security plays an important role in the organization that stores the complete data set in the cloud. The following features make security as the point of attraction for every client.

- DDoS Attack Protection: Distributed denial-of-service attack is the main issue while dealing with cloud storage. The security solutions try to focus on avoiding a large amount of traffic that tends to the organization's data set. Regular monitoring of the traffic disperses the degree of DDoS attack to the stored data set.
- Secure Data: Due to the multi-tenant architecture simultaneously, various clients can perform computation. The security models implement some protocols to encrypt the data during the transaction and storage.
- Regular Compliance: Top security models regularly update the security mechanism by changing the keys to demolish the chance of hijacking the key. If the key is not vulnerable, then the client data and assets will be safe.
- Flexibility: The technique such as the homomorphic encryption process increases flexibility by allowing the user to work with the encrypted data. For any kind of operation, the client needs to decrypt the data which decreases the chance of data loss during the computation process.
- Availability and Support: The presence of appropriate security mechanisms ensures the availability of the data and assets to the client at anytime and anywhere. During storage and computation, the security mechanism completely monitors the process so that any kind of data breach could not happen to the assets. Upon detecting any kind of threats, the server migrates the data to secure the data.

7.3.4 Literature Survey

In this section a brief literature review on different cryptographic models along with their findings and key parameters has been performed. Table 7.1 shows the detailed study of different existing cryptographic models.

Table 7.1 Comparative literature survey.

Paper	Methodology	Results or findings	Parameters used
[9]	Experimental work	Identity-based cryptography, which kills the confused declaration the board in conventional Public Key Infrastructure (PKI) frameworks.	Key size and certificate exchange between the user and the service provider.
[10]	Experimental Work	A homomorphic cryptography system	Plain text and ciphertext public key
[11]	Model-based work	IBTE model for preventing the security attacks	Authorization concept
[12]	Experimental work and survey of various available models	Secure Cloud Storage Protocol (SCSP) for storing the client information efficiently	Cloud strong and DOS attack
[13]	Model-based work	A framework for data mining in cloud computing preventing the attacks	Public key and private key
[14]	Model-based work	A green cloud network which will reduce the server overhead and the cost of storing the data in the cloud	Time of access and cost of storing the data

(Continued)

Table 7.1 Comparative literature survey. (*Continued*)

Paper	Methodology	Results or findings	Parameters used
[15]	Survey work	A survey of existing homomorphic cryptography in a various area)	Homomorphic encryption of the information
[16]	Experimental work	A ciphertext approach attribute-based encryption to attain the adaptable designation of getting to privileges and shared get to benefits together with versatility and fine-grained get to control	Public key and private key, certificate exchange during the communication
[17]	Model-based work and the survey work for comparing the developed model with the existing model.	An ABE process which will make the encryption process faster.	Plain text and ciphertext as an attribute
[18]	Survey work	Different HE algorithms and its usage in the cloud computing environment	HE of the information with different algorithms
[19]	Review Work	PRISMA checklist and CQA method for reviewing the work carried out and retrieved in the various research article	Homomorphic characteristics
[20]	Experimental work.	Usage of the homomorphic cryptography system for handling the feedback from the client side.	FPGA

(*Continued*)

Table 7.1 Comparative literature survey. (*Continued*)

Paper	Methodology	Results or findings	Parameters used
[21]	Model-based work	A cloud storage auditing scheme preventing the duplication for strong privacy protection	Cloud storage
[22]	Model-based Work	A system for DTT with the different gaps between the privacy and efficiency of data storage in a public cloud	Cloud Storage
[23]	Survey Based work	A detailed structure if the Homomorphic encryption characteristics for implementing in the cloud environment	Fully Homomorphic Encryption and Partial Homomorphic Encryption
[24]	Experimental work.	A lossless model for encrypting the data using homomorphic cryptosystem	Distortion Factor while encrypting the data.
[25]	Survey work	A detailed study of homomorphic characteristics of Paillier algorithm	Full HE and partial HE characteristics
[26]	Model-based work	A secure model for storing image data in the cloud	Cloud storage, images, FHE, PHE
[27]	Model-based work	A secure model for storing videos in an encrypted format in the public cloud	Fully homomorphic Encryption and partial homomorphic encryption video data

7.4   Classical Cryptography for Cloud Computing

In this section, the detailed study of existing classical cryptography mechanisms such as RSA, AES, DES, and Blowfish have been studied.

7.4.1   RSA

RSA is asymmetric key cryptography where the public key is being used for the encryption process and the private key is used for the decryption process. There are three different stages known as Key Generation Phase, Encryption Phase, and Decryption Phase [35].

Key Generation

1. Select two prime numbers P and Q
2. Find $N = P \, X \, Q$
3. Calculate $\phi\,(N) = (P-1)\,x\,(Q-1)$
4. Select e such that $gcd\,(\phi\,(N), e) = 1$
5. Calculate $d = e^{-1} mod\,\phi\,(N)$
6. Choose e as public key and d as the private key

Encryption process
Let M be the plain text that is to be stored and C as the calculated ciphertext. Then, C can be calculated as follows:

1. $C = M^e \, mod \, N$

Decryption process
The plain text M can be retrieved back from the ciphertext C as follows:

1. $M = C^d \, mod \, N$

7.4.2   AES

AES works on a block of 128 bits data with three different key sizes such as 128, 192, and 256 bits [32, 33]. It has four different stages as follows:

- Substitution Byte: Each bit of the plain text is being replaced with the substitution bit from the 8-bit S BOX.
- Shift Row: It is being operated on a row basis. Elements of each row are shuffled by a certain offset. The first row will be remaining unchanged, elements of the second row will be shifted 1 bit left, the element of the third row will be shifted 2 bits left, and similarly, the elements of the fourth row will be shifted 3 bits left.
- Mix Column: In this stage, each column will be mapped with a linear function to reform a new input matrix.
- Add Rounded Key: In this step, the subkey is XORed with the input matrix to obtain the ciphertext.

In the case of the encryption, the above-said processes are executed serially, but in the case of decryption, the above-said process is executed in the reverse order.

7.4.3   DES

It utilizes 16 rounds of Feistel cipher structure with the input plain text size as 64 bits. It divides the whole plain text into two equal blocks each of 32 bits. For the encryption process, it makes the uses of a rounded key generator which takes a 48 bits sub-key out of 56 bits of the available key. With one block the sub-key is being combined and the other one will be kept as same for getting the next block of text. The sub-block size is 32 and the subkey size is 48 bits, so the DES uses a P-BOX which expands the block size from 32 bits to 48 bits. After the operation, the expanded block is again compressed into 32 bits with the help of S-Box. This process is repeated 16 times to obtain the ciphertext.

7.4.4   Blowfish

Blowfish is an alternative for the DES algorithm. In this protocol, variable key size starting from 32 bits to 448 bits is taken for each cycle to obtain the ciphertext. The input block size for the Blowfish technique is 64 bits. This is getting popularity because it is unpatented and freely available for all-purpose.

7.5   Homomorphic Cryptosystem

In this section, two homomorphic encryption techniques such as Paillier and RSA have been studied. Both strategies are partial homomorphic. RSA supports multiplicative homomorphic property, whereas Paillier supports the additive homomorphic property.

7.5.1   Paillier Cryptosystem

It was invented by Paillier in 1999. It is public-key cryptography which supports the additive homomorphic property. It has three phases known as key generation, encryption, and decryption phase [34].

Key Generation 5.2

1. Select two prime integers P and Q
2. Calculate $N = P \times Q$
3. Calculate $\lambda = lcm\ (P - 1, Q - 1)$
4. Find g as $gcd\ (L\ (g^{\lambda}\ mod\ n2)) = 1$

   L can be defined as $\dfrac{(x-1)}{n}$, x is the plain text
5. Calculate $\mu = L\ (g^{\lambda}\ mod\ n^2)\square^{-1}$
6. Public key= (n, g) and private key= (λ, μ)

Encryption

1. M is the plain text
2. Choose r as a random integer such as $0 < r < n$
3. $C = g^M, r^n\ mod\ n^2$

Decryption

1. $M = L\ (C^{\lambda}\ mod\ n^2).\mu\ mod\ n$

7.5.1.1   Additive Homomorphic Property

Let E is encryption function and M1 and M2 are two plain texts available for encryption then

$$E(M1 + M2) = E(M1) + E(M2)$$

C1 and C2 are two ciphertexts for M1 and M2, respectively, with two random variable r1 and r2, then

$$C1, C2 = g^{(M1 + M2)}, (r1, r2)^n\ mod\ n^2$$

7.5.2   RSA Homomorphic Cryptosystem

Key Generation [35]

1. Select two prime numbers P and Q
2. Find $N = P \times Q$
3. Calculate $\phi(N) = (P-1) \times (Q-1)$
4. Select e such that $gcd(\phi(N), e) = 1$
5. Calculate $d = e^{-1} \bmod \phi(N)$
6. Choose e as public key and d as the private key IM

Encryption process
Let M be the plain text that is to be stored and C as the calculated ciphertext. Then, C can be calculated as follows:

1. $C = M^e \bmod N$

Decryption process
The plain text M can be retrieved back from the ciphertext C as follows:

$$M = C^d \bmod N$$

7.5.2.1   *Multiplicative Homomorphic Property*

Let E be the encryption function and M1 and M2 are two plain texts available for encryption, then

$$E(M1, M2) = E(M1).\, E(M2)$$

C1 and C2 are two ciphertexts for M1 and M2, respectively, then

$$C1, C2 = (M1, M2)^e \bmod n$$

7.6   Implementation

In this research article, the authors have tried to implement classical RSA, Paillier homomorphic, and RSA homomorphic mechanism in the java environment. The time taken to compute some update operation on the stored data is being calculated and shown that the run time of the homomorphic encryption technique is much faster than classical cryptography. The memory analyzer is being used to measure the memory used by this above-said algorithm while in operation. The above-said algorithms have been implemented in java with a system having 8-GB RAM, Windows 10 OS, and 1-TB HDD, and the ECLIPSE JVM memory analyzer has been used to track the memory used by the algorithms. Security, IO, and UTIL

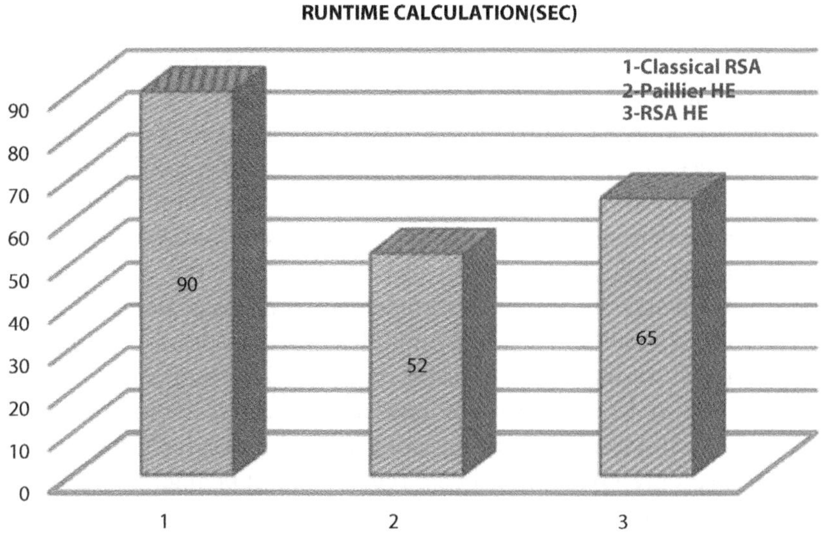

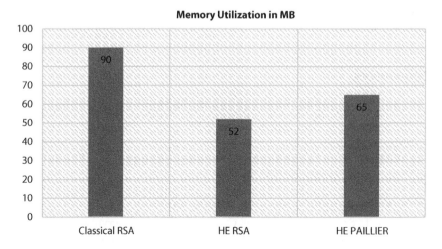

Figure 7.2 Runtime for CRSA, Pallier HE, and RSA HE.

Figure 7.3 Memory analyzer for CRSA, HE RSA, and HE PAILLIER.

packages of java need to be imported to execute algorithms successfully. Figures 7.2 and 7.3 shows the runtime and memory utilization comparison of classical RSA, Pailler homomorphic encryption and homomorphic RSA algorithms respectively.

7.7   Conclusion and Future Scope

This research work has been carried out to investigate the characteristics of classical cryptography and homomorphic cryptosystem. While doing some operation on the stored data in classical cryptography, the time taken to compute is more as compared to the HE cryptosystem. Since in the case of classical cryptography, the ciphertext has to be decrypted first and then only the operation is possible, therefore the time of computation is high. Unlike classical cryptography, the HE cryptosystem allows the user to operate on the ciphertext itself which helps to reduce the computational time. In this work, the author has implemented classical RSA along with HE RSA and HE Paillier for doing multiplication or addition after encryption. The result shows that the time for classical RSA is higher as compared to the other two. In this work, we have also discussed the importance of cryptography in cloud computing along with the disadvantage faced in classical cryptography which is being removed by applying the homomorphic cryptography.

The computation time of RSA and Pallier HE cryptosystem depends upon the key size. If the key size is more, the computation time and cost will also increase severely. The future scope of this work is to reduce the time complexity of the HE cryptosystem while applied to a cloud computing environment.

References

1. Wang, G. and Ng, T.E., The impact of virtualization on network performance of amazon ec2 data center, in: *2010 Proceedings IEEE INFOCOM*, 2010, March, IEEE, pp. 1–9.
2. Wilder, B., *Cloud architecture patterns: using microsoft azure*, O'Reilly Media, Inc., North Sebastopol, CA, 2012.
3. Serrano, N., Gallardo, G., Hernantes, J., Infrastructure as a service and cloud technologies. *IEEE Software*, 32, 2, 30–36, 2015.
4. Zhou, T., Shen, J., Li, X., Wang, C., Shen, J., Quantum cryptography for the future internet and the security analysis, in: *Security and Communication Networks*, 2018.

5. Murali, G. and Prasad, R.S., Comparison of cryptographic algorithms in cloud and local environment using quantum cryptography, in: *2017 International Conference on Energy, Communication, Data Analytics and Soft Computing (ICECDS)*, IEEE, pp. 3749–3752, 2017.

6. Vignesh, R.S., Sudharssun, S., Kumar, K.J., Limitations of quantum & the versatility of classical cryptography: a comparative study, in: *2009 Second International Conference on Environmental and Computer Science*, IEEE, pp. 333–337, 2009.

7. Shabir, M.Y., Iqbal, A., Mahmood, Z., Ghafoor, A., Analysis of classical encryption techniques in cloud computing. *Tsinghua Sci. Technol.*, 21, 1, 102–113, 2016.

8. Kulkarni, G., Gambhir, J., Patil, T., Dongare, A security aspects in cloud computing, in: *2012 IEEE International Conference on Computer Science and Automation Engineering*, IEEE, pp. 547–550, 2012.

9. Ryan, M.D., Cloud computing security: The scientific challenge, and a survey of solutions. *J. Syst. Software*, 86, 9, 2263–2268, 2013.

10. Gagged, G. and Jaisakthi, S.M., Overview on Security Concerns Associated in Cloud Computing, in: *Smart Intelligent Computing and Applications*, pp. 85–94, Springer, Singapore, 2020.

11. Salavi, R.R., Math, M.M., Kulkarni, U.P., A Survey of Various Cryptographic Techniques: From Traditional Cryptography to Fully Homomorphic Encryption, in: *Innovations in Computer Science and Engineering*, pp. 295–305, Springer, Singapore, 2019.

12. Zhang, Y., Yu, J., Hao, R., Wang, C., Ren, K., Enabling efficient user revocation in identity-based cloud storage auditing for shared big data. *IEEE Trans. Dependable Secure Comput.*, 17, 3, 608–619, 2018.

13. Elhabob, R., Zhao, Y., Sella, I., Xiong, H., Efficient certificateless public key cryptography with equality test for internet of vehicles. *IEEE Access*, 7, 68957–68969, 2019.

14. Deng, H., Qin, Z., Wu, Q., Guan, Z., Deng, R.H., Wang, Y., Zhou, Y., Identity-Based Encryption Transformation for Flexible Sharing of Encrypted Data in Public Cloud. *IEEE Trans. Inf. Forensics Secur.*, 15, 3168–3180, 2020.

15. Yang, Y., Huang, Q., Chen, F., Secure cloud storage based on RLWE problem. *IEEE Access*, 7, 27604–27614, 2018.

16. Qiu, S., Wang, B., Li, M., Liu, J., Shi, Y., Toward practical privacy-preserving frequent itemset mining on encrypted cloud data. *IEEE Trans. Cloud Comput.*, 8, 1, 312–323, 2020.

17. Liao, Y., Zhang, G., Chen, H., Cost-Efficient Outsourced Decryption of Attribute-Based Encryption Schemes for Both Users and Cloud Server in Green Cloud Computing. *IEEE Access*, 8, 20862–20869, 2020.

18. Alaya, B., Laouamer, L., Msilini, N., Homomorphic encryption systems statement: Trends and challenges. *Comput. Sci. Rev.*, 36, 100235, 2020.

19. Ahuja, R. and Mohanty, S.K., A scalable attribute-based access control scheme with flexible delegation cum sharing of access privileges for cloud storage. *IEEE Trans. Cloud Comput.*, 2017.

20. De, S.J. and Ruj, S., Efficient decentralized attribute based access control for mobile clouds. *IEEE Trans. Cloud Comput.*, 8, 1, 124–137, 2020.

21. Min Zhao, E. and Geng, Y., Homomorphic Encryption Technology for Cloud Computing. *Proc. Comput. Sci.*, 154, 73–83, 2019.

22. Alloghani, M., Alani, M.M., Al-Jumeily, D., Baker, T., Mustafina, J., Hussain, A., Aljaaf, A.J., A systematic review on the status and progress of homomorphic encryption technologies. *J. Inf. Secur. Appl.*, 48, 102362, 2019.

23. Tran, J., Farokhi, F., Cantoni, M., Shames, I., Implementing homomorphic encryption based secure feedback control for physical systems. arXiv preprint arXiv:1902.06899, 2019.

24. Shen, W., Su, Y., Hao, R., Lightweight Cloud Storage Auditing With Deduplication Supporting Strong Privacy Protection. *IEEE Access*, 8, 44359–44372, 2020.

25. Liu, L., Chen, R., Liu, X., Su, J., Qiao, L., Towards Practical Privacy-Preserving Decision Tree Training and Evaluation in the Cloud. *IEEE Trans. Inf. Forensics Secur.*, 15, 2914–2929, 2020.

26. Brakerski, Z., Fundamentals of fully homomorphic encryption, in: *Providing Sound Foundations for Cryptography: On the Work of Shafi Goldwasser and Silvio Micali*, pp. 543–563, 2919.

27. Zheng, S., Wang, Y., Hu, D., Lossless data hiding based on homomorphic cryptosystem. *IEEE Trans. Dependable Secure Comput.*, 18, 2, 692–705, 2019.

28. Joshi, S., An Efficient Paillier Cryptographic Technique for Secure Data Storage on the Cloud, in: *2020 4th International Conference on Intelligent Computing and Control Systems (ICICCS)*, IEEE, pp. 145–149, 2020.

29. Asuncion, A.E.C., Guadalupe, B.C.T., Yu, W.E.S., Implementation and Analysis of Homomorphic Facial Image Encryption and Manipulation, in: *Proceedings of the 2019 4th International Conference on Multimedia Systems and Signal Processing*, pp. 158–166, 2020.

30. Yan, X., Lu, Y., Liu, L., Wan, S., Ding, W., Liu, H., Exploiting the homomorphic property of visual cryptography, in: *Cryptography: Breakthroughs in Research and Practice*, pp. 416–427, IGI Global, USA, 2020.

31. Babitha, M.P. and Babu, K.R., Secure cloud storage using AES encryption, in: *2016 International Conference on Automatic Control and Dynamic Optimization Techniques (ICACDOT)*, IEEE, pp. 859–864, 2016.

32. Khanezaei, N. and Hanapi, Z.M., A framework based on RSA and AES encryption algorithms for cloud computing services. *2014 IEEE Conference on Systems, Process and Control (ICSPC 2014)*, Kuala Lumpur, pp. 58–62, 2014.

33. Mudepalli, S., Rao, V.S., Kumar, R.K., An efficient data retrieval approach using blowfish encryption on cloud ciphertext retrieval in cloud computing. *2017 International Conference on Intelligent Computing and Control Systems (ICICCS)*, Madurai, pp. 267–271, 2017.

34. Paillier, P., Public-key cryptosystems based on composite degree residuosity classes, in: *International conference on the theory and applications of cryptographic techniques*, Springer, Berlin, Heidelberg, pp. 223–238, 1999.

35. Rivest, R.L., Shamir, A., Adleman, L., A method for obtaining digital signatures and public-key cryptosystems. *Commun. ACM*, 21, 2, 120–126, 1978.

8

Cloud-Based Data Analytics for Monitoring Smart Environments

D. Karthika

Department of Computer Science, School of Computing Sciences, Vels Institute of Science, Technology & Advanced Studies (Formerly Vels University), Chennai, Tamil Nadu, India

Abstract

Wireless communication has made tremendous progress. These developments have sparked new wireless connectivity and networking paradigms. For example, the research community is looking at 5G for automated mobile communications in wireless networks. A recent chapter focuses on the concept of Internet of Things (IoT) as a key element of 5G wireless networks, which aims to connect each unit, such as wireless sensor nodes and home appliances, to the internet. As these technologies grow, they are applied to different real-world problems. Distinct from the maximum relevant application areas is the efficient and smarter monitor of populations. The intelligent city is a vision that extracts information from city systems to take management measures. This vision can be realized by using data and communication skills to track and control these processes. The IoT is used because it would integrate all the city's infrastructure into the internet.

Keywords: Cloud computing, data analytics, IoT, smart cities, wireless technologies

8.1 Introduction

Wireless portfolios can be used as hospitals, highways, trains, and electricity supplies to chart networks like these. To order to pass the readings of the city sensor, local authorities need internet access. The advanced world utilizes knowledge and networking technology for vital data management [1].

Email: d.karthi666@gmail.com

Sachi Nandan Mohanty, Jyotir Moy Chatterjee, Monika Mangla, Suneeta Satpathy and Sirisha Potluri (eds.) Machine Learning Approach for Cloud Data Analytics in IoT, (167–194) © 2021 Scrivener Publishing LLC

Urban grid, intelligent transport, intelligent communication, clever build-ing, intelligent housing, and intelligent services link the whole vision of the urban community. Main structures are interpreted and information col-lected through improved public management and environmental emissions are evaluated, including alternative knowledge analysis techniques. Sensors over this purpose are built to major urban areas as power grids, water and irrigation systems, and reservoirs for petroleum and gas, trains, roads, schools, hospitals, stations, and airports, etc. Insights are one of the big sub-jects of today's infrastructure that contributes itself to the popular trend of social networking and even technological advancement. Apple products also include smartphones, systems, and tablets. Social media, mobile, and laptop developments have as never before changed lifestyles, but insights shift the lives of companies like never. The proliferation of new aspects of the system generated by various types of networks and networks gives businesses useful knowledge and information. The term Business Intelligence (BI), a critical aspect of the results warehouse, was ultimately taken up in its root [2].

All operations—results from integration, pollution, and cleaning, sched-uling and data management, tracking, and research unique types, consul-tancy services, sales and control teams, and system-center users—were still included in BI. A large, diverse, and comprehensive data collection is cre-ated for the use of smart technologies and video/audio channels. To track phenomena of interest with various graphical and heterogeneous measure-ments, sensor devices and networks are used. This also saves, spreads, and analyzes the data for some purposes, including environmental services, the security of air quality, and risk management. For several years, businesses have been accruing data collection, running analyzes of such data in broad data sets, and primarily developing data processing tools [3]. However, the method of disconnecting data production, information management, and technology growth has experienced recent changes, offering companies different market positions. Scalable approaches should integrate the activ-ities of suppliers, producers, service providers, and retailers throughout this scenario. The focus in this section is on data collection and a modern system for the monitoring of urban environmental activities is primarily proposed. The Internet of Things (IoT) is connected to millions of physical sensors and devices to provide heterogeneous, complex, and unstructured data. Many business and scientific projects worldwide focused on IoT data processing to offset costs as well as data maintenance and modeling results.

Powerful database networks infrastructure can effectively handle large programs, and cloud computing can play a crucial role in the IoT para-digm. Cloud storage also provides a broad array of scale-processing and storage features. Therefore, we have built a broad-based data storage cloud architecture that can be implemented and run in different smart environments (e.g., smart cities, home safety, and disaster prevention). Over its associated processes, methodologies, training, and certification, BI as a sector has grown up, is structured, and is now an integral component of this at all large public and private enterprises. Differentiate from documentation and storage BIs and analyses use data mining, analysis, and simulation to provide visibility into the future. It would be inefficient to substitute BI as an umbrella for hypotheses with anything specific to the data. This part grants a detailed step-by-step analysis approach and BI will form the basis. It is thus important that the two meanings be separated and that the two terms are implemented [4].

8.2   Environmental Monitoring for Smart Buildings

Effective protection defines the developments and practices for environmental health identification and monitoring. Advances in technology, engineering, and materials science have opened the way for ever more innovative instruments to be used in environmental monitoring work. Sensor node availability enables fast-to-market speed, which is crucial to the development of new network applications. Embedded sensors remain close to the application-specific hardware from a cost point of view on mobile devices [5]. There are several requirements for the protection of the environment of smart buildings, while there are several limitations and difficulties. The monitoring area and the application scenario both affect requirements and challenges, and the monitoring target, sampling rate, and overall implementation costs are parameters to be considered in the design decisions of the system. At almost the same time, the coexistence of the wireless network and complex changes in the environment are challenges for any proposed solution.

8.2.1   Smart Environments

Each section gives an insight into the main features and facilities in key clever settings like intelligent homes, clever health, and intelligent cities to intelligent factories. The two symmetrical databases are selected for their distinctive scale and complexity, for example, personal-to-business, single user-to-many users, and separate "intelligence" goals. Although there are certainly other types of intelligent environments, we focus as reflective user cases on the four domains. For three main reasons, homes can accommodate intelligent technologies: (i) modern homes already contain many technologies, even though not often linked or interoperable; (ii) controlled

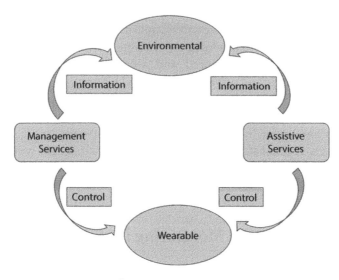

Figure 8.1 Smart environment information system.

environments; and owners that (at least in principle) invest in technology solutions and provide access to them [6].

Intelligent homes are standard in infrastructure. They usually categorize them as funding and administration systems Figure 8.1. Smart home assistive systems are designed to provide users with practical support for themselves which their everyday lives and responsibilities at home. If, for instance, watching the television or listening to music is a concern for individual users, the intelligent home may assist the preparation and setup of the lighting and interactive computers according to consumers' needs through preparing noise examples generated by computer automation, such as turning the laundry machine on. Assistance services can do be tailored to the unique needs of the user, particularly when a user is an elderly person, a disabled person, or a simply ill person, such as environmental support services or e-health services. Tech services cover special smart home capabilities.

For instance, the health and protection of the people or energy management in the house, for example, the regulation of ventilation and energy storage solar panels or the control of electrical and lighting equipment, which minimizes energy usage while satisfying the need for the energy supply. While fundamentally specific, intelligent home services are typically built at the application level of context-aware frameworks, which are focused on common functions and mechanisms. Besides, the building blocks of a house these as windows, doors, the electrical system, the air-conditioning system, the energy production network, sensors, appliances, and so on are at the foundation of home control systems. However, more advanced service companies also require data on the customers, which can be accessed by combining environmentally sustainable and compact cameras these as smartphones, usually paired with their users' devices [7].

Such additional sensors are required to obtain a comprehensive user history that is necessary to transform the intelligent home into an intelligent user-friendly environment. Examples of such details provide the user location (through a localization system), the user's physical environment (through wearable sensors), or the behavior of the user. Nevertheless, such high-level knowledge cannot be accessed by analyzing raw data from sensors directly. This will then be evaluated by appropriate algorithms based usually on signal processing, machine learning, and/or data analysis. The full spectrum of these networks and applications promotes the implementation of a comprehensive and diverse IoT network from a scheme and new technologies (ICT) perspective at least. All these technologies must cover through to the huge spectrum of device/government data collection, storing, and synthesis and to include adequate support for the configuration, overseeing and governance of the information showcase, and the test results on the mechanical movement at the household [8].

8.3   Smart Health

Over the past 20 years, the uses of smart environments and the Web have rapidly expanded due to significant declines in sensor prices and advances in both signal processing techniques and data integration/quality.

8.3.1   Description of Solutions in General

Under the common scheme described in Figure 8.2 are enabling technologies and their use for health care. Several devices, inserted into and/or worn by the person's environment, can collect any data on an ongoing or ongoing basis and analyze it so that the first thing you can provide the patient with details or input is to remind medical staff, the family or other designated persons of the condition [9]. These methods can also be used to monitor medical care in specific contexts, e.g., following surgery or to allow individuals to aware of extensive, healthier, and more self-sufficient lives, e.g., for elderly or disabled people.

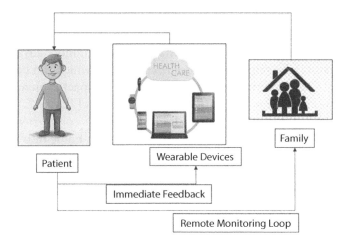

Figure 8.2 Technologies in healthcare.

8.3.2   Detection of Distress

Continuous tracking of people through clinical data or using background/ user activities could describe the physical status of the individual and the ability to increase alerts about pain or many dangerous conditions. Another important reason is that, despite its importance in developing countries, the decline in elderly individuals exists separately. This is, for example, one of Germany's most common sources of emergency and health care in households. Systems need to be developed to analyze, monitor, and consider what kinds of people will be sent for support (medical or ordinary citizen). Drop is one of the main uses of IoT and intelligent communities, including a comprehensive research topic in recent years, for health applications. Many of the most common methods of fall diagnosis is the inertial sensors used by the individual.

With the large variety of devices available and the technology of the last few years, the inertial movement detector has become feasible to detect falling. For instance, the handheld sensors (IMU, GPS, etc.) fuse together to attempt to understand the warning sense of the activity sensor-based algorithm and that false positive. One approach to do then is to attach additional IMU capabilities, such as PIR sensors in the home, to test the person's behaviors with the IMU over the next few minutes after the incident has been detected. In subsequent years, the usage of recording devices in this context has increased. Deep cameras will offer more information and evaluate moving subjects and stationary artifacts more easily. It can be used for situation analysis, behavior detection, and this irregular drop scenario [8–10].

As for 2D cameras, the city of the graphic arts information is given and the pertinence of the different findings and the actual improvement achieved toward what remains to be accomplished is analyzed. Finally, there are other forms of solutions and, for example, a system based on home integrated radar sensors. Drops tend to be very dangerous and demanding (considering both forms of falls). Another form of the condition that may be observed in cardiac and atrial fibrillation, for example. It can be tracked with a smartphone camera or even now with an intelligent clock. The detection involves one of the world's most frequent heart attacks and is now a subject of study using telephones and watches. Cases such as regression can also be detected and evaluated in depression. This device can require intervention to avoid a deterioration of the person's condition as quickly as possible.

8.3.3   Green Protection

As previously highlighted, intelligent homes have been a great challenge and a hot topic for research in recent years [11]. Nevertheless, data from an urban healthcare center could have been used to establish human behavior and to detect changes to the person's health to identify signs of a protection degradation. In this case, the correct segmentation of data throughout uncertain experiments, big multimodality using very distinct data types, the way we can adapt the structures to the person we are tracking, the issue of inferior actions and high-level data from recognized activities, and the efficiency and capacity of different types of identification are many challenges. The recognition of actions is important for health-related applications in smart homes since it provides the basis for the person's well-being, the interaction with the effects, and for use of geriatric scales as ADLs.

The issues are rather complex since the first challenge is that the activities performed are indeed very harder to identify and, secondly, the execution not just to comes down to the individual, but rather the relevance for which it is accomplished. It leads to very complex models for designing and analyzing. Attributes are then duplicated from these detections and identification. The first is to assess the status, for example, of the person being watched in the home for a certain type of problem. The assessment shows the evolution of the person's question to find out whether he or she can no longer live independently. The second type of application is to help individuals carry out these activities with due regard for their disability/illness. It can improve living conditions and relationships at home.

8.3.4   Medical Preventive/Help

All cell sensor with health solutions aims to prevent or help a person who is confronted with a specific condition. Dependence is one of the greatest costs of our healthcare systems and would that the part if it could be modified [12]. A lot of work focuses on taking different types of support into account. Elderly people, for example, provides a system that combines a mobile app that allows the caregiver to provide environmental guidance and a smartphone that supports the person in everyday life. Such technologies require experience so that it can be useful to the customer as rapidly as possible. It typically co-designs for customers. The evaluation or enhancement of the status of individuals with chronic diseases or persistent disorders is indeed one of the major symptoms. In the case of chronic diseases like diabetes, certain electronic devices and applications may be helpful.

The purpose of such systems, which usually rely on measurement equipment and/or mobile devices and many other electrical components, is to help people manage and control the burden of chronic disease or to regulate drug observance. Inside things like the house, tactics can also be applied every day [13]. The objective of this application is to analyze sleep standards so that improvements can be observed and/or quantified and thus abnormalities diagnosed. Sensors and pressure gage are installed into the bed for this purpose. To improve or worsen the living conditions of the person, the long-term development of his needs is necessary. Certain data, for example, can be obtained to long-term track the nature of these data and possibly raise alarms in distress situations, as described previously.

8.4   Digital Network 5G and Broadband Networks

The growing penetration of DERs into distribution networks, such as electric vehicles, photovoltaics, and wind turbines, improves bilateral energy flows and enables customers' habits to be less predictable [14]. Such observability can be achieved through real-time monitoring of the distribution grid, where networking technologies can turn the infrastructure into an intelligent grid. The system uses sophisticated mid-/low-voltage phasor measurement instruments and secure data sharing via the public transmission network.

8.4.1   IoT-Based Smart Grid Technologies

The IoT, the robust and efficient connectivity system, which includes data recovery, collection, transmission, and storage, is one of the newest digital communication technologies. Modern society defines the quality-of-the-art technology to monitor energy sources, automated vehicles, and home appliances and to manage the consumption of electricity, water, and gas. By comparison to other communication technologies, IoT technology has several benefits. One is that by rising energy consumption and costs, system use can be made more efficient [15]. Also, ICT technology is required to guarantee business continuity for service companies. Recent IoT innovations have led by providers, service suppliers, and entrepreneurs, to IoT technology used by smart grids and other creative areas like smart city development, smart buildings, and smart homes.

Throughout this chapter, the IoT web development and system architecture is thoroughly analyzed [16]. A few innovative solutions are proposed, which include wideband execution besides Lorawan, Internet access, Mobile data-A, and blockchain (NB–IoT), low sustainable energy, and ZigBee and Ethernet (BLE). The lengthy-term communication capacities of unlicensed bands are greatly enhanced by both technologies. The most important LPWAN technologies are LoRa, which it supplies with Semtech's reinforced, Sig Fox reinforced, ultra-narrow-belt reinforced (UNB), new enhanced weightless communications, the LTE-M machine type (LTE-M), and NB-IoT 3GPPs. The most deployed LPWAN devices are LoRa and UNB since they use unlicensed frequency bands. The LoRaWAN is a separate LoRa strategy that fits into the topology of stars and cells.

8.5   Emergent Smart Cities Communication Networks

In recent years, energy demand has grown rapidly, with electrical equipment volume and scale increasing steadily. Simultaneously, significant changes are happening in the liveliness subdivision, largely due to traditional to wind transformation, sustainable energy strategies, and more efficient renewable micro-generation [17–19].

Effective electricity network operation depends on the coordination of output and use, which is a major challenge to network control. The arrangement of the grid evolves from a hierarchical and central layout in which large manufacturing units are situated on the land of the grid to a more localized one-stop, local processing system. The result is a more robust and less expensive energy supply than intermittent renewable resources. Energy stocks have increased. A broad management framework for real-time measurement, predictions, and surveillance expertise is required to coordinate efficiency and use effectively. One of the most simple and

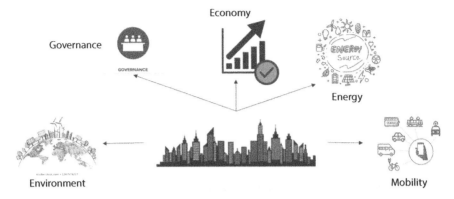

Figure 8.3 Smart cities communication networks.

nuanced development settings is intelligent settlements. It covers growing areas such as climate, economy, mobility, electricity, planning, governance, and other sectors.

In Figure 8.3, numerous relevant concerns, including a range of administrators, such as city managers, supervisors, service providers, and residents, may be competing priorities. Smart societies are not just a technological challenge but also one where the most complex and heterogeneous development barriers arise and technology tend to address specific needs and expectations. In terms of ICT, the development is divided into 10 areas and issues, covering a variety of intelligent cities spanning from e-tourism, e-culture, e-government, intelligent resources to smart networking, and e-health to well-being. In combination with the political issues, the difficulty of technical and open technologies will hinder the development of intelligent cities. Therefore, it is no surprise, especially for the information sharing of technological systems and knowledge is very important as a technology facilitator for smart cities [20].

The most recent developments in this regard are the implementation of new participatory sensing paradigms, in the (cheap) position of data sensing from cities, including the user himself, mobile applications for personal smartphones. Besides also have the enormous benefit of allowing customers to create intelligent cities, in addition to or entirely remove costs associated with the construction and management of capillary sensory devices in the city. Nonetheless, the relative complexity of these techniques has decided to keep them well apart from standardization, and several independent research schemes in smart cities have been attempted.

8.5.1   RFID Technologies

For even a broad frequency range, communication protocols, and device implementations, RFID is the most widely known concept. Consequently, several international organizations, including ISO, ITU, and IEC as well as regional organizations like DIN (Germany), JIS (Japan), and SINIAV (Brazil), have been adopting RFID technologies. The newly applied labels to eliminate unusual use of alphanumeric models such as MI fare or RAIN RFID are further confusing the complexity of RFID. A common approach is to refer to apps that use the same frequency band amen to provide meaning to navigate across the range of RFID technology [21].

8.5.2   Identifier Schemes

As previously pointed out, the RFID would promote a standard way of interpreting identifiers derived from tags to develop transparent IoT systems that typically involve several stakeholders and promote flexible operations. By contrast, specific labeling schemes for a variety of material objects, positions, and even digital things are already widely used in such a manner that RFID in the IoT field is not feasible from a financial or organizational perspective from a clean slate. The main common usage in the recognition of thousands of already addressed objects is authorized distributor protocols (EPC), Sg-1 and EPCglobal, object identification (OID) under the ISO/ITU Standard, Ubiquitous IDs in broad use in Japan, and many other systems commonly employed in QR code and barcode scanner encoding. Although it is not possible to cover each of these schemes in detail, it finds that all schemes remain methodical giving to a comparable decoration. In specific, a program begins with a prefix that defines the following code, i.e., within an EPC context, the prefix of 00110000 is a 96-bit Serialized Global Trade Object (SGTIN-96) integer. The remainder of the code is then typically hierarchically organized to facilitate the distribution of data sharing between regions and organizations.

8.6   Smart City IoT Platforms Analysis System

Almost all types of sensors now have a WLAN connection, which provides the connectivity of the device, with data transmission and reception capacity, into our everyday life. IoT is a concept that makes it possible, at any time and any place, to interact between items. IoT is widely used in various applications, such as home automation, health care, traffic, and development. Through data from sensors scattered around the cities, it is made available with the advent of IoT technology. Big data technology and machine learning algorithms enable citizens and decision-makers to use these urban data for services and solutions [22].

8.7   Smart Management of Car Parking in Smart Cities

It would be fair to say that people who travel through a community to the other side are only responsible for a small part of urban traffic. Many citizens who want to drive to the other end of a town do not move but instead, go around the area to prevent congestion [23]. Then, it is fair to assume that only a few minutes or even a much longer time will be needed for almost everyone else, including taxis. They could spend 30 seconds to 20 minutes on average, depending on the city, looking for space for parking. We can, therefore, infer that parking contributes significantly to congestion in urban cities. As the population of a city grows, the number of vehicles on roads rises and today our society faces the great challenge of a worldwide gridlock.

8.8   Smart City Systems and Services Securing: A Risk-Based Analytical Approach

The critical infrastructures (CI) are the electricity, service, and transportation components necessary for the survival of vital functions of society. Intelligent infrastructure is also an ecosystem that incorporates smart solutions to manage its resources and improve service quality. Land management includes waste management, water management, and energy. The technology standard includes e-government and public utilities, urban mobility, and networking. This is linked to the objective of encouraging economic growth and improving the quality of life of professional city people. Another of the problems faced by smart cities is the volume of data produced by CI subsystems. Such requirements vary by the type, importance, and flexibility of any cybersecurity strategy for smart cities. Providers and end-users, therefore, need to be willing to use any cybersecurity approach. The usability is defined as the efficiency and efficiency of a consumer's activities [24]. A working system meets the requirements of the user. In this sense, the implementation of cyber-fusion centers requires a creative strategy to enable users to make an informed decision-making and to provide throughout-depth information on further developments. Records contained in a standard internal file can create logical hypotheses.

8.9   Virtual Integrated Storage System

The collect servers from a variety of heterogeneous monitoring infrastructures (MIs) and disconnect database device functions that manage separate types of information. This covers instances of both DO-SS and OO-SS in the distributed cloud network that are used to provide a flexible and efficient hybrid database system by unique rules. MI access is collected through the storage of GUI processing [25]. It is an interaction between different databases and communication systems. It is the interfaces. The Knowledge Administrator responsible for virtual data processes all collected data improves remote information selects the correct storage device for the different types of network and eventually adds storage to the storage system. Authentication features are implemented by Identity Administrator and Access Manage modules to control user identity and to provide guidance on accessing data and services. The RESTFUL API allows registered users to access the data.

The core feature of the Info Manager is 1) data extraction and 2) data improvement. System: Cloud Server Administrator is responsible for MI data processing. The results abstraction feature of the program manager is essential to address data fragmentation issues. This presents all tracking and sensed data with a succinct logical description. Distributed workers interact and reflect the exercise setting in which all actions (e.g., data processing) are observed by artifacts (e.g., tracking equipment). The OGC Sensor Web Enabling (SWE) project has taken important first measures for web-based discovery, dissemination, and analysis of sensing data. It points out the interoperability specifications for sensor services through uniform system interfaces. The sophistication of the basic sensor network, its contact information, and several hardware components are the protection of SWE resources from devices built at the top [26].

They expand the SWE definition to define the data currently contained in the paper in the cloud. Although SWE is built into a sensing history to clarify findings, they also have a focus on managing objects, automating querying, and recovery. In particular, the OO-SS norm depends on metadata [27–30]. For monitoring purposes, abstract data following SWE requirements are necessary to connect the organization to its context and to provide a seamless query interface for end-users. To this end, the abundance of data allows context-aware metadata, compatible with

SWE's requirements, to extend the information schema for each object. The OGC-SWE criteria for the incorporation of monitoring systems into the cloud and the dissemination of information to deliver the content were closely watched last year.

This post reflects on data storage problems and presents a new approach to data processing and organization. Two different SWE standards refer to Sensor Observation Device (SOS) and Sensor Alert Service (SAS). Specifically, the SOS norm defines experiences for request, filtering, collection of observations, and data in sensor systems, and the SAS standard describes interfaces for sensor publication and subscription observations. The SOS operator and the SAS assistant, respectively, are part of the data manager can be seen in Figure 8.4.

They are designed to meet expectations, the SWE guideline points out. Also, all the functionalities to identify, view, and capture sensors in a well-defined format are supported by the SOS officer. The definitions are then transmitted as per the O&M (Observation and Measurement) requirements of SWE Sensor [31–33]. The sensor provides models and XML schemes for the definition of sensor systems and processes, and O&M supplies XML schemes and models that reflect the estimation of effects and sensing circumstances. A network to meet the needs of cloud users who need advanced environmental information services is the primary task of the SAS Officer. It supplies information according to the subscription publishing model. A publication for the category of observations (characterized by a specific phenomenon found in a well-defined MI) is available to users using a published publication paper SWE-SAS, an XML document, and one or more comments relating to the same publication.

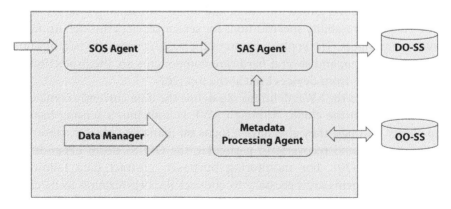

Figure 8.4 Data storage processing.

The constructs cannot be defined in SWE files but can be used to specify the contents of the organization in compliance with SWE specifications only by ordering relevant metadata. This improves the geolocation (e.g., time and place of arrival, user, and expiry time) of the product. The DO-SS is given by the SAS agency for this geolocation information. The object is sent to OO-SS by the information manager portion following the data enrichment process. Therefore, data objects are segregated for the mainte- nance of storage, database, and recovery processes: the description of the metadata is placed in the DO-SS, while the applicant is retained in the OO-SS. The programs are sent to the DO-SS from the end-users' point of view. When data are used for monitoring services, requests are found and planned. The user submits his/her application to the system and the DO-SS collects the information concerned. The recovery process will also provide the key to OO-SS entry when the obtained aid is an entity.

8.10   Convolutional Neural Network (CNN)

With respect to other versions of the neural network, such as multi-layer (MLP), CNN is intended to take many arrays as inputs and then use the local field convolution operator to process information by copying the pupils' image perceptions. It shows excellent productivity in solving computer vision problems, such as picture classification, detection, and interpreta- tion. It is also useful in various ways, including mixed-voice spectral repre- sentations, the physical design of VLSI, multi-media encoding compared to conventional DCT transformation and compressive sensing approaches and the identification of cancer from a variety of pictures changing con- ditions. Moreover, some of the top players recently played a go match in a confusion with AlphaGo, launched by CNN. But CNN's architecture is becoming broader and more complicated to obtain good statistical per- formance and to achieve increasingly challenging targets. At the identical time, more pixels are crammed into one image by high-resolution sensors [35–37]. The preparation and production of CNN is very expensive and limited to implementation due to their slow speed.

Although its conception CNN has studied efficiency and compet- itiveness, it seems to have focused more recently because it has good industrial performance. Any company has introduced profound knowl- edge, which can be routinely used for CNN. The Tensor Processing Unit (TPU) of Google's second generation is built for TensorFlow with a peak performance and an on-chip of 28 MB of 92 TFLOPS. It supports both integer and floating-point calculations that make deep learning more effective. Initiated with a free license for data-intensive automotive goods, NVIDIA introduces an open source Project called NVIDIA Deep Learning Accelerator (NVDLA). They share four key features, including weight sharing, local connection, pooling, and multi-layer use between these different structures. There are several widely used layers, including convolution layers, subsampling layers, and completely entangled layers. In general, after the data there is a coevolutionary layer. The layer of the subsample still parallels the coevolutionary layer. In order to maximize the CNN range, this disparity also occurs.

Technologies of CNN Communication
Whereas RFID systems are used primarily for the recognition of an entity, CNNs are used in the environment for physical interaction. Many smaller sensor actuators are computer-like CNN-tools, like RAMs for top-10kB and 8/15-bit processors, and power limitations, many of them running on a limited source of energy, (e.g., coin cell battery) [34]. The principal cable or digital communications technologies in CNN are discussed in each segment. In most instances, PHY and MAC come from many of these technologies, although some are described as part of a larger protocol stack in Table 8.1.

8.10.1   IEEE 802.15.4

The Wireless Personal Area Network (WPAN) is a hardware device family built for the management and regulation of deployment. The first edition was an important milestone in 2003, when open, focused, and economical connectivity with a focus on accessibility and low energy use was initially established. The platform is more common and the foundation for effective network deployment, including IPv6 and non-IP communication approaches, like ZigBee. Nonetheless, the Times Slotted Channel Humping (TSCH) modes were designed to resolve vulnerabilities in industry contexts in specific contexts. Standard protocol stacks typically, though, for industrial applications like ISA 100.11a and Wireless HART TSCH.

8.10.2   BLE

The Bluetooth mainstream, low-energy version was launched in 2010. BLE will partly reuse Bluetooth and BLE can be activated with a system that uses the standard Bluetooth for low additional costs. Therefore, BLE will collect data from or send commands to the captures and actuators around

Table 8.1 Technologies in CNN.

Model	Layer size	Configuration	Features	Parameter size	Applications
LeNet	7 layers	3C-2S-1F-RBF output layer	-	60,000	Document recognition
AlexNet	8 layers	5C-3S-3F	Local response normalization	60,000,000	Image classification
NIN	-	3mlpconv-global average pooling	mlpconv layer: 1C-3MLP; global average pooling	-	Image classification
VGG	11-19 layers	VGG-16: 13C-5S3F	Increased depth with stacked 3 x 3 kernels	133,000,000 to 144,000,000	Image classification and localization
ResNet	Can be very deep (152 layers)	ResNet-152: 151C2S-1F	Residual module	ResNet-20: 270,000; ResNet-1202: 19,400,000	Image classification; object detection
GoogleNet	22 layers	3C9 Inception-5S1F	Inception	6,797,700	Image classification; object detection

it using its widespread presence on smartphones. The mobile device can also be used as a medium for communication sensors, drives, and the internet. BLE has also become the world's leading supplier of wearables, tablets, and other consumer electronic devices.

8.10.3   ITU-T G.9959 (Z-Wave)

ITU-T G.9959 is a standard that sets the lower layers of Z-Wave. Z-Wave has been designed as a home automation proprietary protocol stack.

8.10.4   NFC

The NFC system is a short-range (e.g., max 0-10 cm) wireless system. It provides inherent safety features as it minimizes unlicensed users' ability for collecting data. The NFC offers various forms of communication for the payment application, e.g., card emulation, reader mode, or peer contact.

8.10.5   LoRaWAN

LoRaWAN is the new group's unauthorized cable gear. Wide Area Low Power (LWGN) networks. LoRaWAN uses the physical layer LoRa infrastructure to improve the connectivity over up to 10 km^2. The topology-based gateway collecting data for 100,000 devices such as sensors provides low infrastructure costs to benefit from fast transfer speeds and bit rates. The gateway offers low infrastructure costs.

8.10.6   Sigfox

Sigfox also offers a broad range of low infrastructure coverage and, at a high cost, is a leading LPWAN wireless technology. The technology is run by a Sigfox company in unlicensed frequency ranges. It is based on a star topology and 10 sq. connection spectrum as other LPWAN technologies. You can get miles.

8.10.7   NB-IoT

Narrowband IoT (NB-IoT) is often recognized as a new technology in the LPWAN network. It is based on a range of licenses and allows several low-bit devices at a single basic platform. In the Release 13 specification, NB-IoT was defined by 3GPP.

8.10.8   PLC

The Protocol for the Power Line (PLC) defines the technology used by power grid networks as a communication tool. PLC is based on wired networking but interferes with this so that it is resistant to media-like errors sharing. Smart home apps are often the PLC models, such as IEEE 1901.2 or ITU-T G.9903 low-bit rates, and associated applications, such as Smart Grid.

8.10.9   MS/TP

Master-Slave/Token Passing (MS/TP) is a cabled device that belongs to the standard family BACnet building automation. Currently, grid power is given to MS/TP phones. While the functions listed in this article are not as restricted as other overviewed technologies, the MS/TP equipment is limited and a small bit rate is provided based on the RS-485 requirements of the physical layer.

8.11   Challenges and Issues

The following hurdles for IoT solutions in intelligent environments are interoperability and standardization, integration and personalization, and identity recognition and virtualization.

8.11.1   Interoperability and Standardization

The IoT definition is primarily motivated by the development of standards spanning all layers, either de facto or de jure, from physical to application levels. Some are introduced although continue to evolve specifically in smart environments [39]. Interoperability between different machines is important, for example, in the background of smart connections for Industry 4.0 networked performance. To deal with this issue, The UA OPC offers a forum for free, scalable, and transparent information between user and system. OPC UA uses standard transport protocols and encodes to ensure communication, for example, as high-end business-service environment among embedded controllers. It offers users, clients, and servers warning and incident notifications to monitor and check their contact credibility from a security perspective. Usually, certain factory management and automation devices and delivery networks are time-sensitive.

Norms are typically not as mature as the smart sector, and in other fields, such as clever home, smart security, or smart cities, are always plentiful. While the prevalence of specifications attests to the maturity of the technology, on the other side, the extensive variety of requirements and numerous significant overlaps suggest that the market is competitive and is growing rapidly and still finding equilibrium. The product's ambiguity concerning requirements is positive in the user's view and reduces the future manufacturer's lock-in, but the reality that requirements are often not easily interoperable leads to standard lock-in. If protocols in a fast-developing industry are quickly obsolete, lock-ins can be troublesome and can hinder future business reforms [40]. Thus, the interoperability of various IoT standards can become crucial in context (e.g., by identifying appropriate gateways).

8.11.2   Customization and Adaptation

A rising tendency in personalization makes increased demands for accessibility and interoperability, both in leisure and in intelligent market environments [41–43]. Current networking and connectivity issues occur for well-functioned sensor and actuator networks to allow IoT to be directly operated by various stakeholders these as cell devices, fogs, club computing, and technology. One essential issue is how the algorithms will change the data processing and support the user of the solution or anyone who gets the best possible interface from the processing. In the previous sections, we have seen that although this issue is solved with significant effort, there are still several obstacles to enable sensors and actuators to function together in the environment. The availability of reliable and validated knowledge and easy installation, learning, and servicing are two characteristics of the significance of the adoption and long-term usage of modern technologies [44].

Two factors such as mobile house environments, connected houses, and creative manufacture are critical when the device is not to be discarded in the cases above. Devices have been stated to be discarded easily for safety or well-being because the awareness given was originally inspiring people, so that information is not enough to encourage use for a long time. For example, if the actions are not detected by an operation tracking program that of the standard that identifies the operation not meeting your use, things would not be included (e.g., wrong IMU/Heartrate adjust requirements for workout applications). That is why such a device "learns" the way the consumer operates in the first few days. Another sign is the difficulty. For example, a variety of experiments in this area attempt to construct mechanisms for monitoring the activity of an older individual in the home to detect behavior changes.

The best part has been that a new scheme is relatively simple to operate, introduce, and serve. Deployment and maintenance are the key problems of hardware and design. However, embedded algorithms help make it easier to use. There are continuing research efforts at the beginning of this issue. The aim is to use software traces and so-called tacit user feedback to continuously change the behavior of the system. Such suggestions are a comment that the operator creates on the system that the behavior he does not like or that the acts of the user match the behavior of the system. Determining how a person resides in an intelligent environment to detect such variances in the data is still very costly and important for the user experience and reliability of such systems.

8.11.3   Entity Identification and Virtualization

To create an integrated and ever increasingly complex connectivity network, IoT technology unites several elements and functions. Organizational identification is a key factor for meeting that task and ensuring that completely integrated systems are designed and completed and that trust remains in scalable and complex operations. This, also, suggests the necessity for formal IoT identification and the support of the Agency Codes resolution and the associated metadata implementation. Remember that IoT organizations may integrate wide-ranging heterogeneous styles of materials, manufacturing objects and equipment, sites, persons, and other live plants, the atmosphere, and building locations. Although there are several explanations that the usage of contact identities has been made, it is not a universal solution, namely, the generally narrow reach of communication, multihomed relationships, the surgical relationships between individuals. However, agency recognition is a core element in the creation of efficient ways of testing confidence ties and regulating access between IoT companies and apps to confidential information. Finally, the recognition in entities is a crucial feature of organization virtualization in IoT, an integral phase in interoperability as it can be monitored and synchronized with physical and electronic assets.

8.11.4   Big Data Issue in Smart Environments

The cloud storage system we incorporate provides heterogeneous control and connectivity to the servers [45]. This allows users to show their needs for metric scale, time interval, information glocalization, and standard data reception design. To explain our main design approaches, we must first highlight the key issues to be addressed in the data management analysis. Investment management includes various communities worldwide in smart environments. Most models would guide site locators to share their knowledge. For example, tenants have information available for network sensing. The cloud storage provider is interested in integrating this information into the system in this case because at the same time the user also has both a set of resources and a database. The type of agreement between the monitoring system manager and cloud storage provider is beyond its influence, but we want to highlight that in such a complex situation, tracking network data is extremely heterogeneous.

8.12   Future Trends and Research Directions in Big Data Platforms for the Internet of Things

Advancing the internet of products and networking things on earth produces compelling demands in a profoundly complicated and complex setting, subject to real research. Data processing and collaboration between artefacts are constantly expanding for high demand in the network and for data to be stored and transferred. Connect protocols are needed not only to allow high-capacity traffic but also to maintain communication between subjects even when wired or wireless connections are interrupted. New strategies should also be designed to store, scan, and retrieve data used in these settings. IoT creates systems like things, people, climate, networking, and governance. The urban system is packed with qualitative knowledge to rapidly maximize the efficiency of resources through its economic, social, and human activities. Based on the technology it will expand vital community networks such as public safety, transit, government, social security, education, and health services [43].

Determining and implementing resource availability and printing, subscription/notification procedures will also improve the management of complex structures. For rational decision-making of joint initiatives, improved test facilities are needed. Using fractured organic methods would also increase data accuracy. Many of us would have difficulty negotiating with them. Modern solutions must be developed to ensure compatible, autonomous, flexible, reliable, and trustworthy goods. They focus on new general structures, hierarchical, and decentralized. Simultaneously, optimal task distribution is sought across high-powered smart devices and IoT networks. New structures and procedures for solving IoT-level privacy and protection problems, like infrastructure. Improved protection strategies could focus on context-conscious control frameworks. Modern energy-saving, energy-efficient, and self-sustainable approaches are needed. In search of new power-efficient systems and technologies, researchers may explore the potential of analytical structures to derive energy from their environment.

Efficient storage, sorting, positioning, and replicating large data inevitably requires the development of specialized hardware and infrastructure to achieve better real-time data access and improved data infrastructure efficiencies [44]. Big data cloud systems are interesting. This approach is preferable to centralized management, which cannot adapt to complex, complete, and dimensional problems. Self-employment also matters at organizational level. Creating and organizing large environments that promote the IoT is easier if autonomous things respond to events arising from context changes. Product shortages and energy consumption derive from unique conditions. New methods are needed to manage energy efficiently and connect to the network routing level at different levels from design level. One challenge is how to implement strategies and assess the quality of solutions. Finally, to maintain confidentiality, privacy, integrity, and availability, issues need to be resolved.

8.13   Case Study

This chapter provides a case study demonstrating how industry 4.0 IoT, cloud, edge computing, and big data technologies could turn a conventional cooler into an interactive device to drive extra value. This experiment provides technical development based on requirements, design, and test (Table 8.2).

A technology-enabled Smart Products and Services (SPS) network. The aim of using IoT in a smart home is to maximize resource usage, provide stability, enable advanced maintenance, and optimize cost-effective system. The case study focused on mass production in Medellin, Refrigerator Antioquia. This project is part of a portfolio of IoT-enabled projects in a proven factory with over 70 years of op-oration. The minimal impact on current production lines is required to convert ordinary household appliances to smart ones. While this paper focuses on refrigerators as a typical home appliance, the same process can make other appliances like washing machines smart. Because of similarities such as network connectivity, restricted features, data volume, data structure, response time, and the most important possibility of incorporating the custom IoT-enabling board into each home appliance, this industrial case study may be extended to all smart home appliances and other home appliances can execute the suggested implementations. Using a single IoT-middle device and mobile app in home applications. Several user acceptance tests were performed for various devices, but the goal is to provide an optimized smart home solution to all appliance systems. In this segment you can find various aspects of an IoT-end-enabled smart appliance network. Finally, IoT's simulation and cloud technology is important. The whole section addresses current challenges, PCB design, network connectivity (Wi-Fi and Bluetooth), edge computing, hardware architecture, software engineering, IoT platforms, real-time security, dashboards, applications, and mobile app development.

Table 8.2 Case study of IoT platforms smart products and systems.

IoT platform	Functionalities	Services	Real life products
AWSIoT	Connecting things, secure interactions, data process, and evev offline interactions of products, services and systems HTTP Web Sockets MQTT	PaaS SaaS IaaS	Messages can be routed to AWSendpoints, e.g. Lambda, Kinesis, S3, Machine Learning, Dynamo, DB, CloudWatch, and Elastic search Service with built-in Kibana integration
Azure IoT	Suite Easy integration with ERP/SAP, CRM/Sales force and Microsoft Dynamics Remote monitoring, predictive maintenance, connectied factory devices HTTPAM QPMQTT	PaaS SaaS IaaS	Tetra Pak (keeping food & drink safely), Rock well AUtomation (Smarter industrial machines), ABUS (Safe guard development), Kennametal (Innovation in metal science)
Google Cloud IoT	Utilized Google's backbone and integrated with Google's web processing, analytics, and machine intelligence MQTTHTTPGCM	PaaS SaaS IaaS	Com Philips, Spotify, Zulity, Scitis, Airbus, GOJEK (logistics & payment), Oden (IoT manufacturing), Motorola, Ocado (Improved customer care and operations with machine learning)
IBM Watson IoT	Machine learning, automated data processing, analyze real-time IoT data, IoT app development supporting Raspberry Pi MQTT	PaaS SaaS IaaS	(improve health outcome for 33.5M members), KONE (Connects 2 million elevators), ISS (Managing 25,000 buildings worldwide), Teradyne (tracking facility utilization)
Open Source IoT	Analytics platform allows aggregating, visualizing and analyzing live data streams in the cloud. HTTPRESt ful MQTTA	PaaS	WSO2 brings fexibility to mobile projects. It provides manufacturers to develop connected products as well as rich integration and smart analytics capabilities.

8.14   Conclusion

This chapter discussed the challenges of using smart city technology and IoT networks via CR and EH technologies. The smart grid depends on heterogeneous and multi-scale communication networks to incorporate new applications and services. To understand it, smart grid operators need to focus on how best to exploit the benefits of these new digital innovations for their daily networking needs and share their experience in determining the imminent. As an advanced risk-based cybersecurity strategy by computer science, this helped reduce cybersecurity risk exposure through a big data fusion center solution. Popular smart city applications with cloud support, connectivity protocols, security mechanisms, storage systems, and prediction capabilities. Although prediction is important in our daily lives, about half of the frameworks have predictive capabilities. This enables smart city dream to be accomplished as the systems can be understood, evaluated, and implemented using communication technologies. It makes smart and efficient community management in terms of public facilities, services, telecommunications, retail, energy, water, etc.

References

1. Abhishek, R. *et al.*, SPArTaCuS: Service priority adaptiveness for emergency traffic in smart cities using software-defined networking. *Proceedings of IEEE International Smart Cities Conference (ISC2)*, Trento, pp. 1–4, 2016.
2. Alparslan, M. *et al.*, Impacts of microgrids with renewables on secondary distribution networks. *Appl. Energy*, 201, 308–318, 2017.
3. Aydeger, A., Akkaya, K., Uluagac, A.S., SDN-based Resilience for Smart Grid Communications. *Proceedings of IEEE Conference on Network Function Virtualization and SDN*, Demo Track, 2015.
4. Aydeger, A., Akkaya, K., Cintuglu, M.H., Uluagac, A.S., Mohammed, O., Software Defined Networking for Resilient Communications in Smart Grid Active Distribution Networks. *Proceedings of IEEE ICC SAC Communications for the Smart Grid*, 2016.
5. Cai, Z., Liu, F., Xiao, N., Liu, Q., Wang, Z., Virtual network embedding for evolving networks. *Proceedings of IEEE GLOBECOM*, pp. 1–5, 2010.
6. Cankaya, H.C., SDN as a Next-Generation Software-Centric Approach to Communications Networks. *OSP*, 33, 2, 1–12, Feb. 2015.
7. Cerroni, W. and Callegati, F., Live migration of virtual network functions in cloud-based edge networks. *Proceedings of the IEEE International Conference on Communications (ICC 2014)*, pp. 2963–2968, 2014.

8. Chiosi, M., Clarke, D., Willis, P., Feger, J., Bugenhagen, M., Khan, W., Fargano, M., Chen, C., Huang, J., Benitez, J., Michel, U., Damker, H., Ogaki, K., Fukui, M., Shimano, K., Delisle, D., Loudier, Q., Kolias, C., Guardini, I., Demaria, E., López, D., Salguero, Ramón, F.J., Ruhl, F., Sen, P., 'Network functions virtualisation', introductory white paper. *Proceedings of SDN and OpenFlow World Congress*, 2012.

9. Chowdhury, N., Rahman, M., Boutaba, R., Virtual network embedding with coordinated node and link mapping. *Proceedings of IEEE INFOCOM*, pp. 783–791, 2009.

10. Dorsch, N., Kurtz, F., Georg, H., Hagerling, C., Wietfeld, C., Software-defined networking for Smart Grid communications: Applications, challenges and advantages. *Proceedings of the 2014 IEEE International Conference on Smart Grid Communications (Smart GridComm)*, Venice, Italy, 3–6 November 2014, pp. 422–427, 2014.

11. Aguilar, S., Vidal, R., Gomez, C., Opportunistic sensor data collection with bluetooth low energy. *Sensors*, 17, 1, 159, 2017.

12. Akl, A., Chikhaoui, B., Mattek, N., Kaye, J., Austin, D., Mihailidis, A., Clustering home activity distributions for automatic detection of mild cognitive impairment in older adults 1. *J. Ambient Intell. Smart Environ.*, 8, 4, 437–451, 2016.

13. Al-Fuqaha, A., Guizani, M., Mohammadi, M., Aledhari, M., Ayyash, M., Internet of Things: A survey on enabling technologies, protocols, and applications. *IEEE Commun. Surv. Tut.*, 17, 4, 2347–2376, 2015.

14. Amato, G., Bacciu, D., Broxvall, M., Chessa, S., Coleman, S., Di Rocco, M., Dragone, M., Gallicchio, C., Gennaro, C., Lozano, H., McGinnity, H., Micheli, A., Ray, A.K., Renteria, A., Saffiotti, A., Swords, D., Vairo, C., Vance, P., Robotic ubiquitous cognitive ecology for smart homes. *J. Intell. Robot. Syst.*, 80, 1, 57–81, 2015.

15. Aziz, A.A., Klein, M.C., Treur, J., An integrative ambient agent model for unipolar depression relapse prevention. *J. Ambient Intell. Smart Environ.*, 2, 1, 5–20, 2010.

16. Bacciu, D., Chessa, S., Gallicchio, C., Micheli, A., On the need of machine learning as a service for the Internet of Things, in: *ACM International Conference Proceedings Series*, ACM, 2017.

17. Baldewijns, G., Claes, V., Debard, G., Mertens, M., Devriendt, E., Milisen, K., Tournoy, J., Croonenborghs, T., Vanrumste, B., Automated in-home gait transfer time analysis using video cameras. *J. Ambient Intell. Smart Environ.*, 8, 3, 273–286, 2016,.

18. Baños-Gonzalez, V., Afaqui, M.S., Lopez-Aguilera, E., Garcia-Villegas, E., IEEE 802.11 ah: A technology to face the IoT challenge. *Sensors*, 16, 11, 1960, 2016.

19. Baronti, P., Pillai, P., Chook, V.W., Chessa, S., Gotta, A., Hu, Y.F., Wireless sensor networks: A survey on the state of the art and the 802.15. 4 and ZigBee standards. *Comput. Commun.*, 30, 7, 1655–1695, 2007.

20. Bellavista, P., Chessa, S., Foschini, L., Gioia, L., Girolami, M., Human-enabled edge computing: Exploiting the crowd as a dynamic extension of mobile edge computing. *IEEE Commun. Mag.*, 56, 1, 145–155, 2018.

21. Bernardino, S., Freitas Santos, J., Cadima Ribeiro, J., The legacy of European capitals of culture to the "smartness" of cities: The case of Guimarães 2012. *J. Conv. Event Tour.*, 19, 138–166, 2018, Taylor & Francis.

22. Bleser, G., Steffen, D., Weber, M., Hendeby, G., Stricker, D., Fradet, L., Marin, F., Ville, N., Carré, F., A personalized exercise trainer for the elderly. *J. Ambient Intell. Smart Environ.*, 5, 6, 547–562, 2013.

23. Bormann, C., Castellani, A.P., Shelby, Z., CoAP: An application protocol for billions of tiny Internet nodes. *IEEE Internet Comput.*, 16, 2, 62–67, 2012.

24. Callaghan, V. and Hagras, H., Preface, Thematic issue: Smart homes. *J. Ambient Intell. Smart Environ.*, 2, 1, 207–209, 2010.

25. Cardone, G., Cirri, A., Corradi, A., Foschini, L., The participact mobile crowd sensing living lab: The testbed for smart cities. *IEEE Commun. Mag.*, 52, 10, 78–85, 2014.

26. Castro-Jul, F., Díaz-Redondo, R.P., Fernández-Vilas, A., collaboratively assessing urban alerts in ad hoc participatory sensing. *Comput. Networks*, 131, 129–143, 2018.

27. Cesta, A., Cortellessa, G., Fracasso, F., Orlandini, A., Turno, M., User needs and preferences on AAL systems that support older adults and their carers. *J. Ambient Intell. Smart Environ.*, 10, 1, 49–70, 2018.

28. Chahuara, P., Fleury, A., Portet, F., Vacher, M., On-line human activity recognition from audio and home automation sensors: Comparison of sequential and non-sequential models in realistic smart homes 1. *J. Ambient Intell. Smart Environ.*, 8, 4, 399–422, 2016.

29. Chin, J., Callaghan, V., Ben Allouch, S., The Internet of Things: Reflections on the past, present and future from a user centered and smart environments perspective. *J. Ambient Intell. Smart Environ.*, 11, 1, 45–69, 2019.

30. Potluri, S., Quality of Service based Task Scheduling Algorithms in Cloud Computing. *Int. J. Electr. Comput. Eng.*, 7, 2, 1088–1095, April 2017.

31. Potluri, S., Efficient Hybrid QoS Driven Task Scheduling Algorithm in Cloud Computing Using a Toolkit: Clouds. *JARDCS*, 12-Special Issue, 8, 1270–1283, 2017.

32. Potluri, S., Optimization model for QoS based task scheduling in cloud computing environment. *IJEECS*, 18, 2, 1081–1088, 2020.

33. Le, D.N., Kumar, R., Nguyen, G.N., Chatterjee, J.M., *Cloud computing and virtualization*, John Wiley & Sons, Hoboken, USA, 2018.

34. Moy Chatterjee, J., Fog computing: beginning of a new era in cloud computing. *Int. Res. J. Eng. Technol. (IRJET)*, 4, 05, 735, 2017.

35. Akhare, R., Mangla, M., Deokar, S., Wadhwa, V., Proposed Framework for Fog Computing to Improve Quality-of-Service in IoT Applications, in: *Fog Data Analytics for IoT Applications*, pp. 123–143, Springer, Singapore, 2020.

36. Chatterjee, J.M., Priyadarshini, I., Le, D.N., Fog Computing and Its security issues, in: *Security Designs for the Cloud, Iot, and Social Networking*, pp. 59–76, 2019.

37. Kumar, A., Payal, M., Dixit, P., Chatterjee, J.M., Framework for Realization of Green Smart Cities Through the Internet of Things (IoT), in: *Trends in Cloud-based IoT*, pp. 85–111, Springer, Cham, 2020.

38. Sujatha, R., Nathiya, S., Chatterjee, J.M., Clinical Data Analysis Using IoT Data Analytics Platforms, in: *Internet of Things Use Cases for the Healthcare Industry*, pp. 271–293, Springer, Cham, 2020.

39. Priya, G., Shri, M.L., GangaDevi, E., Chatterjee, J.M., IoT Use Cases and Applications, in: *Internet of Things Use Cases for the Healthcare Industry*, pp. 205–220, Springer, Cham, 2020.

40. Almusaylim, Z.A. and Zaman, N., A review on smart home present state and challenges: linked to context-awareness internet of things (IoT). *Wirel. Netw.*, 25, 6, 3193–3204, 2019.

41. Almulhim, M. and Zaman, N., Proposing secure and lightweight authentication scheme for IoT based E-health applications, in: *2018 20th International Conference on Advanced Communication Technology (ICACT)*, 2018, February, IEEE, pp. 481–487.

42. Almulhim, M., Islam, N., Zaman, N., A Lightweight and Secure Authentication Scheme for IoT Based E-Health Applications. *Int. J. Comput. Sci. Netw. Secur.*, 19, 1, 107–120, 2019.

43. Alshammari, M.O., Almulhem, A.A., Zaman, N., Internet of Things (IoT): Charity Automation. *Int. J. Adv. Comput. Sci. Appl. (IJACSA)*, 8, 2, 166–170, 2017.

44. Potluri, S., An IoT based solution for health monitoring using a body-worn sensor enabled device. *JARDCS*, 10, 9, 646–651, 2018.

Performance Metrics for Comparison of Heuristics Task Scheduling Algorithms in Cloud Computing Platform

Nidhi Rajak* and Ranjit Rajak

Department of Computer Science and Applications,
Dr. Harisingh Gour Central University Sagar, M.P.

Abstract

Cloud computing is a recent demanding technology and infrastructure paradigm which is using in every field of science and technology. This technology is based on the Internet and apply one principle "pay and usage of computing resources". Scheduling of the tasks is burning area of research in cloud, and it can be defined as the process of mapping of tasks onto the virtual machines and it should give overall minimum scheduling length that is minimize the overall execution time on cloud servers. Here, a very specific graph which is used and is called as Directed Acyclic Graph (DAG) represents of an application in the scheduling problem. A DAG is stated as the collection tasks and communication links with their value. This chapter studies four well-known heuristics of task scheduling algorithms such as HEFT, CPOP, ALAP, and PETS and finds their comparison studies based on performance metrics such as *scheduling length, speedup, efficiency, resource utilization,* and *cost*.

Keywords: DAG, upward rank, downward rank, cloud computing, speedup

9.1 Introduction

Technology is dynamic and it is changing present requirements which are prospective to future demands. Computing capability is growing at a rapid speed in every field and should be solved as fast as compared to earlier time

---

*Corresponding author: nidhi.bathre@gmail.com

Sachi Nandan Mohanty, Jyotir Moy Chatterjee, Monika Mangla, Suneeta Satpathy and Sirisha Potluri (eds.) Machine Learning Approach for Cloud Data Analytics in IoT, (195–226) © 2021 Scrivener Publishing LLC

computing technologies. Simple problems can be solved very easily using conventional systems such as sequential machines but a large or complex problem cannot easily be solved and demands high time consuming. So, to overcome this problem, many computing systems have been developed such as *supercomputing* but it is costly. Now, the era of cloud computing is one of the recent areas of research in the computing science field. The cost of hardware is decreasing on day to day basis and this is enforced by the use of cloud computing. A study [1] found in 2011 that cloud computing is one of the top 10 technologies for future prospective companies and organizations. The evaluation of clouds is shown in Figure 9.1 [2].

There are three aspects for evaluation of cloud as *virtualization, automatic*, and *service-oriented architecture*. The major concern of cloud computing is to better utilize of resources in the era of computing fields with optimal use of technologies. Cloud computing [1] is visible as two things such as *computational paradigm* and *distribution architecture*. There are a number of objectives [3, 4] of cloud computing platforms such as processing of the information with security and fast, providing suitable storage of data, all computation of the service over the Internet.

Scheduling of the tasks onto available resources is one of the present topics of research in cloud computing paradigm. It is formally defined as the mechanism to allocate the tasks onto the virtual machines in such a way so that overall consumption of the processing time would be reduced and improved the performance of the system. Task scheduling is one the example of NP-complete problem [5, 6]. The key components [7] for the

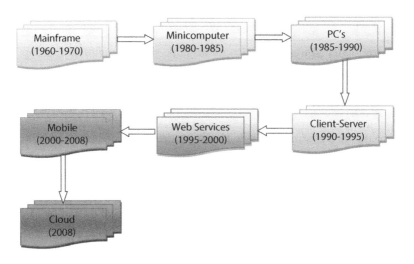

Figure 9.1 Evolution of cloud [2].

tasks scheduling process as follows: cloud servers (processors) performance, selection of the tasks onto cloud servers, and running order of the tasks onto cloud servers. Scheduling of the tasks is divided into two basic parts such as static [8] and dynamic scheduling [9].

This chapter focuses on four well-known heuristics of the task scheduling algorithms such as CPOP, ALAP, HEFT, and PETS algorithms. These algorithms are used as benchmark for comparison with the any new proposed algorithm in cloud computing environment. The detail of the heuristic algorithms is elaborated with the help of example in subsequent section. The comparative analysis of the algorithms uses performance metrics such as *scheduling length, speedup, efficient, scheduling length ratio, resource utilization,* and *cost.*

9.2   Workflow Model

A *workflow model* is used to denoted an application program and it is depicted by Directed Acyclic Graph (DAG) and formally defined by $W_G = (T, E, W)$, where

$T = \{X_1,X_2,X_3,...,X_n\}$ is fixed number of nth tasks.
$E = \{e_{i,j} \in (X_i,X_j)\}$ is edges between any two task X_i and X_j.
$W = \{ (X_i,X_j)| X_i,X_j \in T\}$ *is* data transfer time of the edges two task
     X_i and X_j.

The dependency between tasks should be maintained which is called precedence constraint. Every DAG has an entry and exit task. An entry task X_i of given DAG is defined as $pred(X_i) = \Phi$ which means no any parent tasks of X_i. Similarly, an exit task $succ(X_i) = \Phi$ having no any children tasks. A simple DAG model is shown in Figure 9.2.

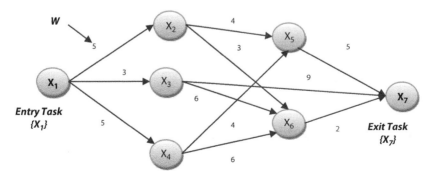

Figure 9.2 Simple DAG model.

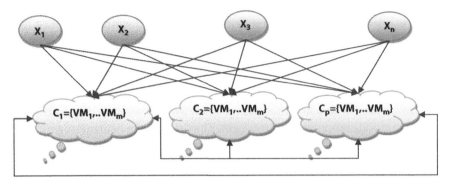

Figure 9.3 Mapping of tasks and virtual machines.

9.3   System Computing Model

It is represented by cloud servers which are communicated in full duplex mode using fast network. Cloud server denoted by $S_G = \{C_s\}$, where $C_s = \{C_1, C_2, \ldots, C_p\}$ is a collection of finite pth cloud servers and each cloud server $C_1 = \{VM_1, \ldots, VM_m\}$, $C_2 = \{VM_1, \ldots, VM_m\}, \ldots, C_p = \{VM_1, \ldots, VM_m\}$ consists of one or more VMs. Here, cloud server's VM are heterogeneous platform and they are worked at a distinct speed. The communication time between two tasks T_i and T_j does not consider if they are communicated in same S_G; otherwise, it would be considered.

Figure 9.3 showed that mapping of tasks onto corresponding cloud servers.

9.4   Major Objective of Scheduling

The major objective of scheduling of the workflow model is to reduce the overall execution time onto the virtual machine. It is mathematically denoted as follows:

$$Sch_{length} = Minimum \{CTT(Exit\ Task\ X_{exit}, Virtual\ Machine\ M)\}$$

where CCT is completion time of the task.

9.5   Task Computational Attributes for Scheduling

These attributes have major role while allocation of the tasks onto VM and details of seven attributes discussed as below [26]:

- Estimated Computation Time(ECT) [10, 26, 27]

$$ECT_{ij} = \begin{bmatrix} ECT_{11} & ECT_{12} & \dots & ECT_{1n} \\ ECT_{21} & ECT_{22} & \dots & ECT_{2n} \\ ECT_{m1} & ECT_{m2} & & ECT_{mn} \end{bmatrix}$$

where ECT_{ij} for the X_i onto VM_j.
- Average ECT (AECT) [11, 26, 27] of a task X_i is defined as

$$AECTi = \frac{\sum_{j=1}^{m} ECTi, j}{m}$$

- Critical Path(CP) [12, 13, 26, 27] is the greatest link from X_{entry} to X_{exit} which is as follows:

$$CP = \underset{path \in DAG}{Max} \{length(path)\}$$

$$length(path) = \sum_{Xi \in T} AECT(Xi) + \sum_{e \in E} T_C(X_i, X_j)$$

- Earliest Start Time EST [14, 26, 27] which is as follows:

$$EST(X_i, VM_j) =$$
$$\begin{cases} 0 & if \ X_i \in Xentry \\ \underset{T_j \in pred(T_i)}{max} \{EFT(X_j, VM_j) + MET(X_i) + T_c(X_i, X_j)\} & otherwise \end{cases}$$

- Minimum Execution Time MET [15, 26, 27] is defined as follows:

$$MET(X_i) = min.\{ECT(X_i, VM_m)\}$$

- Earliest Finished Time EFT [15, 26, 27] is defined as follows:

$$EFT(X_i, VM_j) = ECT_{ij} + EST(X_i, VM_j)$$

- Static Level SL [13, 15, 26, 27]: It can be defined as follows:

$$SL(Xi) = AECT(Xi) + \max_{Xj \in Succ(Xi)} \{SL(Xj)\}$$

9.6   Performance Metrics

Comparison of heuristic algorithms is based on performance metrics which are as follows: *scheduling length, scheduling length ratio, speedup and efficiency, resource utilization, and cost.*

i.   Scheduling Length [15]: It is an important comparison metrics because it gives the overall execution time of the tasks of a given DAG. Formally, scheduling length is defined as the exit task of a given DAG on available virtual machine will take minimum time, i.e.,

$$Scheduling\ Length = Min.\ \{EFT(T_{exit}, VM)\}$$

ii. Scheduling Length Ratio (SLR) [15–17]: It is the ratio of scheduling length and the sum of minimum ECT of critical path (CP_{min}) task in given DAG, i.e.,

$$SLR = \frac{Scheduling\ Length\ of\ Algorithm}{\sum_{T_j \in CP_{min}} Min(ECT_{i,j})}$$

iii. Speedup [17]: It is defined as the ratio of sum of ECT of all the tasks of given DAG on a VM which will take minimum and scheduling length, i.e.,

$$Speedup = \frac{Min.\left[\sum_{j=1}^{m} ECTi, j\right]}{SchedulingLength}$$

Where *m* is number of *VMs*.

iv. Efficiency [17]: It is defined as the ratio of *speedup* and total number of VMs, i.e.,

$$Efficiency = \frac{Speedup}{m} \times 100$$

v. Resource Utilization [18]: It is important metric for cloud computing which has primary objective is to maximize the resource utilization. It is calculated by average resource utilization (ARU).

$$ARU = \frac{\sum_{i=1}^{m} T(VM_i)}{Scheduling \ Length \times m} 100$$

where $T(VM_i)$ is time taken by virtual machine i to finish all tasks of given DAG.

vi. Cost [19]: This metric is defined by following:

$$Cost = \sum E_{ij} \times C(VM_j)$$

where E_{ij} is the running time of X_i on VM_j and $C(VM_j)$ expensive of VM_j per unit time.

9.7 Heuristic Task Scheduling Algorithms

This section will be discussed four well-known heuristic scheduling algorithms such as HEFT [20], CPOP [20], ALAP [12], and PETS [21] in cloud computing environment which is shown in Figure 9.4, and these heuristic algorithms are used as standard algorithms to being comparison with

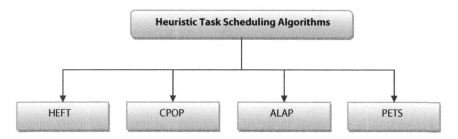

Figure 9.4 Heuristic algorithms.

any new algorithms using various performance metrics. All four heuristic algorithms are based on the priority attribute of the tasks and according to their priority; it will be allocated to the machines. Details of the algorithms are presented in subsequent sections.

9.7.1   Heterogeneous Earliest Finish Time (HEFT) Algorithm

HEFT [20] is a type of list scheduling for heterogeneous platform and it gives good performance with ideal scheduling length. It is worked in two different phase which is as follows:

First Phase: Task Priority
The order of the tasks either ascending or descending is known as the priority for any task. HEFT algorithm uses an *upward rank method* to compute the task's priority of the given DAG. This method is also called a *b-level (bottom level) attribute*. It is denoted by U^{Rank} and it is based on average execution time and average communication time of the tasks. The computation of the priority of the tasks will start from the exit task and move to upward of the DAG. Formally, it is expressed [20] by:

$$U^{Rank}(X_i) = \begin{cases} AET(X_i) + \max_{X_j \in SUC(X_i)} (CT_{i,j} + U^{Rank}(X_j)) & \text{if } X_i \neq X_{exit} \\ AET(X_{exit}) & \text{if } X_i = X_{exit} \end{cases}$$

where:
   X_i is the tasks of the given DAG
   X_{exit} is the last task of the given DAG
   $CT_{i,j}$ is the communication time between the tasks X_i and X_j.
   SUC is a finite set of immediate successor of X_i.
   AET is the average execution time of the task X_i and it can be
      expressed by:

$$AET(X_i) = \frac{\sum_{j=1}^{m} ECT_{i,j}}{m}$$

An Illustrative Example
This section is discussed in detail elaboration of the task priority phase with an example of DAG₁ [14, 26, 27] as shown in Figure 9.5 and ECT

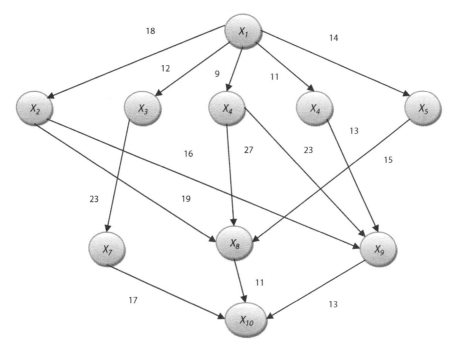

Figure 9.5 DAG1 model with 10 tasks.

[14, 26, 27] value of the tasks also given in Table 9.1. The DAG_1 has 10 tasks$\{X_1, X_2, ..., X_{10}\}$ single entry, single exit tasks, and considered two cloud servers CS_1 and CS_2. The CS_1 consists of two virtual machines VM_1 and VM_2. Similarly, the CS_2 consists of one virtual machine VM_3.

The computation of upward rank (U^{Rank}) of the tasks of the given DAG_1 will be started from the exit task X_{10} and move toward the upward of the DAG_1. The details of the computation [20] are shown in Table 9.2.

Table 9.1 ECT [14, 26, 27] matrix for DAG_1 model.

		X_1	X_2	X_3	X_4	X_5	X_6	X_7	X_8	X_9	X_{10}
CS_1	VM_1	14	13	11	13	12	13	7	5	18	21
CS_1	VM_2	16	19	13	8	13	16	15	11	12	7
CS_2	VM_3	9	18	19	17	10	9	11	14	20	16

Table 9.2 Computation of upward rank of the tasks of DAG_1.

Task(X_i)	AET(X_i)	Computation of $U^{Rank}(X_i)$
X_{10}	$AET(X_{10}) = \dfrac{\sum_{j}^{3} ECT_{i,j}}{3}$ $AET(X_{10}) = \dfrac{21 + 7 + 16}{3}$ $= 14.67$	Task X_{10} is exit task, so that the $U^{Rank}(X_{10})$ will be $AET(X_{10}) = 14.67$, i.e., $U^{Rank}(X_{10}) = AET(X_{10}) = 14.67.$
X_9	$AET(X_9) = \dfrac{18 + 12 + 20}{3}$ $AET(X_9) = 16.67$	$U^{Rank}(X_9) = AET(X_9) + \max\limits_{X_{10} \in SUC(X_9)} (CT_{9,10} + U^{Rank}(X_{10}))$ $U^{Rank}(X_9) = 16.67 + 13 + 14.67 = 44.334$ There is only one successor of X_9 is X_{10}.
X_8	$AET(X_8) = \dfrac{5 + 11 + 14}{3}$ $AET(X_8) = 10$	$U^{Rank}(X_8) = AET(X_8) + \max\limits_{X_{10} \in SUC(X_8)} (CT_{8,10} + U^{Rank}(X_{10}))$ $U^{Rank}(X_8) = 10 + 11 + 14.67 = 35.667$ X_{10} is only one successor of X_8.
X_7	$AET(X_7) = \dfrac{7 + 13 + 11}{3}$ $AET(X_7) = 11$	$U^{Rank}(X_7) = AET(X_7) + \max\limits_{X_{10} \in SUC(X_7)} (CT_{7,10} + U^{Rank}(X_{10}))$ $U^{Rank}(X_7) = 11 + 17 + 14.67 = 42.667$ X_{10} is only one successor of X_7.

(Continued)

Table 9.2 Computation of upward rank of the tasks of DAG$_1$. *(Continued)*

Task(X_i)	AET(X_i)	Computation of U^{Rank}(X_i)
X_6	$AET(X_6) = \dfrac{13+16+9}{3}$ $AET(X_6) = 12.667$	$U^{Rank}(X_6) = AET(X_6) + \max\limits_{X_8 \in SUC(X_6)} (CT_{6,8} + U^{Rank}(X_8))$ $U^{Rank}(X_6) = 12.667 + 15 + 35.667 = 63.333$ X_8 is only one successor of X_6.
X_5	$AET(X_5) = \dfrac{12+13+10}{3}$ $AET(X_5) = 11.667$	$U^{(Rank)}(X_5) = AET(X_5) + \max\limits_{T_9 \in SUC(T5)} (CT_{5,9} + U^{Rank}(X_9))$ $U^{Rank}(X_5) = 11.667 + 13 + 44.334 = 69.00$ X_9 is only one successor of X_5.
X_4	$AET(X_4) = \dfrac{13+8+17}{3}$ $AET(X_4) = 12.667$	X_8 and X_9 are the two successors of X_4. Compute upward rank via X_8 and X_9. Take only maximum between the immediate successors. $U^{Rank}(T_4) = AET(X_4) + \max\limits_{X_8,X_9 \in SUC(X_4)} \{(CT_{4,8} + U^{Rank}(X_8)),(CT_{4,9} + U^{Rank}(X_9))\}$ $U^{Rank}(X_4) = 12.667 + \max\limits_{X_8,X_9 \in SUC(X_4)} \{62.667, 67.334\}$ $U^{Rank}(X_4) = 12.667 + 67.334 = 80.00$
X_3	$AET(X) = \dfrac{11+13+19}{3}$ $AET(X_3) = 14.334$	$U^{Rank}(X_3) = AET(X_3) \max\limits_{X_7 \in SUC(X_3)} (CT_{3,7} + U^{Rank}(X_7))$ $U^{Rank}(X_3) = 14.334 + 23 + 42.667 = 80.00$ X_7 is only one successor of X_3.

(Continued)

Table 9.2 Computation of upward rank of the tasks of DAG_1. (*Continued*)

Task(X_i)	AET(X_i)	Computation of $U^{Rank}(X_i)$
X_2	$AET(X_2)$ $= \dfrac{13+19+18}{3}$ $AET(X_2) = 16.667$	X_8 and X_9 are the two successors of X_2. Compute upward rank via X_8 and X_9. Take only maximum between the immediate successors. $U^{Rank}(X_2) = AET(X_2) + \max\limits_{X_9, X_8 \in SUC(X_2)} \{(CT_{2,8} + U^{Rank}(X_8)), (CT_{2,9} + U^{Rank}(X_9))\}$ $U^{Rank}(X_2) = 16.667 + \max\limits_{X_9, X_8 \in SUC(X_2)} \{54.667, 60.334\}$ $U^{Rank}(X_2) = 16.667 + 60.334 = 77.00$
X_1	$AET(X_1)$ $= \dfrac{14+16+19}{3}$ $AET(X_1) = 13$	$X_2, X_3, X_4, X_5,$ and X_6 are the five successors of X_1. Compute upward rank via $X_2, X_3, X_4, X_5,$ and X_6. Take only maximum between the immediate successors. $U^{Rank}(X_1) = AET(X_1) + \max\limits_{X_2, X_3, X_4, X_5, X_6 \in SUC(X_1)} \{95, 92, 89, 80, 77.33\}$ $U^{Rank}(X_1) = 13 + 95 = 108$

The above table computed the upward rank U^{Ranjk} of the tasks of the given DAG_1 and the U^{Rank} of all 10 tasks is given below:

$U^{Rank}(X_1) = 108$, $U^{Rank}(X_2) = 77$, $U^{Rank}(X_3) = 80$, $U^{Rank}(X_4) = 80$, $U^{Rank}(X_5) = 69$, $U^{Rank}(X_6) = 63.33$, $U^{Rank}(X_7) = 42.667$, $U^{Rank}(X_8) = 35.667$, $U^{Rank}(X_9) = 44.333$, $U^{Rank}(X_{10}) = 14.667$

The task priority of the given DAG computed using U^{Rank} and it would be sorted in decreasing order as per U^{Rank} value. The sorted order of the tasks is X_1, X_3, X_4, X_2, X_5, X_6, X_9, X_7, X_8, and X_{10}. These tasks are used for allocation in the next phase of the algorithm.

Second Phase: VM Selection
This phase is used to select the tasks as per the priority which is computed in the previous section of *task priority phase* and these tasks would be scheduled in the suitable virtual machines which gives the optimal finishing time of the tasks.

VM selection is based on two important attributes such as EST [14] and EFT [15]. Details of the attributes are given below:
Earliest Start Time EST [26, 27] is defined as follows:

$$EST(X_i, VM_j)$$
$$= \begin{cases} 0 & \text{if } X_i \in X_{entry} \\ \max_{X_j \in pred(X_i)} \{EFT(X_j, VM_j) + MET(X_i) + CT_{i,j}\} & \text{otherwise} \end{cases}$$

Minimum Execution Time MET [22, 26, 27] is defined as follows:

$$MET(X_i) = min.\{ECT(X_i, VM_j)\}$$

Earliest Finished Time EFT [26, 27] is defined as follows:

$$EFT(X_i, VM_j) = ECT_{ij} + EST(X_i, VM_j)$$

An Illustrative Example
The sorted order of the tasks is X_1, X_3, X_4, X_2, X_5, X_6, X_9, X_7, X_8, and X_{10}. These tasks would be allocated to available virtual machines as per above given attributes and ECT value of the tasks is given in Table 9.1. The precedence constraints of the tasks should be maintained during the allocation

CS₁	VM₁	0~27 *	27~40 X_2	40~42 *	42~47 X_8			
	VM₂	0~18 *	18~26 X_4	26~42 X_6	42~51 *	51~63 X_9	63~66 *	63~73 X_{10}
CS₂	VM₃	0~9 X_1	9~28 X_3	28~38 X_5	38~49 X_7			

Figure 9.6 Gantt chart for task allocation.

of the tasks. Here, consider two cloud servers CS1 and CS$_2$. CS$_1$ consists of two virtual machines VM$_1$ and VM$_2$. CS$_2$ consists of one virtual machine VM$_3$. For this, the Gantt chart [23] is used to represent the tasks allocation onto VM as shown in Figure 9.6. The HEFT algorithm generates 73 units of scheduling length for the given DAG with 10 tasks.

9.7.2   Critical-Path-on-a-Processor (CPOP) Algorithm

CPOP algorithm [20] is another standard heuristic algorithm which is used for comparison with proposed algorithms. This algorithm is also worked in two phases as mentioned in HEFT algorithm such as *task priority* and *VM selection*. But finding the priority of the tasks of the given DAG$_1$ is based on summation of two ranks value such as upward rank and downward rank. The tasks of CPOP algorithm are either critical path tasks or non-critical path tasks. The critical path tasks would be allocated on same machine which takes minimum execution time and non critical tasks has no such type of condition for allocation of the tasks on same machine. They would be allocated as per EST and EFT attribute of the tasks. It has a priority queue which maintained as per the value of summation rank value.

First Phase: Task Prioritization
This phase is again classified into three major parts such as *prioritization*, *critical path tasks*, and *critical path VM*. Details of these are as follows:

   a. Prioritization
       Task prioritization is based on both upward rank U^{Rank} and downward rank D^{Rank} of the tasks of the given DAG$_1$. It can be expressed by [20]:

$$T^{Priority}(X_i) = U^{Rank}(X_i) + D^{Rank}(X_i)$$

Where

$$U^{Rank}(X_i) = \begin{cases} AET(X_i) + \max_{X \in SUC(X_i)} (CT_{i,j} + U^{Rank}(X_j)) & if\ X_i \neq X_{exit} \\ AET(X_{exit}) & f\ X_i = X_{exit} \end{cases}$$

$$U^{Rank}(X_i) = \begin{cases} \max_{X_j \in PRE(X_i)} \{D^{Rank}(X_j) + AET(X_j) + CT_{i,j}\} & if\ X_i \neq X_{entry} \\ 0 & f\ X_i = X_{entry} \end{cases}$$

where $PRE(X_i)$ as a finite predecessor set of task X_i.
Formal definition of $D^{Rank}(X_i)$ is the greatest distance from X_{entry} to X_i and avoid the average execution time $AET(X_j)$.

  b. Critical Path Tasks

It has a critical path length $|C^P|$ which is the length of the greatest path from X_{entry} to X_{exit} of the given DAG_1. The value of $|C^P|$ is $X^{Priority} (X_{entry})$.

This phase also identify the critical path tasks of the given DAG_1 which is expressed as follows:

It is designated by CP^{SET} and computed [24] as

> *Step 1:* $CP^{SET} = \{X_{entry}\}$
> *Step 2:* $X = X_{entry}$
> *Step 3:* while $X \neq X_{exit}$ then
>   *Find successors of X as X_j*
>   *If $T^{Priority}(X_j) = = |C^P|$ then*
> $CP^{SET} = CP^{SET} U\{X_j\}$
>   *Otherwise*
> $X = X_j$
>   *End While.*
> *Step 4: stop.*

This algorithm helps to compute the all tasks on critical path of the given DAG.

  c. Critical Path VM

It identifies the virtual machine which takes minimum execution time while computing all critical path tasks CP^{SET} on the same VM, i.e.,

$$CP^{VM} = \min_{X_i \in CP^{SET}} \left\{ \sum ECT(X_i) on\ VM \right\}$$

An Illustrative Example
Consider the same example of DAG_1 [14, 26] as shown in
Figure 9.5 and the ECT [14] value of the tasks that is also
given in Table 9.1. The DAG_1 [27] consists of 10 tasks, single
entry, single exit tasks, and considered two cloud servers CS_1
and CS_2. The CS_1 consists of two virtual machines VM_1 and
VM_2. Similarly, the CS_2 consists of one virtual machine VM_3.
The computation of downward rank (D^{Rank}) of the tasks of
the given DAG_1 will be started from the entry task T_{entry} and
move to downward of the given DAG_1. The details of the
computation [24] of downward rank (D^{Rank}) are shown in
Table 9.3 and task priority $T^{Priority}$ computation is shown in
Table 9.4.

The value of $|C^P|$ is 108 and critical path tasks CP^{SET} would
be $\{X_1, X_2, X_9, X_{10}\}$ and minimum execution time taken by
these tasks on VM_2 is 54. So, all CP^{SET} tasks are allocated on
VM_2 during scheduling of the tasks of the given DAG_1.

Second Phase: VM Selection
This phase consists of *ready queue (RQ)* which is initialized by the entry
task of the given DAG_1. The tasks are removed from RQ one by one, and
if removed task T_i belongs to CP^{SET}, then it would schedule onto virtual
machine in CP^{VM} otherwise it would schedule onto a virtual machine
which takes minimum EFT. All successor tasks T_j of Ti would be inserted
into *RQ* as per the value of $T^{Priority}$. Precedence constraint always should be
maintained during the allocation onto a virtual machine otherwise give the
chance to the next low priority task.

An Illustrative Example
The order of the task as per CPOP algorithm is $X_1, X_2, X_3, X_7, X_4, X_5, X_6, X_8$,
and X_{10} of the given DAG_1 in Figure 9.5. The ECT value of the tasks is given
in Table 9.1. Here, consider two cloud servers CS1 and CS_2. CS_1 consists of
two virtual machines VM_1 and VM_2. CS_2 consists of one virtual machine
VM_3. For this, the Gantt chart [23] is used to represent the tasks allocation
onto VMs as shown in Figure 9.7. The CPOP algorithm generates 86 units
of scheduling length for the given DAG_1 with 10 tasks.

Table 9.3 Computation of downward rank of the tasks of DAG$_1$.

Task(X_i)	AET(X_i)	Computation of D^{Rank} (X_i)
X_1	$AET(X_1) = \dfrac{14 + 16 + 19}{3}$ $AET(X_1) = 13$	X_1 is an entry task and it has downward value will be 0, i.e., $D^{Rank}(X_1) = 0$
X_2	$AET(X_2) = \dfrac{13 + 19 + 18}{3}$ $AET(X_2) = 16.667$	X_1 is only predecessor task of X_2. $D^{Rank}(X_2) = \max\limits_{X_{1_i} \in PRE(X_2)} \{D^{Rank}(X_1) + AET(X_1) + CT_{1,2}\}$ $D^{Rank}(X_2) = 0 + 13 + 18 = 31$
X_3	$AET(X_3) = \dfrac{11 + 13 + 19}{3}$ $AET(X_3) = 14.334$	X_1 is only predecessor task of X_3. $D^{Rank}(X_3) = \max\limits_{X_{1_i} \in PRE(X_3)} \{D^{Rank}(X_1) + AET(X_1) + CT_{1,3}\}$ $D^{Rank}(X_3) = 0 + 13 + 12 = 25$
X_4	$AET(X_4) = \dfrac{13 + 8 + 17}{3}$ $AET(X_4) = 12.667$	X_1 is only predecessor task of X_4. $D^{Rank}(X_4) = \max\limits_{X_{1_i} \in PRE(X_4)} \{D^{Rank}(X_1) + AET(X_1) + CT_{1,4}\}$ $D^{Rank}(X_4) = 0 + 13 + 9 = 22$
X_5	$AET(X_5) = \dfrac{12 + 13 + 10}{3}$ $AET(X_5) = 11.667$	X_1 is only predecessor task of X_5. $D^{Rank}(X_5) = \max\limits_{X_{1_i} \in PRE(X_5)} \{D^{Rank}(X_1) + AET(X_1) + CT_{1,5}\}$ $D^{Rank}(X_5) = 0 + 13 + 11 = 24$
X_6	$AET(X_6) = \dfrac{13 + 16 + 9}{3}$ $AET(X_6) = 12.667$	X_1 is only predecessor task of X_6. $D^{Rank}(X_6) = \max\limits_{X_{1_i} \in PRE(X_6)} \{D^{Rank}(X_1) + AET(X_1) + CT_{1,6}\}$ $D^{Rank}(X_6) = 0 + 13 + 14 = 27$

(Continued)

Table 9.3 Computation of downward rank of the tasks of DAG_1. (*Continued*)

Task(X_i)	AET(X_i)	Computation of $D^{Rank}(X_i)$
X_7	$AET(X_7) = \dfrac{7+13+11}{3}$ $AET(X_7) = 11$	X_3 is only predecessor task of X_7. $U^{Rank}(X_7) = \max\limits_{X_1 \in PRE(X_6)} \{D^{Rank}(X_3) + AET(X_3) + CT_{3,7}\}$ $D^{Rank}(X_7) = 62.334$
X_8	$AET(X_8) = \dfrac{5+11+14}{3}$ $AET(X_8) = 10$	X_2, X_4, and X_6 are three predecessor tasks of X_8. $D^{Rank}(X_8) = \max\limits_{X_2,X_4,X_6 \in PRE(X_8)} \{(D^{Rank}(X_2) + AET(X_2) + CT_{2,8}),$ $(D^{Rank}(X_4) + AET(X_4) + CT_{4,8}),(D^{Rank}(X_6) + AET(X_6) + CT_{6,8})\}$ $D^{Rank}(X_8) = 66.667$
X_9	$AET(X_9) = \dfrac{18+12+20}{3}$ $AET(X_9) = 16.67$	X_2,X_4, and X_5 are three predecessor tasks of T_9. $D^{Rank}(X_9) = \max\limits_{X_2,X_4,X_5 \in PRE(X_9)} \{(D^{Rank}(X_2) + AET(X_2) + CT_{2,9}),$ $(D^{Rank}(X_4) + AET(X_4) + CT_{4,9}),(D^{Rank}(X_5) + AET(X_5) + CT_{5,9})\}$ $D^{Rank}(X_9) = 63.667$
X_{10}	$AET(X_{10}) = \dfrac{21+7+16}{3}$ $AET(X_{10}) = 14.67$	X_7,X_8, and X_9 are three predecessor tasks of X_{10}. $D^{Rank}(X_{10}) = \max\limits_{X_7,X_8,X_9 \in PRE(X_{10})} \{(D^{Rank}(X_7) + AET(X_7) + CT_{7,10}),$ $(D^{Rank}(X_8) + AET(X_8) + CT_{8,10}),(D^{Rank}(X_9) + AET(X_9) + CT_{9,10})\}$ $D^{Rank}(X_{10}) = 93.333$

Table 9.4 Computation of task priority $T^{Priority}$ [20] of the tasks of DAG_1.

Task(X_i)	$U^{Rank}(X_i)$	$D^{Rank}(X_i)$	$T^{Priority}(X_i) = U^{Rank}(X_i) + D^{Rank}(X_i)$
X_1	108	0	108
X_2	77	31	108
X_3	80	25	105
X_4	80	22	102
X_5	69	24	93
X_6	63.33	27	90.33
X_7	42.66	62.33	105
X_8	35.66	66.66	102.33
X_9	44.33	63.66	108
X_{10}	14.66	93.33	108

CS_1	VM_1	0~16 *	16~27 X_3	27~34 X_7	34~46 X_5			
	VM_2	0~16 X_1	16~35 X_2	35~65 *		65~77 X_9	77~79 *	**79~86 X_{10}**
CS_2	VM_3	0~25 *		25~42 X_4	42~51 X_6	51~54 *	54~54 X_8	

Figure 9.7 Gantt chart for task allocation.

9.7.3 As Late As Possible (ALAP) Algorithm

ALAP [12] is a scheduling algorithm worked on both heterogeneous and homogeneous platforms. There are two phases of this algorithm such as *task prioritization* and *VM selection.*

Task Prioritization Phase

The task prioritization phase is computed as the difference between *critical path* C^{Path} and *upward rank* U^{Rank} of the tasks X_i of the given DAG_1. It can be expressed as

$$T^{Priority}(X_i) = C^{Path} - U^{Rank}(X_i)$$

C^{Path} is the length of path from entry task to exit task where length is the longest. This attribute is expressed [13] as follows:

$$C^{Path} = \max_{path \in DAG.} \{length(path)\}$$

$$length(path) = \sum_{X_i \in X} AECT(X_i) + \sum_{X_i, X_j \in E} C^{Time}(X_i, X_j)$$

where

$AECT(X_i)$[20] is the Average Estimated Computation Time of task X_i and it can be computed as

$$AECT(X_i) = \frac{\sum_{j=1}^{m} ECT_{i,j}}{m}, \; m \text{ is total number of VMs.}$$

$C^{Time}(X_i, X_j)$ is the Communication time between the tasks X_i and X_j.

E is a finite set of edges of DAG.

X is a finite set of tasks of DAG.

$U^{Rank}(X_i)$ is the longest path from X_i to X_{exit} tasks and it includes the execution time of T_i. Upward Rank is also called *Bottom Level (B-Level)*. $U^{Rank}(X_i)$ is expressed as follows:

$$U^{Rank}(X_i) = \begin{cases} AET(X_i) + \max_{X_j \in SUC(X_i)} (CT_{i,j} + U^{Rank}(X_j)) & \text{if } X_i \neq X_{exit} \\ AET(X_{exit}) & \text{if } X_i = X_{exit} \end{cases}$$

where:

X_i *is the tasks of the given DAG*

X_{exit} *is the last task of the given DAG*

$CT_{i,j}$ *is the Communication Time Between the tasks X_i and X_j.*

SUC *is a finite set of immediate successor of X_i.*

AET *is the Average Execution Time of the task X_i and it can be expressed by:*

$$AET(X_i) = \frac{\sum_{j=1}^{m} ECT_{i,j}}{m}$$

VM Selection Phase
After computing the priority of the tasks of the given DAG_1, it would be sorted for scheduling in cloud server's virtual machines.

This phase decides the selection of a particular virtual machine as per minimum EST and EFT attributes. Details of EST and EFT attributes are as below:

Earliest Start Time EST [26, 27] as follows:

$$EST(X_i, VM_j)$$
$$= \begin{cases} 0 & if \ X_i \neq X_{entry} \\ \max_{X_j \in pred(X_i)} \{EFT(X_j, VM_j) + MET(X_i) + CT_{i,j}\} & otherwise \end{cases}$$

Minimum Execution Time MET [22, 26, 27] as follows:

$$MET(X_i) = min.\{ECT(V, VM_j)\}$$

Earliest Finished Time EFT [26, 27] as follows:

$$EFT(X_i, VM_j) = ECT_{ij} + EST(X_i, VM_j)$$

An Illustrative Example
Consider a DAG_1 [14, 26, 27] as shown in Figure 9.5 and ECT [14, 26, 27] value of the tasks as also given in Table 9.1. This DAG_1 has 10 tasks, single entry, single exit tasks and considered two cloud servers CS_1 and CS_2. CS_1 consists of two virtual machines VM_1 and VM_2. Similarly, CS_2 consists of one virtual machine VM_3.

Critical path of the tasks is shown in Figure 9.8 as the red bold line and the value of C^{Path} is 108. Details computation of the task priority $T^{Priority}$ of the task X_i of the given DAG_1 are shown in Table 9.5.

The sorted the $T^{Priority}$ tasks X_i in ascending order such as X_1, X_3, X_4, X_2, X_5, X_6, X_9, X_7, X_8, and X_{10} of the given DAG in Figure 9.5. ECT value of the tasks is given in Table 9.1, which is used while allocating these onto the virtual machines. Here, consider two cloud servers CS1 and CS_2. CS_1 consists of two virtual machines VM_1 and VM_2. CS_2 consists of one virtual machine VM_3. For this, Gantt chart [23] is used to represent the tasks allocation onto VM as shown in Figure 9.9. The ALAP algorithm generates 73 units of scheduling length for the given DAG with 10 tasks.

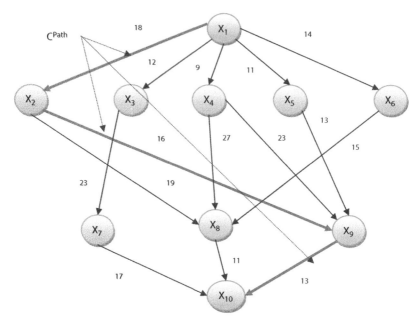

Figure 9.8 DAG model with 10 tasks.

Table 9.5 Computation of the task priority $T^{Priority}$.

Task(X_i)	$U^{Rank}(X_i)$	$T^{Priority}(X_i) = C^{Path} - U^{Rank}(X_i)$
X_1	108	0
X_2	77	31
X_3	80	28
X_4	80	28
X_5	69	39
X_6	63.33	44.667
X_7	42.66	65.333
X_8	35.66	72.333
X_9	44.33	63.667
X_{10}	14.66	93.333

CS_1	VM_1	0~27 *	27~40 X_2	40~42 *	42~47 X_8				
	VM_2	0~18 *	18~26 X_4	26~42 X_6	42~51 *	51~63 X_9	63~66 *	**66~73** **X_{10}**	
CS_2	VM_3	0~9 X_1	9~28 X_3	28~38 X_5	38~49 X_7				

Figure 9.9 Gantt chart for task allocation.

9.7.4   Performance Effective Task Scheduling (PETS) Algorithm

PETS [21] algorithm is worked in three phases such as *sorting of task level, prioritization of task*, and *VM selection*.

First Phase: Sorting of Task Level
This phase is used to find levels with their respective tasks and it is traversed from top to bottom of the given DAG. Each level consists of multiple tasks which are independent and these tasks would be sorted and grouped as appeared in their level. For example, task level sorting of the given DAG as shown in Figure 9.5 is divided into four levels. Level$_1$ consists of entry task X_1, Level$_2$ consists of intermediate tasks X_2, X_3, X_4, X_5, X_6, and so on for the other two levels. Sorting of task level is shown in Table 9.6.

Second Phase: Prioritization of Task
This phase is used to compute the priority and assign to the tasks of the given DAG$_1$. There are three attributes [21] that are designed to compute the priority of the tasks and the attributes are *average execution time (AET), data communication time (DCT)*, and *predecessor task rank (PTR)*. Details of these attributes are given below:

AET of the task T_i is defined as by $AET(X_i) = \dfrac{\sum_{j=1}^{m} ECT_{i,j}}{m}$. For example, the AET of the tasks of the given DAG shown in Figure 9.5 and using

Table 9.6 Sorting of task level.

Level	Task Group
1	$\{X_1\}$
2	$\{X_2, X_3, X_4, X_5, X_6\}$
3	$\{X_7, X_8, X_9\}$
4	$\{X_{10}\}$

the ECT value of the DAG in Table 9.1 Details of AET computation are shown in Table 9.7.

DCT of the task X_i is defined as the summation of communication time of immediate successor tasks X_j of X_i at each level. It can be expressed [21] as

$$DCT(X_i) = \begin{cases} \sum_{j=1}^{s} CT(X_i, X_j), & i < j \quad \text{if } X_i \neq X_{exit} \\ 0 & \text{if } X_i = X_{exit} \end{cases}$$

where s is the total number of tasks in next level.

An example of DCT of the tasks of DAG_1 is given in Figure 9.5. X_1 has five successor tasks X_2, X_3, X_4, X_5, and X_6 and the summation of the communication time CT between X_1 and all its successor tasks is 64. Similarly, DCT computation for rest tasks at each level is shown in Table 9.8.

PTR of the tasks X_i is the greatest rank of immediate predecessors X_j of X_i, and it can be computed[21] as follows:

$$PTR(X_i) = \begin{cases} \max_{T_j \in PRE(T_i)} \{RANK(X_j)\} & \text{if } X_i \neq X_{entry} \\ 0 & \text{if } X_i = X_{entry} \end{cases}$$

where PRE is immediate predecessor tasks X_j of X_i.

RANK of task X_i is computed based on AET, DCT, and PRT of the task. It is computed as follows:

$$RANK(X_i) = Round\{AET(X_i) + DCT(X_i) + PTR(X_i)\}$$

Table 9.7 AET computation.

Task(X_i)		X_1	X_2	X_3	X_4	X_5	X_6	X_7	X_8	X_9	X_{10}
$AET(X_i) = \dfrac{\sum_{j=1}^{3} ECT_{i,j}}{3}$		13	16.67	14.34	12.67	11.67	12.67	11	10	16.67	14.67

Table 9.8 DCT computation.

Task(X_i)	X_1	X_2	X_3	X_4	X_5	T_6	X_7	X_8	X_9	X_{10}
DCT(X_i)	64	35	23	50	13	15	17	11	13	0

Table 9.9 Computation of PTR, RANK, and Priority.

Level	Task(X_i)	DCT(X_i)	AET(X_i)	PTR(X_i)	RANK(X_i)	Priority
1	X_1	64	13	0	77	1
2	X_2	35	16.67	77	129	2
	X_3	23	14.34	77	115	3
	X_4	50	12.67	77	140	1
	X_5	13	11.67	77	102	5
	X_6	15	12.67	77	105	4
3	X_7	17	11	115	143	3
	X_8	11	10	140	161	2
	X_9	13	16.67	140	170	1
4	X_{10}	0	14.67	170	185	1

The priority of the tasks at each level is decided by its rank value. If a task has the greatest rank in their level, then its priority will also be the highest among the tasks. Details of *PRT, RANK,* and *Priority* of the tasks are shown in Table 9.9 of the given DAG_1 in Figure 9.5.

Third Phase: VM Selection
After the computed the priority of the tasks of the given DAG_1, it would be sorted for scheduling in cloud server's virtual machines.

This phase decides the selection of a particular virtual machine as per minimum EST and EFT attributes. Details of EST and EFT attributes as below:
Earliest Start Time EST [26, 27] is defined as follows:

$$EST(X_i, VM_j)$$

$$= \begin{cases} 0 & if \ X_i \in X_{entry} \\ \max_{X_j \in pred(X_i)} \{EFT(X_j, VM_j) + MET(X_i) + CT_{i,j}\} & otherwise \end{cases}$$

Minimum Execution Time MET [22, 26, 27] is defined as follows:

$$MET(X_i) = min.\{ECT(X_i, VM_j)\}$$

CS₁	VM₁	0~21 *	21~32 X₃	32~44 X₅	44~51 *	51~56 X₈	56~63 X₇
	VM₂	0~18 *	18~26 X₄	26~44 *	44~56 X₉	56~63 *	**63~70** **X₁₀**
CS₂	VM₃	0~9 X₁	9~27 X₂	27~36 X₆			

Figure 9.10 Gantt chart for task allocation.

Earliest Finished Time EFT [26, 27] is defined as follows:

$$EFT(X_i, VM_j) = ECT_{ij} + EST(X_i, VM_j)\}$$

Illustrative Example

The order of the tasks as per the *priority* are X_1, X_4, X_2, X_3, X_6, X_5, X_9, X_8, X_7, and X_{10} of the DAG$_1$ in Figure 9.5. The ECT value of the tasks is given in Table 9.1 which is used while allocating these onto the virtual machines. Here, consider two cloud servers CS1 and CS₂. CS₁ consists of two virtual machines VM₁ and VM₂. CS₂ consists of one virtual machine VM₃. For this, Gantt chart [23] is used to represent the tasks allocation onto VM as shown in Figure 9.10. The PETS algorithm generates 70 units of scheduling length for the give DAG with 10 tasks.

9.8   Performance Analysis and Results

The analysis of four heuristics algorithms such as HEFT, CPOP, ALAP, and PETS has done using two directed graphs DAG^1 and DAG^2 as shown in Figures 9.5 and 9.11. This paper discussed six performance metrics in the previous section and they are used as comparison purposed among the four heuristics algorithms. Scheduling length of all heuristic algorithms is found for DAG^1 at the starting of the chapter according the algorithms. Other performance metrics such as efficiency, speedup, SLR, and resource utilization are based on scheduling length. The cost table for DAG^1 is shown in Table 9.10 [25].

Similarly, the computation of scheduling length of all four heuristic algorithms is computed for DAG^2, and value of rest metrics is also shown in table. The ECT table is shown in Tables 9.1 and 9.11 for both DAG^1 and DAG^2 and cost table of DAG^2 is shown in Table 9.12.

The value of all six performance metrics is shown in Table 9.13 [25]. The graphical representation of all performance metrics for four heuristic algorithms is shown in Figures 9.12 to 9.17.

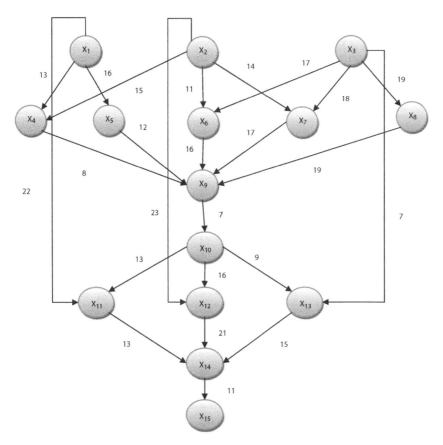

Figure 9.11 DAG$_2$ model with 15 tasks.

Table 9.10 VM rate for DAG[1].

Virtual Machine (VM)	VM$_1$	VM$_2$	VM$_3$
Cost/Unit Time	1.71	1.63	1.21

Table 9.11 ECT [15, 27] matrix for DAG$_2$ model.

	X$_1$	X$_2$	X$_3$	X$_4$	X$_5$	X$_6$	X$_7$	X$_8$	X$_9$	X$_{10}$	X$_{11}$	X$_{12}$	X$_{13}$	X$_{14}$	X$_{15}$
CS$_1$ VM$_1$	17	14	19	13	19	13	15	19	13	19	13	15	18	20	11
CS$_1$ VM$_2$	14	17	17	20	20	18	15	20	17	15	22	21	17	18	18
CS$_2$ VM$_3$	13	14	16	13	21	13	13	13	13	16	14	22	16	13	21
CS$_2$ VM$_4$	22	16	12	14	15	18	14	18	19	13	12	14	14	16	17

Table 9.12 VM cost for DAG².

Virtual Machine(VM)	VM₁	VM₂	VM₃	VM₄
Cost/Unit Time	1.72	1.52	1.69	1.65

Table 9.13 Comparison results.

DAG Models	Scheduling Algorithms	Performance Metrics Results					
		Scheduling Length	Speedup	Efficiency (%)	SLR	Resource Utilization (%)	Cost/Unit Time
DAG¹	HEFT	73	1.74	58.00	1.78	77.12	258.65
	CPOP	86	1.48	49.22	2.09	77.51	301.12
	ALAP	73	1.74	58.00	1.78	77.16	258.65
	PETS	70	1.81	60.33	1.71	80.47	265.39
DAG²	HEFT	152	1.52	38.00	1.71	69.73	702.75
	CPOP	164	1.41	35.25	1.84	64.93	694.92
	ALAP	155	1.49	37.25	1.74	72.74	751.53
	PETS	152	1.52	38.00	1.71	65.13	666.43

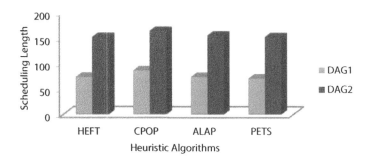

Figure 9.12 Scheduling length.

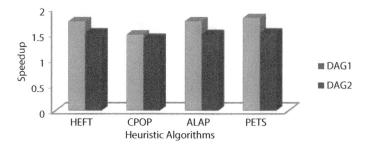

Figure 9.13 Speedup.

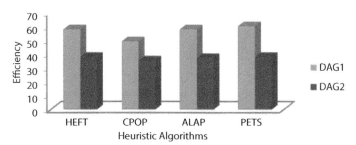

Figure 9.14 Efficiency.

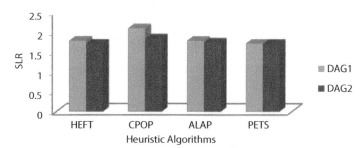

Figure 9.15 SLR.

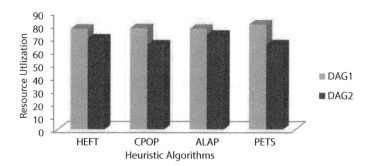

Figure 9.16 Resource utilization.

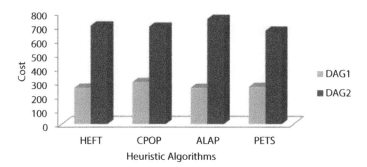

Figure 9.17 Cost.

9.9   Conclusion

This chapter has discussed four heuristic algorithms such as HEFT, CPOP, ALAP, and PETS. These algorithms are used as standard algorithms for comparison purpose with any new proposed algorithms. All four heuristic algorithms are studied in detail and illustrated with help of DAG_1 and DAG_2 with 10 and 15 tasks, respectively. These algorithms are used various attribute to find the priority of the tasks of the given DAG. The comparative studied of the heuristic algorithms has done based on six performance metrics for both DAG with 10 and 15 tasks, respectively.

References

1. Hashizume, K., Rosado, D.G., Fernández-Medina, E., Fernandez, E.B., An analysis of Security Issues for Cloud Computing. *J. Internet Serv. Appl.*, 4, 1, 5, 1–13, 2013.
2. Pachghare, V.K., *Cloud Computing*, PHI, Delhi India, 2016.
3. Zhao, G., Liu, J., Tang, Y., Sun, W., Zhang, F., Ye, X., Tang, N., Cloud Computing: A Statistics Aspect of Users. *First International Conference on Cloud Computing (CloudCom)*, Beijing, China, Springer Berlin, Heidelberg, pp. 347–358, 2009.
4. Zhang, S., Zhang, S., Chen, X., Huo, X., Cloud Computing Research and Development Trend. *Second International Conference on Future Networks (ICFN'10)*, Sanya, Hainan, China, IEEE Computer Society, Washington, DC, USA, pp. 93–97, 2010.
5. Gary, M.R. and Johnson, D.S., *Computer and Intractability: A Guide to the theory of NP Completeness*, W.H freeman, San Francisco CA, 1989.

6. Yadav, A.K. and Mandoria, H.L., Study of Task Scheduling Algorithms in the Cloud Computing Environment: A Review. *Int. J. Comput. Sci. Inf. Technol.*, 8, 4, 462–468, 2017.

7. Kaur, R. and Kaur, R., Multiprocessor Scheduling using Task Duplication Based Scheduling Algorithms: A Review Paper. *Int. J. Appl. Innov. Eng. Manage.*, 2, 4, 311–317, April, 2013.

8. Chung, Y.-C. and Ranka, S., Applications and Performance Analysis of a Compile-Time Optimization Approach for List Scheduling Algorithms on Distributed Memory Multiprocessors. *Supercomputing '92:Proceedings of the 1992 ACM/IEEE Conference on Supercomputing*, Minneapolis, MN, USA, pp. 512–521, 1992.

9. Srinivas, G.N. and Musicus, B.R., Generalized Multiprocessor Scheduling for Directed Acyclic Graphs, in: *Third Annual ACM Symposium on Parallel Algorithms and Architectures*, pp. 237–246, 1994.

10. Zanywayingoma, F.N. and Yang, Y., Effective Task Scheduling and Dynamic Resource Optimization based on Heuristic Algorithms in Cloud Computing Environment. *KSII Trans. Internet Inf. Syst.*, 11, 12, 5780–5802, 2017.

11. Haidri, R.A., Katti, C.P., Saxena, P.C., Cost Effective Deadline Aware Scheduling Strategy For Workflow Applications on Virtual Machines in Cloud Computing. *J. King Saud Univ.- Comp. Info. Sci.*, 32, 6, July 2020.

12. Kwok, Y.-K. and Ahmad, I., Static Scheduling Algorithms for Allocating Directed Task Graphs to Multiprocessors. *ACM Comput. Surv.*, 31, 4, 1–88, December, 1999.

13. Sinnen, O., *Task Scheduling for Parallel Systems*, Wiley Interscience Pulication, Hoboken, New Jersey, 2007.

14. Kumar, M.S., Gupta, I., Jana, P.K., Delay-based workflow scheduling for cost optimization in heterogeneous cloud system. *Tenth International Conference on Contemporary Computing (IC3)*, Noida, pp. 1–6, 2017.

15. Gupta, I., Kumar, M.S., Jana, P.K., Efficient Workflow Scheduling Algorithm for Cloud Computing System: A Dynamic Priority-Based Approach. *Arab. J. Sci. Eng.*, 43, 12, 7945–7960, 2018.

16. Hwang, K., *Advanced Computer Architecture: Parallelism, Scalability, Programmability*, TMH Publishing Company, New Delhi, 2005.

17. Akbar, M.F., Munir, E.U., Rafique, M.M., Malik, Z., Khan, S.U., Yang, L.T., List-Based Task Scheduling for Cloud Computing. *IEEE International Conference on Internet of Things (iThings) and IEEE Green Computing and Communications (GreenCom) and IEEE Cyber, Physical and Social Computing (CPSCom) and IEEE Smart Data (SmartData)*, Chengdu, pp. 652–659, 2016.

18. Kalra, M. and Singh, S., A Review of Metaheuristic Scheduling Techniques in Cloud Computing. *Egypt. Inform. J.*, 16, 3, 275–295, 2015.

19. Benalla, H., Ben Alla, S., Touhafi, A., Ezzati, A., A Novel Task Scheduling Approach Based On Dynamic Queues And Hybrid Meta-Heuristic Algorithms for Cloud Computing Environment. *Cluster Comput.*, 21, 4, 1797–1820, 2018.

20. Topcuoglu, H., Hariri, S., Wu, M.-Y., Performance-effective and low-complexity task scheduling for heterogeneous computing. *IEEE Trans. Parallel Distrib. Syst.*, 13, 3, 260–274, March, 2002.

21. Ilavarasan, E. and Thambidurai, P., Low Complexity Performance Effective Task Scheduling Algorithm For Heterogeneous Computing Environments. *J. Comput. Sci.*, 3, 2, 94–103, 2007.

22. Xavier, S. and Jeno Lovesum, S.P., A Survey of Various Workflow Scheduling Algorithms in Cloud Environment. *Int. J. Sci. Res. Publ.*, 3, 2, 1–3, February, 2013.

23. http://www.gantt.com/

24. Prajapati, K.D., Raval, P., Karamta, M., Potdar, M.B., Comparison of Virtual Machine Scheduling Algorithms in Cloud Computing. *Int. J. Comput. Appl.*, 83, 15, 12–14, December, 2013.

25. Rajak, N. and Shukla, D., Performance Analysis of Workflow Scheduling Algorithm in Cloud Computing Environment using Priority Attribute. *Int. J. Adv. Sci. Technol.*, 28, 16, 1810–1831, 2019.

26. Rajak, N. and Shukla, D., An Efficient Task Scheduling Strategy for DAG in Cloud Computing Environment, in: *Ambient Communications and Computer Systems. Advances in Intelligent Systems and Computing*, vol. 1097, Y.C. Hu, S. Tiwari, M. Trivedi, K. Mishra (Eds.), Springer, Singapore, 2020.

27. Rajak, N. and Shukla, D., A Novel Approach of Task Scheduling in Cloud Computing Environment, in: *Social Networking and Computational Intelligence. Lecture Notes in Networks and Systems*, vol. 100, R. Shukla, J. Agrawal, S. Sharma, N. Chaudhari, K. Shukla (Eds.), Springer, Singapore, 2020.

10

Smart Environment Monitoring Models Using Cloud-Based Data Analytics: A Comprehensive Study

Pradnya S. Borkar and Reena Thakur*

Department of Computer Science and Engineering,
Jhulelal Institute of Technology, Nagpur, India

Abstract

The idea of the Internet of Things (IoT) has emerged in recent years and is growing rapidly. The main aim is to connect real-world things over the cloud to the Internet. The various real-time applications such as farming, weather forecasting uses rain, temperature, moisture, and loam sensors which are connected to an Internet. Thus, various kinds of information such as temperature, moisture, humidity, and rain can be processed later by using data analytics method to identify these and make effective decisions and approaches for monitoring smart environment. Similarly, traders of online shopping uses online data collected through various online shopping clouds through servers to analyze which product is to be more in demand, etc. The reflective transformation in economical system shall be possible in coming years through cloud-based data analytics which can be said as reliable, sustainable, and robust system. The transformation of modernization can only be achieved with persistent usage of information technologies and communication technologies to manage as well as integrate this complete system. Therefore, by providing parallel processing of data and distributed data storage, cloud computing has been envisaged as an emerging technology of making possible this integration. Due to rapid up-gradations in IoT, the Industry 4.0 grows and to handle the issues of large amount of data storage and its processing, cloud came up with variations of data storage and management strategies. Along with support of combination of cloud and IoT, the working styles in many fields become easier. The various challenges and issues have discussed in this chapter.

Corresponding author: rina151174@gmail.com

Sachi Nandan Mohanty, Jyotir Moy Chatterjee, Monika Mangla, Suneeta Satpathy and Sirisha Potluri (eds.) Machine Learning Approach for Cloud Data Analytics in IoT, (227–272) © 2021 Scrivener Publishing LLC

The communication technologies that vary according to the application requirements have been depicted in this chapter. The today's working scenario and life style have been conquered by combination of IoT and cloud. It has been reached to every little part of the human life right from the monitoring of health, farming, smart industries, smart home, metering, video surveillance, etc. This chapter is designed for readers who intend to begin cloud-based data analytics research with detailed knowledge and compile challenges, issues, organize, research avenues, and summarize using cloud. This chapter discusses the overview of the potential applications of cloud computing in smart working systems and case studies. It also describes the main technologies and innovations that will support the smart environment. The organization of the chapter is followed by subsections including introduction, challenges and issues, data models and applications, etc.

Keywords: Internet of Things (IoT), cloud computing, environmental monitoring

10.1   Introduction

The IoT is a paradigm of computerization and communication in which objects of daily life are Internet connected. This contact, assisted through the integration of resource-constrained services, including devices and sensors, allows smart systems to acquire physical realm knowledge, process this information, or perform physical world behavior. IoT assistances include operative source management, increased throughput, and a higher life quality to humans [1]. Hence, IoT is a benefit of development of smart environments [2], including smart homes, cities, health, as well as factories. The advancements in various technical fields are constructing the Internet of Things (IoT) and manageable environment which is smart. The numerous and occurred solutions available offer various features and quality trade-offs, which makes it difficult to identify the most appropriate IoT communication approaches and better results for a specific smart environment. Since all intelligent environments collecting and processing, which act on information, different unique smart environments have at various levels. In addition, various vertical areas (e.g., farming, weather forecasting, health, and online shopping) coming with a variety of necessities and henceforth technology selection that similarly effect strategies of how, where data is managed and in what way information is handled within a particular context.

Recently, IoT as well as cloud computing are common to the people nowadays (IoT). Moreover, researchers are integrating IoT and cloud computing. Through the tendency proceeding further, the associated devices quantity may be multiple times greater in a near future than the amount of individuals coupled. Through 2012, twenty ménage are projected to produce additional Internet road traffic than the whole use of internet to produce in 2008 [5].

10.1.1   Internet of Things

Kevin Ashton (in 1998) firstly introduced IoT, which reflects the impending of Internet and omnipresent computing [5]. Such technical transformation reflects the vision of communication and accessibility. In IoT, a thing is an individual or physical entity also on planet earth which has a unique identifier (UID), expert devices, and the ability to transmit data across a network through a non-communicating useless item and communicating system. IoT includes small items or devices which are also connected to tiny things, anyone can access, and whatever may be Internet part. The objects become communication nodes on the Internet through data transmission, primarily through radio frequency identification tags. Things are not only tangible entities but also electronic entities which conduct certain human as well as environmental activities. Moreover, IoT is a model for hardware and software and also covers connectivity and social dimensions [6]. Specially, a three-layer IoT architecture, with network perception layer, application layer, and perception layer; however, several [7, 8] also added layers like business layer and middleware layer. The fundamental of IoT is the ubiquitous computing foundation, comprised of three components [14]: (a) middleware, (b) hardware, and (c) presentation. As per the authors in [15] and [14], three factors are involved in the IoT environment. IoT architecture, according to the authors in [19], is consists of three layers: network, perception, and application. Figure 10.1 shows the architecture of IoT [19].

The lowermost layer is perception layer in the IoT architecture which gathers environmental data whose main goal is to identify the data after the atmosphere. The data sensing quantity and data collection is completed on perception layer [9]. Detectors, RFID tags, labels with bar code, GPS, and sensor are available on just this layer. Its main objective is to define object/item as well as data collection.

The layer (network) consisting of wireless as well as wired systems gathers data provided by engineering technologies from the perception layer. Network collects the input from the lowermost layer and then transmits it to Internet. This works like network management or center for processing information. It may contain a gateway, having two interfaces wherein one is associated to the sensor network and secondly to Internet.

The network layer then gives data to the middleware layer, the second lowermost layer. Service management and data storage is the main goal of this layer. Its another task includes performing tasks and automatically

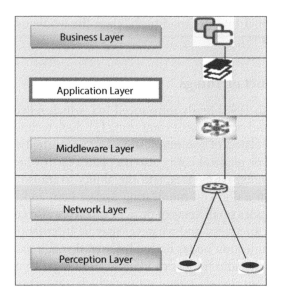

Figure 10.1 Architecture of Internet of Things.

taking decisions based on the outcome. Next, the result of middleware layer is provided to the application layer [8].

This layer is composed of abstract systems that communicate with the end customer to satisfy their needs. This layer gathers information again from middleware layer and provides worldwide technology solutions. Moreover, the application layer introduces the facts in terms of smart city, health, farming, transport, vehicle tracking, home, and many applications [8].

The business layer is the uppermost layer includes make money from service delivered from other layers. The application layer provides data which is then processed to make it knowledge will be transformed into a meaningful service and new services will be generated from existing services.

In fact, the IoT is heterogeneous. IoT's dynamics, intelligence, and versatility make it is a big demand innovation but also renders IoT unstable and insecure. There are currently only early applications in the environmental sector, such as online particulate source monitoring and indoor environmental control systems. The EIoT covers the environmental sciences; however, it has many possible applications in environmental analysis, modeling, and management.

10.1.2 Cloud Computing

The latest development in information technology which is cloud computing brings desktop computing to the entire web, and still users should not worry about managing as well as regulating any of devices. In cloud computing terminology, the customer has to tolerate just an expense of using the service, called as, pay-as-you-go. Cloud computing will turn a smartphone into a major center of data. Cloud computing is an advanced type of parallel computing, distributed, and grid [10]. Cloud computing provides four types of services: PaaS (Platform as a Service), SaaS (Software as a Service), IaaS (Infrastructure as a Service), and NaaS (Networks as a Service) [11]. SaaS refers to a service that is available to the user on a cost-as-you-use base operating over the Internet [12]. User need not save, install, and manage the program. Alternatively, only internet connectivity is required for the SaaS service provider to access the service that was reserved in the cloud. PaaS offers a framework for creating software and services, with the all the required tools and facilities in doing so [13]. NaaS offers the virtual network(s) for users.

The Features of Cloud Computing

1. It is really wide-scale. Cloud platform storage now has greater than one billion computers, Microsoft, IBM, Yahoo, Amazon, and IBM and tens of billions of other "cloud" sites.
2. The Virtualization
   The feature allows the user to use a diverse range of terminal procurement applications from every site. Assets demanded from the "internet," instead of a specific fixed object.
3. Resources Pooling
   This means that now the cloud hosting used a multi-cloud model to drag the computing ability to maintain services to various customers. There really are various assigned and reallocated virtual and physical services which rely on the customer's demand. In particular, the customer does not have influence or information on the area of the resources provided, but can specify position at a higher level.
4. On-Demand Self-Service
   This refers to one of cloud computing's effective and vital functionality, because the user can track the server throughput, functionality, and allocated network capacity on a continuous basis. The consumer can control the computational resources with this feature too.
5. Undemanding Maintenance
   The servers which are easily controlled and its latency is precise minor; also, there are no downtimes except in a few cases. Depending upon the requirement cloud computing

turns up with advancement by creating it increasingly stronger. The new features are more devices coherent and execute likely than older ones together with the fixed bugs.

6. Large Network Access
   Using mobile devices and an internet access, the consumers can connect the data in cloud or publish it anywhere within the cloud. Such features are offered across the network when retrieved through the internet.

7. High Reliability
   Numerous data in the database are kept in the cloud to prevent data loss and improve the reliability. Cloud computing is realer than using local computers.
   Cloud computing is not about a particular application, this can be built together under guidance with ever-changing applications in the "cloud," with a "cloud" being able to support various applications going on simultaneously.

8. High Scalability
   The size of "cloud" can be vigorously scalable to achieve software requirements and consumer scale development [18].

10.1.3 Environmental Monitoring

It is the collection of physical world measurements which determine the status and trends of environmental conditions. This is vital to human health security, environmental sustainability, and policy growth. In many fields, data monitoring system was widely used, particularly in the situation of weather station. The authors proposed [3] real-time, local measurements, and automatic weather station. Several environmental factors are measured continuously in their system. The results are shown via Blynk 1 platform in an Android and iOS application. The system is composed of two parts that are located indoor and outdoor. The author showed another weather station at [4]. The hardware device is based Zigbee wireless technology and Arduino board. It monitors the meteorological data including air temperature and barometric pressure.

The integrated use of IoT and cloud will relate to the execution of a high-speed information technology among the wide-range controlling entities along with the sensors that are properly implemented in the region. Several other applications may correspond to consistent and long-lasting analysis of water levels (for ponds, rivers, and wastewater), air vapour pressure, soil temperatures, and other qualities. Figure 10.2 shows the relation between IoT, cloud and environment monitoring.

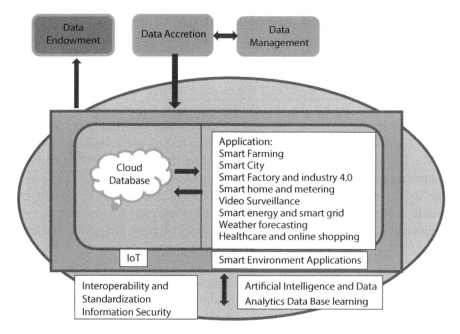

Figure 10.2 Relation between IoT, cloud, and environment monitoring.

Some potential examples are detection of intrusion in dark areas, fire-infrared radiation, or animal recognition [16]. Other areas of application of this nature include agricultural knowledge transfer and intelligent monitoring, intelligent crop management, food safety monitoring, effective harvesting, and forest detection and tracking [17].

A cloud-based data service is able to overcome the frequency energy requirements of reduced energy communications sectors and the omnipresent, rapid retrieval to end-user data [16]. In addition, it allows the management and processing of complex events, produced by sensor-streamed real-time data.

Environmental monitoring is essential to protecting the environment and human health. As the population continues to rise, as industrialization and energy utilize continue to grow, and despite significant progress in controlling pollution, prolonged pollution production remains unavoidable. Thus, the need for monitoring of the environment remains as great as always. Continued advancements in monitoring system creation, deployment, and automation are required to improve monitoring software accuracy and cost-effectiveness. Now it is crucial to generate more scientists and researchers with the education and skills needed to develop and operate monitoring devices effectively and to manage monitoring systems.

10.2   Background and Motivation

Drastically changing inequalities in the ratio of supply to demand which symbolize the advance indicators like environment, momentum, transport, telecommunications, and the marketing has affected the human's day-to-day life. To handle these inequalities, in modern technical societies, the connection has enlarged in such a way that the users are not only connected with the internet but also things are connected which make the term IoT. This is possible because the advancement in manufacturing and communication technology of smart devices. In the world of "IoT", people and things are connected with each other by means of mode of communication which leads the researcher to concentrate on smart devices. Computing parts like sensors, batteries, chips, and sensors have become significantly smaller, quite effective, extra energy-efficient, but less costly. Wireless networking has now become much quicker, the most energy intensive, and wider. These developments allowed the integration of computing technology almost into any item, machine, or environment. These smart objects are connected diversely irrespective of their condition of elements, potentiality to deliver services to the end users. For effective communication of these objects and people, there is a need to design prototypes and patterns. Many other people are already carrying to them an IoT device: a smartphone. Today, several other smart devices have become accessible to users, businesses, as well as cities: smart wearing devices which monitor your fitness and health, voice-activated monitors that support as an assistant, intelligent thermostats which really read how and when to protect your personal relaxed while also conserving energy, smart street lamps that spontaneously enhance or blurred based on number of vehicles or pedestrians or are nearby, etc. To deal with all these components together, there are various challenges and issues which is going to be discussed in Section 10.2.1. Similarly, the various communication technologies and storage systems are discussed in Section 10.2.2.1. The various techniques and data models are explained in Section 10.2.3 which is then followed by application in Section 10.2.6.

10.2.1   Challenges and Issues

The main issues for IoT resolutions are considered in smart atmospheres as follows: a. interoperability and standardization; b. adaptation and personalization; and c. entity recognition and virtualization.

a. Interoperability and Standardization

The creation of standards which identify all layers from both the physical to the higher layers defines the definition of IoT strongly. The most of them have practical relevance in smart environments and are continuing to evolve. For example, in Industry 4.0 interconnected production requires interoperability among various machines in the sense of smart: cities, health, farming, and factories. The OPC UA offers stable, open platform, and scalable for effective machine-to-machine (M2M) communication to address this concern. OPC UA typically uses mode of transmission and encoding to confirm connection, like embedded control systems and high-end innovation service surroundings [20]. This compromises structure functionality for event with alarms alerts, but also provides users, clients, and servers with authentication capabilities for maintaining the confidentiality of their contact from a security perspective. Many industrial systems for monitoring and automation as well as production networks are usually time sensitive. For this reason, many networks follow the IEEE-TSN (Time Sensitive Networking) unified standard [21] to guarantee a specific time supply through manufacturing systems. The manufacturing process in other instances, such as smart cities, health, or home, is not always as innovative as with the smart industry, but it is still visible and wealthy. In addition, the presence of specifications validates the self-awareness of the technology, while attesting to the huge set of standards and the reality they often have considerable conflicts.

From IoT providers' point of view, lack of standardization and interoperability means that the service providers are tied to and must continue with the IoT platform or software provided by a single vendor, which could later carry the potential risk of higher operating costs, product performance, as well as reliability problems [39]. The inconsistency among various IoT systems is helping to momentarily prevent the ecosystem of the IoT service supplier before the IoT industry grows more mature. In particular, support for heterogeneous interfaces of all multiple devices is very expensive for small businesses.

Both academia and industry have stressed the significance of the challenge in IoT as interoperability. By standardizing,

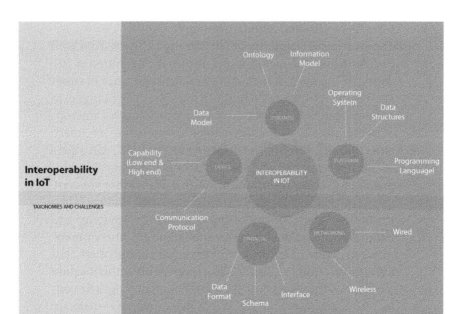

Figure 10.3 Interoperability in IoT.

the factories seek to address the challenges of IoT interoperability as shown in Figure 10.3.

b. Personalization and Adaptation

A recent trend toward personalization is triggering increased emphasis for transparency and interoperability, both in luxury and professional smart environments. Sensing and control networks which run well in separation must aspect new challenges in adaptation and networking to open IoT networks to various stakeholders, realms, and technologies that enable customization. A significant problem is in what way to change the approach the algorithms used through the stored data to provide the solution's user the best possible experience or to someone who takes knowledge from the processing. Two factors are important for long-term adoption and use of emerging innovations: they must provide valuable and validated information which will be fairly easy to set up, recognize, and preserve. For example, smart environments (smart cities, smart homes, and smart manufacturers) or health; all such points are critical in order not to unrestraint the technology. With health or safety, devices are assumed to be abandoned quickly [22] as individuals are motivated by the response styles in at the beginning, but this information is inadequate to motivate long-term usage. For example, if an activity monitoring system is unable to sense the quantity of exercise that one is doing since the threshold that determines it does not ensemble ones use. Hence, during the first few days, such a device will "learn" how the person is behaving. Another example of that is pain. The researcher's aim is to develop a system which will be capable to observe the daily movement of a senior citizen at house to notice variations in her/his behavior and assume any future health-related issues. It is a key problem on the basis of any of this type of distress or health control, as nobody need not initiate too much warning, but we need not miss a case either. The next important attribute is their subjective ease of use, install and maintenance in a latest technology. Installation and proper maintenance is largely an issue of design and technology. However, for ease of use, the embedded algorithms may play a role. Some research groups (e.g., [23–25]) are heading through this issue, are currently underway, and are in their initial phases. The intention is by using device traces to continuously alter the actions of the system, and what has been called subjective and objective user inputs. Analyzing how society behaves well within smart world in order to recognize these data anomalies is very expensive but important for customer experience and device efficiency. If we want even more use and distribution of smart environments and soundscapes in residential care, these systems have to be easy and person-friendly, not the opposite actually.

c. Virtualization and Entity Identification

IoT systems put all together various aspects and functionalities to create interconnected structures of that complexity made up of several interconnected supports. Entity to be identified is a central aspect for dealing this uncertainty, ensuring successful installation and overseeing of entirely functional organizations, as well as ensuring reliable operation in a flexible and responsive context. This, in addition, indicates the need for universal IoT recognition as well as support services to address and link entity codes to related data about data. IoT objects can integrate broadly hetero-geneous types of physical objects, manufactured items and devices, places, individuals and other alive plants and animals, and the physical environment and positions. Identification of entities is a necessary prerequisite for IoT object virtualization, which is called a successful innovation toward the interoperability because of its ability to monitor and configure digital and physical resources across.

d. Machine to Machine Communication

Machine to machine communication can be divided into four major components as shown in Table 10.1: sensor layer collecting data; interaction units/layer relaying the collected information; computing units/layer analyzing the informa-tion; and service layers taking action. Due to the enormous future use of sensors, another challenge is sensor technol-ogy which needs minimal/even zero efforts to maintain and deploy. As per [26], many internal abundant computing plans have declined due to the implementation of sensors is complex next is battery replacement; another is low power sensor design. Because of the increase in number of internet connected devices, do the privacy and security issues [27]. The connected devices can generate data oceans. As per Cisco, in 2008 or 2009, the amount of artefacts on the inter-net exceeded the quantity of humans [28], a phenomenon that accelerates annually. Therefore, in the time ahead, the sum of machine made data will be instructions of greater magnitude.

Table 10.1 Major constituents in M2M and its challenges.

Service	• Computers work for frictionless people and robust people • Generic framework for improving ecosystem creativity
Computation	• The answer to the questions is determined before • Efficient device distribution and cloud intelligence
Communication	• Zero energy efficiency efforts to link huge, compact populations of stationary and moving devices • Complete data privacy and security
Sensors	• Less power, hence no battery shift • Zero touch for installing as well as handling systems

e. Challenges for Database Management

The major challenges in this area are the huge infrastructure potential. In particular, the environmental uncertainty makes it difficult to have adequate analytical resources to deal for rising environmental factors. In addition, security problems are also associated, because risks may be originate in data breaches due to potential violations induced by an infected system or flaw in the communication system.

- Scale, Size, and Indexing

  The magnitude and complexity of the IoT facts would be enormous. Data must be succeeded through liable local rights. Owners of community must determine which resources and data the global network will be made available. Thus, the IoT can perform more on than one level: public and private. Users can access data privately or publically over the public internet. Data quality variations can occur, depending on possession and service level. Progressively trust and credibility mechanisms provide users with information on the quality of information.

- Query Languages

  Structured Query Language (SQL) which relies on structured data is the most projecting examples. Moreover, there are some suggestions for semi-structured data related to query languages, which is more useful of the data available on Internet [31–37].

- Heterogeneity and Integration

  In [38], the author regard an absence of scalable ideal for designing as well as deploying muses over a diverse array of omnipresent devices as among the biggest challenges in making the IoT a reality.

f. Other Challenges

IoT has been instrumental in transforming human existence with greater connectivity and functionality through the today's fast-present Internet networking. Nowadays, IoT becomes more subjective and predictive, combining both the technical and the simulated domain to create a highly personalized, often predictive, culture of today. Besides its promise, IoT is about to address three important issues such as unified interface specifications, privacy, and protection. In addition, the IoT development process would be slow unless those standards are available for smart devices. Failure to address related to data security protection at any IoT joint would not only hamper the growth of IoT but also could also result in lawsuits and social security.

The role of big data, linked to sustainable development, is greatest evident in the energy sector which is faced with productivity and eco-friendly problems related to carbon emission saving [29]. In addition, the usage of renewable and distributed energy production is a crucial component in decreasing carbon dioxide discharges, because the activity of the energy grid accounts for one quarter of global emissions [30].

A number of technological obstacles remain, however, which must be resolved previously the complete IoT dream converts realism. High among these issues are paradigms of usage of internet, proof of identity, behavior and performance, operation and heterogeneity, and also protection, trust, and privacy mechanism technologies. Classical handling is a matter of competition, for example, concurrency, transaction processing, inter-process, and state communication.

The author in [35] classified the IoT paradigm problems into three broader fields which technological challenges, socio-economic challenges, and environmental challenges.

Researchers have witnessed the introduction of several cloud-based IoT systems to consume and process big data replays generated by sensors. Their primary purpose is usually to provide improved services or information by making use of the insights gathered to end consumers. Designing and implementing such platforms however raises new research challenges. The aggregation, processing, and utilization of complex and varied unbounded sources of observation are challenging in general.

10.2.2   Technologies Used for Designing Cloud-Based Data Analytics

Smart environments require various support and services for managing, storing, and collection of data on processing from various sources. The sources mainly concern the devices used in smart environment. The various techniques used in smart environment are as follows. Table 10.2 depicts technological challenges and architecture and heterogeneity.

Table 10.2 Technological challenges and architecture and heterogeneity.

Technological challenges	Architecture and heterogeneity
1. Using the discovery services definition 2. Invention framework comprises of a very well-defined database and a web service interface set	1. Global IoT architecture with electronic software code 2. Operation with object name
1. Offer architecture like OSI-model 2. Ubiquitous end-to-end infrastructure	1. Things layer 2. Adaptation layer 3. Internet and application layer
1. Architecture layered to IoT 2. The author outlined five layers	Layers: 1. Application 2. Middleware 3. Coordination and backbone 4. Access 5. Edge technology
1. Observed customer, creator, service provider, and network provider point of view 2. Interfaces are specified, supporting protocols and necessary standards	Layers: 1. Object sensing 2. Data exchange 3. Information integration 4. Application service
Any intent architecture layered to reflect an IoT device	Layers: 1. Edge technology 2. Access gateway 3. Internet 4. Middleware 5. Application
1. IoT architectures based on the Human Neural and SOF structures 2. Proposed two IoT architecture models: system and universal	1. Management and unified brain-like data center 2. Control nodes distributed which resemble the spinal cord 3. Nets and sensors

10.2.2.1 Communication Technologies

There are various wireless and wired technologies; the technological set includes IEEE 802.11 (Wi-Fi), Digital Enhanced Cordless Telecommunications Ultra Low Energy (DECT-ULE), BLE (Bluetooth Low Energy), LoRaWAN, Sigfox, ITU-T G.9959, NFC (Newfield communication), Narrowband IoT (NB-IoT), and IEEE802.15.4 [16].

- IEEE 802.11 (Wi-Fi)
  IEEE 802.11 is also referred as Wi-Fi and is successful Wireless Local Area Network (WLAN). Power saving mechanism is included in its design but it does not an option for devices which has energy constrained by considering its overall power consumption strategies and complexities. With respect to the use of IEEE 802.11 in actuator or sensor applications, IEEE802.11 has been modified by means of increased range, lower bit, low energy consumption, etc.

- Bluetooth Low Energy (BLE)
  BLE has it prevalent use in smartphones due to its partially reusable Bluetooth hardware and it is used to send and take data from surrounding sensors and actuators. The technologies which promote popular Bluetooth can also facilitate low cost BLE. BLE had been launched in 2010 as the Classic Bluetooth Low Energy Variant [40].

- Digital Enhanced Cordless Telecommunications Ultra Low Energy (DECT-ULE)
  DECT-ULE is the system which is in use during indoor mobile telephony data and voice. It is low energy variant of DECT. Having a good accessibility of DECT equipment [41] is proposed to allow interaction between actuators or sensors and gateway in the home DECT-ULE.

- LoRaWAN
  LoRaWAN is an unregistered wireless band technology that is a part of the developing Class of Low Power Wide Area Networks. LoRaWAN does use LoRa Digital layer skill enables an expanded range of communication to the 10-s range of km. Based on such a star topology which collects a gateway, it offers low data from nearly tens of millions of nodes, including sensor communication costs, at the expense of intense messaging and limiting data rates [42].

- Sigfox
  The other option of wireless technology as LPWAN is Sigfox. By the cost of decreased rate and communication rates, it covers almost maximum amount of devices at long range. The operation of this technology is managed at unlicensed frequency bands. Star topology concept is generally preferable for this wireless technology. The communication ranges in the respect of 10 s of km. This wireless technology has succeeded by the company, also called as Sigfox [42].

- ITU-T G.9959
  ITU-T G.9959 is the lower layer of Z-Wave technology. It is an open-label platform. Z-Wave has emerged as a trade-marked technology and was developed precisely for smart homes applications [43].
- Near-Field Communication (NFC)
  Near-field communication operates at a small range of 10 cm. It prohibits unauthorized devices from capturing of transmitted data and hence this feature offers inherent security properties. The different communication modes are allowed by NFC like peer-to-peer communication, payment applications, and reader mode [44].
- Narrowband IoT (NB-IoT)
  The other category of LPWAN technique is NB-IoT which is considered as one of the emerging technologies [45]. It is focussed on the licensed available spectrum and is identified in the 3GPP release 13. At low bit rates and for a single base station, it provides support for large number of devices.
- IEEE802.15.4
  To allow observing and to monitor and control applications for Wireless Personal Area Networks, IEEE 802.15.4 is one of good wireless technology family. At the first version of its publication, this open source low-rate, selected connectivity which focuses on low energy consumption and on simplicity [46]. It is projected as generic technology, and hence, it is not specifically designed for any particular domain. It supports non-IP-based and IPv6 protocols like Zigbee which has been source for applicable protocol practice architectures.

10.2.3 Cloud-Based Data Analysis Techniques and Models

This chapter describes the key techniques and model which are being used for designing of applications of cloud-based data analysis. The models existing here are based on NoSQL database management systems, MapReduce, and workflows.

10.2.3.1 MapReduce for Data Analysis

The major challenge in internet-enabled devices is the processing of vast volumes of input data. Google [47] proposed MapReduce program to practice this large quantity of data. Now, the MapReduce has been introduced and has proven as an efficient application of handling large data in various domains such as image processing, blog crawling, financial analysis, data analysis, data mining, social machine learning, banking, bioinformatics, healthcare application, and language modeling. It is proven that MapReduce is recognized as important programming model for environments of cloud computing.

MapReduce focuses on locality of data feature to locate the computation jobs close to the data inputted to optimize performance. MapReduce processes large amounts of data which semi-structured or unstructured using number of machines in distributed or parallel environments in contrast to RDBMS. This feature of MapReduce helps to tolerate machine failures. To analyze large amount of data on multiple machines, MapReduce is commonly used to implement algorithms and frameworks for the scalable data analysis.

10.2.3.1.1   MapReduce Hypothesis

The hypothesis of MapReduce model states that user need to state a *Map* and a *Reduce* function and these functions are used in any application that is used to convert input data to output data. A map function forms a pair containing key and value and makes a list of intermediate pairs containing key and value. The intermediate values may have the same intermediate keys which can be then merged by the *reduce* function.

Steps to be Followed by Any Application in MapReduce as shown in Figure 10.4.

1. A job descriptor specifies which MapReduce job to be executed. The job descriptor contains the information of input data, i.e., its location which can be accessed using a distributed file system.
2. The master initiates a variety of mapper and reducer processes on various machines according to the information obtained from job descriptor. Such as at the same instant, the process which reads input data get initiated and starts to read input data. This input data further get partitions into a set of splits; then, these splits get distributed to different mappers.
3. If the partition data is obtained, each mapper method executes the job descriptor map function to produce a list of intermediate key-value pairs. These pairs get grouped further on the basis of keys.

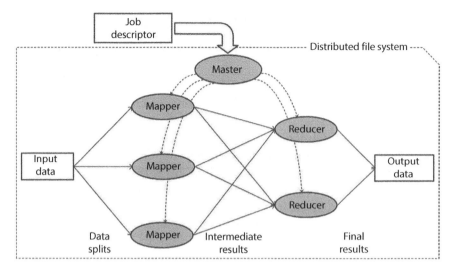

Figure 10.4 Generic MapReduce application execution phases.

4. These clustered pairs of keys are evaluated and the same reducer method is applied to the pairs that have the same keys. Therefore, each reducer process performs the reduction function which the job descriptor has described. Reducer process then combines the same keys to generate small set of values.
5. Finally, the results obtained from each reducer process are to form the final output data get delivered after collecting as per the location identified by task descriptor.

In large storage systems of data such as data center and cluster of computers, Distributed File Systems (DFSs) are the largely acceptable results for MapReduce systems to access the data.

10.2.3.1.2 Framework of MapReduce

To analyze big amounts of data and to develop parallel applications, Hadoop is commonly used MapReduce implementation, and this framework is adopted for development of parallel and distributed applications using various computer languages.

The various Hadoop frameworks are as follows:

a) Distributed File System of Hadoop (HDFS)
   1. This Distributed File System (DFS) provides automatic recovery tolerance for faults.

2. This allows heterogeneous operating system and hardware compatibilities.

3. Hadoop also supports high performance and reliability of the results.

b) Hadoop YARN

This framework is especially for management of scheduling and cluster resource.

c) Hadoop Common

This provides the basic utilities that support Hadoop's other modules. Via the YARN launch in 2013, Hadoop is transitioning from a batch processing program into a batch processing program framework for running a wide range of data applications, including graph analysis, in-memory, and streaming.

10.2.3.1.3   MapReduce Algorithms

All major data mining algorithms such as Support Vector Machines (SVMs) [48], K-means [49], C4.5 [50], and Apriori [51] have been reconfigured in MapReduce over the past few years. Chu *et al.* (2007) showed that MapReduce shows a linear acceleration with an increasing number of processors in a variety of learning algorithms such as Naive Bayes, newly built networks, and probabilistic clustering expectation-maximization.

10.2.3.2   Data Analysis Workflows

The process includes a number of operations, tasks, or activities, which have to be executed to achieve an aim to accomplish a result. Such as, a workflow of data analytics can be described as a series of phases in preprocessing, analyzing, interpretation and post processing. A process can be developed in a functional stage as a program and it can be stated in paradigm or in a computer language. The much more commonly used programming framework used in WMSs is the called as Directed Acyclic Graph (DAG)

10.2.3.2.1   Cloud Workflow Management System

For many applications of data analytics, workflows have been built on high performance computing systems [52]. Out of it, many applications were based on the concept of parallel computing and some of it are of grids.

10.2.3.3   NoSQL Models

Due to rapid change in technology, huge volume of data wants to be managed in different network environments. To control this huge quantity of data, relational database has some limitations which results in performance degradation in analysis and query [53]. Many Databases which are relational have less scalability to manage huge data on many servers.

It has been observed that NoSQL databases are extra extensible as it is not required any manual handling of information or any database management additionally.

10.2.3.3.1   NoSQL Key Features

The important features of NoSQL as demonstrated in [54] are as follows:

- It is capable to scale operation in horizontal fashion on many servers.
- Data replication as well as partitioning can be supported on number of servers.
- It maintains a simple interface for call without binding of SQL.
- It efficiently manages the RAM and distributed indexes for storage of data.
- It has ability to add new attributes during run time.
- It does not support for ACID transactional properties.

10.2.3.3.2   Various NoSQL Systems

The various NoSQL databases are available; all are varied from each other with respect to the solution they provide. Some examples of NoSQL databases are as follows:

- To provide key-value store, a Dynamo of Amazon is used by the author in [55].
- To store documents, MongoDB [56] is the best example.
- To handle extensible record store, Google's Bigtable [57] is used.

The key feature and framework description can be shown in Table 10.3.

Table 10.4 shows the comparison of various algorithms used for various data models [133].

Table 10.3 Description of data models based on key features and framework.

Sr. no.	Model	Key features	Framework
1.	MapReduce	1. Handles large amount of data in cloud computing environment.	Hadoop
2.	NoSQL	1. Does not require manual handling of information. 2. Data replication and partitioning can be supported on number of servers.	MongoDB, Google's Bigtable
3.	Workflows	1. Works in form of phases such as pre-processing, analyzing, interpretation, post-processing, etc.	Directed Acyclic Graph (DAG)

Table 10.4 Comparison of various algorithms used for various data models.

Sr. no.	Algorithms	Characteristic	Search time
1.	R-Tree R*-Tree	Performance bottleneck	O(3D)
2.	Nearest Neighbor Search	Found expensive, in case of searching object is in high-dimensional space	Grows exponentially when with the size of searching space
3.	Decision Tree C4-5	Throughout dataset, practices local greedy search	Observed less time consuming
4.	Hierarchical Neural Network	High rate of accuracy to recognize data	Less time consuming

10.2.4 Data Mining Techniques

Numerous methods and algorithms in data mining are being used to explore the knowledge after databases.

- Classification
  Classification is perhaps the most frequently used data mining approach which uses a set of preclassified instances to

propose a mechanism capable of classifying the record population at large. The process of classifying data includes learning and sorting. In learning, the classification algorithm analyzes the training samples. The data are used in classification to evaluate the correctness of the rules of classification is test data. If the rules are permissible for precision, then it may be applied to a fresh tuples of data [58].

- Clustering
  The unsupervised grouping, called a clustering, is also considered an exploration of data where there is no provision of labeled data. The principal objective of the clustering technique is to distinct the unlabeled data group into some kind of limited and isolated collection of both natural and unknown data structures. No provision is made to provide accurate characterization of non-observed samples generated by a certain distribution of probability. Generally, clustering has two aspects on the basis of which the following can be categorized:
  - Hard clustering: The same entity may refer to a single cluster in hard clustering.
  - Soft clustering: The same entity will refer to various clusters in this clustering [59].
- Regression
  Approach of regression can also be used for forecasting. Analyzing regression will be used to link the relationship among the variables. Parameters are significant variables that are previously specified; the response variables have been trying to anticipate. A lot of real-world issues are not only assumptions, such as this is very hard to forecast if it relies on several dependent variable having complex interactions. Thus, more diverse techniques are also used to predict future values. Neural networks (NNs) may be in use to construct models for classification as well as regression [60].
- Association Rule
  Association as well as correlation are often used to recognize the products which are regularly used from the huge volume of data. Such type of approach supports companies make definite actions, like catalog design, cross-marketing, and study of consumer behavior [61]. Main goal focus on rules that are related to frequently coexisting products, which are used for cross selling, market basket analysis (MBA), and

root cause analysis (RCA). The reason for this is to generate the valuable information that defines connections from a huge amount of data between data objects.

- Neural Networks
  NN is a set of interconnected input components or output components for every relationship and therefore has a volume available. Also, at learning process, by changing weights, it can estimate the right class labels of the input item sets. NNs are then used to extract insights through complex data and then patterns can be extracted using them. They are well designed for inputs and outputs evaluated continuously. NN is the popular mining algorithms that are used in huge data set to detect patterns and trends and are very useful for predicting or predicting conditions [62].

- CURE Algorithm
  CURE algorithm is a hierarchical clustering algorithm which contains data set portioning. A combination of clustering and random sorting is employed for managing a large database. Increasing subset is partially clustered for this algorithm, previously broadly divided from the array of drawn datasets. Instead, selective clusters are clustered once again to establish optimal clusters [63].

- BIRCH (Balanced Iterative Reducing and Clustering Using Hierarchies)
  BIRCH method is a series of Hierarchical clustering algorithms. Since it lowers the amount of input/output activities, it is generally used for especially large databases. Clustering is the data mining algorithm that uses group common items in order to easily classify the data. So, a cluster is a collection of entities and is internally consistent but clearly unlike other cluster objects [64].

- K-means Clustering Algorithm
  This is among the easiest algorithm and unsupervised learning algorithms for very effective resolution of challenging cluster-based issues. This approach uses another simple and easy method to classify a given data set into that set of clusters [65]. K-means–based approach, not having little insight into the relationships between them, is used to combine the various observations that are connected together. A few selected features can be used for real-life objects in such an n-dimensional, where n indicates the

total range of attributes used to define the clusters [66]. When completed, the algorithm will pick k-points in the space of the vectors.

10.2.5   Machine Learning

The techniques are expressed with the technique of machine learning. Artificial Neural Networks (ANN), Random Forests (RFs), Decision Trees (DTs), and SVMs are popular ML techniques that are commonly used for agricultural management.

- Artificial Neural Network (ANN): Since the mid-1990s, ANNs are used primarily for Pattern Recognition (PR) and, in agriculture, attributes mapping [67, 68]. ANNs are also a popular method for classification and regression, such as crop characteristics estimates [69], rainfall and temperature values [70], soil properties [71], irrigation support water content [70], fertilization optimization rates [72], and crop [70]. As a reference, a method for determining field properties of soil and soil component variability was presented in [71]. ANNs have proved to be well-accepted and more reliable but the results obtained of forecast cannot really be standardized. Studies refer to ANNs as an effective device for estimating crop harvest, because the relation among variables is complex and unknown [73, 74].
- Advanced Neural Networks: Like the Adaptive Neuro Fuzzy Inference System (ANFIS) and the deep learning (DL) methods (DLM), these have emerged to tackle a range of drawbacks of traditional ANNs [75, 70]. ANFIS eliminates the typical fuzziness of farming activities and is known for its efficient high dimensionality. DLMs have excellent success in generalization and learn much more quickly than traditional ANNs. The impractical method, uncertainty, and computational complexity of the ANNs led to possible ideas that are easier to train, like RFs, DT and supporting vector machines, with huge probable for forecast applications in agriculture [77].
- Support Vector Machines (SVMs): Dissimilar some additional kernel approaches, the training set have positive critical overview capability and are highly adaptable to the noise. The author in [78] suggested a primary prevention

method for SVM-based sugar beet diseases, using indices of spectral vegetation. Support vector regression was used to retrieve consistent vegetation features, soil mapping, and estimates, but this requires more computational training [79].

- Decision Trees (DT): These are being used regularly in applications of classification, but specified variables may also be taken from continuous soil variables [76] values. The researcher used a Classification and Regression Tree (CART) method to forecast responses of crop changeability to soil property managements and variations techniques. Gradient boosting is a term commonly employed with DTs, enabling greater flexibility and system is to monitor in data modeling [80].

- A DT is a ML classifier based on the tree's data structure which can be used for supervised learning with a procedural modeling approach; each internal node is labeled with an input feature, whereas the arcs that connect a node to several others (children) are labeled with an input data condition that defines the downward path from the root node to the root node.to the leaves

- Random Forests (RFs): These are precise to the over fitting habit trees to its testing set and then are widely known in applications with mapping of attributes, ensuring higher efficiency and higher predictive performance [81, 82]. RFs have comparatively little training time which is easy to parameterise.

- Deep Learning (DL): This is being a very efficient method which adds more difficulty ("depth") to the model by extending classical ANN. The most known use of DL is the classification of images [83]. Such as deep neural networks relate to convolutionary neural networks (CNNs) and are commonly shown in image finding, since it uses a mathematical practice called as convolution to interpret images in non-literal approaches [84]. This allows those networks to recognize partially covered things. Additionally, these complex neural networks are susceptible to over fitting, with a large amount of features and completely connected with dense layers. DL needs large datasets so that the system works well and is acceptable.

Table 10.5 Characteristic of smart data in smart cities.

Sr. no.	Smart city/Smart environment use cases	Data type	Things where processing of data done
1	Smart Traffic	Stream or Massive Data	Edge
2	Smart Healthcare	Stream or Massive Data	Cloud or Edge
3	Smart Environment	Stream or Massive Data	Cloud
4	Smart Weather Prediction	Stream Data	Edge
5	Smart Citizen	Stream Data	Edge
6	Smart Farming	Stream Data	Edge
7	Smart Home	Historical or Massive Data	Cloud
8	Smart Air Controlling	Historical or Massive Data	Cloud
9	Smart Public Place Monitoring	Historical Data	Cloud
10	Smart Human Activity Control	Stream or Historical Data	Edge or Cloud

10.2.5.1 Significant Importance of Machine Learning and Its Algorithms

Table 10.5 shows smart environment, its data types, and where this data is processed in detail [132].

10.2.6 Applications

Importantly, with both the aid of researchers, smart environments also received popularity, but these smart environments are among the most important features of smart cities [104]. Water and green spaces, air quality, waste management, pollution control, waste management, energy conservation, and urban trees control are studied in [105–110] to shape a smart environment, collectively. Table 10.6 gives the overview of ML algorithms for smart environment. Figure 10.5 shows the applications of smart environment.

Table 10.6 Overview of ML algorithms for smart environment.

Sr. no.	ML algorithm	Data processing task
1	Feed Forward Neural Network (FFNN)	Classification or Regression or Feature Extraction or Clustering
2	Support Vector Machine (SVM)	Classification
3	Random Forests (RFs)	Regression or Classification

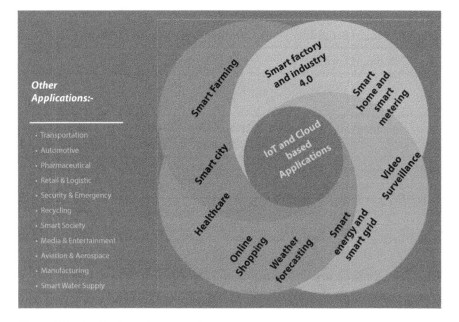

Figure 10.5 Applications of smart environment.

- Smart Farming

  The use of IoT is very crucial in farming. In farming, IoT is often used to monitor soil, to regulate water, to specify fertilizer levels, to track plant production, to identify infection, etc. The detectors, hardware, software, and a few equipment can be monitored. The farmer is able to track the farm and deliver water anywhere across. There are other applications, such as smart agriculture, farm aircraft, livestock tracking, and smart cultivation. It reduces human expense, energy, and effort. It is also known as precision farming.

There are various factors which influence farming systems, such as climate conditions, soil conditions, crop infection and weed control, and water resources. Data scarcity limits current models' ability to incorporate important factors and is reliable enough to gain the trust of the users. Machine learning techniques that emphasize on analyzing data often face difficulties even though large amounts of data are available. Table 10.7 describes the strongest as well as limitations of the ML methods that are used in smart farming.

Over the past decade, the data that is collected on farming from detectors such as crop sensors, hand-held devices or drones has risen exponentially. Presence of spectral, spatial, and time resolution data with high quality will process to detailed and robust representations. Smart farming aim has become the willingness to gather evidence on topsoil and plant unpredictability and react to variance on a fine-scale. Big data use is aimed at supporting this aim but there are numerous challenges.

Table 10.7 Strengthens and weakness of ML techniques in smart farming.

Strengthens	Weaknesses
Do very better with data sources input, e.g., conventional databases with presumed or controlled data	Need tracking of poor quality and inaccurate data Need techniques for data transformation and clustering
Do not claim theoretical preconceived associations	Make very good data-assumptions Conclude homogeneity although there is variance in the inter and intra field Cannot promise successful results forever
Enable rational and tailor-made decision taking using: Estimated yield Form of crop, and identification features Estimation of soil products The detection of diseases and weeds Climate and weather predictions	Requires a significant number of field knowledge-spatial and temporal campaigns, e.g., Cannot apply a guiding principle, difficult to cover all relevant factors Training demand which can be technical and time-consuming Expert expertise on demand, e.g., for shaping

- Smart City

  Smart cities represent best of several wealthiest and more powerful and most complex smart environment scenarios [85, 86]. It includes many domains like the environment, finance, connectivity, resources, development, organization, and some others posing a wide range of relevant challenges and involving different stakeholders, including city officials, managers, providers, and residents, with likely contradictory outlines. It is obvious that smart cities are not only a new challenge in itself, but it is the area where the issues and challenges maybe more complex so heterogeneous, and many expectations and concerns must be addressed by the technological developments. From an ICT viewpoint, the innovations are also transversal to all realms and problems, addressing a range of e-tourism scenarios [87], e-health [92], e-culture [88], smart energy [90], e-government [89], smart mobility [91], to name but a few. Together with political issues [94], the complexity of technological challenges and accessible technologies [93] are obstacles that can hinder the smart city creation. Thus, no wonder which the compatibility of technical standards and solutions is of prime significance, particularly in the area of the IoT, which is universally acknowledged as an important technical enabler for smart cities [95].

- Smart Factory and Industry 4.0

  Industry 4.0 is an evolving industry trend which is getting the advantages of enabling artificial intelligence and environments driving technologies [96]. As it is popular in application areas like smart homes and offices to obtain, process, and act on various types of relevant data sources, smart automated production systems can also benefit from these technologies. The introduction of smart technological solutions in the industrial world has caused a digitalization. This new paradigm is often called the Industrial Revolution of the Fourth Generation-Industry 4.0 [97, 98] and the Future Factory [99]. This envisages smart industries wherein the manufacturing-enabled IoT and Cyber-Physical System [100] set the foundation for producing intelligent systems through smart systems and practices. By harnessing emerging advances in M2M communication, sensor technology, [101], and machine learning [102, 103], smart devices can prepare, monitor, and enhance their individual manufacturing method with limited social interference. Improved retrieval to Industrial IoT (IIoT) data [97] can enable commercial applications from anywhere and on any platform, at any time. The data-intensive nature of smart manufacturing processes, in effect, would allow timely, accurate, and comprehensive record paths resulting in an enhanced view of several processes and activities that was previously impossible. A result is that, the physical and digital worlds become heavily interconnected.

- Smart Home and Smart Metering

  Home-based networks are being described like the area wherever consumers primarily behave: cloud and IoT has a widespread applicability in home environments in which the combined integration of interconnected embedded devices and cloud allows typical in-house operations to be automated. Nonetheless, the integration of software with hardware items allows the transformation of ordinary objects into knowledge machines that can display resources through a web interface integrated across the Web. Most smart-home systems include sensor networks that link intelligent equipment to the Internet for remote monitoring of their activity (e.g., monitoring of the power use of devices to enhance power consumption habits [111]) or remote control (e.g., electricity and air conditioning management [112]). In general, smart lighting has features that lead significant attention from the research community [113, 114] electricity accounts to 19% of universal electrical conservation usage, and interpretations for around 6% of whole greenhouse gas discharges [115]: smart high managing systems have shown to save up to 45% of the energy used for lighting [114]. In this case, the cloud is the strongest choice to create scalable applications with just a few program codes, rendering smart home a simplistic job [116], and providing the tools required for tasks outside the reach of native networks [117]. In this sense, many problems need to be addressed when developing applications, which are primarily linked to the shortage of reliability and consistency. Web-enabled home-based devices and also the communication can be uniform [111]. In addition, device acknowledgment routines are required to allow simple discovery of appliances. There are also questions regarding reliability related to devices not accessible always, device detecting error, and QoS variable [116].

Video Surveillance

Surveillance video is becoming a significant safety and protection feature of the cities today. Smart cameras configured with smart video study can track activities in urban cities for safety and security and offer alert system by acquiring suspicious activities. In [117], author has introduced and concentrated on video monitoring by presenting video content that includes early detection of fire incidents, illegal behavior, and crowd estimate and smart parking system. This research is focused on video-analysis machine learning techniques with better output and incident monitoring with warning generation advantages.

Smart Energy and Smart Grid

Smart electricity and power systems are core constituent of developing smart city structures; these are main part of integrated energy growth plans, as they can not only promote the introduction of renewable energy and transport electrification, but also allow new value-added services related to energy. Electric grid now cover every area of cities, but with the extension of their capacities through competence and data transfers, future urbanization process and facilities not solely connected to their "internal technological activity" would be under gird. The move to clean energy and sustainable cities would require substantial capital investment, expressed in a concise way in phase. IoT with cloud computing can be efficiently combined to even deliver smart energy delivery and utilization management in heterogeneous systems in both the local including wide area.

Usually, IoT nodes involved in these systems have resources for sensing, processing, and communication but minimal resources. Therefore, computational activities can be adequately requested from the cloud, in which more detailed and dynamic decisions are being complete. Cloud acceptance leads to increased robustness through supplying self-caring frameworks and allowing customer involvement and cooperative operation, achieving distributed generation, quality of electric energy, and response to demand [118]. Cloud computing enables massive amounts of information and data from multiple sources to be analyzed and stored through broad networks.

Weather Forecasting

The author [119] recorded and analyzed daily higher and lower temperature, humidity as well as rainfall intensity after a climate station over a 10-year timeslot to support decision-making and predict rainfall by farmers on selecting crop and water resources. In [119], the author used NN model which shows considerable ensemble learning ability but also the authors noted a requirement for fast developments in technologies and software to manage vast volumes of data.

The agriculture relationship with changing weather is bilateral. Although farming is heavily influenced by climate and environment, it really is one of the sectors of the economy that is affecting climate change. Smart farming can minimize emissions by specific tracking of inputs to field temporal and spatial requirements. Proper management of soil, water, fertilizer, and insect will dramatically reduce emissions while preserving crops and reducing costs of production. Innovative machine learning methods have proved useful in mimicking complex, nonlinear problems in the fields of ecology, climate, and the environment [120]. Figure 10.6 shows the various healthcare applications and solutions using IoT.

- Healthcare Applications
  Because of the increase in the population and chronic diseases, the healthcare services are in more demand. The scenario would be more dangerous when the healthcare services would be out of reach; the major part of society would be affected and will be prone to the various diseases.

  Recent technology can help to solve this issue by using the applicability of IoT in healthcare services that make it possible to keep healthcare services in pocket and available

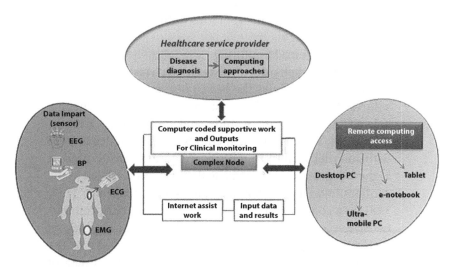

Figure 10.6 Conceptual diagram of IoT healthcare solutions [121].

at lower cost. With the implication of this technology, the routine checkups are now possible at the doorstep or even at patient's house. The combination of cloud with IoT in healthcare system supports more flexibility for data storage and monitoring.

Some health care applications are discussed as follows:

- Glucose Level Detection
  Glucose level detection is possible with aid of sensors implanted in device. Due to metabolic diseases, the level of sugar in blood increases and remains high for long period. This monitoring of blood sugar helps the patient for getting the changing intensity of glucose which can be used to schedule feeding time [122]. The devices supported with sensors provide proper monitoring and sensing of glucose. Still, some significant innovations are demanded in this field.
- Blood Pressure Monitoring
  For supervision of good health, the combination of BP meter with wireless equipment enabled smart mobile goes into a part of BP detecting system [123]. The gadget designed for BP detection relies on the proper functioning of electronic devices. Mostly, the BP gadget body is made with mechanical assembly body with corresponding unit of electronics digital system device incorporating with programmed computing system [124].
- Electrocardiogram Monitoring
  Electrocardiography documents an electrical movement of heart that incorporates the basic pulse estimation and also assures the critical cadence, such as myocardial ischemia, belated QT intermediate study, and multifaceted arrhythmias [125]. The computing methods and techniques assisted with internet facility to electrocardiogram can be used at highest degree [126]. The unusual information related to the cardiopulmonary capacity is consistently detectable [127, 128]. In a condition of integration, the presence of comprehensive recognition software on the basis language analysis of electrocardigram messages in the relevant layer of the internet system tool arranges for the evaluation of data of electrocardiogram graph [129, 130].

- Body Temperature Monitoring
  Observing of body temperature is one of the medicinal facilities provided by combining IOT with mobile application. Using a body temperature sensor built in bit version [131], the concept of a mobile internet computing system is fluctuated. For checking body temperature, the primary framework uses computer program for recording and transmission. Especially in case of infants, it is very important to monitor body temperature during the illness of babies, so to avoid any uncomfortable situation; some wearable sensors can also be used.
- Oxygen Saturation Monitoring
  The gadget designed for continuously monitoring the oxygen saturation of patient which gives the notifications about the wellbeing of patient using computational parameters. This device uses a medical sensor that produces a photoplethsmogram from that we can measure the amount of oxygen saturation and blood volume differences in the muscles. Using hardware filters, this analog waveform has been further analyzed to get Sp02 values and heart rate. Such values are scanned using A2D converters in the ATmega32-based SoC, but are preserved and uploaded in the system continuously.

10.3 Conclusion

The use of cloud computing with IoT is found to be great advancement in technology. With the aid of this technology, it is seems like the world is reachable on single click and the need will be available in a moment. Due to rapid up-gradations in IoT, the Industry 4.0 grows, and to handle the issues of large amount of data storage and its processing, cloud came up with variations of data storage and management strategies. With the help of combination of IoT and cloud, the working styles in many fields become easier. The various challenges and issues have discussed in this chapter. The communication technology varies according to the application requirements that have been depicted in this chapter. The today's working scenario and life style have been conquered by combination of IoT and cloud. It has been reached to every little part of the human life right from the monitoring of health, farming, smart industries, smart home, metering, video surveillance, etc. The various algorithms are also discussed which are mostly used for data analytics. Different data models such as MapReduce and NoSQL are available to analyze data and to handle data storage according to need of system that have been demonstrated here.

References

1. Gomez, C., Paradells, J., Bormann, C., Crowcroft, J., From 6LoWPAN to 6Lo: Expanding the universe of IPv6-supported technologies for the Internet of Things. *IEEE Commun. Mag.*, 55, 12, 148–155, 2017.

2. Cook, D.J. and Das, S.K., How smart are our environments? An updated look at the state of the art. *Pervasive Mob. Comput.*, 3, 2, 53–73, 2007.

3. Farhat, M. *et al.*, A Low Cost Automated Weather Station for Real Time Local Measurements. *J. Eng. Technol. Appl. Sci. Res.*, 7, 3, 1615–1618, 2017.

4. Saini, H.S. *et al.*, Arduino Based Automatic Wireless Weather Station with Remote Graphical Application and Alerts. *3rd IEEE International Conference on Signal Processing and Integrated Networks (SPIN-2016)*, February 2016.

5. Chen, Y.-K., Challenges and Opportunities of Internet of Things, in: *The Proceedings of 17th Asia and South Pacific Design Automation Conference*, Santa Clara, CA, USA, 30 Jan. – 02 Feb., 2012.

6. Kortuem, G., Kawsar, F., Fitton, D., Sundramoorthi, V., Smart Objects and Building Blocks of Internet of Things. *IEEE Internet Comput. J.*, 14, 1, 4451, Jan.-Feb., 2010.

7. Wu, M. *et al.*, Research on the architecture of Internet of things, in: *The Proceedings of 3rd International Conference on Advanced Computer Theory and Engineering*, Beijing, China, 20-22 August, 2012.

8. Khan, R., Khan, S.U., Zaheer, R., Khan, S., Future Internet: The Internet of Things Architecture,Possible Applications and Key Challenges, in: *The Proceedings of 10th International Conference on Frontiers of Information Technology*, Islamabad, Pakistan, 17-19 December, 2012.

9. Uckelamann, D., Harrison, M., Michahelles, F., *Architecting the Internet of Things*, Springer-Verlag Berlin Heidelberg, Spain, ISBN 978-3-642-19157-2, 2011.

10. Zhang, S. *et al.*, Cloud Computing Research and Development Trend, in: *The Proceedings of International Conference on Future Networks*, Sanya, China, 22-24 Jan., 2010.

11. Ma, W. *et al.*, The Survey and Research on Application of Cloud Computing, in: *The Proceedings of 7th International Conference on Computerl Science and Education*, Wuyishan Mountain, China, 02-04 November, 2012.

12. Jadeja, Y. *et al.*, Cloud Computing - Concepts, Architecture and Challenges, in: *The Proceedings of International Conference on Computing Electronics and Electrical Technologies*, Nagercoil, India, 21-22 March, 2012.

13. Zhou, M. *et al.*, Services in the Cloud Computing Era: A Survey, in: *The Proceedings of 4th International Universal Communications Symposium*, Beijing, China, 18-19 October, 2010.

14. Gubbi, J., Buyya, R., Marusic, S., Palaniswami, M., Internet of things (IoT): A vision, architectural elements, and future directions. *Future Gener. Comput. Syst.*, 29, 7, 1645–1660, 2013.

15. Atzori, L., Iera, A., Morabito, G., The internet of things: A survey. *Comput. Networks*, 54, 15, 2787–2805, 2010.

16. Gomez, C., Chessa, S., Fleury, A., Roussos, G., Preuveneers, D., Internet of Things for enabling smart environments: A technology-centric perspective. *J. Ambient Intell. Smart Environ.*, 11, 23–43, 2019. IOS Press.

17. Gomez, C., Oller, J., Paradells, J., Overview and evaluation of bluetooth low energy: An emerging low-power wirelesstechnology. *Sensors*, 12, 9, 11734–11753, 2012.

18. Watteyne, T., Palattella, M., Grieco, L., Using IEEE 802.15.4e time-slotted channel hopping (TSCH) in the Internet of Things (IoT): Problem statement. RFC 7554, 2015. Internet Engineering Task Force, <https://hal.inria.fr/hal-01208395>

19. M. Knight, Wireless Security - How Safe is Z-Wave?, *Comp. & Control Eng. J.*, 17, 6, 18–23, Jan. 2006.

20. Henssen, R. and Schleipen, M., Interoperability between OPC UA and AutomationML. *Proc. CIRP*, 25, 297–304, 2014.

21. Kehrer, S., Kleineberg, O., Heffernan, D., A comparison of fault-tolerance concepts for IEEE 802.1 Time Sensitive Networks (TSN), in: *Emerging Technology and Factory Automation (ETFA)*, Barcelona, pp. 1–8, IEEE, 2014.

22. Clawson, J., Pater, J.A., Miller, A.D., Mynatt, E.D., Mamykina, L., No longer wearing: Investigating the abandonment of personal health-tracking technologies on craigslist, in: *Proceedings of the 2015 ACM International Joint Conference on Pervasive and Ubiquitous Computing*, ACM, pp. 647–658, 2015.

23. A.-B. Karami, A., Fleury, Using feedback in adaptive and user-dependent one-step decision making, in: *25th International Joint Conference on Artificial Intelligence (IJCAI-16) Workshop "Interactive Machine Learning*, AAAI Press/International Joint Conferences on Artificial Intelligence, p. 5, 2016.

24. Karami, A.B., Fleury, A., Boonaert, J., Lecoeuche, S., User in the loop: Adaptive smart homes exploiting user feedback – state of the art and future directions. *Information*, 7, 2, 35, 2016.

25. Rashidi, P. and Cook, D.J., Keeping the resident in the loop: Adapting the smart home to the user. *IEEE Trans. Syst. Man Cybern. – Part A: Syst. Hum.*, 39, 5, 949–959, 2009.

26. Beckmann, C., Consolvo, S., LaMarca, A., Some Assembly Required: Supporting End-User Sensor Installation in Domestic Ubiquitous Computing Environments, *UbiComp 2004, LNCS 3205*, pp. 107–124, 2004.

27. Cha, I., Shah, Y., Schmidt, A.U., Leicher, A., Meyerstein, M.V., Trust in M2M communication. *Veh. Technol. Mag., IEEE*, 4, 3, 69–75, Sept. 2009.

28. CISCO, How the Internet of Things Will Change Everything, http://youtube/ mf7HxU0ZR_Q. CISCO, How the Internet of Things Will Change Everything, http://youtu. be/mf7HxU0ZR_Q (You tube information).

29. Zhou, K., Fu, C., Yang, S., Big data driven smart energy management: From big data to big insights. *Renewable Sustain. Energy Rev.*, 56, 215–225, 2016.

30. Letouzé, E. and Jütting, J., Officials statistics, big data and human development: Towards a new conceptual and operational approach. Data-Pop Alliance White Papers Series, in collaboration with PARIS21(Article), 17, in collaboration with PARIS21(Article), 2014.

31. Abiteboul, S., Querying semi-structured data, in: *6th International Conference on Database Theory, ICDT'97*, vol. 1186, Springer, Delphi, Greece, LNCS, pp. 1–18, 1997.

32. Chamberlin, D., Robie, J., Florescu, D., Quilt: an XML query language for heterogeneous data sources, in: *WebDB (Informal Proceedings)*, pp. 53–62, 2000, (available at http://www.research.att. com/conf/webdb2000/ARTICLES/4. pdf).

33. Heuer, A. and Priebe, D., Integrating a query language for structured and semi-structured data and IR techniques, in: *11th International Workshop Database and Expert Systems Applications*, IEEE, 2000.

34. Cardelli, L. and Ghelli, G., A query language based on the ambient logic, in: *ESOP'01 (invited article)*, (available at http://www.luca. demon.co.uk).

35. Ni, W. and Ling, T.W., Glass: a graphical query Language for semistructured data, in: *DASFAA*, p. 363, 2003.

36. Liu, L., Du, C., Shi, X., Song, H., Lin, Z., RDF-Based representation and query of information in digital library, in: *First IEEE International Symposium on Information Technologies and Applications in Education*, 07, 2007, ISITAE.

37. Cao, Z., Wu, Z., Wang, Y., UMQL: A unified multimedia query language, in: *Third International IEEE Conference on Signal Image Technologies and Internet-Based System*, 2007, SITIS '07.

38. Rellermeyer, J.S., Duller, M., Gilmer, K., Maragkos, D., Papageorgiou, D., Alonso, G., The software fabric for the Internet of Things, in: *IoT 2008: First International Conference on the Internet of Things*, vol. 4952, Springer, Zurich, Switzerland, LNCS, UK, pp. 87–104, 2008.

39. Macaulay, T., *RIoT control: understanding and managing risks and the internet of things*, Morgan Kaufmann, UK, 2016.

40. Castro-Jul, F., Díaz-Redondo, R.P., Fernández-Vilas, A., Collaboratively assessing urban alerts in ad hoc participatory sensing. *Comput. Networks*, 131, 129–143, 2018.

41. Cesta, A., Cortellessa, G., Fracasso, F., Orlandini, A., Turno, M., User needs and preferences on AAL systems that support older adults and their carers. *J. Ambient Intell. Smart Environ.*, 10, 1, 49–70, 2018.

42. Chahuara, P., Fleury, A., Portet, F., Vacher, M., On-line human activity recognition from audio and home automation sensors: Comparison of sequential and non-sequential models in realistic smart homes 1. *J. Ambient Intell. Smart Environ.*, 8, 4, 399–422, 2016.

43. Gomez, C. and Paradells, J., Wireless home automation networks: A survey of Architectures and Technologies. *IEEE Commun. Mag.*, 48, 6, 92–101, 2010.

44. Hong, Y.G., Choi, Y.H., Youn, J.S., Kim, D.K., Choi, J.H., Transmission of IPv6 packets over near field communication. Internet Draft (Work in Progress), Draft Name: Draft-ietf-6lonfc-09, 2015, 2020-08-23.

45. Wang, Y.-P.E., Lin, X., Adhikary, A., Grovlen, A., Sui, Y., Blankenship, Y., Bergman, J., Razaghi, H.S., A primer on 3GPP narrowband Internet of Things. *IEEE Commun. Mag.*, 55, 3, 117–123, 2017.

46. Baronti, P., Pillai, P., Chook, V.W., Chessa, S., Gotta, A., Hu, Y.F., Wireless sensor networks: A survey on the state of the art and the 802.15. 4 and ZigBee standards. *Comput. Commun.*, 30, 7, 1655–1695, 2007.

47. Dean, J. and Ghemawat, S., MapReduce: Simplified data processing on large clusters. *Sixth USENIX Symposium on Operating Systems Design and Implementation (OSDI'04)*, San Francisco, USA, 2004.

48. Sun, Z. and Fox, G., Study on parallel SVM based on MapReduce. *International Conference on Parallel and Distributed Processing Techniques and Applications*, Las Vegas, USA, pp. 16–19, 2012.

49. Ekanayake, J., Pallickara, S., Fox, G., Mapreduce for data intensive scientific analyses. *Fourth IEEE International Conference on e-Science (e-Science'08)*, Indianapolis, USA, pp. 277–284, 2008.

50. Gongqing, W., Haiguang, L., Xuegang, H., Yuanjun, B., Jing, Z., Xindong, W., MReC4.5: C4.5 ensemble classification with MapReduce. *ChinaGrid Annual Conference*, ChinaGrid '09. China, vol. 4, p. 249, 255, 20092009.

51. Lin, M., Lee, P., Hsueh, S., Apriori-based frequent itemset mining algorithms on MapReduce, in: *Proceedings of the Sixth International Conference on Ubiquitous Information Management and Communication (ICUIMC '12)*, New York, USA, 2012.

52. Talia, D., *Workflow systems for science: concepts and tools*, ISRN Software Engineering, London, 2013.

53. Abramova, V., Bernardino, J., Furtado, P., Which NoSQL database? A performance overview. *OJDB*, 1, 2, 17–24, 2014.

54. Cattell, R., Scalable SQL and NoSQL data stores. *SIGMOD Rec.*, 39, 4, 12–27, 2010.

55. De Candia, G., Hastorun, D., Jampani, M., Kakulapati, G., Lakshman, A., Pilchin, A., Sivasubramanian, S., Vosshall, P., Vogels, W., Dynamo: Amazon's highly available key-value store, in: *Proceedings of Twenty-First ACM SIGOPS Symposium on Operating Systems Principles (SOSP '07)*, ACM, New York, NY, USA, pp. 205–220, 2007.

56. Plugge, E., Hawkins, T., Membrey, P., *The Definitive Guide to MongoDB: The NoSQL Database for Cloud and Desktop Computing*, First ed, Apress, Berkely, CA, USA, 2010.

57. Chang, F., Dean, J., Ghemawat, S., Hsieh, W.C., Wallach, D.A., Burrows, M., Chandra, T., Fikes, A., Gruber, R., Bigtable: a distributed storage system for structured data. *OSDI*, 2006.

58. Berkhin, P., Survey of Clustering Data Mining Techniques, Accrue Software, 1045 Forest Knoll Dr., San Jose, CA, 95129, 2002.

59. Nikam, V.B. and Patil, V., Study of Data Mining algorithm in cloud computing using Map Reduce Framework. *J. Eng. Comput. Appl. Sci. (JEC&AS)*, 2, 7, 65–70, July 2013.

60. Voas, J. and Zhang, J., Cloud Computing: New Wine or Just a New Bottle?, Database Systems Journal. *IEEE Internet Comput. Mag.*, III, 3, 71, 2012.

61. Sucahyo, Y.G., CISA: Introduction to Data Mining and Business Intellegence Mansigera, Shivanigoel, Data Mining- Techniques, methods and Algorithms: A review on tools and their Validity. *Int. J. Comput. Appl.*, 113, 18, 22–29 March 2015.

62. Kanungo, T., Netanyahu, N.S., Wu, A.Y., An Efficient k-Means Clustering Algorithm: Analysis and Implementation, *IEEE Trans. Pattern Anal. Mach. Intell.*, https://ieeexplore.ieee.org/xpl/RecentIssue.jsp?punumber=34, 24, 7, 881–892, July 2002.

63. Nikam, V.B. and Patil, V., Study of Data Mining algorithm in cloud computing using Map Reduce Framework, *Journal of Engineering, Computers & Applied Sciences* (JEC&AS), Volume 2, No.7, 2013.

64. Geng, X. and Yang, Z., Data Mining in Cloud Computing. *International Conference on Information Science and Computer Applications*, ISCA, 2013.

65. Mell, P. and Grance, T., *The NIST Definition of Cloud Computing*, U.S.Department of Commerce, Special Publication, Computer Security Division Information Technology Laboratory National Institutes of Standards and Technology, US, 800-145.

66. Talia, D. and Trunfio, P., How distributed data mining tasks can thrive as knowledge services. *Commun. ACM*, 53, 132–137, 2010.

67. Kimes, D.S., Nelson, R.F., Salas, W.A., Skole, D.L., Mapping secondary tropical forest and forest age from SPOT HRV data. *Int. J. Remote Sens.*, 20, 18, 3625–3640, 1999.

68. Wang, F., The use of artificial neural networks in a geographical information system for agricultural land-suitability assessment. *Environ. Plan. A: Economy Space*, 26, 2, 265–284, 1994.

69. Diamantopoulou, M.J., Artificial neural networks as an alternative tool in pine bark volume estimation. *Comput. Electron. Agric.*, 48, 3, 235–244, 2005.

70. Bendre, M.R., Thool, R.C., Thool, V.R., Big data in precision agriculture through ICT: Rainfall prediction using neural network approach, in: *Proceedings of the International Congress on Information and Communication*

Technology. Advances in Intelligent Systems and Computing, S. Satapathy, Y. Bhatt, A. Joshi, D. Mishra (Eds.), pp. 165–175, 2016.

71. Lahoche, F., Godard, C., Fourty, T., Lelandais, V., Lepoutre, D., An innovative approach based on neural networks for predicting soil component variability, in: *Proceedings of the 6th International Conference on Precision Agriculture and Other Precision Resources Management*, pp. 803–816, 2003, Retrieved from http://www.grignon.inra.fr/economie-publique/publi/innovative_approach.pdf.

72. Pokrajac, D. and Obradovic, Z., Neural network-based software for fertilizer optimization in precision farming, in: *Proceedings of the International Joint Conference on Neural Networks (IJCNN '01)*, 2001.

73. Meersmans, J., De Ridder, F., Canters, F., De Baets, S., Van Molle, M., A multiple regression approach to assess the spatial distribution of soil organic carbon (SOC) at the regional scale (Flanders, Belgium). *Geoderma*, 143, 1–2, 1–13, 2008.

74. Paswan, R.P. and Begum, S.A., Regression and neural networks models for prediction of crop production. *Int. J. Sci. Eng. Res.*, 4, 9, 98–108, 2013, Retrieved from https://www.ijser.org/researchpaper/Regression-and-Neural-Networks-Modelsfor-Prediction-of-Crop-Production.pdf.

75. Chandra Deka, P., Patil, A.P., Kumar, P.Y., Naganna, S.R., Estimation of dew point temperature using SVM and ELM for humid and semi-arid regions of India. *J. Hydraul. Eng.*, 24, 2, 190–197, 2018.

76. Chlingaryan, A., Sukkarieh, S., Whelan, B., Machine learning approaches for crop yield prediction and nitrogen status estimation in precision agriculture: A review. *Comput. Electron. Agric.*, 151, 61–69, 2018.

77. Sridharan, M. and Gowda, P., Application of statistical machine learning algorithms in precision agriculture, in: *Proceedings of the 7th Asian-Australasian Conference on Precision Agriculture*, 2017.

78. Rumpf, T., Mahlein, A.-K., Steiner, U., Oerke, E.-C., Dehne, H.-W., Plümer, L., Early detection and classification of plant diseases with support vector machines based on hyperspectral reflectance. *Comput. Electron. Agric.*, 74, 1, 91–99, 2010.

79. Tuia, D., Verrelst, J., Alonso, L., Perez-Cruz, F., Camps-Valls, G., Multioutput support vector regression for remote sensing biophysical parameter estimation. *IEEE Geosci. Remote Sens. Lett.*, 8, 4, 804–808, 2011.

80. Colin, B., Clifford, S., Wu, P., Rathmanner, S., Mengersen, K., Using boosted regression trees and remotely sensed data to drive decision-making. *Open J. Stat.*, 7, 5, 859–875, 2017.

81. De Castro, A., II, Torres-Sanchez, J., Peña, J.M., Jimenez-Brenes, F.M., Csillik, O., Lopez-Granados, F., An automatic random forest-OBIA algorithm for early weed mapping between and within crop rows using UAV imagery. *Remote Sens.*, 10, 3, 285, 2018.

82. Rahmati, O., Pourghasemi, H.R., Melesse, A.M., Application of GIS-based data driven random forest and maximum entropy models for groundwater

potential mapping: A case study at Mehran Region, Iran. *Catena*, 137, 360–372, 2016.

83. Kamilaris, A. and Prenafeta-Boldu, F.X., Deep learning in agriculture: A survey. *Comput. Electron. Agric.*, 147, 70–90, 2018.

84. Andrea, C., Mauricio Daniel, B.B., Jose Misael, J.B., Precise weed and maize classification through convolutional neuronal networks, in: *2017 IEEE Second Ecuador Technical Chapters Meeting*, 2017, doi: 10.1109/ETCM.2017.8247469.

85. Streitz, N., Beyond 's mart-only' cities: Redefining the 'smart everything' paradigm. *J. Ambient Intell. Hum. Comput.*, Springer-Verlag GmbH Germany, 2018.

86. Streitz, N., Charitos, D., Kaptein, M., Böhlen, M., Grand challengesforambientintelligenceandimplicationsfordesign contexts and smart societies. *J. Ambient Intell. Smart Environ.*, 11, 1, 87–107, 2019.

87. Tripathy, A.K., Tripathy, P.K., Ray, N.K., Mohanty, S.P., iTour: The future of smart tourism: An IoT framework for the independent mobility of tourists in smart cities. *IEEE Consum. Electron. Mag.*, 7, 3, 32–37, 2018.

88. Bernardino, S., Freitas Santos, J., CadimaRibeiro, J., The legacy of European capitals of culture to the "smartness" of cities: The case of Guimarães 2012. *J. Conv. Event Tour.*, 19, 138–166, Taylor & Francis, 2018.

89. Lv, Z., Li, X., Wang, W., Zhang, B., Hu, J., Feng, S., Government affairs service platform for smart city. *Future Gener. Comput. Syst.*, 81, 443–451, 2018.

90. Masera, M., Bompard, E.F., Profumo, F., Hadjsaid, N., Smart (electricity) grids for smart cities: Assessing roles and societalimpacts. *Proc. IEEE*, 106, 4, 613–625, 2018.

91. Zawieska, J. and Pieriegud, J., Smart city as a tool for sustainable mobility and transport decarbonisation. *Transp. Policy*, 63, 39–50, 2018.

92. Cook, D.J., Duncan, G., Sprint, G., Fritz, R.L., Using smart city technology to make healthcare smarter. *Proc. IEEE*, 106, 4, 708–722, 2018.

93. Silva, B.N., Khan, M., Han, K., Towards sustainable smart cities: A review of trends, architectures, components, and open challenges in smart cities. *Sustain. Cities Soc*, 38, 697–713, 2018.

94. Krivý, M., Towards a critique of cybernetic urbanism: The smart city and the society of control. *Plan. Theor.*, https://journals.sagepub.com/toc/plta/17/1, Vol 17, Issue 1, 390–397, 2016.

95. Zanella, A., Bui, N., Castellani, A., Vangelista, L., Zorzi, M., Internet of Things for smart cities. *IEEE Internet Things J.*, 1, 1, 22–32, 2014.

96. Preuveneers, D. and Ilie-Zudor, E., The intelligent industry of the future: A survey on emerging trends, research challenges and opportunities in Industry 4.0. *J. Ambient Intell. Smart Environ.*, 9, 3, 287–298, 2017.

97. Gilchrist, A., *Industry 4.0: The Industrial Internet of Things*, Springer, New York, 2016.

98. Lee, J., Bagheri, B., Kao, H.-A., Acyber-physicalsystemsarchitectureforindustry4.0-basedmanufacturingsystems. *Manuf. Lett.*, 3, 18–23, 2015.

99. Karnouskos, S., Colombo, A.W., Bangemann, T., Manninen, K., Camp, R., Tilly, M., Stluka, P., Jammes, F., Delsing, J., Eliasson, J., A SOA-based architecture for empowering future collaborative cloud-based industrial automation, in: *IECON 2012– 38th Annual Conference on IEEE Industrial Electronics Society*, IEEE, pp. 5766–5772, 2012.

100. Monostori, L., Kádár, B., Bauernhansl, T., Kondoh, S., Kumara, S., Reinhart, G., Sauer, O., Schuh, G., Sihn, W., Ueda, K., Cyber-physical systems in manufacturing. *CIRP Ann.*, 65, 2, 621–641, 2016.

101. Verma, P.K., Verma, R., Prakash, A., Agrawal, A., Naik, K., Tripathi, R., Alsabaan, M., Khalifa, T., Abdelkader, T., Abogharaf, A., Machine-to-machine (M2M) communications: A survey. *J. Netw. Comput. Appl.*, 66, 83–105, 2016.

102. Perez, R.A., Lilkendey, J.T., Koh, S.W., Machinelearningfor a dynamic manufacturing environment. *ACM SIGICE Bull.*, 19, 3, 5–9, 1994.

103. Priore, P., de la Fuente, D., Puente, J., Parreño, J., A comparison of machine-learning algorithms for dynamic scheduling of flexible manufacturing systems. *Eng. Appl. Artif. Intell.*, 19, 3, 247–255, 2006.

104. An, J., Le Gall, F., Kim, J., Yun, J., Hwang, J., Bauer, M., Zhao, M., Song, J., Toward global IoT-enabled smart cities interworking using adaptive semantic adapter. *IEEE Internet Things J.*, 6, 3, 5753–5765, Jun. 2019.

105. Zhang, F., Kang, L., Xinyan, X.U., Shen, J., Zhou, A.L.U., Power controlled and stability-based routing protocol for wireless ad hoc networks. *J. Inf. Sci. Eng.*, 33, 4, 979–992, 2017.

106. M.A., A.R., M.H., II, A.M.S., Utilization of the dynamic laser scanning technology for monitoring, locating and classification of the city trees. *Int. J. Inf. Process. Manage.*, 2, 1, 148–159, Jan. 2011.

107. Anagnostopoulos, T., Kolomvatsos, K., Anagnostopoulos, C., Zaslavsky, A., Hadjiefthymiades, S., Assessing dynamic models for high priority waste collection in smart cities. *J. Syst. Software*, 110, 178–192, Dec. 2015.

108. Corbett, J. and Mellouli, S., Winning the SDG battle in cities: How an integrated information ecosystem can contribute to the achievement of the 2030 sustainable development goals: Winning the SDG battle in cities: An integrated information ecosystem. *Inf. Syst. J.*, 27, 4, 427–461, Jul. 2017.

109. Castelli, M., Gonçalves, I., Trujillo, L., Popovič, A., An evolutionary system for ozone concentration forecasting. *Inf. Syst. Front.*, 19, 5, 1123–1132, Oct. 2017.

110. Park, J., Lim, S.B., Hong, K., Pyeon, M.W., Lin, J.Y., An application of emission monitoring system based on real-time traffic monitoring. *Int. J. Inf. Process. Manage.*, 4, 1, 51–57, Jan. 2013.

111. Chen, S.-Y., Lai, C.-F., Huang, Y.-M., Jeng, Y.-L., Intelligent home-appliance recognition over IoT Cloud network, in: *Wireless Communications and Mobile Computing Conference (IWCMC), 2013 9th International*, IEEE, pp. 639–643, 2013.

112. Han, D.-M. and Lim, J.-H., Smart home energy management system using IEEE 802.15. 4 and zigbee. *IEEE Trans. Consum. Electron.*, 56, 3, 1403–1410, 2010, Ye, X. and Huang, J., A framework for Cloud-based smart home, in: Computer Science and Network Technology (ICCSNT). *2011 International Conference on*, December 2011, vol. 2, pp. 894–897.

113. Martirano, L., A smart lighting control to save energy, in: *Intelligent Data Acquisition and Advanced Computing Systems (IDAACS), 2011 IEEE 6th International Conference on*, September 2011, vol. 1, pp. 132–138.

114. Castro, M., Jara, A., Skarmeta, A., Smart lighting solutions for smart cities, in: *Advanced Information Networking and Applications Workshops (WAINA), 2013 27th International Conference on*, March 2013, pp. 1374–1379.

115. Kamilaris, A. *et al.*, The smart home meets the web of things. *Int. J. Ad Hoc Ubiquitous Comput.*, Vol. 7, No. 3, pp 147–154, 2011.

116. Niedermayer, H., Holz, R., Pahl, M.-O., Carle, G., On using home networks and Cloud computing for a future Internet of Things, in: *Future Internet— FIS*, pp. 70–80, München, Germany, Springer, 20092010.

117. Babanne, V., Mahajan, N.S., Sharma, R.L., Gargate, P.P., Machine learning based Smart Surveillance System. *2019 Third International Conference on I-SMAC 2019*.

118. Yun, M. and Yuxin, B., Research on the architecture and key technology of Internet of Things (IoT) applied on smart grid, in: *Advances in Energy Engineering (ICAEE), 2010 International Conference on*, IEEE, pp. 69–72, 2010.

119. Bendre, M.R., Thool, R.C., Thool, V.R., Big data in precision agriculture through ICT: Rainfall prediction using neural network approach, in: *Proceedings of the International Congress on Information and Communication Technology. Advances in Intelligent Systems and Computing*, pp. 165–175, 2016.

120. Chandra Deka, P., Patil, A.P., Kumar, P.Y., Naganna, S.R., Estimation of dew point temperature using SVM and ELM for humid and semi-arid regions of India. *J. Hydraul. Eng.*, 24, 2, 190–197, 2018.

121. Bhattacharya, M., Kar, A., Malick, R.C. *et al.*, Application of Internet Assistance Computation for Disease Prediction and Bio-modeling: Modern Trends in Medical Science, Principles of Internet of Things (IoT) Ecosystem: Insight Paradigm (pp. 1-20), Springer International Publishing.

122. Z.J. Guan, Somatic data blood glucose collection transmission device for Internet of Things. Chin. Patent 202(838), 653, 2013.

123. Dohr, A., Modre-Opsrian, R., Drobics, M., Hayn, D., Schreier, G., The internet of things for ambient assisted living, in: *2010 Seventh International Conference on Information Technology: New Generations*, IEEE, pp. 804–809, 2010.

124. T. Xin, B. Min, J. Jie, Carry-on blood pressure/pulse rate/blood oxygen monitoring location intelligent terminal based on Internet of Things. Chin. Patent 202(875), 315, 2013.

125. Drew, B.J., Califf, R.M., Funk, M., Kaufman, E.S., Krucoff, M.W., Laks, M.M., Macfarlane, P.W., Sommargren, C., Swiryn, S., Van Hare, G.F., Practice standards for electrocardiographic monitoring in hospital settings: an American Heart Association scientific statement from the Councils on Cardiovascular Nursing, Clinical Cardiology, and Cardiovascular Disease in the Young: endorsed by the International Society of Computerized Electrocardiology and the American Association of Critical-Care Nurses. *Circulation*, 110, 17, 2721–2746, 2004.

126. Dash, P., Electrocardiogram monitoring. *Indian J. Anaesth.*, 46, 4, 251–260, 2002.

127. Yang, L., Ge, Y., Li, W., Rao, W., Shen, W., A home mobile healthcare system for wheelchair users, in: *Proceedings of the 2014 IEEE 18th International Conference on Computer Supported Cooperative Work in Design (CSCWD)*, IEEE, pp. 609–614, 2014.

128. Agu, E., Pedersen, P., Strong, D., Tulu, B., He, Q., Wang, L., Li, Y., The smartphone as a medical device: assessing enablers, benefits and challenges, in: *2013 IEEE International Workshop of Internet-of-Things Networking and Control (IoT-NC)*, IEEE, pp. 48–52, 2013.

129. M.-L. Liu, L. Tao, Z. Yan, Internet of Things-based electrocardiogram monitoring system. Chin. Patent 102(764), 118, 2012.

130. Mukhopadhyay, S.C., Wearable sensors for human activity monitoring: a review. *IEEE Sens. J.*, 15, 3, 1321–1330, 2014.

131. Ruiz, M., García, J., Fernández, B., Body temperature and its importance as a vital constant. *Rev. Enferm. (Barcelona, Spain)*, 32, 9, 44–52, 2009.

132. Mahdavinejad, M.S. *et al.*, Machine learning for internet of things data analysis: a survey. *Digital Commun. Networks*, 4, 3, 161–175, August 2018.

133. Thillaleswari, B., Comparative Study on tools and techniques of Big Data Analysis. *Int. J. Adv. Networking Appl. (IJANA)*, 08, 05, 61–66, 2017.

11

Advancement of Machine Learning and Cloud Computing in the Field of Smart Health Care

Aradhana Behura*, Shibani Sahu† and Manas Ranjan Kabat‡

Veer Surendra Sai University of Technology, Burla, Sambalpur, Odisha, India

Abstract

An important application of WSN (Wireless Sensor Network) is WBAN (Wireless Body Area Network) which is utilized to monitor the health by taking the help of cloud computing and clustering, which is a part of machine learning. The sensors can measure certain parameters of human body, either externally or internally. Sensor Nodes (SNs) normally have very limited resources due to its small size. Therefore, an essential design requirement of WBAN schemes is the minimum consumption of energy. Bio-Sensor Nodes (BSNs) or simply called as SNs are the main backbone of WBANs. It is used to sense health-related data such as rate of heart beat, blood pressure, blood glucose level, electrocardiogram (ECG), and electromyography of human body and pass these readings to real-time health monitoring systems. Examples can include measuring the heartbeat and body temperature or recording a prolonged ECG. Several other sensors are placed in clothes, directly on the body or under the skin of a person, and measure the temperature, blood pressure, heart rate, ECG, EEG, respiration rate, etc. Increasing health monitoring needs and self-awareness of the population motivates the need of developing a low energy and maximum lifetime network-based routing protocol. Medical application of the WBANs provides an efficient way for continuous human body monitoring. For example, the sensor monitors a sudden drop of glucose, and then, a signal can be sent to the actuator in order to start the injection of insulin, and we know this from Figures 11.3 and 11.7. WBAN can also be used to offer assistance to the disabled. A paraplegic can be equipped with sensors determining the position of the legs or with sensors attached to the nerves. In addition, actuators positioned

---

Corresponding author: aradhanabehura@gmail.com
†*Corresponding author*: shibanisahu.3g@gmail.com
‡*Corresponding author*: kabatmanas@gmail.com

Sachi Nandan Mohanty, Jyotir Moy Chatterjee, Monika Mangla, Suneeta Satpathy and Sirisha Potluri (eds.) Machine Learning Approach for Cloud Data Analytics in IoT, (273–306) © 2021 Scrivener Publishing LLC

on the legs can stimulate the muscles. Interaction between the data from the sensors and the actuators makes it possible to restore the ability to move.

Keywords: Cloud computing, machine learning, Wireless Body Area Networks (WBANs), dual sink

11.1   Introduction

When the internet was in its infancy the word 'cloud' was used as a metaphor to describe how the complex telephone networks connected. Now, many people and organizations refer to it as 'THE cloud' but it's not a single entity, and it doesn't exist in just the one place. So, what exactly is it?
Cloud is a model of computing where servers, networks, storage, development tools, and even applications (apps) are enabled through the internet. Instead of organizations having to make major investments to buy equipment, train staff, and provide ongoing maintenance, some or all of these needs are handled by a cloud service provider.

There are five key characteristics of a cloud computing environment, as defined by the National Institute of Standards and Technology (NIST):

Internet Access
With a public cloud environment, users "plug into" the data and applications via an internet connection giving anytime, anywhere access.

Measured Service
Cloud is often pay-as-you-go, where you only pay for what you use. Think about how a utility company meters how much water, electricity, or gas is used and charges based on consumption. The cloud is the same.

On-Demand Self-Service
Services can be requested and provisioned quickly, without the need for manual setup and configuration.

Shared Resource Pooling
Cloud often uses the multi-tenancy model. This means a single application is shared among several users. So, rather than creating a copy of the application for each user, several users, or "tenants" can configure the application to their specific needs.

Rapid Elasticity
Cloud platforms are elastic. An organization can scale its resource usage levels up or down quickly and easily as needs change.

Wireless Body Area Networks (WBANs) are WSNs which are designed to interconnect the bio-sensor or actuators and the human body. An important example is aid for the visually impaired. An artificial retina, consisting of a matrix of micro sensors, can be implanted into the eye beneath the surface of the retina. The artificial retina translates the electrical impulses into neurological signals. WBAN can also be found in the domain of public safety where the data is used by firefighters, policemen, or in a military environment. The WBAN monitors, for example, the level of toxics in the air, and warns the firefighters or soldiers if a life-threatening level is detected. The introduction of a WBAN further enables to tune more effectively the training schedules of professional athletes. All these fields are able to manoeuvre WBAN effectively as it requires a low-power consumption because of limited capacity of the battery of each node, and also it requires low latency and a high reliability of communication.

How can a patient able to know its disease and he can take the help of a physician if he stays in another country. This mechanism also helps his time and space. Figure 11.1 introduces about the architecture and message transmission of diseases and describes about the dual sink used in the human body. By considering this, after all, current times as well people adjust it at everyday life occupations of them. Wireless sensors nodes those are embed or wearable makes WBAN inside human body on the basis of QoS (Quality of Service). The independent work of sensors to

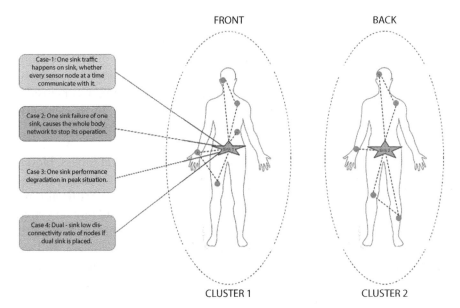

Figure 11.1 Clustering process used in the body for data transmission [1].

sense different human structural information is communicated through wirelessly by outside server for medical purpose [1]. Physical elements of body are observed utilizing sensors that are rate of respiratory, rate of heartbeat, blood pressure, movement of body, levels of glucose, temperature of body, and so on. These assembled body elements, one of two like short level post refined or fresh representatives, are wirelessly sent toward base/sink station for other inspection as well as refining [2, 3]. States of human body are continuously observed through the sensor nodes as well as sensing information is examined for optimal measure. Whether some element(s) are over standard (threshold) span, there is capability of sensors for sending an alert signal [4]. Thus, here, we study dual sink technique utilizing clustering inside body area network (DSCB). This is very important at improving duration of network with effectively using nodes battery time duration. Additionally, connection of nodes toward forward nodes or sink is made certain as utilizing both sink nodes. Inside this protocol, we analyzed the use of that dual sink accompanied by clustering technique. Utilizing clustering technique stables the load of network at sink nodes. At most, nodes opposed to equal cluster transmit sensed information of them as well as another data toward inherent committed sink node that is named by cluster head (CH). It ignores the traffic at one sink by comparing toward sole sink WBANs. By utilizing dual sink aids for keeping relatedness of nodes connected toward arms as well as legs of human too. By forwarding information, every sensor node chooses that finest relay nodes between individual adjacent. It depends on the distance measurement among the data transmission and sink node; then, this transmission rate is very essential for routing. Regarding to motive, calculation of cost function occurs that utilizes route, residual energy, as well as power of transmission. Calculation of SNR link occurs too as well as utilization occurs inside searching power of transmission required as sensor node. Those elements make sure adeptly use of nodes assets for improving capacity of network.

For evolution of WBAN occurs due to immense investigation. By taking an example, examination of individual's (outdoor) corporal fitness, blood pressure, and heart attack like disease occurs through utilizing sensor, cloud, and machine learning technique [5]. Sensors (retina artificial arm chips) [6–8] inside retina can be embed for helping one blind human being for seeing once more. By using WBAN, the sufferers accompanied by heart disease [9], asthma, diabetes, Alzheimer's and Parkinson problem, and so on can be performed [10]. Inside conventional wellness programs, there is a necessity for sufferers for staying inside hospital, yet WBAN confesses these sufferers for continuing through usual everyday schedule of them. It mitigates pharmaceutical work cost and also foundation cost. By using such technique, remote making of diseases detection occurs within sooner. Health observing structures are used for humans sanction for performing everyday ventures continuously that eventually improve life standard of them [11–13]. An important element for that common demand of WBAN is to monitor old humans' health. The growing inhabitants are increasing within whole universe, as well as each further day protection of health cost is enhancing. Above after 50 years, proportion of aged humans is suitably going to be acquiring doubly from 10% to 20% [8, 10, 14]. As well as ratio of this retired person to labors are decreasing inside westernmost earth. Most of the human being number is increasing also. Entirely, these elements are motivating to introduce the WBAN that helps the enhancement of living wellness program. M-health as well as telemedicine [6] get many benefits for this concept.

From Figure 11.1, we know about the clustering process used in the body for data transmission. For clustering purpose we can use C-means, K-means, and optimized clustering (e.g., K-PSO) algorithm. After all, in 2001, the WBANs have concentrated at various techniques according to studies. Those are hardware as well as devices technique, network layer technique, MAC layer technique, as well as security inside WBAN [15]. By putting another way, those areas stated over are main technology areas establishing WBAN technique as well as specify which is become an interesting topic for investigators. As a key parameter of WBANs at time of investigation, there is topic called routing technique. Such routing technologies inside WBANs must take various domains as such kind of networks configuration occurs inside human body. Firstly, whether sensor's power transmission is excessive which is harmful to human body as well as this absorbs excess battery power [16]. Secondly, as corporal classifications that sensor networks which can comfortably give rise to available space attenuation (path-loss/fading), noise, as well as interference, so bandwidth is changeable as well as control of transmission as per protocol's limitation. Thirdly, sensor nodes are connected with anatomy which is transferable, because of body's motion that effects within disjoint accompanied by further nodes. Fourthly, because of duration of battery limitation of sensor nodes' methodical use called more censorious problem [17]. Possibility may occur or not for sending signals whether sensor node dries up of battery power [18].

Because of resources limitation (processing power, memory, as well as battery power), low transmission reach, as well as path-loss, one well-organized energy routing protocol is required for maintenance of WBAN [19]. Various sensor nodes are located in multiple places of a human body. The movable human structure leads to comparative variation of place can happen inside sensor nodes. By taking an example, also movable human body leads to disjoint between nodes as well as sink can happen. It gives rise to large fall rate of packet. Stable Increased-throughput Multi-hop Protocol for Link Efficiency inside WBANs (SIMPLE) is one of multi-hop routing protocol [20]. By achieving efficient energy as well as high duration of network, this utilizes route as well as residual energy elements to choose the afterward hop. Even so, by using one sink, that disjoints problem abides equal. Inside Distance Aware Relaying Energy (DARE)–efficient routing protocol, sufferers inside the hospital unit are observed for various anatomical elements [21]. It utilizes mobile sink node that located in various place of a unit. By mitigating consumption of energy, one on-body relay node located at chest of sufferer is utilized for receiving information against further nodes as well as passes on this toward sink. The on-body relay node has more energy by comparing with further sensor nodes. While locating of sink does not inside interior of human anatomy, remote nodes absorb higher energy with comparing toward neighbor nodes toward sink. Earlier classification statements give one terrible requirement to routing protocols of further traditional WSNs. For performing systematic routing inside WBANs, this should touch censorious operative needs. Those are duration of network addition, energy efficiency, classifications of anatomy, as well as management of position adjustment. Generally, duration of network addition should be regarded incorporating those classifications of anatomy for balanced performance as well as warranty of productive WBAN control. Additionally, WBANs' integration is accompanied by cloud computing shows within starting of recent cost effectual as well as data operated structure. It aids to boost this implicit hospital topic within future. WBAN's policies found at cloud technique possesses more edges like improved efficiency, larger performances, as well as utilities and greater reliability, and even so, this will be quite inside its advance phase as well as might possess various oppositions as well as practical problems [22]. Now, duplicate medicines are available in the market which is dangerous for health of a people. So, IoT-based apps are available in mobile phone. By using mobile phone app, we can predict which medicine is dangerous for our health [28].

11.2   Survey on Architectural WBAN

The WBAN architectural model is classified into four surfaces [7] as in Figure 11.2. The first surface (Surface 1) called BAN surface combines various wireless sensor nodes employing within one restricted physiographic region, so making one Wireless Personal Area Network (WPAN).

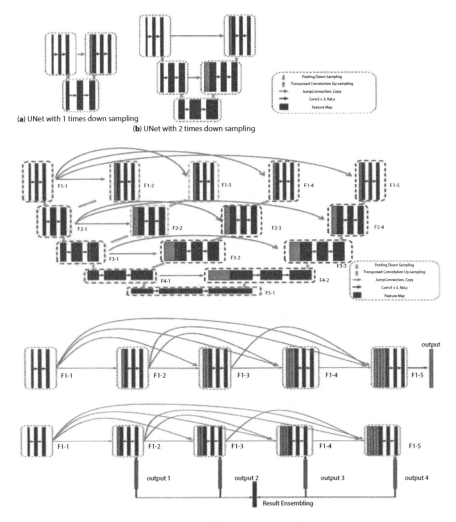

Figure 11.2 Image segmentation using UNet architecture [2, 18].

It depends upon owned style by positioning sensor nodes at human anatomy within mode of wearable sensors stitched inside fabrics, tiny marks (on-anatomy sensor), else placed inside anatomy of human (inside anatomy sensor). Human anatomy is constantly sensed by those sensors by wanted elements as well as sends this toward one outer server directed toward another study. Nodes possess ability of local processing previously transference that is on demand basis. An upper surface one of two locally sends information gathered with the help of sensor nodes else this relays toward median coordinator named sink [23].

Signal-to-noise ratio (SNR), receiver noise figure (RNF), as well as body path-loss (BPL) are three important components that put on sensor node's power of transmission. SNR based upon standard of transmission link. RNF component is based on gadget. Different devices give different results by it. This receiver affects BPL within utilization as well as radio-activity system [24, 25]. Various customer interactivities with gadgets on Surface 2 are there (interactivity surface customer) that importantly perform like access point (AP). The sensor nodes sense information which is sent toward treated server like pharmaceutical server located on hospital by such surface. With the basis of utilized wireless transmission protocol, Surface 2 holds various gadgets like smart phones or PDAs which are based on Bluetooth. Those gadgets gain as well as send information toward Surface 3. Due to observing of populous, by one AP equips various quarters inside home that is also attached with one wired else wireless network such as Wi-Fi [12].

Surface 3 carries decision measuring unit (DMU). This attaches with back end pharmaceutical server located inside hospital by the World Wide Web. This consequently acts every main tasks of computation. The major task of DMU is for collecting information, filtering as well as analyzing this to make decision. Surface 4 is the end surface of such architecture is called Surface 4. This supplies medical management utilities toward staffs with monitoring. The processed information with the help of DMU is communicated with remote pharmaceutical server. Inside hospital, it locates server, at which physician treated build correct conclusions at gained data. Such surface provides importantly dual various tasks called medical management services as well as urgent services.

11.3   Suggested Strategies

11.3.1   System Overview

By indicating Figure 11.1, there is DSBC routing protocol inside the research paper. The expanding duration of network focuses on DSBC protocol, enlarging throughput as well as association. By achieving those targets it uses clustering topic. Every cluster possesses a predetermined as well as attached CH that performs like sink node due to cluster subscribers of them. CH gains information against cluster subscribers of them and collects as well as sends this toward neighbor entry. By utilizing both sink nodes, it provides straight association toward changeable nodes that attached with hands else foots. As well as, this stabilizes burden at a sink node. Afterward, to sense information, every node sends this toward sink node with straightly else by sender node. Sender node uses cost function (CF) for selection. It is calculated for every nearer node that calculates CF that is depended upon path from sink node, power of transmission, as well as residual energy. Utilizing SNR as well as link standard is inspected too. Least CF of nearer node is chosen for sender.

11.3.2   Motivation

What we talk about in literature review, such larger part of suggested strategies utilize a sink node that gains information sensing from sensor nodes as well as sends this toward end server afterward accumulation. Moreover, nearly without protocol inside, WBAN utilizes clustering technology. For this cause, few issues appear that does not possess awareness like:

- At first, there are many possibilities of traffic phenomenon on sink node while every sensor nodes forward information at the same time, mostly on the condition of that censorious information.
- Secondly, WBAN's negligence of one sink node shows within absolute negligence while sink performs like the main hub.
- Thirdly, degradation of action on sink node occurs while several sensor nodes forward information on time that shows for short transport ratio.
- Fourth, to maximize anatomy description, requirement of many sensor nodes occurs as well as whether a cluster proposal is utilized that may generate burden at one sink node.
- Fifth, LOS transmission is needed within several plots that cannot be attained while anatomy is within movement.

Consequently, a routing strategy is presented by us known as DSCB that controls above-named lacks inside WBANs. Inside DSCB protocol, path-loss consequences reduction, load of network leveling, as well as achievement of LOS transmission occurs. Achievement of edges occurs accompanied by using clustering technology as well as formation of both sink nodes at human body.

11.3.3   DSCB Protocol

The suggested routing strategy is presented by us in such part known as Dual Sink Software Defined Networking proposal utilizing clustering inside BAN (DSCB) that improves WBAN's execution as applying clustering strategy between both sinks.

11.3.3.1   Network Topology

DSCB place both the sinks nodes which are called S1 and S2 between 10 sensor nodes at human anatomy. Sink nodes S1 and S2 are dissimilar with further distributed sensors at anatomy. The sink nodes possess superior assets by comparing with further sensor nodes like cell power, transmission power, and memory. Distribution of four sensor nodes occurs at anterior part of human anatomy accompanied by S1 like CH of them as well as four sensor nodes at behind of human anatomy accompanied by S2 like CH of them. A node is located at right hand's anterior part when a node is located at behind of left hand. The waist locates S1 as well as Lumbar locates S2. With the movable part, these nodes which connected toward hands are attached to one of two of sink nodes utilizing LOS transmission. Nodes 1 to 4 as well as, perhaps, 5 united by S1 build cluster 1 at which nodes 6 to 9 as well as feasibly node 10 united by S2 build cluster 2. Whether sensing of censorious information occurs, it is forwarded straightly toward associated CH, nevertheless whether information is not censorious and this is going to chase multi-hop transmission afterward choosing one sender node between nearer nodes. Figure 11.3 shows the suggested DSCB protocol's topology.

11.3.3.2   Starting Stage

Inside such stage [26], two sink nodes (S1 as well as S2) telecasts packets, i.e., "Hello" that carry IDs as well as places of them. On acceptance, every sensor node transmits "Reply" information that carries IDs, place, as well as residual energy. With such procedure, every node plus two sink nodes gain data regarding every further node. To find nearer nodes, this aids.

11.3.3.3   Cluster Evolution

Afterward, recognition of nearer is occurred then upcoming procedure is cluster evolution that occurs by data given before within "Hello" as well as "Reply" texts interchanged. Two sinks are known by CHs as individual clusters of them. CHs give to receive sensed information from sensors, combine, as well as forward this toward neighbor AP. Time periods location

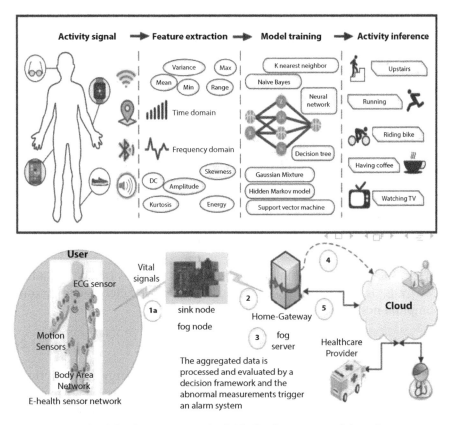

Figure 11.3 Role of cloud computing in the field of body area network [9, 20].

follows cluster evolution toward every cluster participants, occurred with the help of CHs utilizing TDMA protocol.

11.3.3.4   Sensed Information Stage

Activation of sensor nodes occurs just within assigned time period of them or sensor nodes possess snooze way. As sensor node turns agile, this initializes to sense information. That information sensing is inspected for cruciality firstly. If it is critical, it is sent directly to sink node; else, it is sent to sink node via multi-hop.

11.3.3.5   Choice of Forwarder Stage [26, 27]

DSCB calculates sender node with the help of link's SNR, Distance (di) in distinction to sink, Residual energy (E_{Rn}) as well as Transmission power (T_p).

The estimation of threshold considering SNR possesses default inside DSCB protocol that is same with "1". Whether one sensor node does sense little information as well as which is not censorious, this chooses one node in distinction to nearby table of that. After that, numerous hops to sink are added up for selecting nearby direct toward sink. Whether numerous hops possess zero, such node is regarded by straightly attached toward sink as well as so this transmission occurs straightly with no sending node with among. Or SNR of link is computed whether less than 1, for becoming forwarder, it rejects such node as well as it records data of itself. Whether the SNR of link is greater than 1 after that node's function of cost (FC) be about is computed. For calculating sensor node's residual energy (E_{Rn}), this equation is used by us:

$$E_{Rn} = E_{In} - E_{Cn} \qquad (11.1)$$

At which n indicate numerous nodes utilized, E_{Rn} is called as residual energy, E_{In} is called as initial energy as well as E_{Cn} is called as energy consumption node that computes the equation as below.

$$E_{Cn} = E_{Tr} + E_{Re} + E_{Cty} \qquad (11.2)$$

At which E_{Tr} as well as E_{Re} are accordingly, the energy consumption's quantity with the help of node transceiver radio at the time of information's transmission as well as reception as well as E_{Cty} is called as consumption of energy occurred with the help of electronic circuitry of node. The node n_j^i energy absorbs at the time of setup period P_{su}, beginning on time 0 as well as consumption of energy occurred in every round $E_{Rnd\,j}^i$ (ti) is

$$E_{Rnd\,j}^i(ti) = \int_{ti}^{ti+P_{su}} E_{Cn_j}^i(t)\,dt \qquad (11.3)$$

$$= \int_{ti}^{ti+P_{su}} \left(E_{Tr_j}^i(t) + E_{Re_j}^i(t) + E_{Cty_j}^i(t) \right) dt \qquad (11.4)$$

At which $E_{Rnd\,j}^i$ = energy needed with the help of node n_j^i at time of period P_{su} also in every cycle.

For finding energy value needed considering the transmission as well as reception, we use these equations:

$$E_{Tr}(k,di) = E_{Tr\text{-}Cty} * k + E_{Tr\text{-}am}(k, di) \qquad (11.5)$$

$$E_{Tr}(k, di) = E_{Tr-Cty} * k + \epsilon_{am} k di^2 \qquad (11.6)$$

$$E_{Re}(k) = E_{Re-Cty} * k \qquad (11.7)$$

At which "di" = entire distance among receiver Re as well as transmitter Tr. E_{Re} as well as E_{Tr} = consumption of energy fares for every packet with help of receiver as well as transmitter, accordingly. Likewise, E_{Re-Cty} as well as E_{Tr-Cty} = consumption of energy estimates for every bit considering receiver as well as transmitter circuitries of electronics accordingly. k = length of packet at which ϵ_{am} = radio amplifier kind. Loss of co-efficient = l_o that distinct inside human anatomy by comparing with earthly networks; thus, Equation (11.6) is written as l_o as below:

$$E_{Tr}(k, di, l_o) = E_{Tr-Cty} k + \epsilon_{am} n k di^{lo} \qquad (11.8)$$

$$P_n.T = \frac{SNR}{\beta} \qquad (11.9)$$

At which $P_n.T$ = power of transmission as wireless signal as well as β = Path-loss parameter. For finding entire distance di among some sensor node as well as nearby sensor node or sink node of itself, below equation is used:

$$di(n, D_{ts}) = \sqrt{\left(P_n - P_{D_{ts}}\right)^2 + \left(Q_n - Q_{D_{ts}}\right)^2} \qquad (11.10)$$

$$F_n.C = \frac{di}{E_{Rn} * P_n.T} \qquad (11.11)$$

At which $F_n.C$ is function of cost of some node. Afterward computation of nearby F.C, it possesses noted as well as succeeding nearest F.C do computed. One nearer node within minimal F.C does choose like forwarder (Figure 11.4).

11.3.3.6 Energy Consumption as Well as Routing Stage

An important edge with utilizing both sink nodes does which sink's more nodes undergo straight transmission span. Packet data goes sprightly bring of short delay at utilizing single-hop transmission. Inside DSCB, straight transmission happens within various instances. For few instances, this protocol chooses sender node considering routing motive. Consumption of

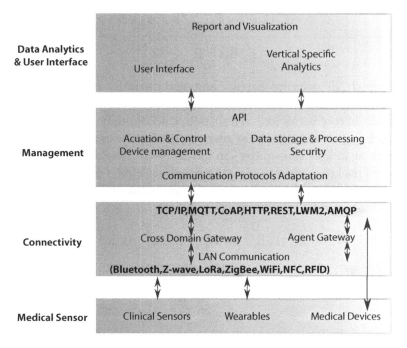

Figure 11.4 Tier health IoT architecture [27].

energy with the help of sensor nodes inside multi-hop transmission indicates [18]:

$$E_{Tr-Mu\ (k,di)} = n^*(E_{Cty} + E_{am})^*k^*L_{EN} \qquad (11.12)$$

$$E_{Re\ -Mu\ (k)} = (n\text{-}1)^*(E_{Cty} + E_{am})^*k \qquad (11.13)$$

$$E_{Tot-\ Mu} = E_{Tr\text{-}M} + E_{Re\text{-}Mu} \qquad (11.14)$$

At which, E_{Tr-Mu} as well as $E_{Re\ -Mu}$ represent energy needed considering transmission as well as reception with help of transmitter as well as receiver accordingly inside multi-hop transmission. k = bits dimensions, di = distance among sink node as well as sensor nodes, E_{Cty} = energy needed considering the transmitters as well as receiver's electronic circuit, E_{am} = for amplifying k numerous bits toward distance di for this energy needed, n = numerous nodes, and L_{EN} = energy loss at a time of communication by medium of transmission. Straight communication's consumption of energy is [5]:

$$E_{Tr-di\,(k,di)} = (E_{Cty} + E_{am})^*k^*L_E \qquad (11.15)$$

$$E_{Tot-di} = E_{Tr-di} \qquad (11.16)$$

At which $E_{Tr-di\,(k,di)}$ = transmission energy of straight transmission.

11.4   CNN-Based Image Segmentation (UNet Model)

Medical image segmentation is the process of automatic or semi-automatic detection of boundaries within a 2D or 3D image in internet-of-medical-things (IoTM) domain. The main difficulty of medical image segmentation is the high variability in medical images. For example, CT images contain a large amount of noise and complex boundaries. Here, we discuss an adaptive fully dense (AFD) neural network for CT image segmentation. By adding the horizontal connections in UNet structure, it can extract various features from all layers adaptively. It uses ensemble training for the output to extract more edge information in the multiple rounds training. To solve complex and large medical image data, it needs many times of up and down sampling process to extract the semantic information features of different regions. Because it is difficult to get the global information from small-scale network, it is often underfitting. Shared encoder structure to combine multiple layers of the UNet is a common way; however, even multiple layers are integrated in a same network structure, the different layers of decoder structure keep independent that cannot improve the usage of the shallow layers of features for network. From Figure 11.2, we know about the architecture of UNet briefly.

At starting, for each register node, BS records each detecting points creates cipher key. In add-on, BS records every confirm utilizers and then generates cipher keys. By keeping identification of detector node with transmitting time-stamp TS, when a sensor node registers with the base station (BS), it stores the record of sensor nodes. To give the additional safety and reliability toward several threads, BS transmits register data. All sensor nodes exist in the network will reply after getting the transmitted message from the BS, by terminating their acknowledgements. In return, this will not forward acknowledgement to BS if a sensor node will not get any message. The BS instantly retransmits the information again to the all the silent nodes. For suggested method accepted that BS is not going to keep any track. To observe patient's physiological data and to trace and detect patients to manage drug administration and doctor's sensor networks are associated in modern health care centers. Different uses are glucose level detectors, organ scanning, general health monitoring, and cancer detection. Inside a human body implanting wireless biomedical sensors is promising though great challenges such as ultra-safety, security, and minimal maintainability of the system are associated.

In this wireless networking for carrying out saturated detecting, a WSN is having many detecting points joined between them, which is utilized in varieties of uses like health and environmental monitoring, surveillance, and security. Permitting, detect, reply to situation in the natural surroundings, detector networking is detecting, computing, and communicating infrastructure and in our daily life. The detectors also range in less passive micro detectors such as "smart dust" as higher range like weather sensing. Their computing resources are totally separate like internet system, which appears the device and application possessed nature of these systems. A very essential way of wireless sensor network enters as for the similar set of events and it has various sensors causing sensing data. For conventional ad hoc networks as various algorithm, protocol has been given, which are not matched in special characteristic. Detector networking is a recent type of wireless networks and such as cellular networks, and MANETs are entirely separated from conventional networks. Like this conventional network, to enhance the high bandwidth efficiency and QoS, the tasks management, routing, and mobility management is executed. Under a high-level mobility situation, these networks perform superior throughput or delay characteristics.

As the battery packs can be changed as required, energy consumption is different concerned matter. Therefore, detector networks are created several points that are drawn for unaccompanied work. In MANETs and cellular networks, congestion is of statistical as compared to the multimedia biased message. The data rate is such that it is so less to 1–100 kb/sec. Aims are extending lifetime of networking system unlike conventional networks that ignore connectivity degradation through aggressive energy management as batteries cannot generally changed for operations in unfriendly or interior area. Distribution of message is primarily one directional in sensor networks from sensor points to sink point.

Enabling differences in between WSN and conventional wireless networks given below are some points of WSNs:

- Detecting point is compactly placed.
- Detecting point is liable to failures.
- Detecting point is restricted with memory, energy, and computing power.

- The topology of a sensor network can be changed frequently.
- Detecting point in WSN is of various orders such as magnitude is greater as compared to points in another conventional Wi-Fi network.
- Where maximum ad hoc networks communicate, data mainly utilize a broadcast communication prototype.
- Node is distributed in a two-dimensional space and cannot be recharged after deployment.
- Nodes are quasi-stationary.
- These are fully depending on communication interval where nodes broadcast in same ranges.
- Nodes based decisions on local information.
- It can be described utilizing GPS, signal strength or direction where nodes are location-aware.
- The energy consumption among nodes is unbalanced. Sensor network do not make any assumptions about:
    - The network length and thickness.
    - The distribution of the nodes.
    - Separation of energy consumption with in nodes.
    - Synchronization of the network.

This model and said assumptions are correct for several real networks. Sensor nodes gather their local information and transmit them to the data center in a sensor network. Regularly, the message is location-dependent, so the nodes have knowledge of their own position through GPS or by different means. Whereas, density is not known. Forwarding the image wavelet coefficients by priority is the fundamental knowledge of the suggested technique. Preserve efficiency using progressive image forwarding attempts by this technique. To organize data packages of many priorities, the wavelet image compression gives at the source. Considering picture dimension is M × N pixels and picture is degraded into r resolution level, then the 2D-DWT is constantly put to r-1 levels. Likewise, data packet priority can be carried out. To obtain each and every priority level at the descend it is optional, only for the primary level 0 which is an important portion of the image energy. We avail an image request-based scenario in this approach. Having a multiple hop transmission, the plea is set up by the main station and then transferred through the in-between nodes. In the request communication procedure, every sensor node complicated having in its memory each request parameters. The very much essential request parameters are QoI (quality of image) which hold priority levels PL and Pc, compression ratio, PSNR, and rate. When achieving a particular processing level, the requested parameters may be gained, based on the wireless implementations.

11.5   Emerging Trends in IoT Healthcare

The emerging trends in cloud computing, mobile applications, and wearable devices facilitate IoT's role for making healthcare a smart and personalized system. Various medical devices, sensors, and diagnostic and imaging devices can be viewed as smart devices or objects constituting a core part of the IoT.

Challenges
- Constrained data processing methods
- Unique identity
- Dynamic and self-adapting self-configuring interoperability
- Integrated into information network

Constrained Data Processing Method
The process of converting raw data using medium-like manual or automatic tools into meaningful output information is as follows:

- Conversion is converting data to another format.
- Validation is ensuring that supplied data is clean, correct and useful.
- Sorting is arranging items in some sequence and/or in different sets.
- Aggregation is combining multiple pieces of data.
- Analysis is the collection, organization, analysis, interpretation, and presentation of data.
- Reporting is list detail or summary data or computed information.
- Presentation data is helpful in taking decisions.
- Characteristics of Unique Identity

Figure 11.3 tells about the fog server. The aggregated data is processed and evaluated by a decision framework and the abnormal measurements trigger an alarm system. IoT schemes have intelligent crossing points which familiarize grounded on the framework. The devices of IoT interfaces permit operators to inquiry about the strategies, display their position, and control them remotely, in connotation with configuration, control, and data management setup. IoT has increased tremendous fame in medical because of its capacity to have applications for which the administrations can be conveyed to shoppers quickly at insignificant expense. An imperative application is the utilization of IoT and cloud innovations to help specialists in giving increasingly successful demonstrative procedures. Specifically, here, we examine electrocardiogram (ECG) information investigation utilizing IoT and the cloud. The slender improvement of Internet availability and its openness from any gadget whenever has made Internet of Things an appealing alternative for creating well-being observing frameworks. ECG information examination and observing comprise a situation that normally appropriates into such situation. ECG represents the important appearance of the contractile action of myocardium of the heart. Such action conveys an exact wave that is reiterated after some phase and that addresses the heart rate. The examination of the condition of the ECG signal is a crucial problem and is the most broadly perceived procedure to deal with distinguish coronary ailment. IoT advancements permit the remote checking of a patient's heart rate, information examination in immaterial time, the notice of therapeutic guide workforce, and experts should these data reveal possibly unsafe situations [1]. Thus, a patient in threat can be checked deprived of embarking to a crisis center for ECG signal examination. Meanwhile, experts and crisis treatment can immediately be informed with respect to cases that require their thought.

- Dynamic and Self-Adapting
  IoT schemes have intelligent crossing points which familiarize grounded on the framework. By taking the help of surveillance camera which can adjust their approaches depends on whether it is night or day. Camera could switch from lower resolution to higher resolution approaches.

IoT devices are to manage themselves, both in terms of their software/hardware configuration and their resource utilization:

1. Energy
2. Communication
3. Bandwidth
4. Medium access

- Self-Configuring
  IoT-based instruments have self-configuring proficiency which permitting a huge number of plans to work collectively

to give convinced functionality. These types of devices have capability to construct themselves, to arrange the networking, and then to fetch newest software renovations with minimal or customer intervention. Self-configuration mainly contains of the activities of neighbor and the discovery of services, organization of network and provisioning of resources.

- Interoperability
  IoT devices provision a large number of communication protocols which are interoperable and can interconnect with the other smart IoT instruments and also takes the help of the infrastructure.

- Integrated Into Information Network
  In human services space, WBAN has happened as a noticeable innovation which is equipped for giving better strategies for ongoing patient well-being checking at medical clinics, refuges and even at their homes. As of late, WBAN has increased incredible intrigue and demonstrated a standout among the most investigated innovations by human services offices on account of its essential job and wide scope of utilization in clinical sciences. WBAN includes correspondence between little sensor hubs with every now and again evolving condition, consequently bunches of issues still should be tended to. A portion of the serious issues are physical layer issues, interoperability and versatility issue, dependability, asset the executives, ease of use, energy utilization, and QoS issues. This exploration paper incorporates an extensive overview of late patterns in WBAN look into, gives forthcoming answers for some serious issues utilizing intellectual methodology, and a proposed idea of cognitive radio (CR)–based WBAN engineering. Hence, a traditional WBAN engineering can be ad-libbed to a versatile, increasingly dependable and proficient WBAN framework utilizing cognitive-based methodology. WBAN is a remote systems administration innovation, in view of radio frequency (RF) that interconnects various little hubs with sensor or actuator capacities. These hubs work in close region to, on or couple of cm inside a human body, to help different restorative region and non-medicinal territory applications [1]. WBAN innovation is profoundly refreshing in the field of medicinal science and human social insurance [2–5]. Additionally, huge commitment is conveyed in the field of Biomedical and

other logical regions [6]. Also, its applications are broad in non-restorative territories like purchaser gadgets and individual diversion. A great deal of research work is experiencing on WBANs. The primary issues concentrated upon are size of system, result precision, hub thickness, control supply, versatility, information rate, vitality utilization, QoS, and real-time correspondence. WBAN hubs use scaled down batteries because of their little size. Thus, the system must work and perform in a power productive way with the goal that the existence term of intensity sources can be augmented. A large portion of the work in this specific space has been on advancement of better MAC conventions for vitality effective preparing. By and by, there are two distinct methodologies of MAC convention planning for sensor systems. Initial one is contention-based MAC convention plan. Case of this sort of MAC convention is Carrier Sense Multiple Access–Collision Avoidance (CSMA/CA). This structure has their hubs needs for channel access before transmitting information. The advantages of CSMA/CA-based conventions incorporate no time synchronization limitations, simple flexibility to arrange varieties, and versatility. The other methodology is schedule-based MAC convention. Case of this sort of convention is a TDMA based, in which time opened access to the channel is given. Henceforth, various clients get isolated availabilities for information transmission. These openings can be of fixed or variable length. Schedule vacancy controller (TSC) is utilized for giving availabilities. The advantages of this methodology are diminished inactive tuning in, over heading, and impact. TDMA-based methodology is very utilized in vitality effective MAC convention [21]. A tale approach of heartbeat fueled the MAC convention is given by [26]. This convention is TDMA-based and utilized for body sensor systems (BSNs). The work incorporates use of heart beat mood to perform time synchronization and consequently gives a vitality proficient MAC layer by evading power utilization related with time synchronization reference point transmission. Utilizing a robot to revive batteries and exchange information can drastically build the life expectancy of a remote sensor arrange. In this, the way of the robot is constrained by waypoints, and the districts where every sensor can be adjusted are featured. We utilize a blend of angle drop and a "numerous voyaging sales rep issue" look calculation to move the waypoints toward districts where sensor hubs can be revived while guaranteeing waypoints remain near one another. An auxiliary well-being remote sensor arrange (WSN) should keep going for quite a long time, yet conventional dispensable batteries cannot continue such a system. Energy is the significant obstruction to supportability of WSNs. Most vitality is devoured by (i) remote transmissions of saw information, and (ii) long-remove multi-jump transmissions from the source sensors to the sink. This paper investigates how to misuse developing remote power exchange innovation by utilizing automated unmanned vehicles (UVs) to support the WSNs. These UVs slice information transmissions from long to short-separations, gather detected data, and recharge WSN's vitality.

11.6   Tier Health IoT Model

The protocol is intended to use as various types of communication smart protocol standards which required to proliferation the flexibility as well as interoperability of the smart system; then, it provides various types of services such as fusion, local storage data aggregation, filtering, actuation, compression, and analysis, and the model of smart e-health protocol has cast-off for fog computing prototype which deals with a hierarchical structural design and an additional reactive scheme. This acts as an intermediate module between the end-users and cloud system which accomplish the advantages by giving priority-based facilities. Figure 11.4 describes about the various types of medical sensor, connectivity, data storage, device management, data analytics, and user interface. Figure 11.5 tells about the modern e-health protocols.

11.7   Role of IoT in Big Data Analytics

Big data platform permits the incorporation and keeping of large volume and variety of information related to healthcare. Figure 11.6 describes about role of IoT in big data analytics.

This can ultimately provide the following:

- Highly configurable information incorporation alerts for real-time disease suffering engagement information customization

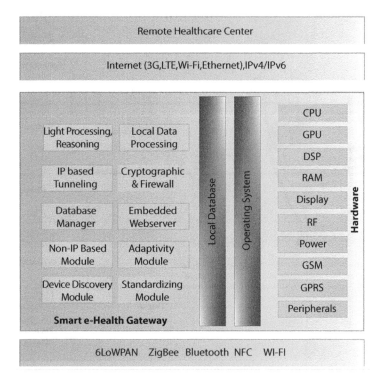

Figure 11.5 Modern e-health protocol [27].

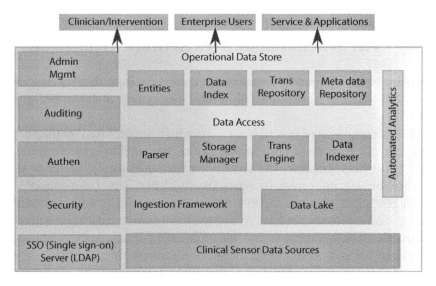

Figure 11.6 Role of IoT and big data in healthcare center [27].

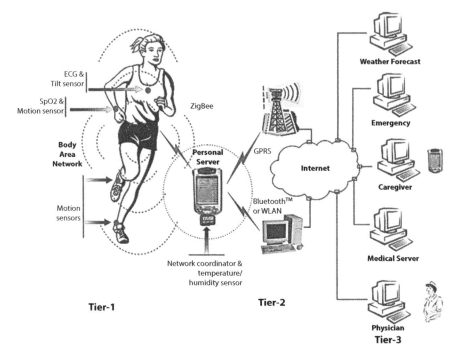

Figure 11.7 WBAN three-tier architecture [21].

by taking the help of parsers; in addition, this system delivers automated message analytics and propels data to patients.

11.8 Tier Wireless Body Area Network Architecture

By using cloud computing, a patient can communicate with physician and the WBAN architecture is basically a three-tier system as shown in Figure 11.7 [21].

This is composed of several biosensors which are deployed on the body. The first tier consists of body sensor nodes, the wireless communication system (devices) becomes the second tier, and the medical center or the application specific center becomes the third tier. Tier 1 consists of an intelligent node which is capable of sensing, processing, and communicating. Some sensors used are ECG sensor for monitoring heart activity, EMB (electromyography) sensor for monitoring muscle activity, consists of a blood pressure sensor and a tilt sensor for monitoring, and many other sensor. Once we collect the data of required parameters from the biosensors, it is transmitted to personal digital assistants (PDAs). Usually, the

PDAs are within the transmission range of the biosensors. The PDA then transmits the data to Tier 2 which can be IEEE 802.15.6 (for implantable nodes), IEEE 802.15.4 (ZigBee), IEEE 802.11 (Wi-Fi), or IEEE 802.15.1 (Bluetooth), etc. In Tier 2, there is an interface in the WBAN sensor nodes through Zigbee or Bluetooth, ZigBee, IEEE 802, and others like Ultra-Wideband (UWB) technology, Zarlink technology, and ANT protocol (Adaptive Network Topology). Wi-Fi cannot provide timing guarantees on packet delivery, while beacon-enabled ZigBee can provide real-time communication by supporting GTS. Zigbee slow rate can be considered as a shortcoming. It is connected with the medical server through mobile telephone networks (2G, GPRS, and 3G) or WLANs—Internet. Its functions are as follows:

- Registers type and number sensor node.
- Manages the network channel sharing, time synchronization, and processing data and send data to the BS.

Next, in Tier 3, we have a set of end points (PDAs) which are linked to a mega database system where the application specific data is analyzed by the specialists in the domain. The communication in WBAN takes place via the sensor nodes. The energy consumed by these nodes tends to finish over a certain period of time; it then becomes of prime importance to restore or replace the batteries of these sensor nodes. In Tier 3, the major functions include the following:

- To authenticate users;
- To save patient data into medical records;
- To analyze the data;
- To recognize serious health cases in order to contact emergency care givers;
- To forward new instruction to user.

Therefore, we need a system which provides us with low energy consumption and maximum network lifetime. Clustering of the nodes is one such solution where the number of direct transmission from source to sink is more. Usually, the clustering approach is good for monitoring applications which require continuous sensor data stream. WBANs are emerging as a technology of great importance in the field of health-care, sports, military, and position tracking. It has a broader area of application because of its characteristics such as portability, real-time monitoring, low cost, and real-time feedback. Efficient data communication and limited energy resources are some of the major issues of WBANs. Despite the recent developments in communication technologies for WBANs, the reliability of packet transmission, especially for emergency and critical data transfer, remains a significant challenge. This may be that most of the existing techniques in WBAN use single-channel for data transmission with no intelligence. The cognitive bonded channel rovides high data rate for emergency and the demanding situation. WBAN consists of low-power sensor nodes where nodes are deployed on or inside the human body to the monitoring of various physiological parameters. It provides the daily activity of the patient and its health condition. WBAN is significantly used in medical applications and health care. In the medical online monitoring environment, WBAN provides low cost and flexibility to monitoring, patient, and medical professionals. Both healthcare and surveillance have been more modified with recent technological advances. Advances in electronics especially in communications technology and microelectronics are leading to more and more personal health monitoring and advanced healthcare products with a wide range of products that already available in our society. Various sensor applications and systems are developed with a wide range of features for heartbeats or temperature, proper insulin level, ECG, and for even wireless pacemakers. The introduction of advanced telecommunications technologies into the healthcare environment and the use of wireless communication solutions for healthcare products have led to increased user-friendliness and accessibility for users and health service providers. In the medical field, WBAN plays an important role to monitor patient health situations for early diagnoses. These sensors sense human body activity and send it to the cluster head or coordinator node. The cluster head is a high power node that collects information from neighboring nodes and sends it to the BS or doctor. Numbers of sensor nodes that can be implanted in the human body, each sensor performs its own functions such as fear detection, heartbeat, blood pressure, etc. In WBAN, some events need high data rate transmission, like in an emergency situation high data rate is required to send the patient health information to the monitoring unit. In wireless communication, CR is a transceiver which senses a frequency spectrum and is capable to concatenate free adjacent channel for high data rate. In CR, the PU, i.e., the primary user to transmit data, has the highest priority to use the channel. If PU is not using the channel and channel is free then it is allocated to the SU (secondary user). Many WBANs coexist, in which multiple WBANs communicate with medical staff for regular health monitoring. These WBANs consist of low-power sensor nodes which have a low data rate. They always rely on a single channel. Due to multiple adjacent WBANs and nearby IoT devices, the co-existence interference affects reliability and overall performance of the system. However, numerous challenges are present in WBANs and their reliability is affected by wireless sensor nodes with limited resources. Also, because of advent and advancement in sensor technology, low-power electronics, and low-power RF design have enabled the development of small, relatively inexpensive, and low-power sensors, called micro-sensors, which can be connected via a wireless network. These wireless micro-sensor networks represent a new paradigm for extracting data from the environment and enable the reliable monitoring of a variety of environments for applications that include surveillance, machine failure diagnosis, and chemical/biological detection. There are two main challenges while designing this kind of networks, namely, communication bandwidth and energy, which are significantly more limited in this kind of WBAN network as compared to any tethered network environment of the same above maintained constraint. These constraints require innovative design techniques to use the available bandwidth and energy efficiently. In order to design good protocols for wireless micro-sensor networks, it is important to understand the parameters that are relevant to the sensor applications. While there are many ways in which the properties of a sensor network protocol can be evaluated, we use the following metrics. They are as follows:

1. Ease of Deployment
   Sensor networks may contain hundreds or thousands of nodes, and they may need to be deployed in remote or dangerous environments, allowing users to extract information in ways that would not have been possible otherwise. This requires that nodes be able to communicate with each other even in the absence of an established network infrastructure and predefined node locations.
2. System Lifetime
   These networks should function for as long as possible. It may be inconvenient or impossible to recharge node batteries. Therefore, all aspects of the node, from the hardware to the protocols, must be designed to be extremely energy efficient.
3. Latency
   Data from sensor networks are typically time sensitive, so it is important to receive the data in a timely manner.
4. Quality
   The notion of "quality" in a micro-sensor network is very different than in traditional wireless data networks. For

sensor networks, the end user does not require all the data in the network because 1) the data from neighboring nodes are highly correlated, making the data redundant and 2) the end user cares about a higher-level description of events occurring in the environment being monitored. The quality of the network is, therefore, based on the quality of the aggregate data set, so protocols should be designed to optimize for the unique, application-specific quality of a sensor network.

It is well known that cloud computing has many potential advantages, and many enterprise applications and data are migrating to public or hybrid cloud. But regarding some business critical applications, the organizations, especially large enterprises, still would not move them to cloud. The market size of cloud computing shared is still far behind the one expected. From the consumer's perspective, cloud computing security concerns, especially data references and privacy protection issues, remain the primary inhibiter for adoption of cloud computing services.

➢ Cloud computing is the delivery of hosting services that are provided to a client over the network. It is a compilation of existing techniques and technologies packaged with a new infrastructure paradigm that offers scalability, elasticity, business agility, faster startup time, reduced management costs, and just-in-time availability of techniques.

Cloud Service Models

Deployment of cloud services are based on the services such as infrastructure as a service, software as a service, and platform as a service.

Cloud Delivery Models

➢ Hybrid cloud: This is a mixture of two or more clouds that have unique entities.
➢ Public cloud: It contains all resources generally inside a company and keeps a lot of sensitive information.
➢ Community cloud: Cloud infrastructure is shared by several clouds, i.e., collection of several clouds. It supports a specific community that has shared concerns.

Application of WBAN can categorized depending on the domain of application. In what follows, we present major WBAN domains of application [21] in Table 11.1.

Table 11.1 WBAN areas of application.

Application	Examples	QoS (Quality of Service) Requirements
Telemedicine	Remote health monitoring Emergency rescue Chronic diseases monitoring Prevention and detection of diseases Daily-life activity monitoring Post-surgery in-home recovery monitoring	Reliability Latency Security Power consumption
Rehabilitation	Daily life and rehabilitation	Reliability Latency Power consumption
Assisted living	Assisted living for elders Treatments of peoples at home	Reliability Latency Security
Biofeedback	User biofeedback activity	Reliability Power consumption

1. WBAN Application for Medical Treatment and Diagnosis
   There are myriad of possibilities where WBANs are useful for diagnosis or treatment of diseases. Many researchers have conducted research in this regard.
   • Remote Patient Monitoring
     Telemedicine and remote patient monitoring are the main applications of WBAN. Telemedicine means diagnosis and treatment of patients located at a remote location using information technology. WBAN has made it possible for delivery of certain healthcare services for patients at a distant location. Using telemedicine, more and more patients can be served. Body sensors collect signals from the body and transfer it to the distant physicians and doctors for processing. Doctors can use this information for health estimation for medical diagnosis and prescription. This will create a smart health care system. Daily-life activities of patients can be monitored to collect vital parameters from the human body.

- Rehabilitation
  Through rehabilitative treatment methods, patients can restore their normal functional capabilities. Proper rehabilitation measures and therapy can enable a person, who has experienced a stroke, to function independently. These patients are constantly monitored to maintain a correct motion pattern. The main application of WBAN in this area includes sensor diversification, data fusion, real-time feedback, and home-based rehabilitation health through devices that constantly monitor bodily activities. This will create awareness regarding certain physiological activities.
- Biofeedback
  Through WBAN, remote monitoring of human body can be done. The data collected by sensors can be accessed to gather valuable parameters from the body. Patients can look after and maintain their health through the mechanism of biofeedback like temperature analysis, blood pressure detection, ECG, etc. Biofeedback means maintaining and improving health through devices that constantly monitors bodily activities. This will create awareness regarding certain physiological activities.
- Assisted Living
  This helps in improving the quality of life. Assisted living technologies enable elderly and disabled people to be monitored at their individual homes. This will lower the healthcare costs. Through these devices and technologies, the condition of the health of the people can be estimated appropriately.

2. WBAN Application for Training Schedules of Professional Athletes
   WBAN further enables to tune more effectively the training schedules of professional athletes.
3. WBAN Application if Public Safety and Preventing Medical Accidents
   Approximately, 98,000 people die every year due to medical accidents caused by human error. Sensor network can maintain a log of previous medical accidents and can notify the occurrence of the same accident and thus can reduce many medical accidents.

4. WBAN Application for Safeguarding of Uniformed Personnel
   WBAN can be used by firefighters, policemen or in a military environment. The WBAN monitors the level of toxics in the air and warns the firefighters or soldiers if a life-threatening level is detected.
5. Application of WBAN in Consumer Electronics
   Next to purely medical applications, a WBAN can include appliances such as an MP3 player, head-mounted (computer) displays, microphone, camera, advanced human-computer interfaces such as a neural interface, gaming purposes, and virtual reality.

11.9 Conclusion

We discussed about WBAN; here, sensor nodes are connected with our body. If any trouble happens in our body, the messages are transferred to the physician and then the physician transfers the health related issue to the specialist through cloud system. Here, we already discussed how cloud computing, machine learning, and wireless sensor network play vital role in smart health care. We discussed a densely connected encoder-decoder structure that shares the coder and integrates the decoders of different depths. The output of multiple decoders is correlated by the densely connected structure. Furthermore, we discussed about an adaptive segmentation algorithm for shallow and deep features using the UNet structure. The horizontal and vertical comparison between the two data sets verified the advantages of the model in the segmentation of complex boundaries. Experiments demonstrated that the depth feature adaptive segmentation algorithm can effectively use the information of different depths and the segmentation results generated by different depth decoders and can learn the final segmentation results from them, thus improving the accuracy of image segmentation.

References

1. Haddad, O., Khalighi, M.A., Zvanovec, S., Adel, M., Channel characterization and modeling for optical wireless body-area networks. *IEEE Open J. Commun. Soc.*, *1*, 760–776, 2020.

2. Qureshi, K.N., Din, S., Jeon, G., Piccialli, F., Link quality and energy utilization based preferable next hop selection routing for wireless body area networks. *Comput. Commun.*, *149*, 382–392, 2020.

3. Shuai, M., Liu, B., Yu, N., Xiong, L., Wang, C., Efficient and privacy-preserving authentication scheme for wireless body area networks. *J. Inf. Secur. Appl.*, *52*, 102499, 2020.

4. Alzahrani, B.A., Irshad, A., Albeshri, A., Alsubhi, K., A provably secure and lightweight patient-healthcare authentication protocol in wireless body area networks. *Wireless Pers. Commun.*, 117, 1, 47–69, 2020.

5. Amjad, O., Bedeer, E., Ali, N.A., Ikki, S., Robust Energy Efficiency Optimization Algorithm for Health Monitoring System With Wireless Body Area Networks. *IEEE Commun. Lett.*, 24, 5, 1142–1145, 2020.

6. Raj, A.S. and Chinnadurai, M., Energy efficient routing algorithm in wireless body area networks for smart wearable patches. *Comput. Commun.*, *153*, 85–94, 2020.

7. Li, H.B., Takahashi, T., Toyoda, M., Mori, Y., Kohno, R., Wireless body area network combined with satellite communication for remote medical and healthcare applications. *Wireless Pers. Commun.*, 51, 697–709, 2009.

8. Yang, G., Wu, X.W., Li, Y., Ye, Q., Energy efficient protocol for routing and scheduling in wireless body area networks. *Wirel. Netw.*, 26, 2, 1265–1273, 2020.

9. Mehrani, M., Attarzadeh, I., Hosseinzadeh, M., Deep-learning based forecasting sampling frequency of biosensors in wireless body area networks. *J. Intell. Fuzzy Syst.*, (Preprint), 1–33, 2020.

10. Hang, S. and Xi, Z., Design and Analysis of a Multi-channel Cognitive MAC Protocol for Dynamic Access Spectrum Networks, in: *Proceedings of the IEEE Military Communications Conference (MILCOM 2008)*, San Diego, CA, USA, 16–19 November 2008, pp. 1–7.

11. Javaid, N., Abbas, Z., Fareed, M.S., Khan, Z.A., Alrajeh, N., M-ATTEMPT: a new energy-efficient routing protocol for wireless body area sensor networks. *Proc. Comput. Sci.*, 19, 224–231, 2013.

12. Nadeem, Q., Javaid, N., Mohammad, S.N., Khan, M.Y., Sarfraz, S., Gull, M., SIMPLE: stable increased throughput multi-hop protocol for link efficiency in wireless body area networks, in: *2013 eighth international conference on broadband and wireless computing, communication and applications BWCCA*, pp. 221–226, 2013.

13. Ahmad, A., Javaid, N., Qasim, U., Ishfaq, M., Khan, Z.A., Alghamdi, T.A., RE-ATTEMPT: a new energy efficient routing protocol for wireless body area sensor networks. *Int. J. Distrib. Sens. Netw.*, 10, 4, 464010, 2014.

14. Ahmed, S., Javaid, N., Akbar, M., Iqbal, A., Khan, Z.A., Qasim, U., LAEEBA: link aware and energy efficient scheme for body area networks, in: *2014 IEEE*

28th international conference on advanced information networking and applications AINA, pp. 435–440, 2014.

15. Tang, Q., Tummala, N., Gupta, S.K.S., TARA: thermal-aware routing algorithm for implanted sensor networks, in: *Proceedings of 1st IEEE international conference on distributed computing in sensor systems*, pp. 206–217, 2005.

16. Ahmed, S., Javaid, N., Yousaf, S., Ahmad, A., Sandhu, M.M., Imran, M., Khan, Z.A., Alrajeh, N., Co-LAEEBA: cooperative link aware and energy efficient protocol for wireless body area networks. *Comput. Hum. Behav.*, 51, 1205–1215, 2015.

17. Cai, X., Li, J., Yuan, J., Zhu, W., Wu, Q., Energy-aware adaptive topology adjustment in wireless body area networks. *Telecommun. Syst.*, 58, 139–152, 2014.

18. Kim, D., Kim, W.Y., Cho, J., Lee, B., EAR: An Environment-Adaptive Routing Algorithm for WBANs, in: *Fourth International Symposium on Medical Information and Communication Technology*, pp. 1–4, 2010.

19. Wang, J., Cho, J., Lee, S., Chen, K.-C., Lee, Y.-K., Hop-based energy aware routing algorithm for wireless sensor networks. *IEICE Trans. Commun.*, 93, 2, 305–316, 2010.

20. Zhou, J., Cao, Z., Dong, X., Xiong, N., Vasilakos, A.V., 4S: A secure and privacy-preserving key management scheme for cloud-assisted wireless body area network in m-healthcare social networks. *Inf. Sci.*, 314, 255–276, 2015.

21. Abidi, B., Jilbab, A., Mohamed, E.H., Wireless body area networks: A comprehensive survey. *J. Med. Eng. Technol.*, 44, 3, 97–107, 2020.

22. Achour, M.H., Mohammed, M.A.N.A., Rachedi, A., On the issues of selective jamming in IEEE 802.15. 4-based wireless body area networks. *Peer Peer Netw. Appl.*, 14, 1, 135–150, 2021.

23. Ullah, A., Said, G., Sher, M., Ning, H., Fog-assisted secure healthcare data aggregation scheme in IoT-enabled WSN. *Peer Peer Netw. Appl.*, 13, 1, 163–174, 2020.

24. Domingos, D., Respício, A., Martinho, R., Reliability of IoT-aware BPMN healthcare processes, in: *Virtual and Mobile Healthcare: Breakthroughs in Research and Practice*, pp. 793–821, IGI Global, 2020.

25. Behura, A. and Kabat, M.R., Energy-Efficient Optimization-Based Routing Technique for Wireless Sensor Network Using Machine Learning, in: *Progress in Computing, Analytics and Networking*, vol. 1119, H. Das, P.K. Pattnaik, S.S. Rautaray, K.-C. Li, (Eds.), pp. 483–496, AISC, Singapore, Springer, Singapore, 2020, https://doi.org/10.1007/978-981-15-2414-1_49.

26. Vimalarani, C., Subramanian, R., Sivanandam, S.N., An enhanced PSO-based clustering energy optimization algorithm for wireless sensor network. *Sci. World J.*, 2016, 2016, https://doi. org/10.1155/2016/86587 60.

27. Sung, W. and Chiang, Y., Improved Particle Swarm Optimization Algorithm for Android Medical Care IOT using Modified Parameters. *J. Med. Syst.*, 36, 6, 3755–3763, 2012.

28. Behura, A., Behura, A., Das, H., Counterfeit product detection analysis and prevention as well as prepackage coverage assessment using machine learning, in: *Progress in Computing, Analytics and Networking*. AISC, vol. 1119, H. Das, P.K. Pattnaik, S.S. Rautaray, K.-C. Li, (Eds.), pp. 483–496, Springer, Singapore, 2020, https://doi.org/10.1007/978-981-15-2414-1_49.

12

Study on Green Cloud Computing—A Review

Meenal Agrawal[1]* and Ankita Jain[2]

[1]D. A. V. V., Indore (M.P.), India
[2]Shri Vaishnav Institute of Management, DAVV, Indore (M.P.), India

Abstract

Cloud computing is evolving as an important information communication technology. Though computing becomes progressively pervasive, the energy consumption attributable to computing is climbing that marked the foundation of Green Computing. In other words, Green Cloud Computing (GCC) is data center architecture of an internet whose objective is to decrease the power consumption of data center and simultaneously secure the performance from users' point of view. One important feature of Green Computing is saving energy or reduction of carbon footprints. It enables wide range of online monitoring, live virtual machine migration, and VM placement optimization. This type of system responds to the period of top use and alters the accessibility of assets dependent on them expanding or contracting the cloud varying. The paper reviews the comprehensive literature on GCC and comes out with research gaps to further explore this field having lots of research potential.

Keywords: Cloud computing, green cloud computing, energy consumption, green information, green computing

12.1 Introduction

The impact of Information and Communication Technologies (ICTs) on the earth during the whole life cycle has been thought of, so as to advance the green and maintainable turns of events. The foundation of

---

*Corresponding author: meenalgarg7587@gmail.com

Sachi Nandan Mohanty, Jyotir Moy Chatterjee, Monika Mangla, Suneeta Satpathy and Sirisha Potluri (eds.) Machine Learning Approach for Cloud Data Analytics in IoT, (307–322) © 2021 Scrivener Publishing LLC

cloud computing has gotten included consideration for its superior adaptability, high accessibility, and unwavering quality. In compatibility of low carbon vitality in the social condition, this stage implies the foundation of Green Cloud Computing (GCC) has got a lot of consideration and examination by both the business and the scholarly community. At the end of the day, cloud computing needs to get green, which implies the cloud administration which mirrors the utilization of vitality under a lot of utilization of vitality standards, and then, it is known as GCC.

The key purpose of GCC is to reuse and use again and again. Such a figuring helps with getting the near enlisting speed by decreasing the utilization of imperativeness. Cloud computing is a working field of ICTs, presenting different kinds of new difficulties for the insurance of condition. The advancements of Green Information Technology have an assortment of area of utilizations; in this manner, they offer adaptability, they are dependable and solid, and they offer elite requiring little to no effort. The upset of Green Information Technology overhauls the advanced systems administration and offers promising natural security possibilities for financial just as for mechanical points of interest. These sorts of advancements can possibly improve productivity of vitality and to diminish carbon impressions and (e-squander). These propelled highlights can change the distributed computing into green distributed computing.

12.2   Cloud Computing

Cloud computing is an illustration utilized by Technology or Information Technology (IT) Service organizations for the conveyance of processing necessities as a support of a heterogeneous network of end beneficiaries. Cloud computing is offering utility-situated IT administrations to clients around the world. It empowers facilitating of uses from purchaser and logical and business areas.

12.2.1   Cloud Computing: On-Request Outsourcing-Pay-as-You-Go

As per Wikipedia, Cloud processing is an assortment of an assortment of registering ideas, wherein a huge number of PCs impart continuously to give a consistent encounter to the client, as though he/she is utilizing a solitary gigantic asset. Time sharing frameworks was the way it was tended to in those days. Even the broadcast communications organizations started offering VPNs (Virtual Private Networks) rather than devoted associations, which were average in QoS however were relatively less expensive in 1990s.

12.3   Features of Cloud Computing

- High agility
- Cost effective
- Device independency
- Location independency
- Sustainability
- Security
- Scalability
- Reliability
- Multi-tenancy

12.4   Green Computing

Green registering is known as the examination and practice of supportable ecological figuring. This sort of green registration is proficient through decrease in general utilization of intensity. This kind of work can be finished through overhauling the system framework by decreasing the quantity of servers, switches, and links or through applying the distinctive force utilization plans and examples.

The different cloud-based server farms are expanding quickly as the interest for asset of PCs. In the meantime, more server farms are appearing and the utilization of vitality of these server farms are likewise expanded. The force mindful booking methods, variable asset of the board, live relocation, and a negligible virtual machine structure in general framework productivity will be inconceivably improved in a server farm-based Cloud with insignificant execution overhead.

GCC contributes to carbon green cloud structure which centers around the outsider thought, which include two sorts of inventories, named as green offer and carbon outflow. These vaults help us to give and utilize the Green organizations from clients and providers both. Green specialists get to the organizations from green offer file and booked organizations according to least CO_2 release.

12.5   Green Cloud Computing

GCC courses of action can save vitality, yet additionally lessen operational costs and upgrade condition maintainability. Cloud computing is giving utility-based organizations to all the customers around the globe. Server ranches made for Cloud computing applications eat up enormous proportions of vitality, adding to high operational costs and a great deal of carbon dioxide spread to the earth. It prompts a critical degree of intensity usage and expanding the proportion of perilous gases in condition. A cloud is a flowed preparing structure containing a variety of interconnected and virtualized PCs. Green Cloud enlisting is used to achieve not simply profitable handling and utilization of figuring system, yet additionally limit vitality usage. It is in like manner called as GREEN IT.

The point of convergence of the current assessment is to give the wide writing studies of various examinations on GCC in India. The current examination in like manner bases on the key issues that have been investigated and applied. The paper does not present new responses for GCC. All things considered, the paper starts with key issues in GCC, covers effective writing audits, and, in conclusion, it ends up with giving assessment openings and giving suggestions and end.

12.6   Models of Cloud Computing

Cloud-based server farms are expanding incredibly in light of the interest for PC asset. Since more server farms are appeared, the vitality utilization of these server farms is additionally expanded by and large. Notwithstanding high vitality utilization, there is an expansion sway on nature by the type of carbon-di-oxide outflows.

Executing sharing of assets, this sort of processing can accomplish dependability and economies of scale. There two fundamental kinds of Cloud computing models:

1. Service based
2. Deployment based

12.7   Models of Cloud Services

   a. SaaS
   b. PaaS
   c. IaaS

Figure 12.1 shows the suggested model of cloud services.

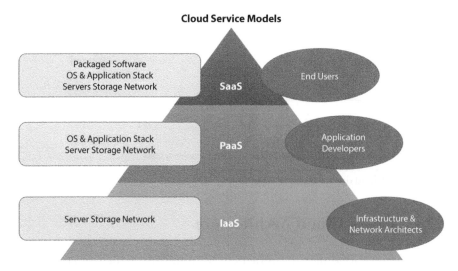

Figure 12.1 Models of cloud services.

a. SaaS: The topmost layer of Cloud computing design, which is a product conveyance model giving on-request access to application, referred to as "On request programming" and is normally valued on a compensation for every utilization premise.

b. PaaS: It facilitates the sending of use without the expense of purchasing dealing with the equipment and programming and provisioning the facilitating capacities. It might likewise incorporate offices for application structure, application advancement, testing, and sending.

c. IaaS: It presents PCs as virtual machines and offers extra assets, for example, images in a virtual collection, square and record-based dimensions, firewalls, consignment balancers, and IP addresses.

12.8   Cloud Deployment Models

Cloud computing is commonly changed assortment of various sort of administrations gave through different organizations. Cloud computing relies upon the sharing of assets utilizing web-empowered gadgets that permit the capacity of different application programming Figure 12.2 shows the suggested models of cloud deployment.

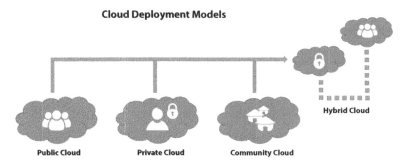

Figure 12.2 Cloud deployment models.

12.9   Green Cloud Architecture

In the Green Cloud plan, customers need to introduce their organization of cloud demands through another middleware known as green authority that manages the assurance of the greenest Cloud provider to serve the customer's solicitation. A green solicitation is of three types:

    a.   Software
    b.   Platform
    c.   Infrastructure

12.10   Cloud Service Providers

Cloud computing services are sellers which give IT as assistance over the Internet. Cloud computing is a term which is utilized for putting away and getting to information over the web. It does not store any information on the hard circle of your PC. Cloud computing causes you to get to your information from a remote server. Cloud computing administrations go from full applications and advancement stages to servers, stockpiling, and virtual work areas. There are different kinds of Cloud computing administrations that are accessible in the market, namely, Amazon Web Service (Aws), Microsoft Azure, Google Cloud Platform, IBM Cloud Services, Kamatera, Vultr, DigitalOcean, Rackspace, Alibaba Cloud, Oracle Cloud, MassiveGrid, LiquidWeb, VMware, and Salesforce. Figure 12.3 shows the suggested model of cloud architecture.

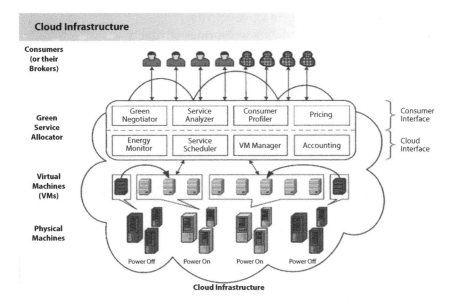

Figure 12.3 Cloud architecture.

12.11   Features of Green Cloud Computing

- Massive scalability
- Highly reliable and fault-tolerance
- Instant application organization
- Intra- and inter-cloud load balance
- Highly virtualized and normalized foundations

12.12   Advantages of Green Cloud Computing

- Reduced time and cost
- Instinctive updates
- Reliability and fault-tolerance
- Ease of use
- Improved storing
- Flexibility
- Reduced vitality utilization
- Reduce vitality utilization of figuring assets during top activity

- Save vitality during inactive activity
- Use eco-accommodating wellsprings of vitality
- Reduce unsafe impacts of registering assets
- Reduce figuring squanders
- No need to introduce or refresh software or hardware
- Access from any program and anyplace
- Unlimited use
- Always on
- Excellent service quality

12.13   Limitations of Green Cloud Computing

- The guideline restriction is the significant expense of acquisition of segments that are required to make the Cloud computing increasingly productive (like cooling gear and carbon discharge rating meter.).
- The high effectiveness delineated by the test system is exceptionally hard to execute in all actuality.
- The upkeep of the gadgets remembered for server farm is additionally a prime restriction. Figure 12.4 shows the suggested cloud and environmental sustainability.

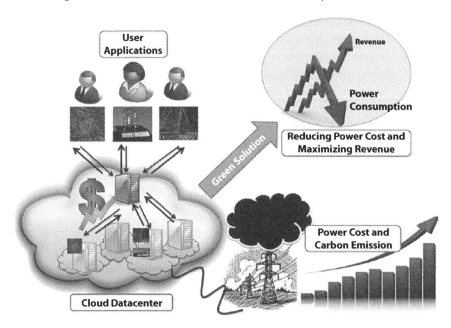

Figure 12.4 Cloud and environmental sustainability.

12.14 Cloud and Sustainability Environmental

These advancements are as of now characterized by commercialization as Cloud computing, which offers pay-more only as costs arise figuring as a utility. Business associations have customarily contributed a lot of capital and time in PC obtaining support.

12.15 Statistics Related to Cloud Data Centers

Cloud advancements are important for organizations that need to embrace business knowledge innovations and other tech-broad arrangements, since getting these gear and programming sent on reason can be a hazardous responsibility for organizations that have changing necessities and pre-requisites. As innovation keeps on getting further developed, a pressing requirement for server farms emerge continually. While innovation expansion is sure, making sense of how to make it less nosy on nature is consistently a test.

Server farms are relied upon to expend the intensity of 73 billion kWh in 2020. Server farm effectiveness and manageability subsequently end up being a significant natural concern.

12.16 The Impact of Data Centers on Environment

In the present time, server farms are vital and center to our mechanical needs. However, their natural effect may be their burden. An article in the New York Times features that a solitary server farm can expend more force than a medium-sized town. What is more, that it is faltering for a great many people to see the harm that server farms could be doing to the earth. Fundamentally, server farms are PCs stacked together that work constantly and therefore get warmed. Presently, this brings the interest for cooling frameworks into the image. The systems to chill off the bountiful measures of PCs use vitality and consume petroleum derivatives, which add to the carbon discharges.

An article on LinkedIn calls attention that 17% of the absolute carbon impression is brought about by server farms. The power expected to run these focuses is almost 30 billion watts. Moreover, these servers squander 90% of the vitality since they run on their full limit all day, every day.

Most recent exploration expresses that, before the finish of 2020, carbon discharge impressions will increment by 20%. This discharge is primarily occurring because of data centers used to accomplish the Cloud computing engineering. Server farms and new innovation selections are for the most part causing this carbon emanation. These data centers utilizes cloud vitality to serve the client produced solicitation and this vitality utilization is the fundamental reason for carbon emission.

12.17   Virtualization Technologies

Virtualization is key technology in today's era. It includes resource, cost, and energy saving. Figure 12.5 shows the suggested model of virtualisation technologies and products.

12.18   Literature Review

Akhare *et al.* [1] proposed a framework that aims to improve QoS (Quality of Service) by providing reduced latency and load balancing at fog layer. This improvement in QoS is achieved with help of data aggregation and load balancing. Mangla *et al.* [10] resulted that tightening the

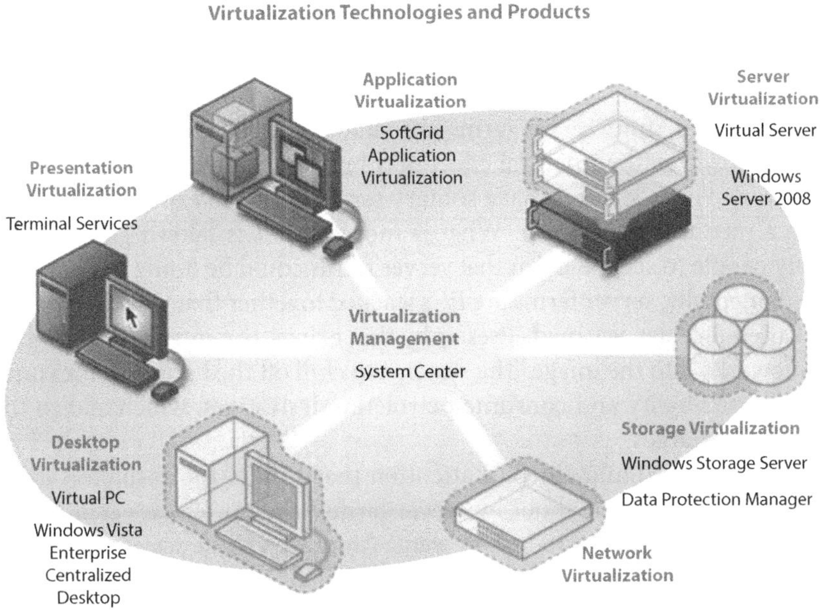

Figure 12.5 Virtualization technologies and products.

environmental regulations and increased concern about climate change among the public. Bindhu and Joe [4] stated about the use of GCC that gives the arrangement of issues of decrease of operational expense and diminishes the carbon impression and its effect on nature. They utilized information mining devices and auto-scaling with limitation fulfillment issues (CSP). Potluri *et al.* [14] talked about the different cloud models utilized in the assembling part to computerize the assembling cycle and how to gauge the nature of administration in assembling frameworks utilizing cloud. Chatterjee *et al.* [5] gives understanding to the elements that accompany the rise of IoT in the furnishings and kitchen producing industry. By actualizing the idea of IoT, organizations are at present assessing how interior information and ranges of abilities relate to the new specialized prerequisites that the developing advanced setting traces and by coordinating inside exploration they are studying IoT and associated items as they continue. Kumar *et al.* [8] introduced an online vitality mindful asset for Transmission Control Protocol/Internet Protocol–based portable cloud applications. In this procedure, they distinguished wellsprings of vitality utilizations in server farms and introduced significant level arrangements.

Radu [15] talked about the commitment of Cloud computing for ecological security like decrease of operational expense to natural assurance and diminishes the impression of carbons. Farooqi *et al.* [7] talked about some innovative thoughts for the home clients just as for cloud server farms to lessen utilization of intensity and CO_2 outflow, they additionally examined an alternate sort of strategies of intensity estimation that measure the force and power of a server farm.

Patil and Kharade [13] analyzed the proficient method to draw the outcomes from the cloud, spare vitality, cost and assets so all the highlights can be accomplished. They examined that embracing green figuring techniques make meaning not just from a moral or good perspective, yet in addition from a business perspective. Mankotia and Bhardwaj [11] drew out the determination and need of green processing with cloud, vitality upgrading strategies and contributing examination proposed by scientists in the green data innovation field.

Kumar and Shekhar [9] discovered that the Cloud computing not just gives the practical just as productivity and adaptability to the web client yet GCC likewise gives the vitality effective processing. In this paper, the scientist discovered a review of GCC that incorporates administrations, favorable circumstances to the general public. Doraya [6] clarified the idea of green processing where all the accessible assets ought to be used in an effective and condition neighborly way. He talked about that there are a few attributes of Cloud computing which advances it as a green registering, yet there are a few issues are should be settled, to make Cloud computing a GCC. Asvale *et al.* [2] broke down that the utilization of vitality and conditions to encourage GCC to spare generally speaking vitality utilization is connected with data correspondence frameworks.

Sandhu *et al.* [16] talked about how green registering can be accomplished through various calculations which can decrease the vitality utilization of cloud server farms which will sequentially diminishes the low emanation of CO_2. They additionally found that this calculation emerges some exploration challenges when such vitality is required. Tawade [18] broke down another thought for assessment of foundation of GCC. These thoughts empower us to chop down server farm vitality costs, along these lines prompting a solid, serious Cloud computing industry. Many end clients would be profited by the diminished vitality bills. This examination likewise supports regular asset, gives green and cost effectiveness, and decreases emanations of carbon, and there is a necessity of virtualization asset movement.

Pandya [12] inspected that the foundation of Cloud Computing contained under server farms to get profited by these advances. The various kinds of strategies, for example, virtualization of processing assets and rest planning for Cloud computing server farms improve the vitality productivity of Cloud computing. Sheme and Fresheri [17] found an outline of explores in the fields of Cloud computing vitality effectiveness enhancements and mindfulness.

Atrey *et al.* [3] investigated the fitting green networks for server farms and afterward put light on green booking calculations that encourage decrease in vitality utilization and CO_2 outflow levels in the current frameworks. Beloglazov and Buyya [19] revolves around virtual machine for the reduction of the vitality use. A creator proposes the dynamic reallocation strategy for VMs and switches off the unused servers which results, huge vitality saving in the authentic Cloud Computing data centers.

12.19   The Main Objective

- The target of the current work is to know the different parts of GCC.
- To understand about Cloud structure and architecture.
- To clarify the concept of Cloud computing and its Green aspect.
- To get Knowledge about various Cloud providers and their working.

12.20   Research Gap

It is contended that examination in assurance of condition is a test which incorporates the two champs and failures. All the difficult works done toward this path are significant and afterward lead to beneficial results. Green Information and Communication innovation is significant in this area. GCC is a noteworthy factor. There is an important hole of examination centered around the security of Cloud computing and on nature of administrations gave by GCC. The quality incorporates fulfillment of client and meets the necessity of ecological security.

Another hole has been found on the structure of a green cloud. The structure of green cloud has two kinds of difficulties: specialized and non-specialized. The specialized perspectives identified with GCC are structuring of programming, virtualization strategies, and warm mindful administration procedures. The non-specialized angles are identified with gauges and inner and universal guidelines in regard to the earth and the interior approaches and techniques of the association.

It unmistakably shows up from the writing that a large portion of the investigations done on GCC was progressively theoretical and theoretical in nature. Thus, alongside calculated and theoretical concentrates, there is have to lead exact investigations in the creating nations like India with an intention to produce mass information about GCC that can be seriously utilized by the analysts and specialist organizations to meet the particular supportable advancement prerequisites of GCC.

12.21   Research Methodology

It is a subjective examination that the ideas were created by the methods for optional information. In this examination, no tallies or measures (non-numerical information) were taken. Rather, the focal point of this investigation was to create and conceptualize models, structure, and speculations through the logical strategy for perception. It attempts to clarify and answer the why and how questions relating to the subject. From a lot of perceptions, content examination was done through recordings, articles in papers, magazines, diaries to determine new recipes, outlines, and models on GCC.

12.22   Conclusion and Suggestions

The current examination had concentrated on the different parts of Green Cloud figuring. These days, Cloud registering is another model that acclimatizes the already existing innovations so as to build the efficiency of utilization of different sorts of assets. The results of utilizing these sort innovations are diverse. At the end of the day, the specialist co-op of this administrations and the creators of the examinations acknowledged by various associations who were keen on natural assurance have given their perspectives on both the good and negative parts of the impacts of Cloud computing on the biological system. To put it plainly, Cloud registering likely makes an agreeable relationship with the earth with the assistance of ICT.

Cloud computing is powerful innovative stage for the clients who are new to pick cloud administrations. Cloud computing organizations can give more vitality effective, increasingly solid and quicker administrations. The cloud suppliers need to limit the utilization of the interest of power and make significant strides in utilizing sustainable power sources as opposed to simply searching for the minimization of cost. It is recommended that scientists can discover different highlights and factors that lead to expand the use of GCC. Numerous clients and specialist co-ops of GCC can be profoundly profited by the discoveries of such explores; in this way, analysts may lead the examination on GCC in their further investigations.

12.23   Scope for Further Research

The extension for additional examination will be the essential undertakings that are required in arranging programming at various levels (OS, compiler, calculation, and application) that support structure wide vitality capability. Moreover, to engage the green cloud data centers, the Cloud providers need to grasp and check existing data center power and cooling plans, power usage of servers and their cooling prerequisites, and apparatus resource use to achieve the best productivity. Thirdly, for arranging the sweeping courses of action in the booking and resource provisioning of uses inside the data center. Last but not the least, the commitment moreover goes to the two providers and customers to guarantee that creating developments does not bring irreversibility.

References

1. Akhare, R., Mangla, M., Deokar, S., Wadhwa, V., Proposed Framework for Fog Computing to Improve Quality-of-Service in IoT Applications, in: *Fog Data Analytics for IoT Applications*, pp. 123–143, Springer, Singapore, 2020.

2. Asvale, O., Jadhav, Y., Kale, P., Tiwatane, N., Survey on Green Cloud Computing Data Centers. *Int. J. Adv. Comput. Sci. Cloud Comput.*, 3, 1, 20–24, 2015.

3. Atrey, A., Jain, N., N.Ch.S.N, I., A Study on Green Cloud Computing. *Int. J. Grid Cloud Comput.*, 6, 6, 93–102, 2013.

4. Bindhu, D. and Joe, M., Green Cloud Computing Solution for Operational Cost Efficiency and Environmental Impact Reduction. *J. ISMAC*, 1, 2, 120–128, 2019.

5. Chatterjee, J.M., Kumar, R., Khari, M., Hung, D.T., Le, D.N., Internet of Things based system for Smart Kitchen. *Int. J. Eng. Manuf.*, 8, 4, 29, 2018.

6. Doraya, D., A Review Paper on Green Cloud Computing-A New form of Computing. *Int. J. Adv. Res. Comput. Sci. Software Eng.*, 5, 7, 1165–1167, 2015.

7. Farooqi, A.M., Nafis, M.T., Usvub, K., Comparative Analysis of Green Cloud Computing. *Int. J. Adv. Res. Comput. Sci.*, 56–60, 2017.

8. Kumar, M., Gupta, D., Jain, S., Research Paper on Green Cloud Computing. *Int. J. Sci. Res. Dev.*, 437–439, 2018.

9. Kumar, S. and Shekhar, J., Green Cloud Computing: An Overview. In *Proceedings of International Multi Track Conference on Sciences, Engineering & Technical Innovations (IMTC-14)*, 1–4.

10. Mangla, M., Akhare, R., Ambarkar, S., Context-Aware Automation Based Energy Conservation Techniques for IoT Ecosystem, in: *Energy Conservation for IoT Devices*, pp. 129–153, Springer, Singapore, 2019.

11. Mankotia, S. and Bhardwaj, A., A Study on Green Cloud Computing. *Int. J. Innovative Res. Comput. Commun. Eng.*, 14339–14343, 2016.

12. Pandya, S.S., Green Cloud Computing. *Int. J. Inf. Comput. Technol.*, 431–436, 2014.

13. Patil, P.S. and Kharade, D., A Study on Green Cloud Computing Technologies. *Int. J. Innovative Res. Comput. Commun. Eng.*, 4, 6, 11141–11148, 2016.

14. Potluri, S., Rao, K.S., Lakshmi, A.V., Quality of Service-Based Cloud Models in Manufacturing Process Automation, in: *Innovations in Computer Science and Engineering*, pp. 231–240, Springer, Singapore, 2019.

15. Radu, L.D., Green Cloud Computing: A Literature Survey. *Symmetry*, 1–20, 2017.

16. Sandhu, G.S., Khurmi, D., Hudiara, D., Green Cloud Computing: A Boon to Technology. *Int. J. Comput. Sci. Technol.*, 31–33, 2015.

17. Sheme, E. and Fresheri, N., A Literature Review: Cloud Computing Energy Aspects Research and Reports. *ICT Innovations Web Proceedings*, pp. 105–110, 2013.

18. Tawade, S.S., Green Cloud: Emerging trends and their Impacts. *Int. Res. J. Eng. Technol. (IRJET)*, 1650–1654, 2015.

19. Beloglazov, A. and Buyya, R. (Eds.), Energy Efficient Allocation of Virtual Machines in Cloud Data Centers. *Proceedings of the 10th IEEE/ACM International Symposium on Cluster Computing and the Grid (CCGrid)*, May 17–20, IEEE Computer Society, Melbourne, Australia, 2010.

13

Intelligent Reclamation of Plantae Affliction Disease

Reshma Banu[1], G.F Ali Ahammed[2] and Ayesha Taranum[1]*

[1]Dept of Information Science & Engineering, GSSS Institute of Engineering and Technology for Women, KRS Road, Metagalli, Mysuru, India
[2]Dept. of Comp. Sc. & Engg. Visvesvaraya Technological University, Centre for Post Graduation Studies, Mysuru, India

Abstract

Identification of Plantae Diseases is emerging as a developing field in India, as agriculture sector plays an important role in socio-economic life. In the early days, irrational methods were used for Plantae disease detection. With specialized and logical headway, dependable techniques through most reduced turnaround time have been created and proposed for early recognition of Plantae infections. In this paper we propose an application of machine learning for the agriculture sector, rendering a particular solution to a problem of analyzing crop diseases which is relied on Plantae images captured using a Smartphone. In the flow of quickening ecological difficulties, for example, water shortage, climatic change, concerns in regards to nourishment supply, security and the inconvenient natural effects, feasible farming is a critical step to adapt to a quickly developing total population. The scope of cultivation which is plausible outreaches short-term yield amplification and efficiency steered exploitation of resources.

Keywords: Plantae, convolution neural network (CNN), acquisition, verticillium

*Corresponding author: ezhan123@gmail.com

Sachi Nandan Mohanty, Jyotir Moy Chatterjee, Monika Mangla, Suneeta Satpathy and Sirisha Potluri (eds.) Machine Learning Approach for Cloud Data Analytics in IoT, (323–346) © 2021 Scrivener Publishing LLC

13.1 Introduction

Terror attack of Locust in the sky!!! Farmer's very trouble 30 May 2020—this was the tag line of one of the esteemed newspaper. Gujarat is the epicenter of the current crisis, with over 6,000 hectares being affected over the last 2 weeks. Disturbingly, the rapacious swarms have wreaked havoc on crops like mustard, castor, cumin, fennel, wheat, and others, putting the fate of immeasurable farmers at risk. News information says that around 45 teams of the central and state government are functioning on getting relief of the pests by spraying insecticide in North Gujarat. The government also reportedly plans to press drone-mounted sprays into action in the affected area to oppose the troublemaker. Around 3,200 hectares have been affected by the swarms, official told The Times of India [1]. The official said that the leaves and moisture due to good rainfall in Rajasthan were what was drawing desert locusts. Farmers were found in the fields using out-of-date methods of driving away locusts with loud noises.

According to the Locust Warning Organization (LWO), under the Ministry of Agriculture, there are four locust species originate in India; they are desert locust (Schistocerca gregaria), which is the most significant nuisance species. Diminutive locust desert swarm, "which consumes as much in 1 day as about 10 elephants, 25 camels, or 2,500 people", the LWO has informed.

Identification in plantae afflictions is emerging as a developing field in India, as the agriculture sector has a significant position in socio-economic life. In the early days, irrational methods were used for plantae affliction disease [2]. With specialized and logical headway, dependable techniques through most reduced turnaround time have been created and proposed for early recognition of plantae infections. Figure 13.1 provides a sample of afflictions.

Figure 13.1 Plantae affliction sample 1.

An application of intelligent reclamation for the agriculture sector, rendering a particular solution to a problem of analyzing crop afflictions, which is relied on plantae pictures, captured using a Smartphone [4]. In the flow of quickening ecological difficulties, for example, water shortage, climatic change, concerns in regard to nourishment supply, security, and the inconvenient natural effects, feasible farming is a critical step to adapt to quickly developing total inhabitants. Cultivation possibility, which is plausible, has a quick-fix yield amplification and competence resource exploitation [5].

Center of attention on detecting and diagnosing crop afflictions using the intelligent reclamation algorithm. intelligent reclamation expounds computer being programmed to be able to optimize a performance criterion using data or past experience [6]. It is considered as the most dynamic and progressive form of technology. Figure 13.2 provides a sample of afflictions of rice plantae

The ability of intelligent reclamation to process data and patterns in huge amount in real-time is helping to create a new framework for problem-solving. Agriculture is changing rapidly and, with it, the landscape through which afflictions spread. It discovers the factors that influence the invasion and persistence of new pathogenic strains in plantae [7, 8]. The current diagnostic procedure involves specialists venturing out to various pieces of the world and outwardly evaluating the plantae by centering at the indications of burden on the leaves. This methodology is accepted conflicting and emotional; for one specific plantae, it is not unusual for experts to disagree on a ranking. If the farmer identifies an unusual change in the color or pattern of the leaf, he must collect the sample and take it to the laboratory. In rural areas, the agricultural laboratories might not offer services at the required time. This is a dull and tedious undertaking; sometimes, solutions offered may likewise not be precise [9].

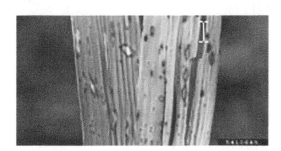

Figure 13.2 Plantae affliction sample 2.

A Smartphone-based symptomatic framework is presented which can be utilized by a rancher to get the field's condition of wellbeing progressively [10, 39]. Farmer uses a Smartphone to capture a picture of the affliction leaf, upload it to the server, and find the outcome in terms of discomfort and severity level. Figure 13.3 provides the image of plantae afflictions of the third sample.

The application can be used by the farmer on various plants in the field to predict the condition of scope and schedule suitable interventions, and focus on detecting and diagnosing crop afflictions using the intelligent reclamation algorithm can be much faster and accurate [11].

The objective is to present an application of intelligent reclamation in the field of agriculture, detecting a particular problem of diagnosis of crop afflictions, and give suggestive measures based on plantae pictures taken with smartphones. Plant disease identification is emerging as a developing area in India, since agriculture plays an important role in socio-economic life. During the early days, irrational methods were used for plant disease detection [12, 13]. With specialized and logical headway, dependable techniques through most reduced turnaround time have been created and proposed for early recognition of plant infections we suggest applying machine learning to the agricultural sector, which will offer a specific solution to the problem of analyzing crop diseases, which is relied on plant pictures captured using a Smartphone [14, 40].

In the flow of quickening ecological difficulties, for example, water shortage, climatic change, concerns in regard to nourishment supply, security, and the inconvenient natural effects, feasible farming is a critical step

Figure 13.3 Plantae affliction sample 3.

to adapt to a quickly total population changing [15]. The cultivation spectrum, which is possible, includes short term yield amplification and efficiency steered resource utilization.

Concept focuses at detecting and diagnosing crop diseases using a machine learning algorithm. Machine learning expounds computers being programmed to be able to optimize a performance criterion using data or past experience. It is considered as the most dynamic and progressive form of technology. The ability of machine learning to process a lot of information and perceive designs in real time is helping to create a new framework for problem-solving. Agriculture is changing rapidly, and with it, the landscape through which diseases spread. This concept discovers the factors that influence the invasion and persistence of new pathogenic strains in plants [16, 17].

The current diagnostic procedure involves specialists making a trip to different territories of the nation and outwardly evaluating the plants by taking a gander at the manifestations of the disease that manifest on the leaves [18, 41]. This approach appears to be inconsistent and very subjective; for one specific plant, it is not unusual for experts to disagree on a ranking. The goal of this definition is to present utilization of AI in the field of horticulture, detect a particular problem of crop disease diagnosis, and offer suggestive steps based on smartphone pictures taken from plants [42].

13.2 Existing System

> In the existing system, if the farmer identifies an unusual change in the color or pattern of the leaf, he must collect the sample and take it to the laboratory [19].
> In rural areas, the agricultural laboratories might not offer services at the required time.
> This is a dull and tedious assignment; here and there, arrangements offered may likewise not be exact.

13.3 Proposed System

> The farmer uses a Smartphone for incarcerate the diseased folio picture, uploads the same for server, and finds the result in terms of the disease and level of severity [20].

- The application can be used on different plants in the field, by the farmer to anticipate the state of field health and schedule suitable strategies [43].

➢ A Smartphone-based monitoring device is introduced that can be used by a farmer to obtain the field's health in real time.

13.4 Objectives of the Concept

➢ To detect and classify various crop diseases using machine learning.

➢ To provide a solution in terms of detecting the diseases and suggesting immediate actions.

➢ To implement mobile applications so as to assist the producer.

13.5 Operational Requirements

An operational prerequisite characterizes the capacity of the framework or its segment, where the capacity is depicted as a conduct determination among yields and information sources. Useful prerequisites may incorporate estimations, specialized subtleties, information control, handling, and other explicit highlights that characterize what the framework is intended to accomplish [44]. The operational necessities of the "Machine Learning for Plant Disease Detection" are as follows:

1. Picture Acquisition: Picture acquisition is the creation of a digitally encoded representation of the visual characteristics of a leaf picture. The first stage of the system is the acquisition of a picture, because the picture has to be obtained in order to apply different methods of processing [21].

2. Picture Segmentation: Picture segmentation method of dividing digital picture to many division. The objective differentiation designed to abridge the division of a picture which provides valid results [22, 45].

3. Feature Extraction: In picture processing, feature extraction begins with preliminary information and produce determined qualities that are planned to be useful and nonexcess, encourages ensuing learning and speculation steps,

and, now and again, guides the cycle, to better human understandings [46].

4. Comparison: It is a classification technique that is formally defined by a Euclidean distance. When Labeled data are generated, the algorithm produces an optimal hyperplane that categorizes new instances [47].

5. Convolution Neural Network (CNN): When the image passes through one convolution layer, the output of the primary layer becomes the input of the second layer. This is often reaching to happen with each alternative convolutionary layer. Once every convolution operation, the nonlinear layer is extra. It is AN activation operation that brings along nonlinear properties [23, 24, 48]. While not this property, a network would not are adequately powerful and provides a model supported response variable.

13.6   Non-Operational Requirements

A non-functional requirement assesses procedure of an arrangement with precise behaviors. It should contrast with functional requirements which explain particular behaviors or functionality. The main non-functional requirements for "Machine Learning for Plant Disease Detection" are as follows:

> Adaptability: The elements in the application should be designed to ensure accessibility and should be well-matched above Marshmallow, installed in all smartphones.

> Usability: Application is user friendly, and every farmer is able to download the application on their mobile phones and use it for the detection of diseases using the plant leaves.

> Quick Response: The farmer uploads picture of the diseased plant folio to server of the application, picture will be measured with the database of leaves, and the respective output is available immediately.

> Maintainability: The Admin can maintain complete data accumulated in the cloud server. A huge set of pictures is stored in the database, and maintaining all of them is a necessary function. He can delete the users and add new pictures if required.

> Efficiency: All the core elements should be able to provide optimal performance.

13.7   Depiction Design Description

During this design phase, the architecture of the system is built up. This stage starts with the necessity report conveyed during the prerequisite stage and guides the necessity in the development stage. The engineering characterizes the instrument, its interfaces, and its practices. Engineering is the deliverable structure archive. The structure record sets out an arrangement for the execution of the necessity [49]. Framework engineers can by and large be relied upon to have two primary parts: framework examination and framework structure. More significance is given to understanding the subtleties of a current framework in framework investigation [50, 53]. The structure archive sets out an arrangement to execute the prerequisite. Framework engineers can by and large be relied upon to have two fundamental parts: framework investigation and framework structure. In framework investigation, more accentuation is set on understanding the subtleties of a current or proposed system furthermore, choosing whether or not the proposed framework is alluring and whether the current framework needs improvement [51, 52].

The prerequisite assurance and particular includes investigation. It includes setting up wants for all framework components and afterward planning these necessities to programming structures. The conventional methodology is to arrange changed over information through framework stream graphs that help future framework improvements and encourage correspondence with clients. In any case, the framework stream outline is a physical framework instead of a consistent one. Maybe the most basic factor in the structure of the framework is the nature of the product [25, 26]. The customary methodology is to compose changed over information through framework flowcharts, which uphold future framework advancements and encourage correspondence with clients. In any case, the framework stream diagram speaks to a physical framework as opposed to an intelligent one. Maybe, the most basic factor is the plan of a framework that influences the nature of the product [54, 55].

13.8   System Architecture

System architecture as shown in Figure 13.4 describes flow of the system. After the picture is captured, it is sent in the cloud, the Keras (neural network API) along with the TensorFlow (software library by Google) to the server in the cloud in binary format, which will be transformed to grayscale

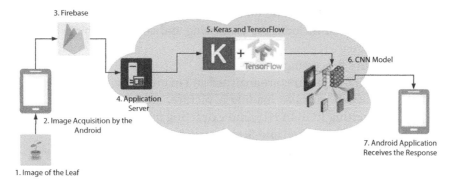

Figure 13.4 System architecture for machine learning for plant disease detection.

picture [26]. The pictures are trained using the CNN model. For classification, CNN model is used where there are numerous convolution layers, which increases the accuracy with every convolution.

The picture depicts as a two-dimensional array of pixels by means of amount in each position. To determine coordinating an element to an image fix, the CNN model duplicates every pixel in the element by the estimation of the relating pixel in the picture [27, 56]. At that point, it includes the appropriate responses and partitions the complete number of pixels in the element. When contrasting two pictures, if any pixel esteems do not coordinate, the images do not match. To complete the process, the process is repeated, lined up the feature with every possible picture patch.

13.8.1   Module Characteristics

The following stepwise procedure to be followed:

- Picture acquisition
- Picture processing
- Feature extraction and segmentation
  Image processing
  Picture segmentation
- Classification

> Picture Acquisition
  Picture acquisition is formation of a digitally determined illustration for visual description of a leaf's picture. The primary stage of the scheme is the picture acquisition because

the picture has to be obtained to apply various processing methods. It includes the processing and compression of the picture.

➤ Picture Processing
  The digital pictures are analyzed and manipulated to improve quality. It includes loading a picture, enhancing contrast, converting RGB to HIS, and extracting features.

➤ Feature Extraction and Segmentation
  In picture handling, the extraction of highlights starts with estimating of primer information that get determined qualities with the point of which are expected to be instructive and non-repetitive, encourages subsequent information and disentanglement steps, and prompts better human translation [28, 57].
  Picture division is a cycle of parceling a computerized picture into numerous fragments. The point of division is to rearrange and change the portrayal of an image which gives considerable and simpler approach to dissect [29, 58].

➤ Classification
  Arrangement incorporates two periods of preparing and testing utilizing any classifier. In the preparation stage, the classifier is prepared utilizing the estimation of the qualities and its particular objective qualities. This certified classifier is then used to order the image highlights [30, 31].

13.8.2 Convolutional Neural System

At the point when the image goes through a convolution layer, the yield of the principal level turns into the contribution of the subsequent layer. What is more, this will occur with each other convolutionary layer [32, 59]. After every convolution activity, the nonlinear layer is included. It has an initiation work, which unites nonlinear properties. Without this property, the system would not be adequately extraordinary and would not have the option to do so reaction variable is displayed.

13.8.3 User Application

➤ Login Page: After the registration process, the user shall proceed to login page, and user provides email address and the password to enter into the activity page.

> Upload Picture: In the activity page, the user has an option to upload the picture of the diseased leaf. The pixel range of the picture is set to a threshold, and the user is expected to upload a picture of the same range.
> Clear Picture: If the user wants to change the picture he has already uploaded, the user clicks on the clear option and uploads other pictures.

13.9   Design Diagrams

13.9.1   High-Level Design

A flowchart is a graph that portrays a cycle, framework, or PC calculation. They are utilized in the structure and development of straightforward cycles or projects. Like different kinds of charts, they help picture what is happening, helping to comprehend the cycle, and maybe additionally finding more subtle highlights inside the cycle, including such blemishes and bottlenecks.

There are various kinds of flowcharts where each type has its own arrangement of boxes and documentations.

Figure 13.5 represents the flowchart for user where the user logs into the mobile application using his email and password. In the activity page, the user uploads the picture and submits the picture. The pixel range of the picture is set to a threshold; the user is expected to upload a picture of the same range [33, 34]. After the picture has been uploaded, picture processing begins, and noise removal and conversion to grayscale picture take place. The grayscale picture is used to extract features such as the color of the leaf, gradient, width, and height of the leaf. Features extracted are classified based on the type of the disease. Result is displayed to the user, which describes the name of the disease [35, 60].

13.9.2   Low-Level Design

The diagram depicts the interactions between objects in sequential order.

Figure 13.6 represents the sequence diagram for user where the user logs into the mobile application using his email and password. In the activity page, the user uploads the picture and submits the picture. The pixel range of the picture is set to a threshold; the user is expected to upload a picture of the same range [36]. After the picture has been uploaded, picture

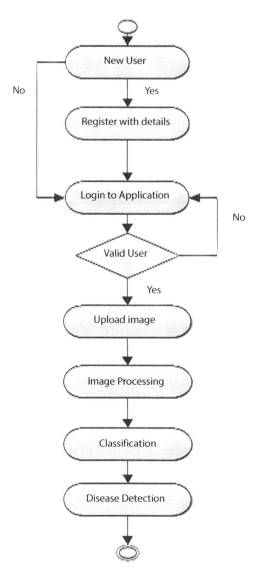

Figure 13.5 Flowchart for user.

processing begins; noise removal and conversion to the grayscale picture take place. The grayscale picture is used to extract features such as the color of the leaf, gradient, width, and height of the leaf [37, 38]. The features extracted classify the type of the disease. The result is displayed to the user, which describes the name of the disease.

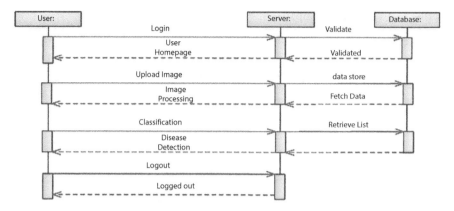

Figure 13.6 Sequence diagram for user.

13.9.3   Test Cases

Table 13.1 provides the test cases which have been carried out with respect to the work.

13.10   Comparison and Screenshot

Figure 13.7 shows that when the user clicks on the mobile application for the first time, the user will be directed to registration page and asked to fill the details such as name, email address, and set the password.

Figure 13.8 depicts the registration process; the user will be directed to the login page users email address, and the password will be entered into the activity page.

Figure 13.9 shows the activity page, and the user has an option to upload the picture of the diseased leaf. The pixel range of the picture is set to a threshold; the user is expected to upload a picture of the same range.

Figure 13.10 displays how user uploads the diseased folio picture of rice.

Figure 13.11 shows steps after the picture has been uploaded. Picture processing begins, and noise removal and conversion to grayscale picture take place.

Figure 13.12 depicts how features are being extracted as of the uploaded picture grayscale picture used to haul out features such as the color of the leaf, gradient, width, and height of the leaf. The features extracted will classify the type of the disease.

Figure 13.13 provides the insight where the result is displayed to the user, which describes the name of the disease. When the diseased rice folio picture is uploaded, the result is displayed as Bacterial Folio Blight.

Table 13.1 Test cases comparison.

Test case no.	Description	Expected output	Actual output	Result
1	The picture pixels are not in the range of 0 to 255	Upload an picture which is in the range of 0 to 255	Upload an picture which is in the range of 0 to 255	Successful
2	The picture pixels are in the range of 0 to 255	dispensation of the Picture begins	Processing of the Picture begins	Successful
3	The uploaded picture does not belong to the five crops chosen for the concept	Displays the message "Upload an picture of the specified crop"	Displays the message "Upload an picture of the specified crop"	Successful
4	The uploaded picture is not in jpeg format	Displays the message "Upload an picture which is in jpeg format"	Displays the message "Upload an picture which is in jpeg format"	Successful
5	Internet connection is not available	Displays the message "Internet Connection is required"	Displays the message "Internet Connection is required"	Successful

In Figure 13.14, when the diseased rice folio picture is uploaded, the result is displayed as Brown Folio Spot.

In Figure 13.15, when the diseased rice folio picture is uploaded, the result is displayed as Verticillium wilt of cotton along with the suggestive measure.

In Figure 13.16, it describes that when a healthy picture is uploaded, the result after classification is displayed as unable to find disease.

Figure 13.7 Registration page for the user.

Figure 13.8 Login page for the user.

Upload image

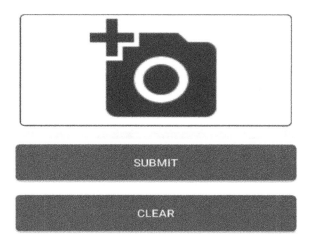

Figure 13.9 Picture acquisition from the user.

Upload image

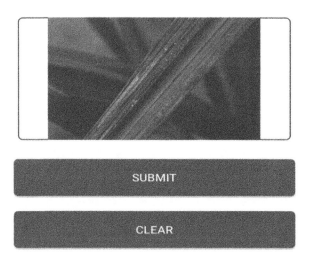

Result

Figure 13.10 Uploading the picture to the application.

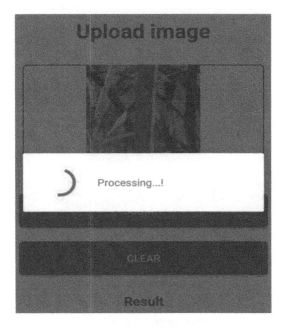

Figure 13.11 Picture processing for the uploaded picture.

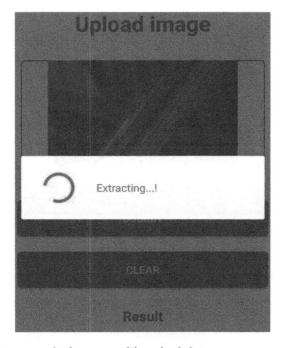

Figure 13.12 Extracting the features as of the uploaded picture.

Upload image

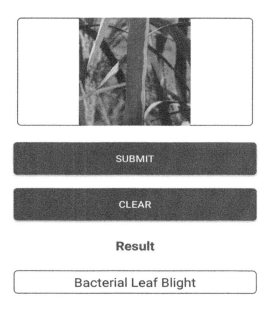

Figure 13.13 Result after classification displayed as Bacterial Folio Blight.

Upload image

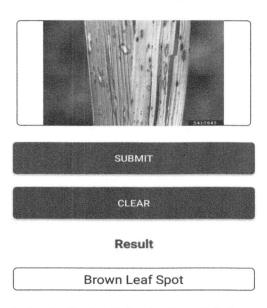

Figure 13.14 Result after classification displayed as Brown Folio Spot.

Figure 13.15 Result after classification displayed as Verticillium wilt of cotton along with the suggestive measures.

Figure 13.16 When a healthy picture is uploaded, the result after classification is displayed as unable to find disease.

13.11   Conclusion

The adaptable application gives minute outcomes and teaches the farmer whether the picture contains a healthy folio or an unhealthy leaf. If the folio is debilitated, then the particular illness and insurances to be taken appeared. The proposed system identifies the disease, classifies it, and responds with the type of disease identified and also describes the preventive measures required. CNN provides better classification and ensures proper detection of the diseased leaves. The farmers can utilize this application or early detection of diseases, which, in turn, reduces the crop failure ratio.

One of the future things to work includes the execution of low-power first-time offline type of useful application that can give an essential examination so as to can be ratified once the application has been made gadget executes on the web. This flexible application centers around the illnesses stressed over rice, ragi, wheat, cotton, and maize. The application can be improved by including data trial of various plants and their diseases.

References

1. Mangla, M., Akhare, R., Ambarkar, S., Context-Aware Automation Based Energy Conservation Techniques for IoT Ecosystem, in: *Energy Conservation for IoT Devices*, pp. 129–153, Springer, Singapore, 2019.
2. Akhare, R., Mangla, M., Deokar, S., Wadhwa, V., Proposed Framework for Fog Computing to Improve Quality-of-Service in IoT Applications, in: *Fog Data Analytics for IoT Applications*, pp. 123–143, Springer, Singapore, 2020.
3. Deokar, S., Mangla, M., Akhare, R., A Secure Fog Computing Architecture for Continuous Health Monitoring, in: *Fog Computing for Healthcare 4.0 Environments*, pp. 269–290, Springer, Cham, 2021.
4. Potluri, S., Quality of Service based Task Scheduling Algorithms in Cloud Computing. *Int. J. Electr. Comput. Eng.*, 7, 2, 1088–1095, April 2017.
5. Potluri, S., A study on technologies in cloud-based design and manufacturing. *IJMPERD*, 8, 6, 187–192, 2018.
6. Potluri, S., Software virtualization using containers in google cloud platform. *IJITEE*, 8, 7, 2430–2432, May 2019.
7. Potluri, S., Simulation of QoS-Based Task Scheduling Policy for Dependent and Independent Tasks in a Cloud Environment, in: *Smart Intelligent Computing and Applications*, vol. 159, pp. 515–525, May 2019.
8. Potluri, S., Quality of Service-Based Cloud Models in Manufacturing Process Automation, in: *Lecture Notes in Networks and Systems*, vol. 32, pp. 231–240, 2019.

9. Potluri, S., Optimization model for QoS based task scheduling in cloud computing environment. *IJEECS*, 18, 2, 1081–1088, 2020.
10. Potluri, S., IOT Enabled Cloud Based Healthcare System Using Fog Computing: A Case Study. *J. Crit. Rev.*, 7, 6, 1068–1072, 2020, ISSN-2394-5125.
11. Potluri, S., Improved quality of service-based cloud service ranking and recommendation model. *TELKOMNIKA Telecommun. Comput. Electron. Control*, 18, 3, 1252–1258, June 2020, ISSN: 1693–6930, accredited First Grade by Kemenristekdikti, Decree No: 21/E/KPT/2018 DOI: 10.12928/TELKOMNIKA.v18i3.11915.
12. Potluri, S., A Hybrid PSO Based Task Selection and Recommended System for Cloud Data. *Test Eng. Manage.*, 83, 10210–10217, March-April 2020, ISSN: 0193-4120.
13. Potluri, S., A Hybrid Self-Adaptive PSO and QoS Based Machine Learning Model for Cloud Service Data. *Test Eng. Manage.*, 83, 23736–23748, May-June 2020, ISSN: 0193-4120.
14. Le, D.N., Kumar, R., Nguyen, G.N., Chatterjee, J.M., *Cloud computing and virtualization*, John Wiley & Sons, USA, 2018.
15. Jha, S., Kumar, R., Chatterjee, J.M., Khari, M., Collaborative handshaking approaches between internet of computing and internet of things towards a smart world: a review from 2009–2017. *Telecommun. Syst.*, 70, 4, 617–634, 2019.
16. Chatterjee, J.M., Kumar, R., Khari, M., Hung, D.T., Le, D.N., Internet of Things based system for Smart Kitchen. *Int. J. Eng. Manuf.*, 8, 4, 29, 2018.
17. Sujath, R., Chatterjee, J.M., Hassanien, A.E., A machine learning forecasting model for COVID-19 pandemic in India. *Stochastic Environ. Res. Risk Assess.*, 34, 1, 2020.
18. Chatterjee, J., IoT with Big Data Framework using Machine Learning Approach. *Int. J. Mach. Learn. Networked Collab. Eng.*, 2, 02, 75–85, 2018.
19. Moy Chatterjee, J., Fog computing: beginning of a new era in cloud computing. *Int. Res. J. Eng. Technol. (IRJET)*, 4, 05, 735, 2017.
20. Iwendi, C., Bashir, A.K., Peshkar, A., Sujatha, R., Chatterjee, J.M., Pasupuleti, S., Jo, O., COVID-19 Patient Health Prediction Using Boosted Random Forest Algorithm. *Front. Public Health*, 8, 357, 2020.
21. Kumar, A., Chatterjee, J.M., Díaz, V.G., A novel hybrid approach of SVM combined with NLP and probabilistic neural network for email phishing. *Int. J. Electr. Comput. Eng.*, 10, 1, 486, 2020.
22. Sannakki, S.S. and Rajpurohit, V.S., Classification of Pomegranate Diseases Based on Back Propagation Neural Network. *Int. Res. J. Eng. Technol. (IRJET)*, 2, 02, 2015.
23. Banu, R., Modeling of Secure Communication in Internet-of-Things for Resisting Potential Intrusion, in: *3rd Computational Methods in Systems and Software*, vol. 2, Springer, Cham, 2019, https://link.springer.com/chapter/10.100 7%2F978-3-030-31362-3_38.

24. Banu, R. and Taranum, A., Framework for Secured Transmission between communicating nodes with the internet host in IOT. *Int. J. Disaster Recovery Bus. Contin. (IJDRBC)*, 11, 1, 1370–1380, 2020.

25. Chatterjee, J.M., Priyadarshini, I., Le, D.N., Fog Computing and Its security issues. *Security Designs for the Cloud, Iot, and Social Networking*, pp. 59–76, 2019.

26. Choudhuri, A., Chatterjee, J.M., Garg, S., Internet of Things in Healthcare: A Brief Overview, in: *Internet of Things in Biomedical Engineering*, pp. 131–160, Academic Press, 2019.

27. Chaki, J., Parekh, R., and Bhattacharya, S., Plant leaf recognition using texture and shape features with neural classifiers, *Pattern Recognition Letters*, 58, 61–68, 2015.

28. Shri, M.L., Devi, E.G., Balusamy, B., Chatterjee, J.M., Ontology-Based Information Retrieval and Matching in IoT Applications, in: *Natural Language Processing in Artificial Intelligence*, pp. 113–130, Apple Academic Press, 2020.

29. Yun, S., Xianfeng, W., Shanwen, Z., Chuanlei, Z., Pnn based crop disease recognition with leaf image features and meteorological data. *Int. J. Agric. Biol. Eng.*, 8, 4, 60, 2015.

30. Jain, V. and Chatterjee, J.M. (Eds.), *Machine Learning with Health Care Perspective: Machine Learning and Healthcare*, vol. 13, Springer Nature, 2020.

31. Chatterjee, J.M., COVID-19 Mortality Prediction for India using Statistical Neural Network Models. *Front. Public Health*, 8, 441, 2020.

32. Kumar, A., Payal, M., Dixit, P., Chatterjee, J.M., Framework for Realization of Green Smart Cities Through the Internet of Things (IoT), in: *Trends in Cloud-based IoT*, pp. 85–111, Springer, Cham, 2020.

33. Sujatha, R., Nathiya, S., Chatterjee, J.M., Clinical Data Analysis Using IoT Data Analytics Platforms, in: *Internet of Things Use Cases for the Healthcare Industry*, pp. 271–293, Springer, Cham, 2020.

34. Priya, G., Shri, M.L., GangaDevi, E., Chatterjee, J.M., IoT Use Cases and Applications, in: *Internet of Things Use Cases for the Healthcare Industry*, pp. 205–220, Springer, Cham, 2020.

35. Raj, P., Chatterjee, J.M., Kumar, A., Balamurugan, B., *Internet of Things Use Cases for the Healthcare Industry*, Springer International Publishing, 2020.

36. Garg, S., Chatterjee, J.M., Le, D.N., Implementation of Rest Architecure-Based Energy-Efficient Home Automation System, in: *Security Designs for the Cloud, Iot, and Social Networking*, pp. 143–152, 2019.

37. Kumar, P.S., Kumar, A., Rathore, P.S., Chatterjee, J.M., An On-Demand and User-Friendly Framework for Cloud Data Centre Networks with Performance Guarantee, in: *Cyber Security in Parallel and Distributed Computing: Concepts, Techniques, Applications and Case Studies*, pp. 149–159, 2019.

38. Chatterjee, J.M., Kumar, R., Pattnaik, P.K., Solanki, V.K., Zaman, N., Preservação de privacidadeemambienteintensivo de dados. *Tour. Manage. Stud.*, 14, 2, 72–79, 2018.

39. Tripathy, H.K., Acharya, B.R., Kumar, R., Chatterjee, J.M., Erratum to: Machine Learning on Big Data: A Developmental Approach on Societal Applications, in: *Big Data Processing Using Spark in Cloud*, pp. E1–E1, Springer, Singapore, 2018.

40. Barbedo, J.G.A., Digital image processing techniques for detecting, quantifying and classifying plant diseases. *Springer Plus*, 2, 660, 1–12, 2013.

41. Agrawal, G.H., Galande, S.G., Londhe, S.R., Leaf disease detection and climatic parameter monitoring of plants using IOT. *Int. J. Innov. Res. Sci. Eng. Technol.*, 4, 10, 9927–9932, 2015.

42. Almusaylim, Z.A. and Zaman, N., A review on smart home present state and challenges: linked to context-awareness internet of things (IoT). *Wirel. Netw.*, 25, 6, 3193–3204, 2019.

43. Almulhim, M. and Zaman, N., Proposing secure and lightweight authentication scheme for IoT based E-health applications, in: *2018 20th International Conference on Advanced Communication Technology (ICACT)*, 2018, February, IEEE, pp. 481–487.

44. Almulhim, M., Islam, N., Zaman, N., A Lightweight and Secure Authentication Scheme for IoT Based E-Health Applications. *Int. J. Comput. Sci. Netw. Secur.*, 19, 1, 107–120, 2019.

45. Using Wireless Sensor Technology. *Int. J. Adv. Res. Electr., Electron. Instrum. Eng.*, 3, 12, 2014.

46. Bharwad, V.S. and Dangarwala, K.J., Recent research trends of plants disease detection. *Int. J. Sci. Res.*, 4, 12, 843–845, 2015.

47. Potluri, S., An IoT based solution for health monitoring using a body-worn sensor enabled device. *JARDCS*, 10, 9, 646–651, 2018.

48. Potluri, S., Health record data analysis using wireless wearable technology device. *JARDCS*, 10, 9, 696–701, 2018.

49. Banu, R. and Taranum, A., Detection of TCP Xmas Scan using Pattern Analysis. *Third International Conference on Electrical,Electronics Communication, Computer Technologies and Optimization Techniques*, Dec 2018.

50. Nguyen, V.V., Pham, B.T., Vu, B.T., Prakash, I., Jha, S., Shahabi, H., Tien Bui, D., Hybrid machine learning approaches for landslide susceptibility modeling. *Forests*, 10, 2, 157, 2019.

51. Tripathy, H.K., Acharya, B.R., Kumar, R., Chatterjee, J.M., Machine learning on big data: A developmental approach on societal applications, in: *Big Data Processing Using Spark in Cloud*, pp. 143–165, Springer, Singapore, 2019.

52. Islam, M., Dinh, A., Wahid, K., Detection of potato diseases using image segmentation and multiclass support vector machine. *2017 IEEE 30th Canadian Conference on Electrical and Computer Engineering (CCECE)*, IEEE Journal.

53. Patil, S.B. and Bodhe, S.K., Leaf Disease Severity Measurement Using Image Processing. *Int. J. Eng. Technol.*, 3, 5, 297–301, 2011.

54. Patil, S. and Chandavale, A., A survey on methods of plant disease detection. *Int. J. Sci. Res.*, 4, 2, 1392–1396, 2015.

55. Ampatzidis, Y., De Bellis, L., Luvisi, A., iPathology: Robotic applications and management of plants and plant diseases. *Sustainability*, 9, 6, 1010, 2017.

56. Breukers, A., Kettenis, D.L., Mourits, M., Werf, W.V.D., Lansink, A.O., Individual-based models in the analysis of disease transmission in plant production chains: An application to potato brown rot. *Acad. Sci.*, 90, 1–3, 112–131, 2006.

57. Ghosal, S., Blystone, D., Singh, A.K., Ganapathysubramanian, B., Singh, A., Sarkar, S., An explainable deep machine vision framework for plant stress phenotyping. *PNAS*, 115, 18, 4613–4618, 2018.

58. Pantazi, X.E., Moshou, D., Tamouridou, A.A., Automated leaf disease detection in different crop species through image features analysis and one class classifiers. *Comput. Electron. Agric.*, 156, 96–104, 2019.

59. Prakash, B. and Yerpude, A., A survey on plant disease identification. *Int. J. Adv. Res. Comput. Sci. Softw. Eng.*, 15, 3, 313–317, 2015.

60. Keoh, S.L., Kumar, S.S., Tschofenig, H., Securing the Internet of Things: A Standardization Perspective. *IEEE Internet Things J.*, 1, 3, 265–275, 2014.

14

Prediction of the Stock Market Using Machine Learning–Based Data Analytics

Maheswari P. and Jaya A.*

Department of Computer Applications, B.S Abdur Rahman Crescent Institute of Science and Technology, Chennai, India

Abstract

The economy is the foremost part of any countries establishment of an asset in stock market is a financial barometer. A barometer is data points that represent trends in the market. Indian stock market has two exchanges, and the oldest stock exchange is the Bombay Stock Exchange (BSE). In terms of volume, The National Stock Exchange is the largest stock exchange. Exchanges are the actual prices where stocks are bought and sold. Whereas an index is a grouping of company stocks that measures changes in the broader stock market or a sector of the stock market. Two Indian market indexes are Sensex and Nifty. Earlier prediction of the stock market was usually forecasted by the financial professionals. Nowadays, with the advancement of data analytics and machine learning techniques computer professionals also embraced prediction. Machine learning and data analytics are some of the most existing recent technologies.

This study aims to predict the five sectors like pharmaceuticals, banking, fast-moving consumer goods, power, and automobile sectors. From the five sectors selected, the following companies are selected: pharmaceutical sector: Cipla and Torrent Pharma; banking sector: ICICI bank and SBI; FMCG sector: ITC and Hindustan Unilever; power sector: Adani Power Ltd. and Power Grid Ltd; and automobile Sector: Mahindra & Mahindra and Maruti Suzuki Ltd.

The above company's stock prices are predicted by the machine learning technique, i.e., linear regression, and by deep learning technique, i.e., long short-term memory (LSTM), which are used. Using the above techniques, stock prices are predicted more accurately, therefore, help the investors to gain more profits.

Corresponding author: jayavenkat2007@gmail.com

Sachi Nandan Mohanty, Jyotir Moy Chatterjee, Monika Mangla, Suneeta Satpathy and Sirisha Potluri (eds.) Machine Learning Approach for Cloud Data Analytics in IoT, (347–374) © 2021 Scrivener Publishing LLC

Keywords: Stock market, prediction, linear regression, long short-term memory (LSTM), machine learning, deep learning

14.1 Introduction of Stock Market

The world is going digital. The Internet has brought a revolution in the world of financial business. In the top 10 countries, India is in second place with the maximum number of internet users more than 560 million in 2020[1]. The Internet is one of the most innovative technologies creating a major paradigm shift. It has philosophically affected the way that shoppers watch motion pictures, tune in to music, purchase items, trade items, and communicate. It has additionally had a tremendously positive effect on contributing particularly for financial specialists. Before the creation of Internet innovation, the investor's smartest choice was to go to the neighborhood library to peruse budgetary writing and investigation firms and securities like stocks, bonds, and mutual funds.

The investor's need to contact the organization directly for the recent budgetary report might have consumed more time and expensive regarding the postage for huge budgetary reports. Investors are coordinated by the firm's relation department and need to wait for the budgetary report to be printed. With the help of the Internet, investors can find the budgetary report instantly from the Securities and Exchange Commission (SEC) website.

The stock market is the heart of the global financial systems. The organization needs a stock market to raise capital for it's business. Investors are protected and safeguard trustworthiness by the regulators. Since the stock market is the core component of the financial systems. During bull markets, investors feel to invest in the investment that will also raise the market value. Bear markets would cause the opposite effect. The economy may slow down due to this reduction in investment activity.

The stock market is an exchange where buying, selling, and issuance of shares of publicly held companies take place. A company wants to share its assets and earrings with the general public because it needs money. An organization can either get cash from someone or raise it by selling some portion of the organization which is known as issuing stocks.

---

[1]www.internetworldstats.com/top20.htm

14.1.1 Impact of Stock Prices

Stock prices are influenced by numerous variables that can estimate the stock ascent or fall. The fluctuation of the stock prices affected ultimately the buyers and sellers of stocks.

- ➢ Supply and demand
- ➢ Earnings and expectations
- ➢ Economic indicators
- ➢ Industry conditions
- ➢ Chasing the biggies
- ➢ News
- ➢ Market sentiment
- ➢ Pandemic (COVID-19)

Nowadays, during the pandemic situation, the prediction of the stock market is becoming increasingly more complex. This study aims to improve the prediction of the stock price and maximize the profit for the investors. New financial technology innovations are bringing investing and trading are becoming more and more data-driven. Machine learning allows us to validate, test, and execute them more efficiently. Machine learning uses the historical data learns from it and then predicts the trends. Data analytics and machine learning are the most in ultimatum domains in the industry. One of which is to predict the stock market.

Stock markets are hard to predict. Only a few months back, stock markets were trading high. The black swan named Coronavirus appeared suddenly and tumble-down the bull market. In India on 25th March 2020. Our Prime Minister Mr. Narendra Modi declared a 3-week nationwide lockdown and he said that social distancing is the only way to break the cycle of infection[2]. The words social distancing and lockdown were unheard of until the Coronavirus emerged. Many countries have been forced to lockdown that prevents the movements of the citizens unnecessarily. Due to social distancing issues and limitations of movements, the well-being and economy of the various nations are being under threat. GDP of the entire world has dropped drastically [3]. The effect of the virus had been developed greater every day and swallowing the past decade growth of the country's economy. Investors have to tolerate that the organizations are halted. The world economy has been wrapped with the uncertainty of thick clouds.

---

[2]www://economictimes.indiatimes.com

The major sector that came out to be a winner is the pharmaceuticals, life sciences, and pathology sector. May it be children, adults, or the elderly, in the wake of the COVID-19 spread, the majority of the human population would wish to have enough health medication and facilities handy. Once a vaccine is successfully developed, the shape of our current pharmaceutical industry would change for good. Every single human being would require a dose and provide for the demand at hand will be on the shoulders of our pharmaceutical industry. These people would be providing for a noble cause, but to make a fortune for them is more than certain.

The rest of the paper consists of the following: Section 14.2 provides a background of related works in stock prediction using machine learning, deep learning, and data analytics. Section 14.3 provides a financial prediction framework. Section 14.4 discusses the implementation and discussion of the result. Section 14.5 provides the conclusion and future enhancement.

14.2   Related Works

In [1], the prediction model uses Auto-ARIMA and Holt-Winters models are implemented. The portfolio optimization incurred more profit and reduce loss. This helps individuals and corporate investors. Research work in [2], forecasts the future value of GOOGL and NKE assets. The proposed RNN based on LSTM has shown a promising result. The found the finest sets for the length of the data and the number of training periods that suit their assets and maximize their prediction accuracy.

In [3], the authors proposed a numerical model to predict the COVID-19 spread. The model utilizes linear regression (LR), multilayer perception (MLP), and vector autoregression (VAR). The model showed that the MLP model has a better performance than LR and VAR. In [4], the authors proposed a system train recurrent neural network. They have used the past 5 years of Google stock prices. The model used opening and closing price for each day. Simple sentimental analysis has the ability of 40% of the market inconsistency in market return.

In [5], the authors constructed the deep learning hybrid stock market prediction model CEEMD-PCA-LSTM. The proposed model use CEEMD is an order smoothing and breakdown module. PCA reduces the aspect of the breakdown IMFs component. LSTM has predicted the closing price of the next trading day for each module.

In [6], authors proposed Deep Stock trend Prediction Neural Network (DSPNN) a module that constructs market indicator vectors of the target stock. Information module clusters the investors' profile of trading behaviors and trading feature matrices construct the transaction behaviors of the investors' clusters on the target and the relevant stocks. The accuracy of the single stock is 60% of the Chinese A share market.

In [7], authors applied ARIMA to acquired historical distribution rules. The proposed method is based on the historical price information of assessing the distribution likelihood of future stock fluctuations keeps away from the huge loss [8] applied WEKA tool counts different algorithms which are used to economic data in Ecuadorian stock exchanges (BVQ and BVG).

In [9], the authors proposed the framework using historical stock prices that helps the investors in the future. Proposed techniques collect data transform, analyze, and present to the investor. In [10], the authors approach uses a Hadoop-based pipeline that learns from the past data and based on the streaming updates decisions are predicted in US stocks.

In [11], the authors used supervised machine learning is limited and explained only fundamental. In [12], authors predicted the stock with the help of news headings. Sentiment analysis is used by calculating the polarity score prediction that is performed. In [13], all observations and inferences in the paper are computation, analysis, and the prediction that uses machine learning.

In [14], authors implemented the artificial neural network, SVR, RF, and LSTM with the daily close price. SVR method has obtained greater accuracy than the neural network.

In [15], authors have finely measure ARIMA's boundaries and attempted the various fusions of the exogenous features and saw through test assessment that the nearness of Google Trends information by and large improved the estimates. In [16], authors have proposed an algorithm that worked on the views ideas of their investors on the shares. Security exchange is such a field where perspectives on the clients will matter. The views of the experts have affected a lot to the traders those who want to enter into the market. The unsupervised and supervised learning–dependent methods help to find the results in a better way.

In [17], based on the comparative study, authors have implemented, support vector machine (SVM) showed to be the maximum effective and achievable model in predicting the stock price, in favor of the opinions of the tweets. Utilizing the machine learning systems to estimate cheap contrasted with the base survey then led to the extent the general public sentiment.

In [18], authors applied VADER, SentiWordNet, and TextBlob on StockTwits information to check whether they can raise the precision of sentiment analysis. Logistic regression, linear SVM, and Naive Bayes classification are used as a starting point and related to the results of applying lexicon-based prototypes along with machine learning models. Because of our outcomes, in addition to the fact that VADER outperforms AI techniques in removing assessment from budgetary web-based life, similar to Stock-Twits. In [19], the authors applied descriptive statistics and analysis variability and central tendency and plot the data in a histogram.

The idea behind the stock market prediction utilizing machine learning, data analytics, and deep learning in the early stages is discussed. Based on those ideas, the proposed system has been implemented.

14.3   Financial Prediction Systems Framework

The financial prediction systems framework defines the conceptual financial prediction systems. Figure 14.1 illustrates the flow of the control from one phase to another phase that helps to predict the stock prices.

14.3.1   Conceptual Financial Prediction Systems

The proposed conceptual financial prediction systems comprise three phases. Phase 1 is the historical data. In financial prediction systems, historical data is retrieved from the Yahoo finance website using python libraries panda reader. The retrieved data consists of 60 days with a daily frequency of historical data is used for the prediction of the closing price of the respective stock. Phase 2 consists of a machine learning module and a deep learning module. In the machine learning module, the LR model is used to predict the closing price of the stock. In deep learning module, long short-term memory (LSTM) is used for the predicting the closing price of the stock given. Phase 3 consists of prediction of stock prices, and visualization is used.

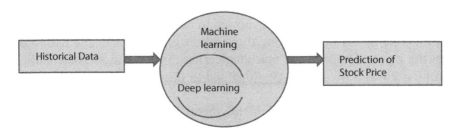

Figure 14.1 Conceptual financial prediction systems.

Data Source

In this research work, predicting the stock prices of a public listed company in Nifty using past stock prices. The historical prices are collected from the Yahoo finance using python libraries pandas_reader. The closing price is used to predict the stock prices in this research work. Past 60 days prices are used in LR model and LSTM model from pharmaceuticals, banking, fast-moving consumer goods (FMCG), power, and automobile sectors. From the five sectors selected, the following companies are selected: pharmaceutical sector: Cipla Limited and Torrent Pharma; banking sector: ICICI Bank and SBI; FMCG sector: ITC and Hindustan Unilever; power sector: Adani Power Ltd. and Power Grid Ltd.; and automobile sector: Mahindra & Mahindra and Maruti Suzuki Ltd. This research work covers different companies stocks from the period of 28th April 2020 to 30th July 2020[3]. The closing price of the stock for the various companies which are selected in each sector like pharmaceuticals, banking, FMCG, power, and automobile sectors are predicted using Linear Regression (LR) and Long Short Term Memory (LSTM).

Sample Dataset

Dataset consists of various attributes like date, open, high, low, close, total trade quantity, and turnover Lacs. The date represents the market session date of the respective stock. Open and close represent the initial and ending price of the respective stock. High and low represents the maximum and minimum price of the respective stock. Volume represents the total number of trades executed on the stock throughout the market session. Figure 14.2 depicts the sample dataset used in the financial prediction system.

14.3.2   Framework of Financial Prediction Systems Using Machine Learning

LR is one of the essential types of machine learning where we train a model to predict the behavior of your stock price based on certain attributes. In the machine learning module, the LR algorithm is used. LR is a measure of regression analysis. It is supervised learning. Regression analysis is a system of predictive modeling that benefits the investors to find out the association between attributes that are used as input and the objective variable.

---

[3]https://in.finance.yahoo.com/

☒ MARUTI1.NS

	A	B	C	D	E	F	G
1	Date	Open	High	Low	Close	Volume	
2	4/28/2020	5090	5120	4990.25	5052.7	1172062	
3	4/29/2020	5100	5100	5011.05	5068.45	1038094	
4	4/30/2020	5122	5425	5122	5358.8	2341081	
5	5/4/2020	5096	5130.25	4840	4886.3	1742771	
6	5/5/2020	4995	5029.55	4800	4829.85	1570620	
7	5/6/2020	4841.2	5000	4710	4843.25	2214528	
8	5/7/2020	4899.5	4935.35	4735	4749.3	1530808	
9	5/8/2020	4874	4879	4637.5	4654.15	1828141	
10	5/11/2020	4750	5014.6	4730.15	4937.8	3176473	
11	5/12/2020	4914	4985	4690.05	4951.3	3124672	
12	5/13/2020	5250	5317.45	4986.25	5036.1	3304845	
13	5/14/2020	4905	5145	4852.15	5114.05	2590674	
14	5/15/2020	5110	5123.2	4961.15	5100.4	2182462	
15	5/18/2020	5080.4	5095	4680.55	4720.95	3164086	
16	5/19/2020	4842	4900	4755.75	4805.3	2108177	
17	5/20/2020	4754	4920	4745.5	4891.95	1518296	
18	5/21/2020	4890	5073.8	4851.05	5050.1	1868166	
19	5/22/2020	5010	5150	4930.75	5134.3	1935875	
20	5/26/2020	5200	5285.8	5160.65	5246.15	1508751	
21	5/27/2020	5270	5291	5135.4	5244.4	1534655	
22	5/28/2020	5267	5495	5220	5468.35	2325084	
23	5/29/2020	5375	5666.75	5375	5610.8	3386733	
24	6/1/2020	5690	5864.65	5666.9	5793.6	2340994	
25	6/2/2020	5797.75	5849	5625.1	5690.1	2110719	

Figure 14.2 Sample dataset used in the financial prediction system.

LR provides a strong statistical method to discover the association between certain attributes. LR creates the preeminent predictive accurateness for linear association although it is slightly complex to outliers and the mean of the reliant on attributes. The cost function is used to discover the finest values for a_0 and a_1 which provide the finest line suitable for the closing stock prices. This will minimize the accuracy between the predicted stock price and the actual stock price. The cost function is otherwise known as the mean squared error (MSE) function. Figure 14.3 depicts the flow of control LR that helps to predict the closing price of the stock.

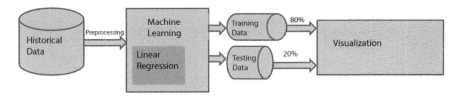

Figure 14.3 Illustration of linear regression in financial prediction systems.

14.3.2.1   *Algorithm to Predicting the Closing Price of the Given Stock Data Using Linear Regression*

The algorithm below describes predicting the closing price using LR.

Input data: Date, Open, Close, High, Low, and Volume of the particular stocks from Yahoo finance.
Step 1: Begin
Step 2: import Sklearn libraries
Step 3: import pandas libraries
Step 4: loading the dataset of the particular stock
Step 5: Declaring the variables x and y
Step 6: Splitting the training and testing data
Step 7: fitting the regressor using x train and y train
Step 8: finding the regression coefficient and predict the test data
Step 9: printing the root mean square error
Step 10: visualizing the line plot.
Step 11: stop the execution
Output data: The closing price of the particular stock is visualized. The closing price is predicted accurately.

14.3.3   Framework of Financial Prediction Systems Using Deep Learning

A deep learning module is a method of machine learning module without human supervision able to learn. Neural networks to carry out the process of the machine learning module. In this research work, LSTM is used for predicting the closing price of the given stock. LSTM models are the powerful model used in time series data. The model can predict an arbitrary number of steps into the future. It consists of cell state, hidden state, input gate, forget gate, and output gate. For implementing the prediction of stock prices, TensorFlow provides a good sub-API (called RNN API). Illustration of LSTM is depicted in Figure 14.4.

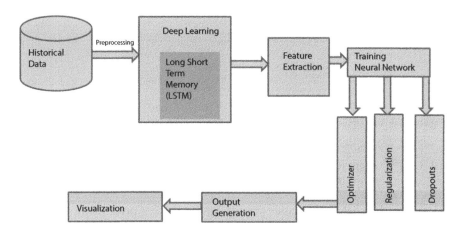

Figure 14.4 Illustration of long short-term memory (LSTM) in financial prediction systems.

14.3.3.1 Algorithm to Predict the Closing Price of the Given Stock Using Long Short-Term Memory

The algorithm below describes predicting the closing price using LSTM

Input data: Date, Open, Close, High, Low, and Volume of the particular stocks from Yahoo finance.

Step 1: Begin

Step 2: import all the required libraries

Step 3: loading the dataset of the particular stock

Step 4: Feature Extraction, in this phase features are taken into the neural network

Step 5: In training Neural Network phase information is served to the neural network and trained the information for the prediction allocating the arbitrary biases and masses.

> *Step 5.1: Optimizer shows a vital role to increase the accuracy of the model. The proposed model used Adam (Adaptive Movement Estimation) is used to fast the algorithm meets the least price. It calculates the adaptive learning rates for each attributes based on its past gradients.*

> *Step 5.2: Regularization is another important aspect of training the model. This phase has made sure that weights should not be too large, hence overfit. Proposed model used Tikhonov regularization.*

> *Step 5.3: Dropouts are used for creating the neurons further stronger and allows to calculate the trend without concentrating on anyone neuron.*

Step 6: Output Generation, this stratum will generate the output value by the output layer RNN compared with the objective value. Using the back propagation algorithm the acquired output value is reduced.

Step 7: Visualization: a rolling analysis of a financial prediction system is frequently used to evaluate the system strength over the period.

Output data: The closing stock price of the particular stock is visualized. The closing stock price is predicted accurately.

14.4   Implementation and Discussion of Result

The financial prediction systems framework utilizes the LR module and LSTM module. This system framework uses date, open, close, high, low, and volume of the particular stocks from the Yahoo finance website. The algorithms are used to predict the closing price of the given stock. System framework aims to predict the five sectors like pharmaceuticals, banking, FMCG, power, and automobile sectors. From the five sectors selected, the following companies are selected: pharmaceutical sector: Cipla and Torrent Pharma; banking sector: ICICI Bank and SBI; FMCG sector: ITC and Hindustan Unilever; power sector: Adani Power Ltd. and Power Grid Ltd; and automobile sector: Mahindra & Mahindra and Maruti Suzuki Ltd.

14.4.1   Pharmaceutical Sector

Globally, the leading source of generic drugs in India. The pharmaceutical sector in India has an important position in the world market supplies over 50% of worldwide demand for various vaccines, 40% of generic demand in the US, and 25% of all medicine in the UK. India has a large pool of scientists and engineers with the potential to steer the industry. Indian pharmaceutical firms supplied 80% of the antiretroviral drugs used globally to combat AIDS (Acquired Immune Deficiency Syndrome)[4].

14.4.1.1   Cipla Limited

Cipla Limited is a multinational company that manufactures and sells pharmaceutical products in India, the United States, South Africa, and internationally. The company deals with the pharmaceutical ingredients and formulations in various areas for the treatment of respiratory, cardiovascular disease, arthritis, diabetes, weight control, and depression[5].

---

[4]https://www.ibef.org/industry/pharmaceutical-india.aspx
[5]https://www.cipla.com

Figures 14.5 and 14.6 depict the actual stock price and predicted stock price of the closing price for the pharmaceuticals sectors of Cipla company using LR and LSTM, respectively. The root mean square error (RMSE) value of LR and LSTM are 4.05 and 5.19, respectively.

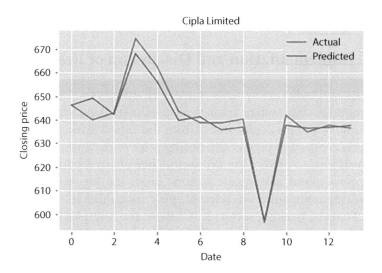

Figure 14.5 Prediction of closing price—Cipla Limited (linear regression).

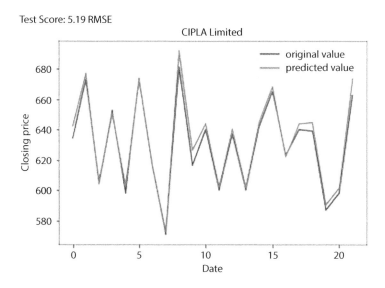

Figure 14.6 Prediction of closing price—Cipla Limited (LSTM).

14.4.1.2   Torrent Pharmaceuticals Limited

Torrent Pharmaceuticals Limited is dynamic in the healing areas of central nervous system (CNS), anti-infective pain management, diabetology, and cardiovascular segments[6].

Figures 14.7 and 14.8 depict the actual stock price and predicted stock price of the closing price for the pharmaceuticals sectors of Torrent company using LR module and LSTM, respectively. The RMSE value of LR and LSTM is 18.93 and 38.05, respectively.

14.4.2   Banking Sector

The banking sector is an economic sector holding financial assets. The banking sector includes the regulation of banking activities by government organizations, insurance, debts, stockholder services, and credit cards. It has 20 public sector banks and 22 private sector banks[7].

14.4.2.1   ICICI Bank

Industrial Credit and Investment Corporation of India (ICICI) bank is an Indian multinational, private sector banking, and financial services. It has 5,275 branches and 15,589 ATM across India[8].

Figures 14.9 and 14.10 depict the actual stock price and predicted stock price of the closing price for the banking sectors of ICICI Bank Limited using LR and LSTM, respectively. The RMSE value of the LR model and LSTM model is 4.36 and 6.20, respectively.

14.4.2.2   State Bank of India

State Bank of India is a worldwide open area banking and budgetary administrations. It is the largest bank in India with a 23% market share by assets and 25% of the total deposits and loan market[9].

Figures 14.11 and 14.12 depict the actual stock price and predicted stock price of the closing price for the banking sectors of State Bank of India using the LR model and LSTM model, respectively. The RMSE value of LR and LSTM is 1.63 and 1.96, respectively.

---

[6]https://www.torrentpharma.com/
[7]https://www.ibef.org/industry/banking-india.aspx
[8]https://www.icicibank.com/
[9]https://www.onlinesbi.com

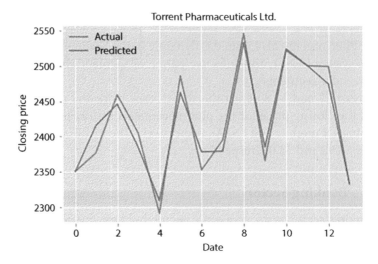

Figure 14.7 Prediction of closing price—Torrent Pharmaceuticals Limited (linear regression).

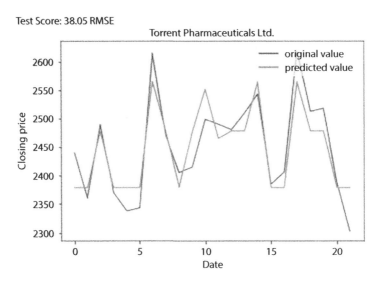

Figure 14.8 Prediction of closing price—Torrent Pharmaceuticals Limited (LSTM).

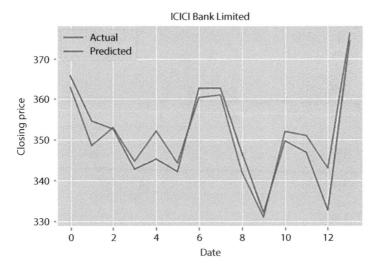

Figure 14.9 Prediction of closing price—ICICI Bank (regression).

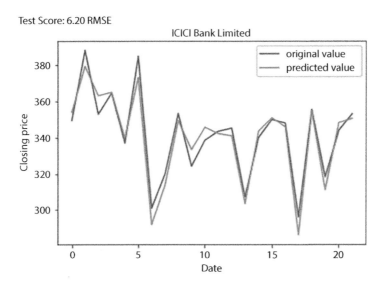

Figure 14.10 Prediction of closing price—ICICI Bank (LSTM).

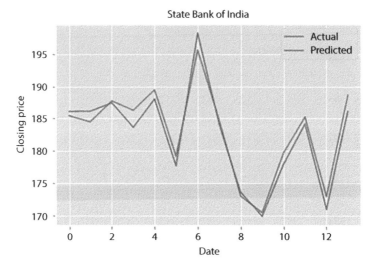

Figure 14.11 Prediction of closing price—SBI Bank (regression).

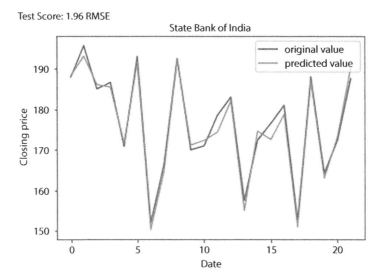

Figure 14.12 Prediction of closing price—SBI Bank (LSTM).

14.4.3 Fast-Moving Consumer Goods Sector

FMCG is otherwise known as consumer packaged goods (CPG) that are sold rapidly and the price is moderately low. Products include non-durable household goods like packaged foods, candies, cosmetics, dry goods, fruits, vegetables, milk, gum, soda, and other consumables[10].

---

[10]https://www.ibef.org/industry/fmcg.aspx

14.4.3.1   ITC

Imperial Tobacco Company of India Limited (ITC) is a private sector company with FMCG, hotels, agribusiness, information technology, packaging, and paperboards. ITC is the leading FMCG marketer[11].

Figures 14.13 and 14.14 depict the actual stock price and predicted stock price of the closing price for the FMCG sectors of ITC Limited using the LR model and LSTM model, respectively. The RMSE value of LR and LSTM is 1.98 and 2.96, respectively.

14.4.3.2   Hindustan Unilever Limited

Hindustan Unilever Limited (HUL) is a British-Dutch multinational company. It is an Indian Subsidiary of Unilever. Their products include beverages, food, cleaning agents, personal care products, FMCG, and water purifiers. Their portfolio had 35 products brands in 20 categories[12].

Figures 14.15 and 14.16 depict the actual stock price and predicted stock price of the closing price for the FMCG sectors of Hindustan Unilever Limited using LR model and LSTM model, respectively. The RMSE value of LR and LSTM is 12.71 and 37.98, respectively.

14.4.4   Power Sector

The power sector is the most diversified in the world. In Asia, India has ranked fourth. There are conventional and non-conventional sources. Conventional sources are natural gas, oil, hydro coal, lignite, and nuclear power. Non-conventional sources are solar, domestic waste, wind, solar, and agricultural[13].

14.4.4.1   Adani Power Limited

Adani Power Limited is India's largest private thermal power producer. It is the principal organization to set up a coal-based supercritical warm force venture enrolled under the Clean Development Mechanism (CDM) of the Kyoto convention on the planet[14].

Figures 14.17 and 14.18 depict the actual stock price and predicted stock price of the closing price for the Power sectors of Adani Power Limited using the LR model and LSTM model, respectively. The RMSE value of LR and LSTM is 0.24 and 0.76, respectively.

---

[11]https://www.itcportal.com
[12]https://www.hul.co.in/
[13]https://www.ibef.org/industry/power-sector-india.aspx
[14]https://www.adanipower.com

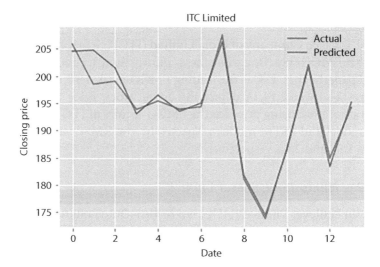

Figure 14.13 Prediction of closing price—ITC (regression).

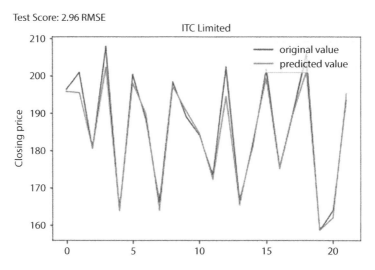

Figure 14.14 Prediction of closing price—ITC (LSTM).

14.4.4.2   Power Grid Corporation of India Limited

Power Grid Corporation of India Limited is India's leading electric power transmission service. The power grid is an Indian state-owned Maharatna company. Its original name was National Power Transmission Corporation Limited. The transmission network is 153,635 circuit kilometers[15].

---

[15]https://www.powergridindia.com/

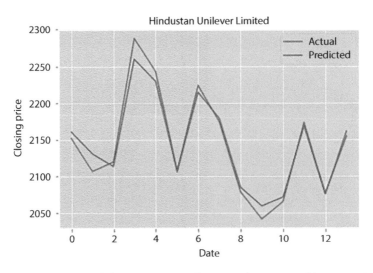

Figure 14.15 Prediction of closing price—Hindustan Unilever Limited (regression).

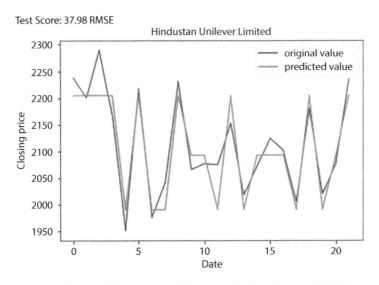

Figure 14.16 Prediction of closing price—Hindustan Unilever Limited (LSTM).

Figures 14.19 and 14.20 depict the actual stock price and predicted stock price of the closing price for the Power sectors of Power Grid Corporation of India Limited using the LR model and LSTM model, respectively. The RMSE value of LR and LSTM is 0.90 and 1.86, respectively.

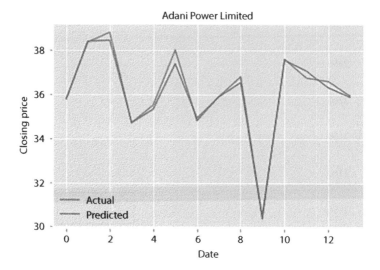

Figure 14.17 Prediction of closing price—Adani Power Limited (regression).

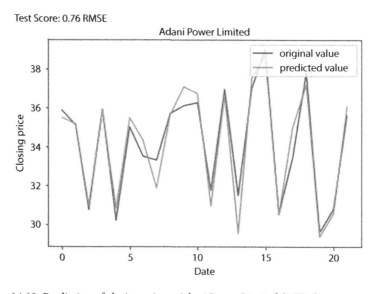

Figure 14.18 Prediction of closing price—Adani Power Limited (LSTM).

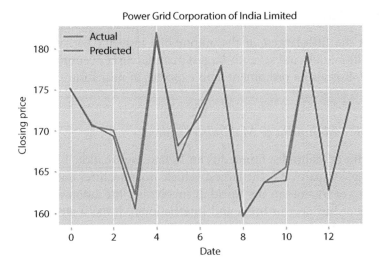

Figure 14.19 Prediction of closing price—Power Grid Corporation of India Limited (regression).

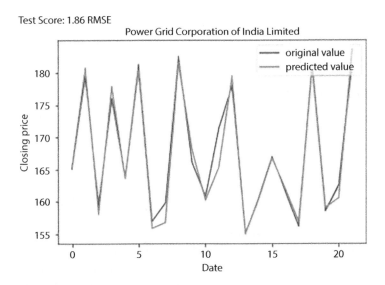

Figure 14.20 Prediction of closing price—Power Grid Corporation of India Limited (LSTM).

14.4.5 Automobiles Sector

India is the fifth-largest in the automobile industry with sales reaching 3.81 million units and seventh-largest manufacturer of commercial vehicle in 2019. It is also a prominent auto exporter in near future, where strong growth is expected[16].

14.4.5.1 Mahindra & Mahindra Limited

Mahindra & Mahindra Limited is an Indian multinational vehicle manufacturing company. It is the largest vehicle manufactures and largest manufacturer of tractors in the world. It involves in the automotive and farm equipment business in India and International. It has a strategic alliance with Ford Motor Company[17].

Figures 14.21 and 14.22 depict the actual stock price and predicted stock price of the closing price for the Automobiles sectors of Mahindra & Mahindra Limited using LR model and LSTM model, respectively. The RMSE value of LR and LSTM is 5.65 and 10.50, respectively.

14.4.5.2 Maruti Suzuki India Limited

Maruti Suzuki India Limited is known as Maruti Udyog Limited in the past. It is a vehicle producer in India. It has a 56.21% owned subsidiary of the Japanese Suzuki Motor Corporation. It has the facilitation of pre-owned car sales, car financing, and fleet management[18].

Figure 14.23 and 14.24 depict the actual stock price and predicted stock price of the closing price for the Automobiles sectors of Maruti Suzuki India Limited using the LR model and LSTM model, respectively. The RMSE value of LR and LSTM is 43.26 and 517.77, respectively.

14.4.6 Comparison of Prediction Using Linear Regression Model and Long-Short-Term Memory Model

Table 14.1 compares the prediction of the closing price of the respective stock. The accuracy is calculated by the RMSE value.

Based on the performance of the LR model and LSTM model to conclude that the LR model has a lower error than the LSTM model. Finally, Table 14.1 depicts that, comparing RMSE value, the prediction of the closing price

---

[16]https://www.ibef.org/industry/india-automobiles.aspx
[17]https://www.mahindra.com
[18]https://www.marutisuzuki.com/

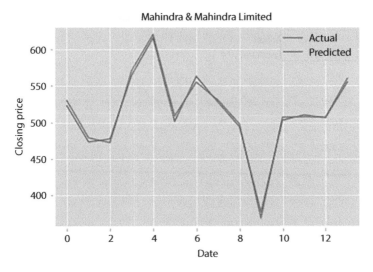

Figure 14.21 Prediction of closing price—Mahindra & Mahindra Limited (regression).

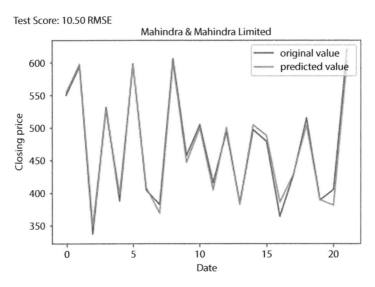

Figure 14.22 Prediction of closing price—Mahindra & Mahindra Limited (LSTM).

using LR has a better result than the prediction of the closing price using LSTM. The stock prices are predicted during the pandemic (COVID-19) situation. According to Table 14.1, the LR model and LSTM model have predicted more accurate in positive stocks like Adani Power, Power Grid Corporation of India, ITC, SBI, Cipla, and ICICI since the RMSE is very less compared to negative stocks like Torrent Pharmaceuticals Limited,

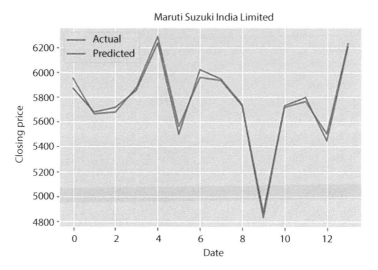

Figure 14.23 Prediction of closing price—Maruti Suzuki India Limited (regression).

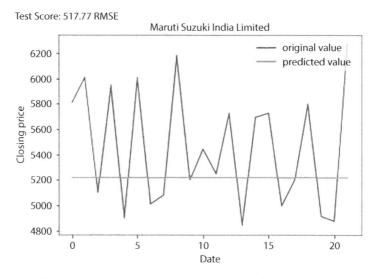

Figure 14.24 Prediction of closing price—Maruti Suzuki India Limited (LSTM).

Hindustan Unilever Limited, Mahindra & Mahindra Limited, and Maruti Suzuki Limited since the RMSE value of the negative stocks are higher than the positive stocks. The companies have been more affected by the impact of COVID-19 due to national lockdown where factories were shut down, 50% of workers were constrained, disruption in production/supply logistics, and social distancing, which are the major factors that affect the stock prices of the negative sectors.

Table 14.1 Comparison of RMSE value for linear regression model and long short-term memory (LSTM) model.

S. no	Company name	Linear regression	Long short-term memory (LSTM)
1	Cipla Limited	4.05	5.19
2	Torrent Pharmaceuticals Limited	18.93	38.05
3	ICICI Bank	4.36	6.20
4	SBI Bank	1.63	1.96
5	ITC	1.98	2.96
6	Hindustan Unilever Limited	12.71	37.98
7	Adani Power Limited	0.24	0.76
8	Power Grid Corporation of India Limited	0.90	1.86
9	Mahindra & Mahindra Limited	5.65	10.50
10	Maruti Suzuki India Limited	43.26	517.77

14.5 Conclusion

The proposed system is used for the precise predicting techniques using LR, and LSTM units. It helps the investors to predict the stock values. The stock prices are calculated during the pandemic (COVID-19) situation. By comparing the RMSE value, the prediction of the closing price using the LR model has more accuracy than the LSTM model. To conclude, the result showed that there is a strong correlation between the actual stock prices and predicted stock prices. Positive stocks during the pandemic have predicted accurately, i.e., RMSE (0.24) in the LR model and RMSE (0.76) in the LSTM model. In negative stocks, except Maruthi Suzuki, all other stocks have a slight deviation from the actual stock prices to the predicted stock prices. Maruthi Suzuki cut production by 98% in May due to the impact of the Corona virus[19].

---

[19]https://www.business-standard.com/article/companies/maruti-cuts-production-by-98-in-may-amid-coronavirus-pandemic-120060901484_1.html

14.5.1 Future Enhancement

The attractiveness of the stock market trading is emerging tremendously promptly by which the researchers are boosted to discover a new system for predicting the stock prices using new methodology. Future research includes discussion forums and economic news feeds. Stacked LSTM and CNN LSTM models can be used to predict stock prices. To improve the accuracy and minimize the errors other factors like news headlines, industry condition, earnings, and market sentiment must be considered.

References

1. Roy, S., *Stock Market Prediction and Portfolio Optimization Using Data Analytics, Computational Intelligence in Data Mining. Advances in Intelligent Systems and Computing*, vol. 990, pp. 367–381, Springer, Singapore, 2020.
2. Moghar, A. and Hamiche, M., Stock Market Prediction Using LSTM Recurrent Neural Network. *International Workshop on Statistical Methods and Artificial Intelligence (IWSMAI 2020)*, vol. 170, ScienceDirect Procedia Computer Science, pp. 1168–1173, 2020.
3. Sujath, R., Chatterjee, J.M., Hassanien, A.E., A machine learning forecast model for COVID–19 pandemic in India. *Stochastic Environ. Res. Risk Assess.*, 34, 959–972, 2020. https://doi.org/10.1007/s00477-020-01827-8.
4. Sarkar, A., Sahoo, A.K., Sah, S., Pradhan, C., LSTMSA: A Novel Approach for Stock Market Prediction Using LSTM and Sentiment Analysis. *International Conference on Computer Science, Engineering and Applications (ICCSEA)*, Gunupur, India, pp. 1–6, 2020.
5. Zhang, Y., Yan, B., Aasma, M., A novel deep learning framework: Prediction and analysis of financial time series using CEEMD and LSTM. *Expert Syst. Appl.*, 159, 113609–113630, 2020.
6. Long, J., Chen, Z., He, W., Wu, T., Ren, J., An integrated framework of deep learning and knowledge graph for prediction of stock price trend: An application in Chinese stock exchange market. *Appl. Soft Comput.*, 91, 106205, June 2020.
7. Wang, F., Li, M., (Member, IEEE), Mei, Y., Li, W., Time Series Data Mining: A Case Study With Big Data Analytics Approach, Special Section On Big Data Technology And Applications In Intelligent Transportation, IEEE Access publication January 14, 2020, 8, 14322–14328, 2020.
8. Edgar, P., Torres, P., Hernández-Álvarez, M., *Stock Market Data Prediction Using Machine Learning Techniques*, Á. Rocha, *et al.*, (Eds.), ICITS 2019, AISC 918, pp. 539–547, Springer Nature Switzerland AG, 2019.

9. Al Armouty, B. and Fraihat, S., Data Analytics and Business Intelligence Framework for Stock Market Trading. *2019 2nd International Conference on new Trends in Computing Sciences (ICTCS)*, 2019.

10. Peng, Z., Stocks Analysis and Prediction Using Big Data Analytics. *2019 IEEE,International Conference on Intelligent Transportation, Big Data & Smart City (ICITBS)*, 2019.

11. Pahwa, K. and Agarwal, N., Stock Market Analysis using Supervised Machine Learning. *International Conference on Machine Learning, Big Data, Cloud and Parallel Computing (Com-IT-Con)*, India, 14th-16th Feb 2019, ©IEEE, 2019.

12. Kompella, S. and Chilukuri, K.C., Stock Market Prediction Using Machine Learning Methods. *Int. J. Comput. Eng. Technol. (IJCET)*, 10, 3, 20–30, 2020, May-June 2019, IAEME Publication.

13. Vats, P. and Samdani, K., Study on Machine Learning Techniques In Financial Markets. *Proceeding of International Conference on Systems Computation Automation and Networking 2019*, 2019, 978-1-7281-1524-5.

14. Nikou, M., Mansourfar, G., Bagherzadeh, J., *Stock price prediction using DEEP learning algorithm and its comparison with machine learning algorithms*, John Wiley & Sons, Ltd, Volume 26, Issue 4, Pages: 151–203, October/December 2019, 20 September2019.

15. Carta, S., Medda, A., Pili, A., Recupero, D.R., Saia, R., Forecasting E-Commerce Products Prices by Combining an Autoregressive Integrated Moving Average (ARIMA) Model and Google Trends Data. *Future Internet*, 11, 5, 2019.

16. Borole, R., Govilkar, S., Duble, D., Sonawane, M., Stock prediction marketing using machine learning. *Int. J. Adv. Res., Ideas Innovations Technol.*, 5, 1, 28, 4, 63–83, 2019.

17. Mankar, T., Hotchandani, T., Madhwani, M., Chidrawar, A., Lifna, C.S., Stock market Prediction based on social sentiments using Machine learning. Published in *International Conference on Smart City and Emerging Technology (ICSCET)*, IEEE, 2018.

18. Sohangir, S., Petty, N., Wang, D., Financial Sentiment Lexicon Analysis. *12th IEEE International Conference on Semantic Computing*, 2018.

19. Alraddadi, R., Statistical Analysis of Stock Prices in John Wiley & Sons. *J. Emerg. Trends Comput. Inform. Sci.*, 6, 1, 38–47, 2015.

Web Citations

1. www.internetworldstats.com/top20.htm

2. https://economictimes.indiatimes.com/news/politics-and-nation/india-will-be-under-complete-lockdown-starting-midnight-narendramodi/articleshow/74796908.cms

3. https://in.finance.yahoo.com/
4. https://www.ibef.org/industry/pharmaceutical-india.aspx
5. https://www.cipla.com/home
6. https://www.torrentpharma.com
7. https://www.ibef.org/industry/banking-india.aspx
8. https://www.icicibank.com/
9. https://www.onlinesbi.com/
10. https://www.ibef.org/industry/fmcg.aspx
11. https://www.itcportal.com/
12. https://www.hul.co.in/
13. https://www.ibef.org/industry/power-sector-india.aspx
14. https://www.adanipower.com/
15. https://www.powergridindia.com/
16. https://www.ibef.org/industry/india-automobiles.aspx
17. https://www.mahindra.com/
18. https://www.marutisuzuki.com/
19. https://www.business-standard.com/article/companies/maruti-cuts-production-by-98-in-may-amid-coronavirus-pandemic-120060901484_1.html

15

Pehchaan: Analysis of the 'Aadhar Dataset' to Facilitate a Smooth and Efficient Conduct of the Upcoming NPR

Soumyadev Mukherjee, Harshit Anand, Nishan Acharya, Subham Char, Pritam Ghosh and Minakhi Rout*

School of Computer Engineering, Kalinga Institute of Industrial Technology (Deemed to be) University, Bhubaneswar, Odisha, India

Abstract

The Government of India has sanctioned Rs. 3,941.35 crore for maintaining the National Population Register (NPR). The "usual residents" of a nation are reflected in the NPR. Any individual who has stayed in an area for the past six months or plans to stay in an area for the next six months is referred to as a "usual resident". "Aadhar" is an authentic identity number comprising of 12 digits that can be issued at will by people who reside in the nation or individuals who hold passports of India, subjective to their demographic and biometric information. Analyzing the "Aadhar Dataset" and drawing meaningful insights out of the same will surely ensure a fruitful result and facilitate a smoother conduct of the upcoming NPR. The sole objective of "Hadoop" in this research is storing and processing huge amount of semi structured data. Hence, our proposed work uses "Hadoop" for processing the data gathered. The input data is processed using MapReduce and finally the result is loaded into the Hadoop Distributed File System (HDFS).

Keywords: National population register, aadhar, identity crisis, UIDAI, big data, hadoop, mapreduce, HDFS, tableau

Corresponding author: minakhi.routfcs@kiit.ac.in

Sachi Nandan Mohanty, Jyotir Moy Chatterjee, Monika Mangla, Suneeta Satpathy and Sirisha Potluri (eds.) Machine Learning Approach for Cloud Data Analytics in IoT, (375–390) © 2021 Scrivener Publishing LLC

15.1 Introduction

The Indian Government will shortly be coming up with a plan to maintain and update the "National Population Register" (NPR) nationwide. A sudden outbreak of COVID-19 has brought the entire procedure to a halt. Let us have a sight at what this NPR is all about. A list of usual residents of the nation is what the NPR comprises of. The same is being maintained right from the grassroots level including *panchayats* and suburbs to the state and national levels subject to the Citizenship Act of 1955 as well as the 2003 issued Citizenship Rules. It is the compulsion of every individual residing in India to be a part of the NPR. Any individual who has stayed in an area for the past 6 months or plans to stay in an area for the next 6 months is referred to as a "usual resident".

India witnessed a lot of protest against the "Citizenship Amendment Act" (CAA). "Identity crisis" is expected to be an obvious consequence of the same when blended with the "National Register of Citizens", people believe. The protests involving the CAA has compelled the state governments to pause the process of gathering data to facilitate the NPR for the time being. A particular section of the society might fall prey to this is what the authorities fear. NPR is not merely a census exercise; there are several other reasons solid enough to worry about the same, and it might result in the government putting its residents under custody and monitor their activities strictly; this turn is a major threat to the constitutional rights and the secular image of the nation. The "Aadhar" getting linked up with NPR plays a crucial role here.

We do all fear that someday our identity will be at stake. It is the desire of every individual being a part of this nation to call himself/herself a citizen of this country. "Aadhar" has been issued to most of the folks with certain exceptions and anomalies which if not taken care of will put forth a huge problem in front of the government. Soon, The Registrar General of the country is expected to request the Unique Identification Authority of India (UIDAI) to check credentials of people for making them a part of the recently planned NPR process, and fresh collection of biometrics would otherwise be a tedious task. However, there are many who have not yet verified their "Aadhar" credentials despite of being a part of this nation for a very long period of time. Do not you think they are citizens too? Do not they deserve the right to be referred to as Indians? They do.

Problems that may be encountered:

Lost Aadhar: Many times, individuals lose their Aadhar cards. For instance, Raghu, a fisherman residing near Puri, lost his Aadhar card during "Fani" and did not reissue the same.

Irrelevant and fake Aadhar Numbers: Possessing a fake identity is an offense; however, the story of duplicate Aadhar numbers being circulated is no more an unsaid tale. It is well known that many individuals possess more than one cards and pose a major threat to the proper governance.

Unrecognized immigrants: Aadhar cards have not been issued in bordering states like Assam as many immigrants have forcefully entered the state from Bangladesh. "Rohingyas" coming from Myanmar have come across similar problems too.

Linking Issues: Many innocent people have missed the deadline. Ahalya, a cancer patient from Cuttack, could not be a part of the process as she had no one to support her and take her for the formalities.

Updation of biometrics: The biometric information of an individual changes gradually over a span of time and has to be updated to avoid anomalies. However, a huge number of incorrect credentials pose an immense problem to the progress of the nation.

The following steps will resolve:

1. Spot out the age group more prone to the anomalies associated with the Aadhar Database and resolve the same.
2. Figure out the count of Aadhar cards accepted and directly facilitate the NPR.
3. Figure out the count of Aadhar cards not accepted across states, districts, and blocks and the reason behind the same.
4. Verify biometric and other personal credentials and update the same, if not
5. Check if the mobile number is linked with the Aadhar or not.
6. Resolve all peculiarities for valid citizens by passing on the results to UIDAI.
7. Spread a social message across the nation that there is no need to panic, proper analysis of data resulting in meaningful insights will protect your identity and help the government in resolving conflicts.

15.2 Basic Concepts

Hadoop offers five daemons with each daemon possessing a Java Virtual Machine: A) DataNode, B) NameNode, C) JobTracker, D) Secondary NameNode, and E) TaskTracker. One storing data and metadata, DataNode

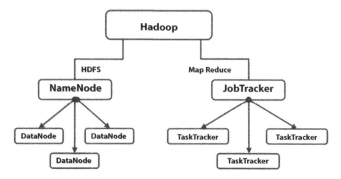

Figure 15.1 Apache Hadoop architecture.

and NameNode, form a part of HDFS, and TaskTracker and JobTracker, which monitor and perform the job, form a part of MapReduce layer (Figure 15.1).

Hadoop core architecture comprises of the following:

- MapReduce: It is a programming methodology implemented using "Hadoop". The same has been improvised for fields to work on and anatomize huge data sets facilitating scalability, reliability, and fault tolerance. "Map Phase" and "Reduce Phase" are used for analysis and anatomization of data. Figure 15.2 depicts the MapReduce Framework.
- The Hadoop Distributed File System (HDFS): It facilitates data storage and ensures high reliability, scalability, and fault tolerance. It combines storage resources which scale subject to inquiries and is highly inexpensive. HDFS works in

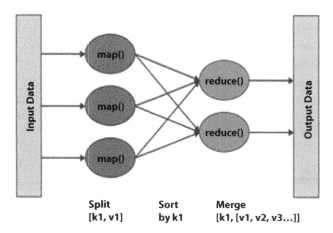

Figure 15.2 MapReduce framework.

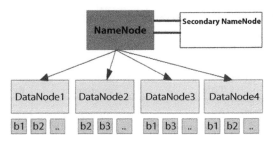

Figure 15.3 Hadoop master-slave architecture.

association with MapReduce. It takes into account data in any format be it audio, video, picture, or text irrespective of basic structure and, by default, ensures a large bandwidth. Hadoop Master-Slave Architecture has been depicted in Figure 15.3.

We are using HDFS in our project because of the following reasons:

→ Large Dataset: Current population of India is more than 1.3 billion; if we want to analyze data for that amount of people, then the dataset will be huge. That much huge amount of data cannot be processed by normal file system. That is why to get a smooth workflow we need to use HDFS.

→ Data Replication: We are working with a large dataset, so occurrence of unfortunate situations like hardware failure, crashing of a node is pretty common. In such situations, data loss may occur. To overcome this kind of problem, HDFS provides a feature called data replication. The data is replicated across a number of machines in the cluster by creating replicas of blocks.

→ Scalability: Our main goal in this work is to analyze the "Aadhar" dataset using Hadoop and facilitate a smoother maintenance of the NPR. So, our project must be scalable in order make it a dynamic project, because every year we may need to add new Aadhar data to our dataset. This can be achieved by using HDFS. In HDFS, we can scale up the infrastructure by adding more racks or clusters to our system.

→ Data Locality: In older systems, the data is brought at the application layer and then worked upon. In this research work, as a consequence of the huge bulk of data, bringing data to the application layer lowers down the overall performance.

In HDFS, we fetch the analysis part to the data nodes, the place where data resides. Hence, with HDFS, we are not moving computation logic, instead transferring data to the computation logic.

15.3   Study of Literature Survey and Technology

Table 15.1 Literature review.

S. no.	Author and year	Title	Proposed approach	Review
1	Mohit Dayal *et al.* (2016) [1]	An Anatomization of Aadhaar Card Data Set-A Big Data Challenge.	Analyzing the UIDAI Data Set for various inquiries using "Hadoop Cluster" and "Pig Latin".	->Apache Pig does not have explicit Data Schema. ->Entirely distributed Hadoop Cluster implementation.
2	D. Durga Bhavani *et al.* (2019) [2]	Big Data Analytics on Aadhaar Card Dataset in Hadoop Ecosystem.	Model to observe fluctuations in enrollment as a consequence of demonetization and PAN linkage in UIDAI Data Set using Hadoop and Hive.	->Row Level updates and Real-Time Queries are not much likely to be handled. ->Hive Latency is generally very high. ->Sub-queries are not supported.
3	R. Jayashree (2020) [3]	Analysis of Aadhaar Card Dataset Using Big Data Analytics.	Prototype for the retrieval of Blood Donor details and Crime Investigation using Sqoop (SQL + Hadoop) and Hive.	->Inefficient Data Transfer from RDBMS to Hadoop. ->Highly based on Market Research. ->Issues in handling sub-queries and inline queries.
4	K. Ramya *et al.* (2019) [4]	Big Data Applications in Aadhar Card Fraud Detection.	Data mining techniques in classification of Naive Bayesian (NB), c4.5 and Back Propagation (BP) to identify patterns leading to fraud.	->Network Paralysis may occur while using BP. ->Overfitting of Data Model likely to occur.

(Continued)

Table 15.1 Literature review. (*Continued*)

S. no.	Author and year	Title	Proposed approach	Review
5	Mrs. Lakshmi Piriya. S *et al.* (2018) [5]	Aadhar Based Data Migration, Analysis and Performance using Big Data Analytics and Data Science.	Proposal to use HDFS in Data Calibration, Data Wrangler in Data Cleansing, R in Data Analytics, and MapReduce Tools in Architecture Testing.	->Obscure solution rather than elucidated approach. ->Based on statistical summaries and Data Quality Visuals.

15.4 Proposed Model

The dataset is divided into smaller blocks which are primarily processed by "Map Phase" in parallel followed by "Reduce Phase". Hadoop framework arranges the output of the "Map Phase" which is then fed to "Reduce Phase" to initiate parallel reduce tasks. The file system stores the processed results. The model has been proposed based on the literature survey performed, please refer to Table 15.1 for a detailed literature review.

MapReduce retrieves data from HDFS. It takes input dataset in the form of key-value pair and further breaks down for effective analysis. Then, the number of rejections is mapped to corresponding states and shuffled accordingly. The number of entries rejected per state is the reduced output. The final result is sent to the authorities for corrective measures. Please refer to Figure 15.4 for a snapshot of the input dataset.

In our research we will be using five MapReduce key functions to get the desired output/outcome. The functionalities of each functions are as follows:

- UID_Mapper.java: Filters the header and writes to mapper output.
- UID_Reducer.java: Aggregate values for each state and outputs state wise identity.

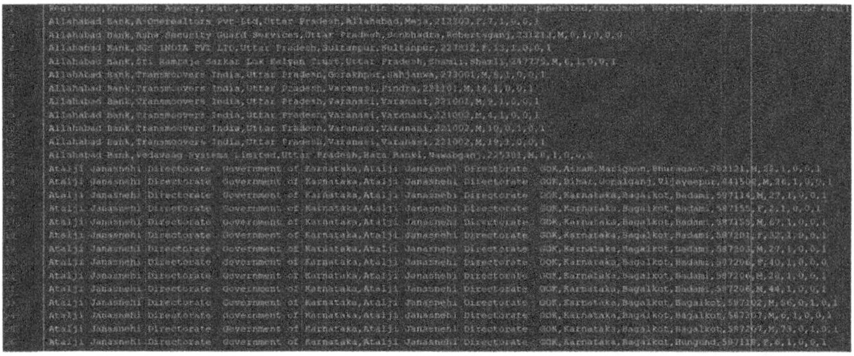

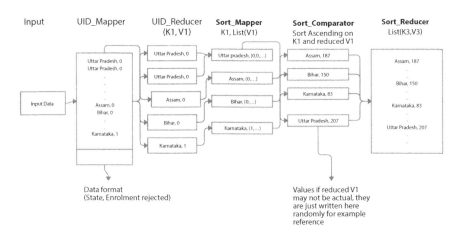

Figure 15.4 Input dataset snap.

- Sort_Mapper.java: Receive output from previous UID_ Mapper – Reducer phase and shuffle (x,y1) and (x,y2) pair into (x,(y1,y2)) form.
- Sort_Comparator.java: Sorts and reduces the output in descending order.
- Sort_Reducer.java: Swap (x,y) pair into (state,count) format and produce output.
- Driver.java: It is the main driver program for the MapReducer job. Please refer to Figure 15.5 for the detailed steps involved in the MapReduce Job.

Use case diagrams outline the usefulness of a framework utilizing the on-screen characters and use cases (Figure 15.6). The actors here are the

Figure 15.5 MapReduce job.

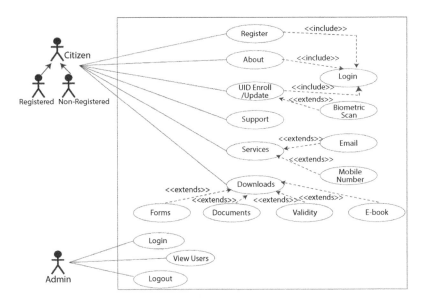

Figure 15.6 Use case diagram.

citizens, and the Admin of the system and Register, Enroll, Login, Support, Download, Check Validity, etc., are the various use cases. The class diagram (Figure 15.7) asserts the static structure of a framework. Various classes that we have used are Aadhar_Base, Appointment (appli_id, date, and time), Verification (Verification_id, status_id, application_id), etc. The ER diagram shows the relation between the entities which here are Citizen, Enrolling Agency, Supervisor, CIDR, UIDAI Admin, and the Government (Figure 15.8).

15.5   Implementation and Results

Having done intensive research, we have found out the following outputs which correspond to the 'Aadhar' dataset anatomization using Hadoop. Figures 15.9, 15.10 and 15.11 respectively denotes the Histogram of Age, Histogram of Logarithm of Age and Aadhar Applicants by Gender. This can help the government to figure out why the applications are rejected, i.e., the reasons behind the disapproval. This can also help the UIDAI Admin to make amendments to the existing database which can thereby contribute in removing ambiguities and clearing confusions. Hence, a smoother conduct for the upcoming NPR Programme can be assured. Figure 15.12, Figure 15.13 and Figure 15.14 depicts the percentage of overall applications

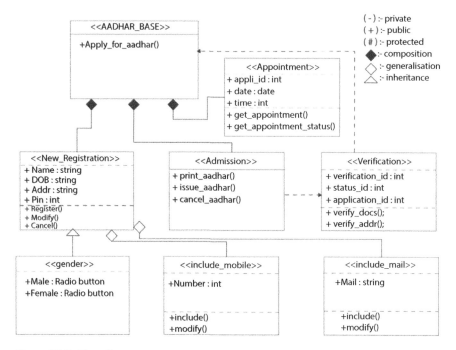

Figure 15.7 Class diagram.

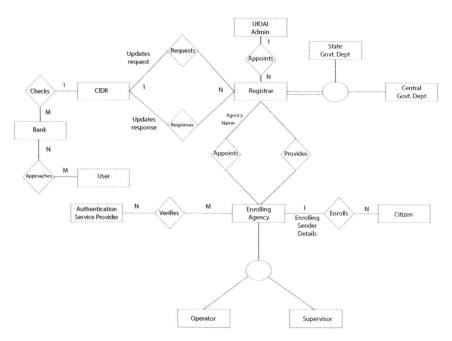

Figure 15.8 Entity relationship diagram.

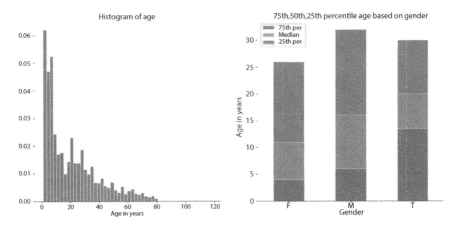

Figure 15.9 Histogram of age.

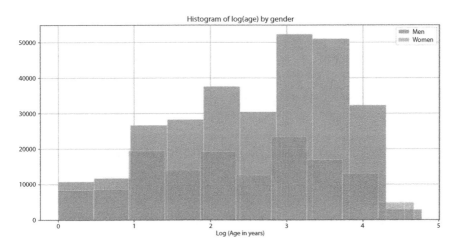

Figure 15.10 Histogram of logarithm of age.

by state, percentage of Aadhar Cards generated per state and percentage of Aadhar Cards rejected per state respectively. Percentage of emails and mobiles registered with Aadhar Cards can be found in Figure 15.15 and Figure 15.16 respectively.

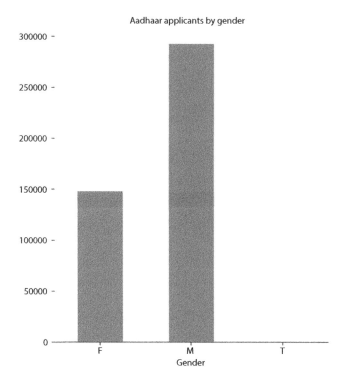

Figure 15.11   Aadhar applicants by gender.

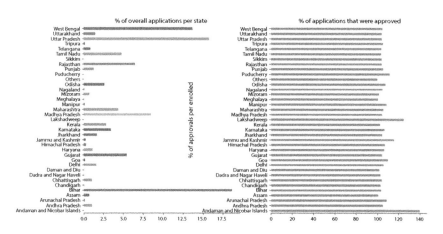

Figure 15.12   Percentage of overall applications per state.

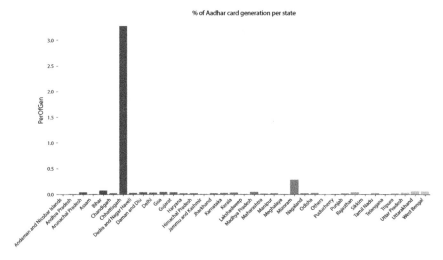

Figure 15.13 Percentage of aadhar cards generated per state.

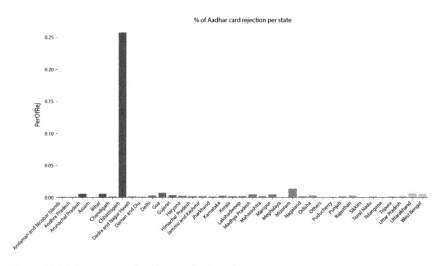

Figure 15.14 Percentage of aadhar card rejected per state.

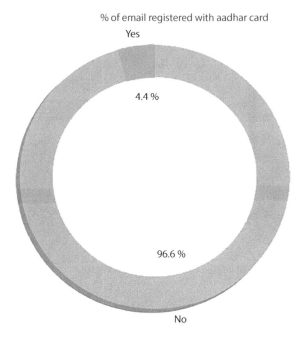

Figure 15.15　Percentage of emails registered with aadhar card.

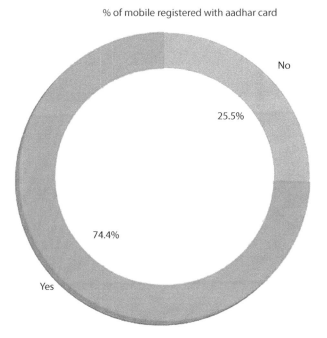

Figure 15.16　Percentage of mobiles registered with aadhar card.

15.6 Conclusion

After having concluded the analysis, authorities can undertake prompt measures to counter the anomalies observed in the 'Aadhar' dataset, and the citizens will, in turn, breathe a sigh of relief. Ambiguous results will be filtered out helping the State and Central Governments to resolve conflicts. The proposed idea is an attempt to sort out the long standing dilemma post the CAA. It has been observed that the number of female applicants for Aadhar is less than the number of male applicants. It has also been noticed that a lot of Aadhar applications are getting rejected, and many approved applications contain ambiguous results, showcasing the inefficiency of the registration process. The need of the hour is to resolve all anomalies and to facilitate a smoother conduct of the upcoming NPR Program. Let each and every individual being a part of this beautiful nation be proud of his/her identity and let us all cheer together, "Mera Aadhar, Meri Pehchaan".

References

1. Dayal, M. and Singh, N., An Anatomization of Aadhaar Card Data Set-A Big Data Challenge. *International Conference on Computational Modeling and Security*, CMS, 2016.
2. Durga Bhavani, D., Rajeswari, K., Srinivas Naik, N., Big Data Analytics on Aadhaar Card Dataset in Hadoop Ecosystem, in: *First International Conference on Artificial Intelligence and Cognitive Computing. Advances in Intelligent Systems and Computing*, vol. 815, R. Bapi, K. Rao, M. Prasad (Eds.), Springer, Singapore, 2019.
3. Jayashree, R., Analysis of Aadhaar Card Dataset Using Big Data Analytics, in: *Emerging Trends in Computing and Expert Technology*. COMET 2019. Lecture Notes on Data Engineering and Communications Technologies, vol. 35, D. Hemanth, V. Kumar, S. Malathi, O. Castillo, B. Patrut (Eds.), Springer, Cham, 2020.
4. Kou, Y., Lu, C.-T., Sirwongwattana, S., Huang, Y.-P., Survey of fraud detection techniques, *in IEEE International Conference on Networking, Sensing and Control* (IEEE, 2004), vol. 2, pp. 749–754, 2004.
5. Lakshmi Piriya, S. and Sri Nithi, T., Aadhar Based Data Migration, Analysis and Performance using Big Data Analytics and Data Science. *International Conference on Computing Intelligence and Data Science (ICCIDS 2018)*, Department of Computer Studies Sankara College of Science and Commerce Saravanampatty, Coimbatore.
6. Howe, D., Costanzo, M., Fey, P., Gojobori, T., Hannick, L., Hide, W., Hill, D.P., Kania, R., Schaeffer, M., St Pierre, S., Twigger, S., White, O., Rhee, S.Y.,

Big data: The future of biocuration. *Nature*, International Weekly Journal of Science, 455, 47–50, 4 September 2008.

7. Lynch, C., Big data: How do your data grow? *Nature*, International Weekly Journal of Science, 455, 7209, 28–29, 2008.

8. Jacobs, A., The pathologies of big data. *Commun. ACM - A Blind Person's Interaction with Technology*, 52, 8, 36–44, August 2009.

9. Meena, I., Aravind, R., Sarker, V., Sanjudharan, M.S., Healthcare analysis using hadoop framework. *IJSART*, 4, 14, 300–306, 2018.

10. Linda, B., Analysis of the Social Security Number Validation Component of the Social Security Number, Privacy Attitudes, and Notification Experiment, in: *Report of Census 2000 Testing, Experimentation, and Evaluation Program*, 2003.

11. Madhavi, V., Parallel Processing of cluster by Map Reduce. *Int. J. Distrib. Parallel Syst. (IJDPS)*, 3, 1, 167–179, 2012.

12. Wu, X., Zhu, X., Wu, G.Q., Ding, W., Data mining with big data. *IEEE Trans. Knowl. Data Eng.*, 26, 1, 97–107, 2014.

13. Abawajy, J., Comprehensive analysis of big data variety landscape. *Int. J. Parallel Emergent Distrib. Syst.*, 30, 5–14, 2015.

14. Matturdi, B., Zhou, X., Li, S., Lin, F., Big data security and privacy: A review. *IEEE Trans. Content Min.*, 2014. https://doi.org/10.1109/access.2014.2362522

15. Miller, H. and Mork, P., From Data to Decisions: A Value Chain for Big Data. *IT Professional*, 15, 1, 57–59, 2013.

16. Fisher, D., DeLine, R., Czerwinski, M., Drucker, S., Interactions with big data analytics. *Interactions*, 19, 3, 50–59, May 2012, For journal.

17. Tan, P.-N., Kumar, V., Steinbach, M., *Introduction to data mining*, First Edition, 2012.

18. Dufrasne, B., Warmuth, A., Appel, J. *et al.*, Introducing disk data migration, in: *DS8870 Data Migration Techniques*, pp. 1–16, IBM Redbooks, 2017.

19. Xia, D., Li, H., Wang, B., Li, Y., Zhang, Z., A Map Reduce-based nearest neighbor approach for big-data-driven traffic flow prediction. *IEEE Trans.*, 2169–3536, 2016. https://doi.org/10.1109/access.2016.2570021

20. Boyd, D. and Crawford, K., Six Provocations for Big Data. *Social Science Research Network: A Decade in Internet Time: Symposium on the Dynamics of the Internet and Society*, 21 September 2011.

16

Deep Learning Approach for Resource Optimization in Blockchain, Cellular Networks, and IoT: Open Challenges and Current Solutions

Upinder Kaur[1]* and Shalu[2]

[1]Department of Computer Science & Technology, Akal University, Talwandi Saboo, Punjab, India

[2]Department of Computer Science, Baba Farid College, Bathinda, Punjab, India

Abstract

Blockchain is the emerging technology to promote decentralized services in the distributed systems, with enhanced security, privacy, transparency, reliability, and robustness in a distributed manner. This chapter first outlines the current blockchain techniques and consortium blockchain framework and, after that, considers the application of blockchain with cellular 5G network, big data, IoT, and mobile edge computing. After that, we cover the aspects of machine learning and deep learning to bring intelligence in the blockchain applications. Here, we start with the open challenges for the resource management and allocation techniques in the existing techniques and motivation to the use of machine learning and deep learning–based resource allocation techniques in blockchain and its applications in future networks, IoT, and mobile edge computing. In the end, we provide the comprehensive study of the existing machine learning–deep learning–based resource optimization and allocation techniques in blockchain with it application in the future cellular network, IoT, and mobile edge computing. We also provide a framework for resource optimization and allocation for the future cellular networks, IoT, and mobile edge computing in collaboration with blockchain technology using machine learning–deep learning approach. It also concludes the

*Corresponding author: drupinder2016@gmail.com

Sachi Nandan Mohanty, Jyotir Moy Chatterjee, Monika Mangla, Suneeta Satpathy and Sirisha Potluri (eds.) *Machine Learning Approach for Cloud Data Analytics in IoT*, (391–428) © 2021 Scrivener Publishing LLC future research directions involving machine learning–deep learning in intelligent resource optimization and allocation techniques.

Keywords: Blockchain, deep learning, resource optimization, mobile edge computing, IoT, cellular networks, machine learning

16.1   Introduction

In this chapter, we proposed the vision of a deep learning approach with the integration of blockchain technology in various applications. As the emerging technology blockchain is an open database that is immutable, transparent, more secure, and reliable based on decentralized computing. Authors in [2, 3] presented the blockchain for next-generation cellular networks for cost-effective administration with dynamic access to spectrum efficiently. Some other authors [53] utilized the blockchain technology for the vehicular edge networks. They used a blockchain smart contract to design data sharing technique in vehicular networks. They used proof of work based on mining and required huge resources and energy consumption. In [6], the author discussed the mobile edge computing solutions for boosting the communication speed and provided seamless communication in heterogeneous networks and device-to-device communication. The authors [8–10] proposed caching schemes to resolve the backhaul congestion problems in mobile edge computing. They also proposed some offloading strategies to minimize task duration in the case of heterogeneous networks. There is a big challenge for optimizing the computing resources and caching issue on the mobile edge servers due to versatility in the time-variant, channels, requirements, and heterogeneity in emerging 5G cellular networks. Some authors worked on high-performance computing algorithms to overcome the demands of upcoming cellular networks.

The artificial intelligence (AI) branch has great potential in handling the issues in 5G cellular networks, blockchain, and IoT other emerging technologies. Some researchers worked on the integration of blockchain with AI in wireless networks for intelligent networks. AI can be integrated with cloud computing, cellular networks, mobile edge computing networks, and IoT networks to facilitate intelligent and secure resource management. The branch of AI, reinforcement learning (RL), that can be more generic, deals with a problem-solving approach and explicit programming. RL can be processed sequentially and automatically adjust the policies by observing the result and behavior. The authors in [11] focused on the deep RL (DRL) approach to handling the caching issue in mobile edge computing. Further, the author [12] designed an application to address the expansion of the network scale and in-depth feature discovery. The author [13] presented a deep learning–based algorithm for traffic control and potentially reduced the offloading time. Some others worked on a secure and intelligent framework for future generation networks integrate with blockchain.

The era of machine learning triggers a huge interest in DRL in various research fields. The authors [21–24] presented deep learning development models for computer vision, resource optimization, pattern recognition, and speech synthesis. Some of them presented a comprehensive report on application and open issues in the deep learning approach. Others summarized the principals, evolutionary methods, architecture, and core algorithms for DRL. The authors [26] highlight the remarkable achievement of deep neural networks in blockchain, IoT, and cellular networks. Further, [78] presented a survey on more application areas of deep learning. The author [32] shed more light on the deep learning potential in mobile edge computing, and popular application in IoT and blockchain.

16.1.1   Aim

There were numerous research articles published in the scope of machine learning integrated with blockchain to date on different aspects of emerging technology. Some researchers presented comprehensive surveys with a focus on the integration of machine learning with blockchain on specific fields and application areas. The proposed chapter covers the details of fundamental aspects of a deep learning–based approach in integration blockchain with IoT and 5G cellular networks.

There are survey articles that provide the integration of blockchain and 5G networks, authors [8] provide adoption of blockchain for secure 5G networks resource management. The author [7] focused on the potential of blockchain in industry 4.0. Further, [10] presented the analysis of blockchain application in handling the privacy issues for smart technology like IoT, smart grid, and healthcare. The author [9] presented blockchain for 5G IoT applications. Some other researchers presented a systematic survey on D2D caching techniques for content sharing and 5G networks. Our work is different from other as we did research mainly focused on the deep learning techniques in integration with blockchain, architecture, research challenges, and future directions for 5G cellular networks and IoT. The comparison of this chapter with the existing paper is given in Table 16.1.

Table 16.1 Comparison of existing surveys in blockchain and machine learning.

Reference	Title	Technology	Major contributions	Limitations
[1]	Deep Learning in mobile and wireless networking: A survey	IoT, ML, blockchain	The author presented a detailed study of deep learning techniques in mobile and wireless networking, IoT, signal processing	Discussed the deep learning approach but not covered blockchain application
[2]	Machine Learning Adoption in Blockchain-based smart applications	ML, Blockchain, smart applications	The author focused on the use of machine learning integrated with blockchain and smart applications	They missed the deep learning approach
[3]	Blockchain for 5G-enabled IoT for industrial automation	Blockchain, 5G, IoT	The author presented the comprehensive view of blockchain in for 5G enabled IoT in various applications like smart home, smart city, industry 4.0	Machine learning and deep learning is not considered
[4]	Machine learning for resource management for cellular and IoT networks	Machine learning, deep learning, IoT, 5G networks	In this, authors provided the taxonomy, machine learning approaches in IoT and 5G networks	They did not cover it with blockchain technology
[5]	Deep learning–based IoT for secure smart city	Deep learning, IoT, blockchain, smart cities	In this, author presented the methodological flow of SDN with blockchain technologies for smart cities	They covered blockchain and IoT technologies only
[6]	Adaptive resource allocation in future networks with blockchain	Mobile edge computing, blockchain, deep reinforcement learning	In this, author provides the systematic framework of the future wireless networks and open issues and future directions	They missed the IoT technologies

(*Continued*)

Table 16.1 Comparison of existing surveys in blockchain and machine learning. (*Continued*)

Reference	Title	Technology	Major contributions	Limitations
[7]	Blockchain for industrial 5G networks blockchain, IoT The paper only provided the concept of	Blockchain, 5G, and IoT networks	The author provides the content for the applications of blockchain in 5G networks and industry 4.	Machine learning, deep learning, specific use cases are missing
[8]	Blockchain for 5G network management	Blockchain, deep reinforcement learning	In this, author presented adoption of blockchain in the 5G network resource management and deep learning techniques	They missed focusing on other 5G technologies, D2D communications, IoT
[9]	Blockchain for UAV	Blockchain technology, UAV	The author presented a viewpoint for use of blockchain in solving UAV networks issues	They missed the focus on blockchain applications in 5G networks domain
[10]	Blockchain and 5G networking	Blockchain technology, D2D communication	They provides complete survey on D2D communication in 5G	They missed focus on role of blockchain in other 5G services
Our Paper	Blockchain for resource management in 5G cellular and IoT networks and deep learning techniques	Blockchain, IoT, deep learning, 5G cellular networks	Here, we are presenting a comprehensive survey of integration of blockchain with deep learning in 5G cellular and IoT networks	

16.1.2   Research Contribution

The proposed work covers all the concepts of deep learning to be applied in blockchain applications with IoT and 5G cellular networks. The following are the research contributions of this chapter:

- We presented a review of the existing survey on blockchain-empowered IoT and 5G cellular network services.

- We presented a systematic discussion on the potential of blockchain using machine learning and deep learning for resource management in 5G and IoT networks.
- Based on the study, we summarized the open issues, research challenges, and further future research directions.

16.1.3   Organization

This chapter is organized as follows. Section 16.1 covers the introduction of the chapter. Section 16.2 highlights the details of the background related to blockchain, IoT, 5G, machine learning, and deep learning. The summarized architecture, taxonomy, is detailed in Section 16.3. Section 16.4 presented the discussion on the open issues, research challenges, and further future research directions. In the Section 16.5, we concluded the chapter.

16.2   Background

In this chapter, we illustrate the analysis of existing surveys and provide the benefits with their limitations in applications of blockchain in cellular networks and IoT. The author in [14] explained the blockchain technology with their key requirements, consensus algorithms, and blockchain platforms with their pros and cons. The author [42] provided a detailed study of blockchain in decentralized blockchain consensus mechanism with BFT (Byzantine Fault Tolerance) strategies, other mining protocols, and hybrid protocols. In [13], author gave a complete survey on the permissionless blockchain technology and observed the system performance, cost of participation, and topologies adopted with design to improve the efficiency of blockchain technology. Further in [43], author investigates the security factors, authentication, privacy, access control, resource utilization, and quality assurance in blockchain technologies. The authors in [44–47] provide a comprehensive view of the applications of blockchain technology in smart cities, edge computing, IoT with increased efficiency, traceability, more transparency, and security of the system at low cost.

In the [49–52], authors provided the detailed applications of the machine learning approach in wireless sensor networks, optical communication networks, cognitive radio networks, software-defined networks. Some of the authors in [45, 54] investigate the applications of the deep learning approach to add intelligence in communication networks at different layers and IoT networks. They provided a review of the machine learning techniques for traffic classification, network controls in communication networks. In [57–59, 70], authors addressed the security issues, threats, machine learning approach in data mining and detection system. They also covered critical security issues in monitoring security threats. Nowadays, the machine learning technique is considered as promising technologies in integration with other technologies. Both machine learning and blockchain is used with integration in IoT, 5G cellular networks, and cloud computing to improve the overall performance. The author in [61] provides the integration.

16.2.1   Blockchain

Blockchain technology is distributed ledger technology that can provide an immutable set of transactions. It is more secure, reliable, and transparent technology. All the transactions in blockchain are managed in a tamper-proof ledger. It also has a consensus mechanism for attaching a new block to the chain. It offers ample of opportunities to manage untruthful parties by decentralized strategies of transaction governance. The key features of this technology are decentralization, privacy, transparency, auditability, and immutability. Due to its potential in various applications, it gained much attention for mobile networks, cloud computing, IoT, mobile edge computing, and infrastructure commissioners. Distributed ledger–based technology [22] used distributed databases for organizing hash tree, with irreversible and tamper-proof transaction management. Its consensus mechanism ensures the integrity of the transaction and guarantees the consistency of the transaction. The consensus mechanism performance parameters are transaction throughput, security, and scalability that also depend upon application scenarios. Proof of work, BFT, and proof of stake are the commonly used consensus mechanism.

The distributed ledger technology can be benefited for all the upcoming and emerging technologies. The transparency in the blockchain is the value for both end-users and the service providers. This is an ideal technology to track the history of all the transactions that are occurred. These features help in a revolutionary change in improving the current system efficiency and reliability [32]. In the paper [33], the author presented blockchain as the infrastructure as a service on the cloud with the feasibility that trade can be done in a distributed manner without centrally managed. Further, they incubate BaaI (blockchain as an Infrastructure) which managed a strong link between the end-user and the service provider. For this, blockchain acts as the backbone in distributed resource management technique and keeps the transparent transaction record. This incubates the new wings to resource management in blockchain applications—5G networks, IoT, cloud computing, etc. The automated blockchain-enabled technology provides complete resource management application in various fields.

16.2.2   Internet of Things (IoT)

The emerging technology IoT integrates the internet with the objects and is called the new technique as IoT. It is a powerful technique that can sense, actuate, dynamic behavior, and better networking. The IoT devices are found everywhere- smart homes, smart vehicles, smart transport systems, intelligent grids smart E-health, etc. IoT applications generates huge amount of heterogeneous data. The IoT has several key features that it's a highly dynamic environment, high power computing devices required for efficient functionality to IoT devices, and needs a federated system for secure resource management in IoT devices. The dynamic nature of IoT helps to work across the large geographical area, but need more scalable models and low latency response time algorithms. It can be integrated with the other technologies—cloud computing, blockchain, mobile edge computing for the deployment of ingestion bandwidth, processing, and better resource management services. The IoT devices provide a large-scale geographically locality and can be scale-up the resources to empower the real-time services of IoT devices. They can work in distributed decentralized networks and promising technology for future electronics devices, micro-grids, etc.

16.2.3   5G Future Generation Cellular Networks

The 5G is popularly known as the next-generation cellular communication networks. The 5G technologies have three broad services—enhanced mobile broadband, ultra-low latency communication and reliability, and massive MIMO. The next generation of the mobile networks to be rolled out the key characteristic of the 5G networks is the high data rate at the speed of 10 Gbps, high scalability for massive machine communication, networks slicing and software-defined networks, better network virtualization, and device-to-device communications. The integration of blockchain and machine learning in 5G cellular networks provides a great perspective to manage the research challenges in implementation. In this, we covered the 5G cellular resource management with deep learning and blockchain technology.

16.2.4 Machine Learning and Deep Learning Techniques

Machine learning is border term, categories into supervised, unsupervised, and RL techniques. In this, supervised learning is a technique where we can estimate then do prediction based on unknown parameters. The existing techniques used for supervised learning are Bayes classifier, vector support method, decision tree, random forest, and many more. The unsupervised learning is opposite to the previous one, they are used in a heuristic manner. Here, the data unlabeled and used to train the data. RL is a technique that learns from the environment. Q-learning is the most popularly used deep learning technique. Machine learning is used in several applications load balancing, spectrum sharing, sensor device management, channel utilization, energy trading, etc.

16.2.5 Deep Reinforcement Learning

The DRL is the branch of AI that can solve complex problems. It is a sequential learning technique that can adjust to the policies and gives rewards accordingly. They mainly focused on the Markov decision process that consists of an environment and has a set of agents [14, 15]. Machine learning followed through deep learning has basic paradigm learning. The agents perform an important role by applying meaning actions. Further, the action gives feedback to improve the output action because when the agent interacts with the environmental setup it gets rewards as the feedback signal. The main target is to achieve an optimized solution. Recently, this approach gained popularity in a wide range of applications. The DRL techniques have two main categories— model-based and model-free [16].

In a model-based deep learning approach, the agent can get access to the model environment. The environment function helps the agent to predict the probabilities and transaction states. The agent can predict better choices by understanding the environment. This approach helps plan policy. The author in [18] presented the model-based predictive control, where the agent predicts the environment and gives an optimal solution. The agent learns the environment and prepares new plans after every interaction in the system. In other [19] research areas, the author used model-based deep learning to train the agent and use agent experience to give probable solutions. Some of the best available deep learning techniques are given in Figure 16.1.

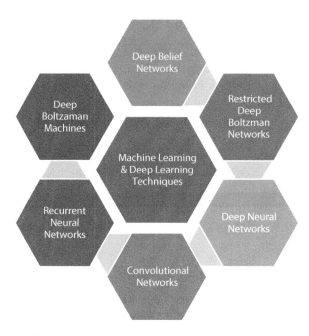

Figure 16.1 Deep learning techniques.

In a model-free deep learning approach, the agent learns the ground truth and use different aspects of the environment. This is the best approach as it is complex to train the model that can be exploited by agents. Thus, more feasible and can incubate multiple factors for rewards. The main agenda is to train the agent with the best optimal solution. The deep learning approach attracted researchers where a large no of possible states can be considered as a feedback output. The model-free approaches are Deep Q networks, Asynchronous Advantage Actor-Critic, deep policy gradient, and distributed proximal policy optimization. In [107–110], authors used a deep learning approach in AI gaming, automatic driving, and robotics. In [19], the author gave deepMind solutions for Atari video games. Further, [80] worked on actor centric mechanism, where different actors were deployed with different threads of CPU. Thus, it improves the training of agents in CPU processing. In [73], the author presented distributed proximal policy optimization. They implemented this approach on multi-threading CPU and apply different strategies to train the agents. Many other researchers applied the deep learning approach in solving more complex problems. In [110], a game-based agent has used that defeat the real-time multi-agent in the game. In [110–112], authors focused on the Markov decision process to train the switching policies, routing in networks, tracking control systems, and others. The ability of deep learning to work efficiently in high dimensionality makes this more useful in next-generation computing.

16.3   Deep Learning for Resource Management in Blockchain, Cellular, and IoT Networks

This section presented the current solutions of a deep learning approach in integration with blockchain for 5G cellular networks and IoT networks. Deep learning is the machine learning technique based on artificial neural networks that have multiple layers between the input and output layers. The deep learning network trained the data set based on the environment and performs an action based on this. This has huge potential in problem-solving—prediction, categorization, resource allocation, classification, speech synthesis, natural language processing, etc. The process used in deep learning is to perform feature extraction and then do further classification in various layers. There are multiple layers in which first find the patterns and then further recognized the complex problems to optimize the solution for further layers. A large amount of data can be arranged and managed using deep learning. As this is a powerful technique in for high-level features extraction, it is suitable in blockchain, IoT, and 5G networks because it can exploit the large amount of unlabeled data using the different deep learning models. Some existing deep learning models are shown in Figure 16.1. Deep Boltzmann network has two layers of neurons and in [42] author used this for network communications. They suggest the deep learning reduces the complexity of the complex task. It has great potential with technologies like blockchain, 5G networks, SDN, IoT, and cloud applications. In deep learning, the agents learn by themselves and experience the solutions by maximizing the effort in generating long-term rewards. Its major disadvantage is the large set of data need to train and test before use in any application. In [43, 44], authors presented the applications of deep neural networks in various domains. The author in [45] presented the deep learning for the prediction analysis in IoT networks. Some other researchers in [46, 47] presented the advanced level deep Q learning techniques. The further section provides the summarized research done in the blockchain, future generation networks, and IoT networks using machine learning and deep learning techniques.

16.3.1   Resource Management in Blockchain for 5G Cellular Networks

Blockchain technology mainly has three types of blockchain: public, private, and consortium blockchain. Table 16.2 showed the blockchain services in future generation communication networks. A public blockchain is a traditional approach in which anyone can participate. The summarized architecture view is shown in Figure 16.2. For the integration of blockchain, IoT, 5G networks, and deep learning approach. Private blockchain is mastered by some specific organization and the consortium-based blockchain used permission nodes to create new blocks. Generally, blockchain has three components—transactions, blocks records, and a consensus algorithm. When a transaction occurred it is encrypted and signed digitally. The block is packed with a cryptographically tamper-proof node block. The consensus algorithm helps invalidate the block and in terms of consistency and order. In a future generation, communication network security is a big issue. So, the application of blockchain is considered for secure and privacy-preserving future networks. Blockchain has the potential to improve the 5G cellular network services. In this chapter, we summarized the detail of the services offered by blockchain for 5G cellular networks. Table 16.2 provides the details of the key services of blockchain in 5G cellular networks. The integration of blockchain in future generation networking communication promises better services including data sharing, network virtualization management, resource management, federated learning, privacy services, and spectrum management. The main focus is to take potential of blockchain is secure and immutable decentralized transparent services of blockchain in future generation communication networks.

This section provides the resource in the future generation networks and discusses in detail the prospective of blockchain and machine learning–deep learning in resource management in future generation network communication.

16.3.2   Deep Learning Blockchain Application for Resource Management in IoT Networks

The popularity of deep learning encourages researchers to develop the application of deep learning in upcoming technologies. The author in [48] proposed the cognitive IoT network with the implementation of Q learning approach of deep learning. It helped in the optimization of packets transmitted in multiple channels. This enhances the overall network efficiency in IoT networks. Some authors worked on the [49–51] deep

Table 16.2 Blockchain services in 5G future generation communication networks.

Resources	References	Technology	Findings
Data collection and Sharing	[11–14, 34]	Blockchain, IoT, DRL, 5G	• Presented storage and sharing scheme for decentralized storage management • Secure sharing scheme was presented for industrial IoT • Integration of blockchain and fog for data sharing • They presented energy-efficient framework for secure data collection and sharing • DRL-based approach in which blockchain-enabled efficient improve data sharing and collection scheme proposed with etherum blockchain and DRL for 5G networks and created the same environment.
Device-to-Device Communication	[31, 30]	Blockchain, DRL, 5G networks	• Presented caching content at mobile devices and reduces data traffic using ML • Presented DRL approach to address the resource management using blockchain and 5G networks
Network Virtualization Management	[15–17, 37]	Blockchain and 5G cellular networks	• A blockchain approach to support MVNOs with wireless network virtualization • They presented a secure virtual machine orchestration system • The architecture proposed for blockchain-based network virtualization • DL-based blockchain framework for network resource management was presented

(*Continued*)

Table 16.2 Blockchain services in 5G future generation communication networks. (*Continued*)

Resources	References	Technology	Findings
Federation Learning	[21, 22, 27, 36]	Blockchain and 5G cellular networks	• Blockchain-based federated learning architecture proposed • Proposed blockchain-based nonrepudiation and tamper resistance federation learning methodology • Proposed deep learning–based deep chain framework • FDC—federated DRL approach for data collaboration in blockchain applications
Spectrum Management	[23–26, 30]	Blockchain and 5G cellular networks	• Proposed secure spectrum sharing in CRN • Blockchain-based secure spectrum sensing platform proposed • Unlicensed spectrum sharing scheme proposed with blockchain • Presented DRL approach to address the resource management using blockchain and 5G networks
Resource Management	[18–20, 28–40]	Blockchain, IoT, deep learning, cloud computing	• Presented architecture for mobile edge computing • Blockchain-based resource allocation strategy for IoT • Presented blockchain radio access network • Proposed network resource management using deep learning • Presented adapted resource allocation in future generation networks using a deep learning approach

(*Continued*)

Table 16.2 Blockchain services in 5G future generation communication networks. (*Continued*)

Resources	References	Technology	Findings
			• Secure spectrum based incentive scheme presented • Intelligent resource management scheme with DRL and blockchain was presented • Blockchain empowers resource management and sharing for future generation networks
Content Caching	[30, 38]	DRL, blockchain, 5G networks	• Presented DRL approach to address the resource management using blockchain and 5G networks • DRL blockchain approach for addressing open challenges
Energy Trading	[32, 33, 35, 39, 41]	DRL, ML, blockchain, 5G networks	• They presented the ML approach that is used for smart vehicles and mechanisms for energy trading with blockchain • They proposed V2V energy trading framework with ML and blockchain techniques • Deepcoin—blockchain and DRL based for energy trading in smart grids • Intelligent resource management scheme with DRL and blockchain was presented • Proof of deep learning is proposed for energy recycling blockchain

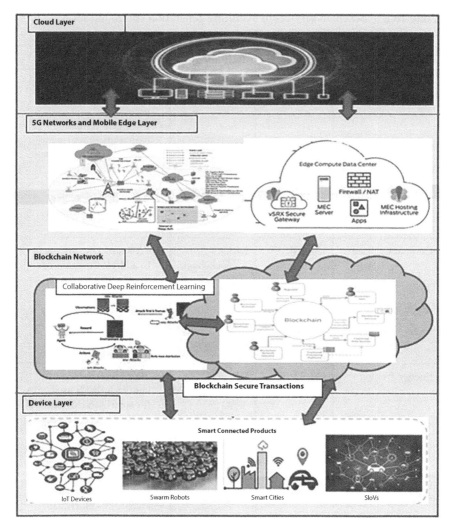

Figure 16.2 Summarized architectural view of the integration of deep learning and blockchain technologies empowered IoT and 5G generation networks.

learning–based approach in spectrum sharing and sensing. Some authors presented the deep learning technique in the MIMO and NOMA technologies also. Similarly, others framed the deep neural network for load prediction and balancing in the IoT networks in [52]. In [53], the author proposed a deep learning technique for spectrum management by using primary and secondary users and created an automated learning platform. Further in [54], a deep recurrent neural network approach proposed for channel selection, spectrum access, and carrier sensing. They claimed the

Table 16.3 Summarized taxonomy for resource management using deep reinforcement learning/machine learning blockchain approach in IoT networks.

Resources	References	Technology	Findings
Resource Allocation in Vehicular Networks	[56, 57, 113]	IoT, blockchain, machine learning, DRL,	• Proposed relocation mapping with DRL approach for vehicle-to-vehicle communication • DRL technique for resource allocation in vehicular networks IoT • Resource allocation–based DRL algorithm for orchestration in vehicular networks
Spectrum Sharing	[53, 55]	IoT blockchain, DRL	• Deep Q–based learning for spectrum sharing • Proposed power allocation for multicellular technology
Content Caching	[114]	IoT, DRL, blockchain	• DRL framework for cache replacement technique in multi-timescale resource management
Traffic Scheduling and Duty Cycle	[58, 59, 82]	IoT, DRL, ML	• Energy-efficient resource scheduling is presented using Machine Learning • Smart home resource scheduling technique is presented using deep Q learning in IoT networks • ML-based traffic scheduling is proposed in a real time scale.

(*Continued*)

Table 16.3 Summarized taxonomy for resource management using deep reinforcement learning/machine learning blockchain approach in IoT networks. (*Continued*)

Resources	References	Technology	Findings
Resource Allocation for QoS	[60–63]	IoT, ML, Wireless Networks	• Machine learning and cloud used together for resource allocation and beam management in wireless IoT networks • The presented mixture of supervise/unsupervised Machine learning to optimize the QoE • ML scheme for energy efficiency in the IoT network • DRL algorithm–based approach to sense inference and noise in IoT networks
Power Allocation	[64]	IoT, blockchain, machine learning	• Presented ML-based approach for low power transmission in IoT devices using LoRA3
Inference Management	[65–68]	IoT, 5G networks	• Q learning algorithm for power and inference management in IoT and 5G networks • Proposed a mechanism for inference level detection for radio channels • Presented inference detection and identification model in real-time traffic in IoT networks

(*Continued*)

Table 16.3 Summarized taxonomy for resource management using deep reinforcement learning/machine learning blockchain approach in IoT networks. (*Continued*)

Resources	References	Technology	Findings
Device-to-Device Communication	[71–77]	ML, IoT, blockchain	• Worked on improving the spectral efficiency and energy efficiency • Presented device-to-device communication problems-caching, security, and privacy • Machine learning–based approach for resource allocation in the distributed device-to-device system • Q learning–based technique presented for optimal resource allocation in device-to-device networks. • DRL-based approach to improve and provides optimal resource allocation to the device-to-device communication networks • Q learning–based approach for power resource management and reduce energy consumption in IoT networks
Clustering and Data Aggregation	[75–80]	ML DRL, IoT	• Presented algorithm for decreasing clustering time and increase efficiency based on k- means clustering algorithm • Presented hybrid ML approach for active learning SVM for IDS management

(*Continued*)

Table 16.3 Summarized taxonomy for resource management using deep reinforcement learning/machine learning blockchain approach in IoT networks. (*Continued*)

Resources	References	Technology	Findings
			• Multilayer clustering using ML for intrusion detection was proposed • SAX ML technique for handling density-based clustering • Presented IoT device access control mechanism using ML (INSTRUCT) • Deep Q learning proposal for resource allocation and cluster hear selection and resource allocation mechanism in vehicular networks
Resource and cell selection	[81–85]	ML, DRL, blockchain, IoT	• DRL-based algorithm proposed for multi-band spectrum sensing • Extreme ML algorithm for sensing scheme for multiple primary users. And get accurate complex channel states • Bayesian ML technique for heterogeneous spectrum states in the ML process • Proposed intelligent spectrum mobility management model for IoT networks • Presented spectrum mobility between two different modes using TACL algorithm

(Continued)

Table 16.3 Summarized taxonomy for resource management using deep reinforcement learning/machine learning blockchain approach in IoT networks. (*Continued*)

Resources	References	Technology	Findings
Traffic and Mobility Patterns	[86–90]	DRL, blockchain, IoT	• Presented IoT traffic classification using the ML approach • Presented analyzed details of real-time packet header using ML SVM and BP approach • DRL-based framework for traffic forecast in IoT networks • Presented OFDM channel estimation and signal detection using DRL approach • DRL-based traffic learning model and capturing traffic path detection and forwarding
Heterogeneous Networks	[62, 91–93]	ML, blockchain, IoT	• The ML-based scheme proposed for mobility management in heterogeneous networks • Presented Fuzzy Logic–Based approach for reducing energy consumption. • ML framework for Radio Access in heterogeneous networks. • Resource allocation technique proposed for cognitive radio networks using ML
MIMO	[94–100]	ML, DRL, Blockchain, IoT	• ML-based Bayesian learning approach presented to address channel estimation issues

(*Continued*)

Table 16.3 Summarized taxonomy for resource management using deep reinforcement learning/machine learning blockchain approach in IoT networks. (*Continued*)

Resources	References	Technology	Findings
			• ML-based artificial neural networks approach proposed for MIMO channel estimation problems • DRL-based approach proposed to address MIMO pilot contamination issues. • ML-based algorithm presented for link adaption in the MIMO system. • The ML-based algorithm proposed to the modulation scheme and coding rate in the MIMO system • ML-based approach for handling grouping problem in massive MIMO systems. • ML-based approach for beam allocation in MIMO networks
NOMA	[101–106]	ML, DRL, Blockchain, IoT	• ML-based approach for spectral performance and handling multiuser for NOMA techniques • Presented DRL-based approach for solving NOMA networks problem • Presented NOMA techniques for handling multi-users in BS with DRL approach • They used ML-based online adaptive filters for NOMA transmissions

(*Continued*)

Table 16.3 Summarized taxonomy for resource management using deep reinforcement learning/machine learning blockchain approach in IoT networks. (*Continued*)

Resources	References	Technology	Findings
			• Q learning–based technique for transmission and dynamic downloading in NOMA transmissions • They presented NOMA based management of multi-cell networks with ML approach • NOMA technique to address heterogeneous IoT network with DRL-based RNN model

maximization of the network throughput using a deep learning approach. In Table 16.3, we summarized taxonomy and the deep learning base block-chain techniques used for resource management in IoT networks. Table 16.3 provides the summarized resource management techniques for blockchain-empowered IoT networks with the machine learning approach.

16.4   Future Research Challenges

In this section, the open research challenges in adopting the machine learning approach and DRL approach to address the various issues for blockchain application in resource management in 5G future generation networks and IoT networks. The open challenges are related to the emerging blockchain technology and some issues related to the future generation 5G and IoT networks interoperability. How machine learning approach will helps in problem solving, after that issue of using ML and DRL techniques with blockchain technology. The research challenges related to this is given in Figure 16.3.

16.4.1   Blockchain Technology

The future generation promising technology, blockchain, provides the limited number of nodes in the blockchain networks. So, scalability is a major

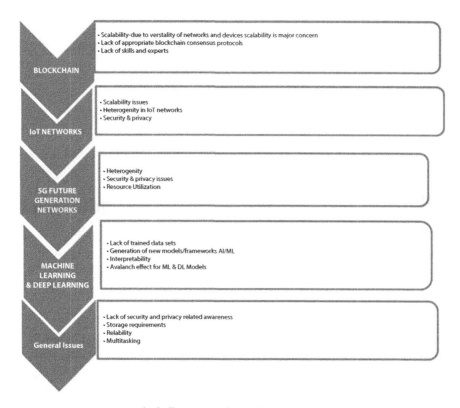

Figure 16.3 Open research challenges and future directions.

issue in servicing the blockchain empowers 5G and IoT networks. We also need consensus protocols for the validity of blockchain technology. Due to the development in blockchain, the availability of the standard platform and experts is very less. So, we there is need of more skills to address the emerging issues of blockchain in different application domains. All the other research issues are discussed below.

16.4.1.1   Scalability

The scalability of blockchain in IoT and 5G cellular networks becomes a major issue, where the lakhs of users need to be served and need to be scale to be up. The blockchain integration with the IoT and 5G cellular future generation networks need to be proceeding with high computational capabilities for handling a large amount of data and transactions. In [106], the author addressed the salability problem in maintain resource lanes for sharing lanes and multiple transactions chain maintained in parallel.

So, scalability needs to handle the fast processing of all the transactions in distributed decentralized networks. The computational power is limited to the resources available in the application domain. So, the scalability of transactions is appreciated when the growing demand of the user needs independent lanes for transactions. Further, the processing of scalability in these technologies is still a challenging task. The scalability in hybrid blockchain, IoT networks, resource lanes, and the hybrid consensus in the emerging technologies is an open challenge. The various ML models are trained to address the scalability issue. The improper handling of the scalability issue leads to delay in processing transactions. The present ML and DRL techniques are trained with the limited capacity data sets that have significantly difficult to handle scalability issues. Thus, the more diversified algorithms need to be a frame in this versatile environment to address the scalability difficulties.

16.4.1.2   Efficient Consensus Protocols

In the blockchain environment, we are having blockchain consensus protocols in the middle layer of the blockchain environment. In [107–109], several consensus protocols like proof of learning, proof of work, proof of useful work, proof of training quality, and proof of DL were proposed. The validity of the assigned work is validated by the validator committee in the blockchain consensus protocol. Further, the consensus ranking and consensus block will be sent to the validator to reach in a consensus after some iteration. Thus, the complex computation is required to solve these huge hash-based calculations in the blockchain. In [107], the author proposed the proof of DL was proposed to validate the blockchain transaction and train the data set using the DRL approach. The valid proof of the transaction block is created only if the DRL model is produced for the same. Further, in [110], the author presented the proof of useful work to validate the blockchain-based cryptocurrency with the DRL train model and mined a new block when the trained model exceeds its threshold limit. Thus, proper consensus mechanisms are required to address these growing issues.

16.4.1.3   Lack of Skills and Experts

In the blockchain technology, there lacked the number of skilled personnel and researchers that still worked on various models, architecture, and the framework for blockchain application in different domains. Thus, this affects the popularity of this technology.

16.4.2   IoT Networks

16.4.2.1   Heterogeneity of IoT and 5G Data

The heterogeneous nature of both networks has multiple compatibility issues while servicing various applications. The data generated in IoT networks and 5G cellular networks are heterogeneous and multidimensional so the exact features and information cannot be predicted. Thus, while training such data need to pretreatment like cleansing, ordering, and preprocessing because the fusion of this variety of data leads to false prediction. So, this plays an important role in the training of the data set and feature selection for testing data sets in heterogonous environments. For instance, smart homes IoT networks data is generated by the sensors and humans. But the data used in this application must be collected at a certain central server, in which data collected for different sources combined and trained accordingly that can able to cope up with data anomalies and more prediction accuracy can be achieved.

16.4.2.2   Scalability Issues

The emerging blockchain technology has many scalability bottlenecks in terms of the number of nodes in blockchain and that also constraint the performance. Some researchers presented the work suffered from huge processing time for transactions to the nodes in the blockchain due to block size restrictions. Thus, scalability is the major issue while integrating blockchain in versatile growing IoT networks.

16.4.2.3   Security and Privacy Issues

The large gigantic quantity of data produced by IoT devices is exposed to the greater threat security and privacy. The integration of blockchain to IoT networks is also subjected to verification before storing in a public ledger and still privacy preservation is a major issue. Some of the research worked on the lightweight cryptographic algorithms for resource-specific computation and storage services to ensure data security and privacy in IoT devices. Few blockchain gateways are proposed for the preserving security of the users in the IoT devices.

16.4.3   5G Future Generation Networks

16.4.3.1   Heterogeneity

The data generated in 5G cellular networks are heterogeneous and multidimensional so the exact features and information cannot be predicted.

Thus, while training such data need to pretreatment like cleansing, ordering, and preprocessing because the fusion of this variety of data leads to false prediction. So, this plays an important role in the training of the data set and feature selection for testing data sets in heterogonous environments. The researchers focused on this issue and some proposed solutions with a machine learning approach to optimized heterogeneity in blockchain-enabled 5G networks.

16.4.3.2   Security and Privacy

In 5G cellular networks, utilizing blockchain solution has major security and privacy issues. The existing solution was badly suffering from serious security issues. The acceptance of blockchain has various security and privacy issues, and the consensus protocol development needs significant testing before deploy in real-time 5G cellular networks. Researchers worked on the consensus protocols that suffered from serious security attacks. They also provided that critically analyses the smart contract due to improper code. Thus, the security and privacy is an open challenge in integration blockchain for 5G solutions against the security threats.

16.4.3.3   Resource Utilization

The researcher emphasizes on the efficient use of resource scheduling and optimization in the future generation 5G networks. To manage multiple heterogeneous resources in 5G cellular networks, researches provided a blockchain framework with machine learning. Few of them gave solutions for PoW blockchain consensus protocols. The resources deal with the device-to-device communication, SDN, and network virtualization, and the efficient coordination between 5G and blockchain is need for an efficient solution. Only a few researchers explored the consensus protocol in this regard. Thus, the quantitative analysis of resource utilization with blockchain-empowered 5G networks is a sensitive research issue.

16.4.4   Machine Learning and Deep Learning

The trends of building an intelligent system have made a drastic change in machine learning and deep learning techniques. Due to the emergence of new IoT networks, it is really difficult to train machine learning and deep learning technology for a greater level of abstraction in real-time analysis. Research put their efforts to build a new system for deep learning to use in blockchain and emerging 5G and IoT networks.

16.4.4.1   Interpretability

When we apply DRL models, interpretability is required to get a deep insight into the machine learning model. They need to be trained as per the policies of the blockchain for IoT and future generation networks to take all the accurate decisions and predictions. The training of DRL techniques needs proper insight into deep learning models for proper prediction. Deep learning models like artificial neural networks, deep neural networks, CNN and RNN are more difficult to interpret results. For greater accuracy, further models need to make that can interpret and high accuracy rate. The overall performance of DRL models can be quantified on parameters like computation power, learning capability, reliability, and more accuracy. The existing algorithms can be improved with repeated experimental testing data and training sets.

16.4.4.2   Training Cost for ML and DRL Techniques

The data set for the experimental models required to be trained. But the cost to train the ML and DRL models especially the real-time data applications. The training is required to keep the data set up to mark for accurate prediction. The overall retraining of the data set is the continuous learning process in real-time data environments. The system model framework needs to be taken for the initial data training process and keep the learning process in continuous mode for the maintaining accuracy level. Thus, the cost of providing the initial training depends on the complexity of the deep learning model used for the process as the sufficient amount of data is need to train for the testing purpose also.

16.4.4.3   Lack of Availability of Data Sets

The ML and DRL models/algorithms are completely based on the amount of training data set. The emerging technologies are subject to the collection of real-time data sets. The artificial synthesis of data sets is a challenging task as compared to the training the actual data sets. The lack of availability of proper data sets for a particular application domain also gives rise to another major issue that is the uniformity of data sets in heterogeneous environments.

16.4.4.4   Avalanche Effect for DRL Approach

This is the desirable characteristic of the secure algorithms that the minor change in the input reflected in output also. The use of ML and DRL approached helped to train the system from these vulnerable adverse security threats. So, preprocessing is required before actual training of the data. In [112], the author discusses the guarantee to the integrity of input data set data. Thus, the necessary measures are needed to be taken for the actual data count and trained input data set to maintain the integrity.

16.4.5   General Issues

16.4.5.1   Security and Privacy Issues

In the emerging technologies, due to the availability of large data sets, the communication has security and privacy issues. The critical aspect of this is that being secure technology blockchain is still suffering from attacks in various application domains—security of etherum platform breached results in loss of $50 million worth of ether as mention in [110]. The consensus blockchain brought thus serious issues that led to etherum platform. The numerous ML approaches were proposed by the researchers to solve these issues. Some focused on intrusion detection and develop DRL-based mechanism to significantly solve the security and privacy issue.

16.4.5.2   Storage

Blockchain technology has open research areas because; a large amount of data will be generated by IoT devices networks and 5G cellular networks. So, the integration of blockchain in IoT and 5G cellular networks cannot directly use distributed ledgers. The particular information needs to be stored separately before transaction verification. The concept to handle the storage requirement is to combine blockchain with better storage distributed databases that can accommodate a large amount of data in blockchain block nodes. Some research also proposed blockchain storage as a service. The block in the blockchain is replicated and need more storage space to complete the transaction. That leads to the major concern and burden on blockchain-empowered IoT and 5G technologies to limit the participation in the blockchain system.

16.4.5.3 Reliability

The nature of ML and DRL algorithms is very sensitive to the change of data. The prediction mechanism used in adversarial learning changes action and rewards. Thus, the reliability of any model and algorithm depends upon the data set and changes lead to change in output also. Even a few changes may lead to a drastic change in the output prediction. Therefore, the reliability of any model/algorithm referred to the input of learning algorithms and the further processing of data, their classification policies change the outcomes. In [111], the author predicts that adding noise in the trained data set can manipulate the outcome as well. The attackers can target the ML and DRL algorithms and models based on their feature selection. They provide that attackers manipulate the input data set with the additional features and they get desired outcomes. Therefore the resource allocation policies in IoT network requires proper reliability check. In IoT networks, if the resource allocation policies and data.

16.4.5.4 Multitasking Approach

This approach depends upon the complexity of the specific problem domain. The ML and DRL model need to be trained according to the specific type of data required. If the problem domain is changing continuously, then the solution should contain the reassessment and retain the data model is required. Sometimes, the data model needs to be restructured for real-time applications like traffic patterns in IoT and 5G cellular networks; the difficulty arises in train the data and preserves the changes. Therefore, the proposed model or algorithm must be tested for their multitasking approach according to the application domain. The complexity of the problem domain and level of depth might be different and decision-making versatility in different applications.

16.5 Conclusion and Discussion

The blockchain is the emerging technology, and the integration of blockchain with ML and DRL approach for future generation 5G networks and IoT networks has a significant effect. In this chapter, we explore the opportunities available with the emergence of ML and DRL in blockchain to empower the 5G future generation communication networks and IoT networks. The work is motivated by the increasing trends of machine learning and DRL to future intelligent technologies. In this chapter, we presented the comparative study of the existing survey in the area of blockchain-empowered 5G and IoT networks. We also provided the background knowledge of machine learning, deep learning, blockchain, resource management, IoT, and future generation 5G communication networks. Then, we provide the taxonomy of the resource management services utilizing the machine learning and deep learning techniques for integration of blockchain and in blockchain integrate IoT and blockchain integrate 5G. Here, we focused on intelligent resource management instead of the traditional approaches. The resource management taxonomy in the 5G generation networks is summarized in Table 16.2 and provides the existing solution with the technology used. The resource concerned is network virtualization, resource management, data collection and sharing services, federation learning, and spectrum management. The major concern is utilizing the issue focused on machine learning and deep learning. Similarly, the resources addressed in IoT networks are resource allocation in vehicular networks, spectrum sharing, content caching, traffic scheduling, QoS, power allocation, inference management, device-to-device communication, cell selection, MIMO, NOMA, and traffic mobility patterns. Table 16.3 provides the taxonomy for resource management in blockchain-empowered IoT networks. The integration of machine learning and deep learning for the intelligent resource allocation and management and decision-making process especially for the large-scale versatile heterogeneous, complex, distributed, and dynamically 5G and IoT networks. The heterogeneity of emerging technology needs intelligent scalability, efficient, and reliable networks. In the end, we conclude the open issues and research challenges in integrating the ML and DRL approach with blockchain to empower the 5G future generation networks and IoT networks. We categories the open research challenges with respect to technological and general issues in Figure 16.3. We provide the detailed the future research challenges in blockchain, IoT networks, 5G networks, and utilizing machine learning and deep learning. The study of existing research work concluded that blockchain with machine learning and deep learning prospective to practically empower the emerging large-scale fully heterogeneous 5G future generation networks and IoT networks.

The main finding is the blockchain potential in offering decentralized, immutable, and transparent transactions and eliminates the centralized network resource management. Then, it also covers the importance of machine learning techniques for intelligent resource management and provides better network services. Finally, blockchain can be accepted in the establishment of blockchain-enabled 5G and IoT services. The availability of blockchain uplifts the shape and future of emerging technologies. This chapter will be helpful for those who study the resource management services in 5G and IoT blockchain-empowered networks utilizing machine and deep learning approach.

References

1. Zhang, C. *et al.*, DL in Mobile and Wireless Networking: A Survey. *IEEE Commun. Surv. Tut.*, 21, 3, 1–67, 2019.
2. Bhatia, Q. *et al.*, ML Adoption in Blockchain-Based Smart Applications: The Challenges, and a Way Forward. *IEEE Access*, 8, 474–489, Dec 2019.
3. Mistry, I. *et al.*, Blockchain for 5G-enabled IoT for industrial automation: A systematic review, solutions, and challenges. *J. Mech. Syst. Signal Process., Elsevier*, 135, 1–21, 2020.
4. Hussain, F. *et al.*, Machine Learning for Resource Management in Cellular and IoT Networks: Potentials, Current Solutions, and Open Challenge. *J. IEEE Commun. Surv. Tut.*, 22, 2, 1–26, 2019.
5. Singh, S.K. *et al.*, A Deep Learning-based IoT-oriented Infrastructure for Secure Smart City. *J. Sustain. Cities Soc.*, 60, 1–22, 2020.
6. Guo, F. *et al.*, Adaptive Resource Allocation in Future Wireless Networks with Blockchain and Mobile Edge Computing. *J. Trans. Wireless Commun.*, 19, 3, 1689–1703, 2019.
7. Jovovi, I. *et al.*, Innovative application of 5G and blockchain tech. *J. Endorsed Trans. Netw. Intell. Syst.*, 18, 6, 1–6, 2019.
8. Dai, Y. *et al.*, Blockchain and DRL empowered intelligent 5G beyond. *IEEE Netw.*, 33, 3, 10–17, 2019.
9. Mehta, P. *et al.*, Blockchain envisioned UAV networks: challenges, solutions, and comparisons. *J. Comput. Commun.*, 151, 518–538, 2020.
10. Prerna, D. *et al.*, D2D content caching techniques in 5G: a taxonomy, solutions, and challenges. *J. Comput. Commun.*, 153, 48–84, 2020.
11. Zhang, Y. *et al.*, A blockchain-based framework for data sharing with fine-grained access control in decentralized storage systems. *IEEE Access*, 6, 38437–38450, 2018.
12. Krieger, U.R. *et al.*, A fog comp. architecture to share sensor data using blockchain functionality, in: *Int. Con. IEEE ICFC*, pp. 31–40, 2019.
13. Zhang, X. *et al.*, Adaptive blockchain-based electric vehicle participation scheme in smart grid platform. *J. IEEE Access*, 6, 25657–25665, 2018.
14. Nguyen, C. *et al.*, Secrecy Performance of the UAV enabled cognitive relay network, in: *IEEE Third Int. Conf. on ICCIS*, pp. 117–121, 2018.
15. Alshammari, A. *et al.*, Edge computing enabled resilient wireless network virtualization for the internet of things, in: *proc. of IEEE Third Int. Con. on CIC*, pp. 155–162, 2017.
16. Pujolle, G. *et al.*, Securing virtual machine orchestration with blockchains, in: *First Cyber Security in Networking Conference*, pp. 1–8, 2017.
17. Rebello, G.A. *et al.*, Securing configuration management and migration of VNF using blockchain, in: *IEEE/IFIP NOMS*, pp. 1–9, 2018.
18. Chen, L. *et al.*, 2. Etra: efficient three-stage resource allocation auction for mobile blockchain in edge computing, in: *proc. of 24th Int. Con. on ICPADS*, IEEE, pp. 701–705, 2018.

19. Leung, V.C. *et al.*, Resource allocation for video transcoding and delivery based on mobile edge computing and blockchain, in: *Proc. of IEEE Global Communications Conference*, pp. 1–6, 2018.
20. Wang, J. *et al.*, Prototype design and test of blockchain RAN, in: *proc. Of IEEE Int. Con. on Communications Workshops*, pp. 1–6, 2019.
21. Bennis, M. *et al.*, Blockchained on-device federated learning. *J. IEEE Commun.*, 24, 6, 1279–1283, 2019.
22. Niyato, D. *et al.*, Incentive mechanism for reliable federated learning: a joint optimization approach to combining reputation and contract theory. *J. IEEE IoT*, 6, 6, 10700–10714, 2019.
23. Bilén, S.G. *et al.*, Blockchain-enabled spectrum access in CRN, in: *proc. of Wireless Telecomm. Symposium*, pp. 1–6, 2017.
24. Zubow, A. *et al.*, Smart contracts for spectrum sensing as a service. *J. IEEE Trans. Cogn. Commun. Netw.*, 5, 3, 648–660, 2019.
25. Gazda, J. *et al.*, Blockchain-based intelligent network management for 5G and beyond, in: *proc. Of Third Int. Con. on AICT*, pp. 36–39, 2019.
26. Samdanis, K. *et al.*, On multi-access edge computing: a survey of the emerging 5G network edge cloud architecture and orchestration. *IEEE Commun. Surv. Tut.*, 19, 3, 1657–1681, 2017.
27. Zhang, J. *et al.*, Deep chain: Auditable and privacy-preserving DL with blockchain-based incentive, *IEEE Transactions on Dependable and Secure Computing Early Access*, 1–1, 2018.
28. Guo, S. *et al.*, Trusted Cloud-Edge Network Resource Management: DRL-driven Service Function Chain Orchestration for IoT. *J. Internet Things*, 7, 7, 1–13, 2019.
29. Guo, F. *et al.*, Adaptive Resource Allocation in FWN with Blockchain and Mobile Edge Computing. *J. IEEE Trans. Wirel. Commun.*, 19(3), 1–15, 2019, 2956519.
30. Dai, Y. *et al.*, Blockchain and Deep Reinforcement Learning Empowered Intelligent 5G Beyond. *J. Intell. Netw.: Cogn. Computing ML*, 33, 3, 1–10, May 2019.
31. Kang, J.J. *et al.*, Blockchain for Secure and efficient Data Sharing in Vehicular Edge Comp. and Nets. *J. IEEE IoT*, 99, 1, 1–13, 2018.
32. Kang, J. *et al.*, Enabling Localized P2P Electricity Trading Among Plug-In HEV Using Consortium Blockchains. *J. IEEE Trans. Industr. Inform.*, 13, 6, 3154–64, 2017.
33. Li, Z.Z. *et al.*, Consortium Blockchain for Secure Energy Trading in Industrial IoT. *J. IEEE Trans. Industr. Inform.*, 14, 8, 3690–3700, 2017.
34. Liu, C.H. *et al.*, Blockchain-enabled Data Collection and Sharing for Industrial IoT with Deep Reinforcement Learning. *J. IEEE Trans. Industr. Inform.*, 15, 6, 1–11, 2018.
35. Ferrag, M.A. *et al.*, DeepCoin: A Novel Deep Learning and Blockchain-Based Energy Exchange Framework for Smart Grids. *J. IEEE Trans. Eng. Manage.*, 67, 4, 1–13, 2019.

36. Yin, H. *et al.*, FDC: –A Secure Federated DL Mechanism for Data Collaborations in the Internet of Things. *J. IEEE IoT*, 7, 7, 1–12, 2020.

37. Garg, S. *et al.*, DL based Blockchain Framework for Secure SDN. *IEEE Trans. Ind. Inf.*, 17, 1, 1–11, 2020.

38. Jameel, F. *et al.*, RL in Blockchain-Enabled IIoT Networks: A Survey of Recent Advances and Open Challenges. *J. Sustainability*, MDPI, 12, 12, 1–12, 2020.

39. Xu, C. *et al.*, Intelligent Resource Management in Blockchain-Based Cloud Datacenters. *J. IEEE Cloud Comput.*, 4, 6, 1–10, 2017.

40. Xu, H. *et al.*, Blockchain-enabled resource management and sharing for 6G communications. *J. Digit. Commun. Netw.*, 6, 3, 261–269 2020.

41. Chenli, C. *et al.*, Energy-recycling Blockchain with Proof-of-Deep-Learning, in: *Int. conf. on blockchain and cryptocurrency*, May 2019, IEEE.

42. Chen, Z. *et al.*, A survey on DL for big data, *IF*, 42, 146–157, 2018.

43. Vassanelli, S. *et al.*, Applications of DRL to biological data. *IEEE Trans. NN LS*, 29, 6, 2063–2079, Jun 2018.

44. Saad, W. *et al.*, Learning How to Comm. in the IoT: Finite Resources and Heterogeneity. *IEEE Access*, 4, 7063–7073, Nov 2016.

45. Budinska, B.B. *et al.*, Adv. and disadv. of heuristic and multi-agents approaches to the solution of the scheduling problem. *IFAC*, 33, 13, 367–372, May 2000.

46. Debbah, M. *et al.*, Wireless network design in the era of DL: Model-based, AI-based, or both?, in *Jol. of Electrical Engineering and Systems Science*, arXiv:1902.02647v1, 1–43, Feb 2019.

47. Gong, S. *et al.*, App. of DRL in communications and networking: A survey, in *IEEE Communications Surveys & Tutorials,* 21, 4, 3133–3174, 2018.

48. Song, Y. *et al.*, A new DL based transmission scheduling mechanism for the cog. IoT. *IEEE IoT J.*, 5, 4, 1–1, 2017.

49. Cho, D. *et al.*, Deep cooperative sensing: Cooperative spectrum sensing based on CNN. *IEEE Trans. VT*, 68, 3, 1–1, 2019.

50. Kim, M. *et al.*, Deep cooperative sensing: -Coop. spectrum sensing based on CNN. *IEEE Trans. Veh. Technol.* 68, 3, 3005–3009, 2018.

51. Niyato, D. *et al.*, DRL based modulation and coding scheme selection in cognitive HNets. *IEEE Trans. on Wireless Comms*, 18, 6, 3281–3294, 2018.

52. Kim, J.M. *et al.*, A load balancing scheme based on DL in IoT, in the *Jol. of Cluster Comput.* 20, pp. 873–878, Springer, Oct. 2016.

53. Du, X. *et al.*, Resource Mang. for future mobile networks: Arch. and tech, in the *Jol. of Comput. Netw. Elsevier,* 129, 2, 392–398, Elsevier, 2018.

54. Saad, W. *et al.*, Proactive resource management in LTE-U systems: A DL perspective, –[CoRR, vol. abs/1702.07031, 2017.

55. Hossain, E. *et al.*, A D- Q Learning method for downlink power allocation in multi-cell networks, in https://-arxiv.org/pdf/1904.13032.pdf, April 2019.

56. Hossain, E. *et al.*, DL for radio resource allocation in multi-cell networks, -CoRR, https://arxiv.org/pdf/1904.13032v1.pdf, 2018.

57. Yin, H. *et al.*, Integrated networking, caching, and computing for connected vehicles: A DRL approach. *IEEE Trans. Veh. Technol.*, 67, 1, 44–55, Jan 2018.

58. George, N.K. *et al.*, A comparison of RL based approaches to appliance scheduling, in: *2016 2nd Int. Con. on Contemporary Comp. and Info. (IC3I)*, pp. 253–258, Dec 2016.

59. Hu, P. *et al.*, Cellular network traffic scheduling with DRL, in: *AAAI*, 2018.

60. Verbelen, T. *et al.*, Discrete event simulation for efficient and stable resource allocation in coll. Mob. cloudlets, in: *Simulation Modelling Practice and Theory*, vol. 50, pp. 109–129, 2015.

61. Zorzi, M.M. *et al.*, An ML approach to QoE–based video admission control and resource allocation in wireless systems, in: *2014 13th Annual Mediterranean Ad Hoc Networking Workshop*, pp. 31–38, Jun 2014.

62. Shihada, B. *et al.*, Enhanced ML scheme for energy-efficient resource allocation in 5g heterogeneous cloud RCN, in: *IEEE 28th Annual Int. Sym. on Personal, Indoor, and -Mobile Radio Comm. (PIMRC)*, pp. 1–7, Oct 2017.

63. Alizadeh, M. *et al.*, Resource management with DRL, in: *Proceedings of the 15th ACM Workshop on Hot Topics in Networks, ser. HotNets*, pp. 50–56, 2016.

64. Sidhu, R. *et al.*, Powering the IoT through embedded ML and Lora, in: *2018 IEEE 4th World Forum on IoT*, pp. 349–354, Feb 2018.

65. Fan, Z., Gu, X., Nie, S., Chen, M., D2D power control based on supervised and unsupervised learning, in: *Third IEEE Int. Con. on Computer and Comm. (ICCC)*, pp. 558–563, 2017.

66. P.L. *et al.*, Using ML for adaptive interference suppression in WSN. *IEEE Sens. J.*, 18, 21, 8820–8826, 2018.

67. Gidlund, M. *et al.*, Real-time interference identification supervised learning: Embed. coexistence awareness in IoT devices. *IEEE Access*, 7, 835–850, 2019.

68. Wang, X. *et al.*, Collaborative distributed q-learning for rach congestion minimization in MIoT networks. *IEEE Commun. Lett.*, 23, 4, 1–1, 2019.

69. Ansari, R., II, 5G device–to–device-networks: Techniques, -challenges, and - prospects. *IEEE Syst. J.*, 12, 4, 3970–3984, Dec 2018.

70. Vucetic, B. *et al.*, Localized small cell caching: A ML approach based on rating data. *IEEE Trans. Commun.*, 67, 2, 1663–1676, Feb 2019.

71. Maghsudi, S. *et al.*, Channel selection for network-assisted device-to-device-comm. via no-regret bandit learning with calibrated forecasting. *IEEE Trans. Wirel. Commun.*, 14, 3, 1309–1322, Mar 2015.

72. Miyanaga, Y. *et al.*, An autonomous learning-based algorithm for joint channel and power level selection by device-to-device- pairs in HNets cellular networks. *IEEE Trans. Commun.*, 64, 9, 3996–4012, Sept 2016.

73. Luo, Y. *et al.*, Dynamic resource allocations based on Q-Learning for device-to-device-communication in CN, in: *2014 11th Int. Comp. Con. on Wavelet Active Media Tech. and Info. Processing*, pp. 385–388, Dec 2014.

74. AlQerm, I. *et al.*, Energy-efficient power allocation in multitier 5G nets. using enhanced online learning. *IEEE Trans. Veh. Technol.*, 66, 12, 11 086–11 097, Dec 2017.

75. Thakral, A. *et al.*, Novel technique for prediction analysis using normalization for an improvement in k-means clustering, in: *2016 Int. Con. on Info. Tech.-The Next-Generation IT Summit on the Theme-IoT: Connect your Worlds*, pp. 32–36, 2016.

76. Kumari, V.V. *et al.*, A semi-supervised IDS using active learning SVM and fuzzy c-means clustering, in: *Int. Con. on I-SMAC (IoT in Social, Mobile, Analytics, and Cloud) (I-SMAC)*, pp. 481–485, 2017.

77. Khan, A. *et al.*, A novel learning method to classify data streams in the IoT, in: *2014 IEEE National Software Engg. Con.*, pp. 61–66, 2014.

78. Ochiai, H. *et al.*, nstruct: A clustering-based identification of valid comm. in the Internet of things networks, in: *5ᵗʰ Int. Con. on IoT: Systems, Management, and Security*, Oct 2018, pp. 228–233.

79. O.Y.-J., *et al.*, Semi-supervised multi-layered clustering model for ID. *Sci. Direct*, DCN, 4, 4, 227–286, Nov 2018.

80. Pourkhalili, A. *et al.*, A cluster-based vehicular cloud architecture with learning-based resource management. *JSC*, 71, 4, 1401–1426, Apr 2015.

81. Koivunen, V. *et al.*, RL method for energy-efficient cooperative multiband spectrum sensing, in: *IEEE Int. Workshop on ML for Signal Processing*, pp. 59–64, Aug 2010.

82. Kuang, H. *et al.*, Cooperative spectrum sensing using extreme ML for CRN with multiple primary users, in: *IEEE Third Advanced IT, Electronic and Automation Control Con.*, pp. 536–540, 2018.

83. Vucetic, B. *et al.*, Mobile collaborative spectrum sensing for HNets.: A bayesian ML approach. *IEEE Trans. SP*, 66, 21, 5634–5647, 2018.

84. Li, Z., Wu, W., Liu, X., Qi, P., Improved cooperative spectrum sensing model based on ML for CRN. *IET Commun.*, 12, 19, 2485–2492, 2018.

85. Kumar, S. *et al.*, Intelligent spectrum management based on transfer actor-critic learning for rateless transmissions in CRN. *IEEE Trans. Mob. Comput.*, 17, 5, 1204–1215, 2018.

86. T.T., *et al.*, Traffic prediction for dynamic traffic engg., Jul 2015, vol. 85, Elsevier, pp. 34–60.

87. Xu, X. *et al.*, *A learning-based multimodel Integrated framework for dynamic traffic flow forecasting*, vol. 85, pp. 407–430, Springer, Mar 2018.

88. Qiao, M. *et al.*, Real-time multi-application network traffic identification based on ML. *J. Ann.*, 9377, 473–480, 2015.

89. Y., *et al.*, *Learning-based network path planning for traffic engineering*, vol. 92, pp. 59–67, Elsevier, Sep 2018.

90. Juang, B.H. *et al.*, Power of DL for channel estimation and signal detection in -OFDM systems. *IEEE Wireless Commun. Lett.*, 7, 1, 114–117, February 2018.

91. Omar, M.S. *et al.*, Multi-objective optimization in 5G hybrid networks. *IEEE IoT J.*, 5, 3, 1588–1597, June 2018.

92. Vasudeva, K. *et al.*, Fuzzy logic game-theoretic approach for energy-efficient operation in hetnets, in: *IEEE Int. Con. on Comm. Workshops*, pp. 552–557, May 2017.

93. Perez, J.S., ML aided cognitive rat selection for 5G HetNets, in: *International Black Sea Conference on Communications and Networking*, IEEE, pp. 1–5, 2017.

94. Ting, P. *et al.*, Channel estimation for massive MIMO - using gaussian-mixture bayesian learning. *IEEE Trans. on Wireless Comm.*, 14, 3, 1356–1368, 2015.

95. Zhao, Y. *et al.*, Mobile location-based on SVM in MIMO communication systems, in *Int. Con. on Information, Networking, and Automation*, vol. 2, pp. V2–360, IEEE, 2010.

96. Choi, J. *et al.*, DL based -pilot allocation scheme for 5G massive MIMO system. *IEEE Comms. Letters*, 22, 4, 828–831, 2018.

97. Gao, X. *et al.*, ML-based link adaptation method for MIMO system, in - *29th Annual Int. Symp. on Personal, Indoor, and Mobile Radio Comm.* pp. 1226–1231, IEEE, 2018.

98. Heath, R.-W. *et al.*, Adaptation in convolutionally coded MIMO-OFDM wireless systems through supervised learning and SNR ordering. *-IEEE Trans. on vehicular Technology*, 59, 1, 114–126, 2010.

99. Maciel, T.-F. *et al.*, A low complexity solution for resource allocation and SDMA grouping in massive MIMO systems, in *15th IEEE ISWCS*, pp. 1–6, 2018.

100. Wang, J. *et al.*, An ML framework for resource allocation assisted by CC. *-IEEE-Network*, 32, 2, 144–151, 2018.

101. Higuchi, K. *et al.*, NOMA for cellular future radio access, in: *IEEE 77th (VTC Spring)*, pp. 1–5, 2013.

102. Ding, Z. *et al.*, NOMA: Common myths and -critical questions. *IEEE Wireless Communications*, 19, 1536–1284, 2018, arXiv preprint arXiv:-1809.07224.

103. Sari, H., DL for an effective non-orthogonal multiple access scheme. *IEEE Trans. Veh. Technol.*, 67, 9, 8440–8450, 2018.

104. Poor, H.V. *et al.*, RL based NOMA power allocation in the presence of smart jamming. *IEEE Trans. Veh. Technol.*, 67, 4, 3377–3389, 2018.

105. Mohajer, A. *et al.*, A Novel Approach to Efficient Resource Allocation in NOMA HNets: Multi-Criteria Green Resource Management. *Appl. AI*, 32, 7–8, 583–612, 2018.

106. Liu, M. *et al.*, Deep cognitive perspective: Resource allocation for NOMA based HetNets IoT with imperfect SIC. *IEEE IoT J.*, 6, 2, 2885–2894, 2018.

107. Li, B. *et al.*, Energy-recycling blockchain with PoDL, in *Proc. of IEEE Int. Conference on Blockchain and Cryptocurrency*, IEEE, 14–17 May 2019, arXiv preprint arXiv:1902.03912, 2019.

108. Maharjan, S. *et al.*, Blockchain and FL -for privacy-preserved data sharing in the industrial internet of things. *IEEE Trans. Industr. Inform.*, 69, 4, 4298–4311, 2019.

109. Saez, Y. *et al.*, Coin. AI– A PoUW scheme for blockchain-based distributed DL. *MDPI Jol. Entropy,* 21, 723–740, 2019, arXiv preprint arXiv:1903.09800.

110. Siegel, D. *et al.*, Understanding the DAO attack, Web. http://www. coindesk. com/understanding-dao-hack-journalists, 2016.

111. Agrawal, R. *et al.*, Mining association rules between sets of items in large DB. *ACM-Sigmod Rec.*, 22, 2, 207–216, 1993.

112. Raman, R.K. *et al.*, Promoting distributed trust in ML and computational simulation via a blockchain network. *Jol. of arXiv preprint*, 1–13, 2018, link- arXiv:1810.11126.

113. Ye, H. *et al.*, Toward intelligent Veh. Nets.: machine learning framework, in *the journal of IEEE Internet of Things*, vol. 6, pp. 124–135, 2019.

114. Tabassum, H. *et al.*, Deep Learning for Radio Resource Allocation in Multi-Cell Networks, in *the J. of IEEE Network*, vol. 33, issue 6, pp. 188–195, 2018.

17

Unsupervised Learning in Accordance With New Aspects of Artificial Intelligence

Riya Sharma, Komal Saxena and Ajay Rana*

Amity Institute of Information Technology, Amity University U.P., Noida, India

Abstract

Artificial Intelligence (AI) has evolved and there are many new generations that are taking place for the management of data and intelligence learning. In this chapter, we will discuss the various methods that keep evolving as a major concern in the place of unsupervised learning for the AI. Being an underlying model or the hidden structure for the distribution in the data of unsupervised learning is that any one can only have input data formed up with no corresponding output variables. Being a machine learning task, this type of learning has numerous types of hidden patterns or the underlying structures which combats to give input data in order to learn about the data more rigorously. Later knowing about the applications, you will be going to see how the edge cutting open source AI technologies are evolving that can be used to take out the machine learning projects to the next level. This involves a number of lists of the different open source machine learning platforms which have the ability to use the unsupervised data as a framework for the machine learning. Some of them are as listed which you will have more brief view later on, these are TensorFlow, Keras, Scikit-learn, Microsoft Cognitive Toolkit, etc. Since unsupervised learning is also used to draw inferences from the different datasets which again consists the data without the labeled responses. Going in with the applications of the unsupervised learning, you will also discover new machine learning algorithm which is going to be more evolved in upcoming market.

Keywords: TensorFlow, unsupervised, cognitive, inferences, labeled responses, machine learning, open-source

*Corresponding author: ajay_rana@amity.edu

Sachi Nandan Mohanty, Jyotir Moy Chatterjee, Monika Mangla, Suneeta Satpathy and Sirisha Potluri (eds.) *Machine Learning Approach for Cloud Data Analytics in IoT*, (429–460) © 2021 Scrivener Publishing LLC

17.1   Introduction

The main objective is to understand machine learning is to distinguish and investigate regularities and conditions in information and integrity. Principal component analysis (PCA) and clustering are two examples of the unsupervised learning plans that are generally utilized in getting know about information and applications [1]. Like administered learning plans, unaided taking in continues from a limited example of preparing information. This implies the scholarly ideas are stochastic factors relying upon the specific (irregular) preparing inset. This opens the inquiry of power and speculation: how vigorous are the educated ideas to change and commotion in the preparation set, and how well will they perform on another (test) datum? Speculation is a key theme in the hypothesis of directed learning, and critical advancement has been accounted for [2]. The most generally relevant mathematical results were as of late distributed by Murata *et al.*, depicting the asymptotic speculation capacity of directed calculations that are persistently defined. The point of this paper is to broaden the hypothesis of Murata *et al.* to unaided learning and show how it might be utilized to enhance the speculation execution of PCA and bunching [3].

The expansion of current application based upon Hadoop and NoSQL makes new operational difficulties for IT groups in regards to security, consistence, and work process bringing about hindrances to more extensive appropriation of Hadoop and NoSQL [4]. Exceptional information volume and the multifaceted nature of overseeing information across complex multi-cloud framework just further compounds the issue [5]. Luckily, ongoing improvements in Artificial Intelligence (AI)–based information in the form of unsupervised learning, the board instruments are helping associations address these difficulties which bring about the discrete need of unsupervised learning [6]. The sheer volume and assortments of the present big data fits an AI-based methodology, which diminishes a developing weight on IT groups that will before long become unreasonable. This conveys various dangers to the venture that may sabotage the benefit of receiving more up to date stages, for example, NoSQL and Hadoop, and that is the reason I accept AI can help IT groups undertaking the difficulties of information the board [7]. Next, how about we look in more detail at these key operational difficulties? From a security and examining viewpoint, the venture availability of these frameworks is still quickly advancing, adjusting to developing requests for severe and granular information get to control, validation and approval, introducing a progression of difficulties [8].

Right off the bat, Kerberos, Apache Ranger, and Apache Sentry speak to a few of the devices endeavor use to make sure about the Hadoop and NoSQL database; however, regularly, they were seen as mind boggling to actualize and oversee and troublesome in nature [9]. This may just be an element of item development as well as the hidden intricacy of the difficult they are attempting to address [10]. However, the recognition stays in any case. Secondly, classifying and caring critically the Personally Identifiable Information (PII) from leakage is a contest as the ecology compulsory to accomplish PII on big data platforms has not mature yet to the stage wherever it would gain full acquiescence confidence [11].

17.2   Applications of Machine Learning in Data Management Possibilities

For CIOs and CISOs concerned over safekeeping, agreement and success SLAs, it is really hard to distinguish that ever-raising dimensions and variations of data, and it is not persuasively believable aimed at an officer or level a line-up of administrators and data scientists to crack these encounters [12]. Luckily, machine learning here can help with unsupervised algorithms.

A division of deep learning and machine learning observations might be appointed to achieve this [14]. Approximately talking, machine/deep learning methods can be confidential as also unsupervised learning, supervised learning, or strengthening learning:

- The supervised learning contains the learning from the data that is by now "labeled" which is the arrangement and "result" for each data idea is recognized in advance [15].
- Equally, the unsupervised learning, such as the k-means clustering will be used as soon as the data is "unlabeled" which is an alternative way of maxim that the data is unsystematic [16].
- The machine learning depends on the part of rules or restraints distinct upon a system to regulate a best-known strategy to achieve an objective.

A prime for what method was be determined for which issue is being resolved is the key frame work done alongside of machine learning [17]. As an example, could be supervised learning device such as an arbitrary jungle can be used to create a frontline or baseline, for what institutes "normal" behavior for an organization [18], by seeing through applicable character-istics, then that uses that front or baseline to examine irregularities which are been lose from that baseline. Such type arrangement may be uses for perceiving threat fears for an organization [19]. That is mainly appropriate in classifying error occurrences and threats which would be slowly evolv-ing into the nature and would not encode the data once at on one occasion which can be rather progressively being over the time [20].

Though, as an initial in the training in which the data is used in typi-cal recreation named as unlabeled, there interpreted supervised learning methods somehow are useless [21]. While in case of unsupervised learning might appear as a normal and appropriate fit which is a substitute method that can possibly will results the further precise methods of models includes a pre-processing action to allocate labels to unlabeled data in such a move that make it functioning for the supervised learning [22]. Alternative moti-vating phase of engagement of data is using the deep learning method is to classify, tag, and mask the PII data as earlier discussed [23]. Making them consistent expressive and static ideology of data may be used for that purpose, by means of deep learning allows understanding for the precise formats (Even tradition PII types [24]) which is used in an association. Convolutional Neural Networks (CNNs) have been positively used for the image processing, thus discovering the usage for PII acquiescence is another interesting opportunity to get the information [25].

17.2.1 Terminology of Basic Machine Learning

Before we dive into the many forms of AI, how about taking a look into a basic and for the most part utilized in AI and guide to help in formation of the thoughts we familiarize with are discernible: the email or the spam channel [26]. We need to construct an easy-going system that takes in mes-sages and appropriately sorts out them as either "spam" or "not spam." This is a straight to the point characterization issue [27].

Here is a touch of AI phrasing as a boost: the info factors into this issue are the content of the messages [29]. These info factors are otherwise called highlights or indicators or free factors. The yield variable in which what we are attempting in foresee that is the mark of "spam" or "not spam" [30]. This is otherwise called an objective variable, subordinate variable, or reac-tion variable (or a long since this is a major grouping issue).

This arrangement models the AI preparation on its own is known as the preparation set; thus, every distinct model should be known as a preparation case or test as shown in the Figure 17.1 [31]. Throughout the

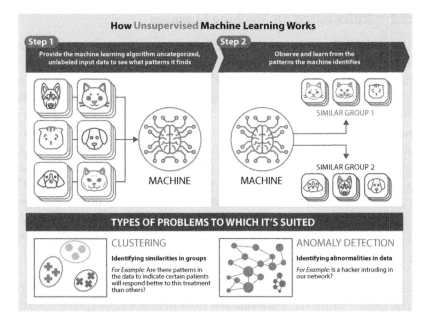

Figure 17.1 Working for machine learning algorithm [167].

preparation, the AI is endeavoring in limiting its cost capacity or blunder rate, or encircled all the more emphatically, to expand its worth capacity—for that situation, this proportion is effectively arranged into messages [32]. This AI effectively streamlines for a negligible blunder rate during preparing. Its mistake rate is determined by contrasting the AI's anticipated name and the genuine name [33]. Be that as it may, what we care about most is the manner by which well the AI sums up its preparation to at no other time seen messages [34]. It will be a genuine test for the AI which can effectively arrange messages which are never observed utilizing that in what it has realized via preparing for the models in the preparation set [35]. This speculation blunder or out-of-test mistake is the primary concern we use to assess AI arrangements. This set should be never foreseen the cases which are identified as the *test set* or *holdout set* (since the data is seized out from the exercise). If we have to select a numerous *holdout sets* as since the data is in the seized out from the exercise) [36]. This may be an intermediate holdout which can be known as the *validation sets* [37].

To make it all together, the methodology used in AI trains on the training data known as the experience set which is to improve its error rate (*performance* [38]) in flagging spam (*task*), which can ultimately create a successful criterion in such a manner that tells how well the *experience* being generalized throughout the formation error cycle [39].

17.2.2   Rules Based on Machine Learning

Utilizing the principles-based methodology, we can plan a spam channel with express standards to get spam, for example, banner messages with "u" rather than "you," "4" rather than "for," "Purchase NOW," and so forth [40]. Yet, this framework would be hard to keep up after some time as trouble-makers change their spam practices to sidestep the standards. On the off chance that we utilized a guidelines-based framework, we would need to habitually change the principles physically just to keep awake to-date [41]. Likewise, it would be over the top up in thinking about all of the standards that we would need to make to make this a well-working framework [42].

Rather than a standards-based methodology, we can utilize AI to pre-pare on the e-mail information and consequently plot rules to accurately hail malignant email as spam. This AI-based framework could be con-sequently balanced after some time also [43]. This framework would be a lot less expensive to prepare and keep up [44]. In this straightforward email issue, we might be able to handcraft rules, be that as it may, for some, issues, handcrafting rules are not practical in any way [45]. For instance, think about planning a self-driven vehicle an envision drafting the rules for how the vehicle ought to act in every single case it ever experiences [46]. This is an obstinate issue except if the vehicle can learn and adjust on its own dependent on its experience. We could likewise utilize AI frame-works as an investigation or information revelation apparatus to increase further knowledge onto the difficult we are attempting to fathom [47]. For instance, in the email spam channel model, we can realize which words or expressions are generally prescient of spam and perceive recently develop-ing vindictive spam designs.

17.2.3   Unsupervised vs. Supervised Methodology

This field of AI has two significant cores which are managed and unaided into the learning aspect and a lot of sub-core threads that connect the two of the methodologies [48]. In supervised learning, the AI specialist approaches marks, which can use it to improve its presentation on some algorithmic assessments. In the e-mail spam channel issue, we are having a dataset of messages with all the content inside every single e-mail [49]. We additionally know that which of these messages are spam or not (the supposed names) [50]. These names are truly important in helping the reg-ulated learning AI separates the spam messages from the rest.

As in case of unsupervised learning, the names are not accessible. In this way, the errand of the AI specialist is not very much characterized, and execution cannot be so obviously estimated [51]. Contemplate the e-mail spam channel issue, this time without marks. Presently, the AI specialist will endeavor to comprehend the basic structure of messages, isolating the database of messages into various gatherings to such an extent that messages inside a gathering are like each other yet not the same as messages in different gatherings [52].

This supervised learning issue is less plainly characterized much more than the managed learning issue and firmer for the AI operator to understand [53]. Yet, whenever took care of well, the arrangement is all the more impressive [54]. Here is the reason: the solo learning AI may discover a few gatherings that this later label as being "spam"— yet the AI may likewise discover bunches that its later labels as being "significant" or order as "family," "proficient," "news," "shopping," and so forth [55]. At the end of the day, in light of the fact that the issue does not have a carefully characterized task, the AI specialist may discover intriguing examples well beyond what we at first were searching for. Also, this unsupervised framework is superior to the directed framework at finding new examples in future information, making the solo arrangement nimbler on a go-ahead premise. It is the intensity of supervised learning [56]. The pros and cons of unsupervised learning are supervised learning will wallop unsupervised learning at barely characterized assignments for which we have all around characterized designs that do not change a lot after some time and adequately enormous, promptly accessible named datasets [57]. Be that as it may, for issues where examples are obscure or continually changing or for which we do not have adequately huge marked datasets, unaided adapting genuinely sparkles.

Rather than being guided by marks, the supervised learning works by learning the hidden skeleton of the information on which it has been prepared [58]. This is done by attempting to generated a boundaries based on the quantity models which are accessible as the example of the datasets on a distinguish feature of unmistakeable portrayal of the information. For instance, all the pictures that seem as though seats will be gathered, all the pictures that appear as though mutts will be assembled, and so forth [59]. Obviously, the solo learning AI itself cannot name these gatherings as "seats" or "mutts" however since comparable pictures are assembled, people have a lot less difficult marking task. Rather than naming a large number of pictures by hand, people can physically name all the unmistakable gatherings, or the names that has to apply on all the individuals inside each gathering [60]. After the underlying preparing, if the supervised learning in AI discovers pictures that do not have a place with any of the named gatherings, the AI will make separate gatherings for the unclassified pictures, setting off a name the new, yet-to-be-marked gathered information of pictures. Supervised learning makes already unmanageable issues progressively feasible and is a lot nimbler at finding concealed examples both in the recorded information that is accessible for preparing and in future information [61]. Also, we currently have an AI approach for the gigantic troves of unlabeled information that exist on the planet [62]. Despite the fact that unaided learning is less skilled than directed learning at understanding explicit, barely characterized issues, it is better at handling increasingly open-finished issues of the solid AI type and at summing up this information. Similarly, as significantly, unaided learning can address a large number of the basic issue's information researchers experience when building AI arrangements [63].

17.3   Solutions to Improve Unsupervised Learning Using Machine Learning

Ongoing accomplishments of AI which have been in the accessibility of lots of information, propels in PC equipment and cloud-based assets, and advancements in AI calculations. Be that as it may, these triumphs have been in for the most part slender AI issues, for example, picture characterization, PC vision, discourse acknowledgment, common language handling, and machine interpretation [64]. To take care of progressively goal-oriented AI issues, we have to open the estimation of solo learning. We should investigate the most well-known difficulties information researchers undergo when the building arrangements of information is helping to design supervised learning as we can see in the diagram that how the data is converted and being used as an output after processing [65].

17.3.1   Insufficiency of Labeled Data

In the event that AI stayed a rocket transport, information will be the fuel, this without the parts of the rocket and engine the rocket cannot fly [66]. Yet, not being all information is made equivalent. In concern to utilize managed calculations, we require loads of marked information, which

Figure 17.2 Data Processing by machine learning.

sometimes results in more expensive in generation. Along supervised learning, we can consequently name unlabeled models [67]. Here is the means by which this will work as per the constraints, we would bunch all the models and afterward apply the marks from named guides to the unlabelled ones inside a similar group which can be seen in above Figure 17.2. Unlabeled models would get the mark of the named ones they are generally like [68].

17.3.2   Overfitting

On the off chance that the AI calculation learns an excessively unpredictable capacity dependent on the preparation information, it might perform inadequately on at no other time seen occasions from the holdout sets, for example, as the *approval set* or the *test set* [69]. In this situation, the calculation has over-fit the preparation information and by separating a lot from the clamour in the information [70]—and has helpless speculation blunder. So, the calculation is retaining the preparation information as opposed to figuring out how to sum up information dependent on it. To attain this, we can present unsupervised learning as a distribution [71]. Distribution is a procedure used to diminish the multifaceted nature of an AI calculation, helping it catch the sign in the information without altering an excessive amount to the commotion [72]. This is one such type of distribution. Rather than taking care of the first info information legitimately into a directed learning calculation, we can take care of another portrayal of the first information that we produce.

17.3.3   A Closer Look Into Unsupervised Algorithms

Presently, if we direct our concentration towards issues for which we still don't have classified names. Rather than attempting to make expectations, unaided learning calculations will attempt to become familiar with the basic distribution of the information [73].

17.3.3.1   Reducing Dimensionally

On the group of calculations, which is known as dimensionality decrease calculations, extends the first high-dimensional information to a low-dimensional space, sifting through the not really applicable highlights and keeping; however, much of the intriguing ones as could reasonably be expected [74]. Dimensionality decrease permits unaided learning AI to all the more successfully recognize examples and all the more effectively unravel enormous scope, computationally costly issues (frequently including pictures, video, discourse, and text).

As far as the dimensionality concerns, it tells about the complex rigidity traversal outputs being converted from one and another [75].

The other thing which can be remember during understanding is that when the high dimension of data is mergers throughout the procedure then the labeled data cannot be changed as the data is travelling in a structured manner so that any changes during the execution of the cycle is not allowed [76]. Moreover, the inclination is a boosting calculation utilized when we manage a great deal of information to make a gauge with high gauge power [77]. Improving is really a group of learning calculations which consolidates the count of a few base estimators so as to improve strength over a solitary estimator [78].

Thus, it can be altered to understand the various things during the movement of the data in the dimensional form.

17.3.3.2   Principal Component Analysis

This way to deal with culture of the hidden attributes of information is to distinguish between highlights for which the arrangement of highlights is being generally significant in clarifying the fluctuation on the occurrences in the information [79]. Neither all the highlights are equivalent—for certain highlights, the qualities in the dataset do not change a lot, and these highlights are less helpful in clarifying the dataset [80]. For different highlights, the qualities may fluctuate significantly—these highlights merit investigating in more prominent details of information for a better model for helping it, this configuration separates the information [81].

According to PCA algorithm, the calculation results in finding the low dimensions portrayal for the information while holding however much of the variety as could reasonably be expected [82]. The quantity of measurements which are been left significantly littler than that of the quantity of measurements for the full *datasets* (i.e., the quantity of complete highlights). This loses a portion in the difference in the low dimensions space, yet in the hidden information is simpler to distinguish, permitting to perform undertakings like grouping all the more productively [83]. Thus, some few variations of PCA will investigate later on. These incorporate smaller than usual bunch variations, for example, steady PCA, nonlinear variations, for example, bit PCA, and inadequate variations, for example, meagre PCA [84].

17.3.4   Singular Value Decomposition (SVD)

Alternative way in dealing with learning the basic about the information is to decrease in the position of the first lattice of highlights to a littler position to such an extent that the first framework can be reproduced utilizing a straight blend of a portion of the vectors in the littler position network is known as SVD [85]. To create the less position lattice, SVD keeps the vectors of the first framework that have the most data (i.e., the most elevated solitary worth). The littler position lattice catches the most significant components of the first element space [86].

17.3.4.1   Random Projection

A comparable dimension decrease algorithm includes prominent targets from a high dimensional space to such space of inferior dimensionalities in a manner so that the detachments between the points are well-looked-after [87]. This can be using moreover an *arbitrary Gaussian matrix* or a *random sparse matrix* to complete this [88].

17.3.4.2   Isomax

It is a type of machine learning approach where this algorithm learns the geometric intrinsic of data learning by estimating the geodesic or the curved distance between each point and to its neighbors rather of Euclidean distance [89]. This algorithm uses this method then to embed the real high-dimensional space to of a low-dimensional space [90]. This implants high-dimensional information into a space of only a few measurements, permitting the changed information to be pictured [91]. In this a few dimensional space, comparative occurrences are displayed nearer together and disparate occasions are demonstrated further away.

17.3.5   Dictionary Learning

A methodology recognized as word reference learning includes learning the portrayal of the funda mental information [92]. On this agent, components are basic vectors, and each example in the dataset is spoken to as the weight vector and can be remade as a weighted aggregate of the delegate components. The agent components that this solo learning creates are known as the word reference [93].

By making such a word reference, this calculation can proficiently distinguish the most striking delegate components of the first element space to fill the ones with the most non-zeroes loads [94]. The delegate components that are less substantial will have not many nonzero loads [94]. As with PCA, word reference learning is superb for learning the fundamental structure of the information, which will be useful in isolating the information and in distinguishing intriguing examples [95]. One regular issue with unlabeled information is that there are numerous free signals implanted together into the highlights we are given [96]. Utilizing autonomous segment investigation or Independent Component Analysis (ICA), we can isolate these mixed signs into their individual parts. After the detachment is finished, we can reproduce any of the first highlights by including a blend of the individual segments we create [97]. ICA is usually utilized in signal handling errands (for instance, to distinguish the individual voices in a sound clasp of a bustling café).

17.3.6   The Latent Dirichlet Allocation

Solo learning can likewise clarify a dataset by realizing why a few pieces of the dataset are like one another [98]. This requires learning in secret components inside the dataset—a methodology known as inactive Dirichlet distribution (LDA). For instance, think about a report of text with many, numerous words. These words inside an archive are not absolutely arbitrary; rather, they display some structure [99]. This can be demonstrated as imperceptibly components known as subjects. In the wake of preparing, LDA can clarify a given report with a little arrangement of subjects, where for every point there is a little arrangement of much of the time utilized words [100]. This is the shrouded structure the LDA can catch, to make us understand better clarify a formerly unstructured corpus of text [101].

17.4   Open Source Platform for Cutting Edge Unsupervised Machine Learning

All the patterns, as referenced above of machine learning, are very useful and look encouraging in granting uncommon consumer loyalty [102]. The dynamic elements of ever-developing businesses further push the pertinence of machine learning patterns. Computerized reasoning (AI) innovations are rapidly changing pretty much every part in our life. As how we impart to the methods, we use for transporting the data progressively dependent on them. In view of these fast headways, enormous measures of ability and assets are committed to quickening the development of the innovations [103]. Here is a rundown of 7 best open source AI advancements you can use to take your AI ventures to the following level [104].

17.4.1   TensorFlow

At first discharged in 2015, TensorFlow is an open source AI system that is anything but difficult to utilize and send over an assortment of stages. It is one of the most very much kept up and broadly utilized systems for AI [105]. Made by Google for supporting its exploration and creation targets, TensorFlow is currently broadly utilized by a few organizations, including Dropbox, eBay, Intel, Twitter, and Uber. TensorFlow is accessible in Python, C++, Haskell, Java, Go, Rust, and most as of late, JavaScript [106]. You can likewise discover outsider bundles for other programming dialects. The structure permits you to create neural systems (and significantly other computational models) utilizing flowgraphs [107].

17.4.2   Keras

At first discharged in 2015, Keras is an open source programming library intended to rearrange the production of profound learning models. It is written in Python and can be sent on head of other AI innovations, for example, TensorFlow, Microsoft Cognitive Toolkit (CNTK), and Theano [108]. Keras is known for its ease of use, seclusion, and simplicity of extensibility. It is reasonable in the event that you need an AI library that takes into account simple and quick prototyping, bolsters both convolutional and repetitive systems, and runs ideally on the two CPUs (focal preparing units) and GPUs (illustrations handling units) [109].

17.4.3   Scikit-Learn

At first discharged in 2007, scikit-learn is an open source library created for AI. This customary structure is written in Python and highlights a few AI models including characterization, relapse, bunching, and dimensionality decrease [110]. Scikit-learn is structured on three other open source ventures—Matplotlib, NumPy, and SciPy—and it centers around information mining and information examination [111].

- Programming and development
- Red Hat Developers Blog
- Programming cheat sheets

17.4.4   Microsoft Cognitive Toolkit

At first discharged in 2016, the Microsoft Cognitive Toolkit (recently alluded to as CNTK) is an AI arrangement that can enable you to take your AI ventures to the following level [112]. Microsoft says that the open source system is fit for "preparing profound learning calculations to work like the human mind." Some of the fundamental highlights of the Microsoft Cognitive Toolkit incorporate exceptionally advanced segments equipped for taking care of information from Python, C++, or Brain Script, capacity to give effective asset utilization, simplicity of joining with Microsoft Azure, and interoperation with NumPy [113].

17.4.5   Theano

At first discharged in 2007, Theano is an open source Python library that permits you to effortlessly form different AI models [114]. Since it is probably the most established library, it is viewed as an industry standard that has propelled advancements in profound learning [115].

At its core, it allows you to simplify the course of defining, improving, and evaluating mathematical terminologies. Theano is fit for taking your structures and changing them into productive code that incorporates with NumPy, effective local libraries, for example, BLAS and local code (C++) [116]. Besides, it is upgraded for GPUs, gives effective emblematic separation, and accompanies broad code-testing abilities [117].

17.4.6   Caffe

At first discharged in 2017, Caffe (Convolutional Architecture for Fast Feature Embedding) is an AI system that centers around expressiveness, speed, and seclusion [118]. The open source system is written in C++ and accompanies a Python interface. Caffe's principle highlights incorporate an expressive design that motivates advancement, broad code that encourages dynamic turn of events, quick execution that quickens industry arrangement, and an energetic network that animates development [119].

17.4.7   Torch

At first discharged in 2002, Torch is an AI library that offers a wide cluster of calculations for profound learning [120]. The open source system gives you advanced adaptability and speed when taking care of AI ventures—without causing superfluous complexities all the while. It is composed utilizing the scripting language Lua and accompanies a basic C usage [121]. A portion of Torch's key highlights incorporate N-dimensional exhibits, direct polynomial math schedules, numeric improvement schedules, productive GPU backing, and backing for iOS and Android stages [122].

17.5 Applications of Unsupervised Learning

The effect of machine learning is very engaging, as it has caught the consideration of numerous organizations, regardless of their industry type [123]. For the sake of the game, machine learning has really changed the basics of businesses for better [124].

The hugeness of machine learning can be brought about by the way that $28.5 billion was distributed in this innovation during the principal quarter of 2019, as announced by Statista. Considering the importance of machine learning, we have concocted patterns that are going to clear a path into the market in 2020 [125]. Coming up next are the eagerly awaited machine learning patterns that will modify the premise of enterprises over the globe [126].

17.5.1 Regulation of Digital Data

In this day and age, information is everything. The rise of different advancements has moved the enhancement of information [127]. Be it the car business or the assembling segment, information is producing at a phenomenal pace. Yet, the inquiry is, "is all the information pertinent?" All things considered, to unwind this puzzle, machine learning can be conveyed, as it can sort any measure of information by setting up cloud arrangements and server farms [128]. It just channels the information according to its criticalness and raises the utilitarian information, while deserting the piece [129]. Thusly, it spares time permits associations to deal with the consumption, also. In 2020, a huge measure of information will be delivered, and ventures will require machine learning to order the significant information for better productivity [130].

17.5.2 Machine Learning in Voice Assistance

As indicated by the eMarketer concentrate in 2019, it was evaluated that 111.8 million individuals in the US would utilize a voice aide for different purposes. In this way, it is very apparent that voice collaborators are a significant piece of businesses [131]. Siri, Cortana, Google Assistant, and Amazon Alexa are a portion of the popular instances of savvy individual aides. AI, combined with AI, helps in preparing activities with the most extreme precision [132]. In this manner, Machine Learning is going to assist ventures with performing muddled and critical errands easily while improving efficiency. It is normal that in 2020, the developing territories of examination and speculation will chiefly concentrate on producing specially crafted Machine Learning voice help [133].

17.5.3 For Effective Marketing

As indicated by the eMarketer concentrate in 2019, it was evaluated that 111.8 million individuals in the US would utilize a voice aide for different purposes [134]. In this way, it is very apparent that voice collaborators are a significant piece of businesses [135]. Siri, Cortana, Google Assistant, and Amazon Alexa are a portion of the popular instances of savvy individual aides [136]. AI, combined with AI, helps in preparing activities with the most extreme precision. In this manner, machine learning is going to assist ventures with performing muddled and critical errands easily while improving efficiency. It is normal that in 2020, the developing territories of examination and speculation will chiefly concentrate on producing specially crafted machine learning voice help [137].

17.5.4 Advancement of Cyber Security

Lately, the internet has become all the rage. As announced by Panda Security, around 230,000 malware tests are made each day by programmers, and the goal to make the malware is consistently completely clear [138]. Also, with the PCs, systems, projects, and server farms, it turns out to be much progressively tricky to check the malware assaults.

17.5.5 Faster Computing Power

Industry experts have begun getting a handle on the intensity of fake neural systems, and that is on the grounds that we as a whole can anticipate the algorithmic achievements that will be required for supporting the critical thinking frameworks [139]. Here, AI and machine learning can address the unpredictable issues that will require investigations and directing dynamic limit [140]. Furthermore, when every last bit of it is deciphered, we can hope to encounter ever-blasting registering power. Undertakings like Intel,

Hailu, and Nvidia have just equipped to enable the current neural system handling by means of custom equipment chips and clarify capacity of AI calculations [141].

When the organizations make sense of the processing capacity to run machine learning calculations logically, we can hope to observe more force communities, who can put resources into creating equipment for information sources along the edge [142].

17.5.6   The Endnote

Without hold, we can say that machine learning is going large step by step, and in 2020, we will encounter included uses of this creative innovation [143]. Also, why not? With machine learning, ventures can conjecture requests and settle on fast choices while riding on cutting edge machine learning arrangements [144]. Overseeing complex assignments and keeping up exactness is the way to business achievement, and machine learning is impeccable in doing likewise [145].

17.6   Applications Using Machine Learning Algos

17.6.1   Linear Regression

To comprehend the working usefulness of this calculation, envision how you would organize arbitrary logs of wood in expanding request of their weight [146]. There is a trick; be that as it may—you cannot gauge each log. You need to figure its weight just by taking a gander at the tallness and bigness of the log (visual investigation) and organize them utilizing a mix of these noticeable boundaries [147]. This is the thing that straight relapse resembles.

In this procedure, a relationship is built up among free and ward factors by fitting them to a line. This line is known as the relapse line and spoke to by a straight condition $Y = a * X + b$. In this equation,

   Y – Dependent Variable
   a – Slope
   X – Independent variable
   b – Intercept

These constants a and b are subsequent based on dropping the sum of squared modification of distance between data points and lapse line [148].

17.6.2   Logistic Regression

Logistic Regression estimates the likelihood of event of an occasion by fitting information to a logit capacity, and it is otherwise called logit relapse [149]. Strategic Regression is utilized to appraise discrete qualities (generally double qualities like 0/1) from a lot of autonomous factors. It predicts the likelihood of an occasion by fitting information to a logit work. It is additionally called logit relapse [150].

- Include interaction terms
- Eliminate features
- Regularize techniques
- Use a non-linear model

17.6.3   Decision Tree

It is one of the most well-known AI calculations being used today; this is a managed learning calculation that is utilized for characterizing issues [151]. It functions admirably characterizing for both straight out and constant ward factors. In this calculation, we split the populace into at least two homogeneous sets dependent on the most critical properties/autonomous factors [152].

17.6.4   Support Vector Machine (SVM)

In SVM, each fact element as a point trendy n-dimensional space with the value of seprate feature and provides the rate of a particular association. These lines called classifiers can be castoff to divide the data and plot them on a diagram [153].

17.6.5   Naive Bayes

A Naive Bayes classifier accepts that the nearness of a specific component in a class is disconnected to the nearness of some other element [154]. Regardless of whether these highlights are identified with one another, a Naive Bayes classifier would consider these properties autonomously while computing the likelihood of a specific result. A Naive Bayesian model is anything but difficult to construct and valuable for huge datasets [155]. It is basic and is known to beat even profoundly complex arrangement strategies [156].

17.6.6   K-Nearest Neighbors

For this, Kenn can be utilized for both characterization and relapse. Be that as it may, yet more often than not for Kenn utilizing characterization issues in the business. K closest neighbors is a basic calculation that stores every single accessible case and groups new cases by a mainstream vote of its k neighbors [157].

- Before profitable to select KNN must reflect below things
- KNN is computationally higher
- Variables must be normalized, or else higher range variables can bias the algorithm
- Data still requires to be pre-processed.

17.6.7   K-Means

It is basic and simple to characterize a given informational indexes over a specific number of groups. What is more, it is a sort of solo calculation. Information focuses inside a bunch are homogeneous and heterogeneous to honourable gatherings [158].

How K-implies structures groups:

- The K-implies calculation decisions k measure of focuses
- Each information point strategies a bunch with the nearest centroids
- It now makes new centroids dependent on the current group individuals.

With the above centroids, the nearest separation for every information point is resolved. This procedure is visit until the centroids do not change [159].

17.6.8   Random Forest

Arbitrary Forest is an image term for an outfit of choice trees. Random Forest is a gathering of choice trees [160]. To classify another article dependent on highlights, each tree gives an arrangement, and we state the tree votes in favor of that class. Each tree is set up and developed as follows:

- If the quantity of cases in the preparation set is N, at that point, an example of N cases is taken aimlessly. This example will be the preparation set for developing the tree [161].
- If there are M input factors, a no m << M is expressed with the end goal that at every hub, m factors are chosen aimlessly out of the M, and the best isolated on this m is utilized to partitioned the hub [162]. The estimation of m is thought interminable during this procedure. Each tree is developed to the most considerable degree conceivable [163]. There is no turning.

17.6.9   Dimensionality Reduction Algorithms

In this day and age, an enormous number of information is being put away and investigated by corporate and government areas and research associations [164]. As an information researcher, you realize that this crude information contains a ton of data and the test is in ordering noteworthy structures and factors.

17.6.10   Gradient Boosting Algorithms

Inclination is a boosting calculation utilized when we manage a great deal of information to make a gauge with high gauge power as shown in Figure 17.3 below [165]. Improving is really a group of learning calculations which consolidates the count of a few base estimators so as to improve strength over a solitary estimator [166].

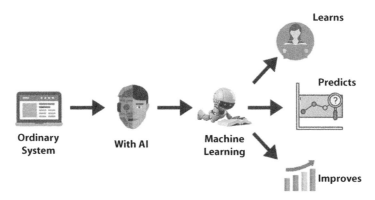

Figure 17.3 Different AI-based machine learning used systems [168].

References

1. Destefanis, G., Barge, M.T., Brugiapaglia, A., Tassone, S., The use of principal component analysis (PCA) to characterize beef. *Meat Sci.*, 56, 3, 255–259, 2000.
2. Destefanis, G., Barge, M.T., Brugiapaglia, A., Tassone, S., The use of principal component analysis (PCA) to characterize beef. *Meat Sci.*, 56, 3, 255–259, 2000.
3. White, T., *Hadoop: The definitive guide*, O'Reilly Media, Inc., O'reilley, 43–79, 2012.
4. Nandimath, J., Banerjee, E., Patil, A., Kakade, P., Vaidya, S., Chaturvedi, D., Big data analysis using Apache Hadoop, in: *2013 IEEE 14th International Conference on Information Reuse & Integration (IRI)*, IEEE, pp. 700–703, 2013.
5. Steiner, J.G., Clifford Neuman, B., Schiller, J., II, Kerberos: An Authentication Service for Open Network Systems, in: *Usenix Winter*, pp. 191–202, 1988.
6. Kohl, J.T., Clifford Neuman, B., Theodore, Y., The evolution of the Kerberos authentication service, IEEE, Reprinted with permission from distributed Open Systems, F.M.T. Braizen and D. Johansen (eds.), pp. 78-94, 1994.
7. Burrell, J., How the machine 'thinks': Understanding opacity in machine learning algorithms. *Big Data Soc.*, 3, 1, 430, 2016, 2053951715622512.
8. Demšar, J., Zupan, B., Leban, G., Curk, T., Orange: From experimental machine learning to interactive data mining, in: *European conference on principles of data mining and knowledge discovery*, Springer, Berlin, Heidelberg, pp. 537–539, 2004.
9. Maloof, M.A. (Ed.), *Machine learning and data mining for computer security: methods and applications*, Springer Science & Business Media, Springer, pp. 47–64, 2006.
10. Dunjko, V. and Briegel, H.J., Machine learning & artificial intelligence in the quantum domain: a review of recent progress. *Rep. Prog. Phys.*, 81, 7, 074001, 2018.
11. Syam, N. and Sharma, A., Waiting for a sales renaissance in the fourth industrial revolution: Machine learning and artificial intelligence in sales research and practice. *Ind. Market. Manage.*, 69, 135–146, 2018.
12. Kovačević, A., Dehghan, A., Filannino, M., Keane, J.A., Nenadic, G., Combining rules and machine learning for extraction of temporal expressions and events from clinical narratives. *J. Am. Med. Inf. Assoc.*, 20, 5, 859–866, 2013.
13. Baldwin, J.F., Lawry, J., Martin, T.P., The application of generalised fuzzy rules to machine learning and automated knowledge discovery. *Int. J. Uncertainty Fuzziness Knowledge-Based Syst.*, 6, 05, 459–487, 1998.
14. Baldwin, J.F., Lawry, J., Martin, T.P., The application of generalised fuzzy rules to machine learning and automated knowledge discovery. *Int. J. Uncertainty Fuzziness Knowledge-Based Syst.*, 6, 05, 459–487, 1998.

15. Love, B.C., Comparing supervised and unsupervised category learning. *Psychon. Bull. Rev.*, 9, 4, 829–835, 2002.

16. Fritzke, B., Growing cell structures—a self-organizing network for unsupervised and supervised learning. *Neural Networks*, 7, 9, 1441–1460, 1994.

17. Radford, A., Metz, L., Chintala, S., Unsupervised representation learning with deep convolutional generative adversarial networks. *arXiv preprint arXiv:1511.06434*, 2015.

18. Hastie, T., Tibshirani, R., Friedman, J., Unsupervised learning, in: *The elements of statistical learning*, pp. 485–585, Springer, New York, NY, 2009.

19. Abdullah, M., Iqbal, W., Erradi, A., Unsupervised learning approach for web application auto-decomposition into microservices. *J. Syst. Software*, 151, 243–2575, 2019.

20. Kim, Y.S., Nick Street, W., Menczer, F., Feature selection in unsupervised learning via evolutionary search, in: *Proceedings of the sixth ACM SIGKDD international conference on Knowledge discovery and data mining*, pp. 365–369, 2000.

21. Yang, Y., Liao, Y., Meng, G., Lee, J., A hybrid feature selection scheme for unsupervised learning and its application in bearing fault diagnosis. *Expert Syst. Appl.*, 38, 9, 11311–11320, 2011.

22. Novotney, S., Schwartz, R., Ma, J., Unsupervised acoustic and language model training with small amounts of labelled data, in: *2009 IEEE International Conference on Acoustics, Speech and Signal Processing*, 2009, April, IEEE, pp. 4297–4300.

23. Wang, J., Zhu, X., Gong, S., Li, W., Transferable joint attribute-identity deep learning for unsupervised person re-identification, in: *Proceedings of the IEEE Conference on Computer Vision and Pattern Recognition*, pp. 2275–2284, 2018.

24. Dietterich, T., Overfitting and undercomputing in machine learning. *ACM Comput. Surv. (CSUR)*, 27, 3, 326–327, 1995.

25. Jbabdi, S., Sotiropoulos, S.N., Savio, A.M., Graña, M., Behrens, T.E.J., Model-based analysis of multishell diffusion MR data for tractography: how to get over fitting problems. *Magn. Reson. Med.*, 68, 6, 1846–1855, 2012.

26. Bartlett, P.L., Long, P.M., Lugosi, G., Tsigler, A., Benign overfitting in linear regression. *Proc. Natl. Acad. Sci.*, 117, 48, 30063–30070, 2020.

27. F. Weng and L. Zhao, Unified treatment of data-sparseness and data-overfitting in maximum entropy modeling. U.S. Patent 8,700,403, issued April 15, 2014.

28. Oates, T., PERUSE: An unsupervised algorithm for finding recurring patterns in time series, in: *2002 IEEE International Conference on Data Mining, 2002. Proceedings*, 2002, December, IEEE, pp. 330–337.

29. Hinton, G.E., Dayan, P., Frey, B.J., Neal, R.M., "The" wake-sleep" algorithm for unsupervised neural networks. *Science*, 268, 5214, 1158–1161, 1995.

30. Solberg, T.R., Sonesson, A.K., Woolliams, J.A., Meuwissen, T.H.E., Reducing dimensionality for prediction of genome-wide breeding values. *Genet. Sel. Evol.*, 41, 1, 1–8, 2009.

31. Hinton, G.E. and Salakhutdinov, R.R., Reducing the dimensionality of data with neural networks. *Science*, 313, 5786, 504–507, 2006.

32. Gandhi, J., Basu, A., Hill, M.D., Swift, M.M., Efficient memory virtualization: Reducing dimensionality of nested page walks, in: *2014 47th Annual IEEE/ACM International Symposium on Microarchitecture*, IEEE, pp. 178–189, 2014.

33. Wold, S., Esbensen, K., Geladi, P., Principal component analysis. *Chemometr. Intell. Lab. Syst.*, 2, 1–3, 37–52, 1987.

34. Abdi, H. and Williams, L.J., Principal component analysis. *Wiley Interdiscip. Rev.: Comput. Stat.*, 2, 4, 433–459, 2010.

35. Schölkopf, B., Smola, A., Müller, K.-R., Kernel principal component analysis, in: *International conference on artificial neural networks*, Springer, Berlin, Heidelberg, pp. 583–588, 1997.

36. Golub, G.H. and Reinsch, C., Singular value decomposition and least squares solutions, in: *Linear Algebra*, pp. 134–151, Springer, Berlin, Heidelberg, 1971.

37. Van Loan, C.F., Generalizing the singular value decomposition. *SIAM J. Numer. Anal.*, 13, 1, 76–83, 1976.

38. Mairal, J., Ponce, J., Sapiro, G., Zisserman, A., Bach, F.R., Supervised dictionary learning, in: *Advances in neural information processing systems*, pp. 1033–1040, 2009.

39. Tosic, I. and Frossard, P., Dictionary learning. *IEEE Signal Process. Mag.*, 28, 2, 27–38, 2011.

40. Kreutz-Delgado, K., Murray, J.F., Rao, B.D., Engan, K., Lee, T.-W., Sejnowski, T.J., Dictionary learning algorithms for sparse representation. *Neural Comput.*, 15, 2, 349–396, 2003.

41. Blei, D.M., Ng, A.Y., Jordan, M., II, Latent dirichlet allocation. *J. Mach. Learn. Res.*, 3, Jan, 993–1022, 2003.

42. Krestel, R., Fankhauser, P., Nejdl, W., Latent dirichlet allocation for tag recommendation, in: *Proceedings of the third ACM conference on Recommender systems*, pp. 61–68, 2009.

43. Aksu, D., Üstebay, S., Aydin, M.A., Atmaca, T., Intrusion detection with comparative analysis of supervised learning techniques and fisher score feature selection algorithm, in: *International Symposium on Computer and Information Sciences*, Springer, Cham, pp. 141–149, 2018.

44. Huang, J., Lin, A., Narasimhan, B., Quertermous, T., Agnes Hsiung, C., Low-Tone, H., Grove, J.S. *et al.*, Tree-structured supervised learning and the genetics of hypertension. *Proc. Natl. Acad. Sci.*, 101, 29, 10529–10534, 2004.

45. Abadi, M., Agarwal, A., Barham, P., Brevdo, E., Chen, Z., Citro, C., Corrado, G.S. *et al.*, Tensorflow: Large-scale machine learning on heterogeneous distributed systems. *arXiv preprint arXiv:1603.04467*, 2016.

46. Girija, S.S., Tensorflow: Large-scale machine learning on heterogeneous distributed systems. *Software available from tensorflow. org*. 39, 9, 2016.

47. Gulli, A. and Pal, S., *Deep learning with Keras*, Packt Publishing Ltd, 215–224, 2017.

48. Jin, H., Song, Q., Hu, X., Auto-keras: An efficient neural architecture search system, in: *Proceedings of the 25th ACM SIGKDD International Conference on Knowledge Discovery & Data Mining*, pp. 1946–1956, 2019.

49. Seide, F., Keynote: The computer science behind the microsoft cognitive toolkit: an open source large-scale deep learning toolkit for Windows and Linux, in: *2017 IEEE/ACM International Symposium on Code Generation and Optimization (CGO)*, IEEE, pp. xi–xi, 2017.

50. Pathak, S., He, P., Darling, W., Scalable deep document/sequence reasoning with cognitive toolkit, in: *Proceedings of the 26th International Conference on World Wide Web Companion*, pp. 931–934, 2017.

51. Mei, T. and Zhang, C., Deep learning for intelligent video analysis, in: *Proceedings of the 25th ACM international conference on Multimedia*, pp. 1955–1956, 2017.

52. C. Brockett, E. Breck, W. Dolan, Unsupervised learning of paraphrase/translation alternations and selective application thereof. U.S. Patent 7,552,046, issued June 23, 2009.

53. Netzer, Y., Wang, T., Coates, A., Bissacco, A., Wu, B., Ng, A.Y., NIPS Workshop on Deep Learning and Unsupervised Feature Learning, 2011 on Google Publication.

54. G.W. Brown, Method and apparatus for power regulation of digital data transmission. U.S. Patent 6,226,356, issued May 1, 2001.

55. Yeung, K., 'Hypernudge': Big Data as a mode of regulation by design. *Inf. Commun. Soc.*, 20, 1, 118–136, 2017.

56. Sokol, K. and Flach, P.A., Glass-Box: Explaining AI Decisions With Counterfactual Statements Through Conversation With a Voice-enabled Virtual Assistant, in: *IJCAI*, pp. 5868–5870, 2018.

57. R. Sepe Jr, Voice actuation with contextual learning for intelligent machine control. U.S. Patent 6,895,380, issued May 17, 2005.

58. C.O. Emmett, II, Deborah Dahl, and Richard Mandelbaum. Voice activated virtual assistant. U.S. Patent Application 13/555,232, filed January 31, 2013.

59. Forkuor, G., Hounkpatin, O.K.L., Welp, G., Thiel, M., High resolution mapping of soil properties using remote sensing variables in south-western Burkina Faso: a comparison of machine learning and multiple linear regression models. *PloS One*, 12, 1, e0170478, 2017.

60. Chu, C.-T., Kim, S.K., Lin, Y.-A., Yu, Y.Y., Bradski, G., Olukotun, K., Ng, A.Y., Map-reduce for machine learning on multicore, in: *Advances in neural information processing systems*, pp. 281–288, 2007.

61. Chen, J., de Hoogh, K., Gulliver, J., Hoffmann, B., Hertel, O., Ketzel, M., Bauwelinck, M. *et al.*, A comparison of linear regression, regularization, and

machine learning algorithms to develop Europe-wide spatial models of fine particles and nitrogen dioxide. *Environ. Int.*, 130, 104934, 2019.

62. Witten, I.H. and Frank, E., Data mining: practical machine learning tools and techniques with Java implementations. *ACM Sigmod Rec.*, 31, 1, 76–77, 2002.

63. Chaudhuri, K. and Monteleoni, C., Privacy-preserving logistic regression, in: *Advances in neural information processing systems*, pp. 289–296, 2009.

64. Cheng, W. and Hüllermeier, E., Combining instance-based learning and logistic regression for multilabel classification. *Mach. Learn.*, 76, 2–3, 211–225, 2009.

65. Bui, D.T., Tuan, T.A., Klempe, H., Pradhan, B., Revhaug, I., Spatial prediction models for shallow landslide hazards: a comparative assessment of the efficacy of support vector machines, artificial neural networks, kernel logistic regression, and logistic model tree. *Landslides*, 13, 2, 361–378, 2016.

66. Dietterich, T.G. and Kong, E.B., Machine learning bias, statistical bias, and statistical variance of decision tree algorithms. Technical report, Department of Computer Science, Oregon State University, 1995.

67. Dietterich, T., Overfitting and undercomputing in machine learning. *ACM Comput. Surv. (CSUR)*, 27, 3, 326–327, 1995.

68. Tong, S. and Koller, D., Support vector machine active learning with applications to text classification. *J. Mach. Learn. Res.*, 2, Nov, 45–66, 2001.

69. Xuegong, Z., Introduction to statistical learning theory and support vector machines. *Acta Autom. Sin.*, 26, 1, 32–42, 2000.

70. Rebentrost, P., Mohseni, M., Lloyd, S., Quantum support vector machine for big data classification. *Phys. Rev. Lett.*, 113, 13, 130503, 2014.

71. Rodriguez-Galiano, V., Sanchez-Castillo, M., Chica-Olmo, M., Chica-Rivas, M. J. O. G. R., Machine learning predictive models for mineral prospectivity: An evaluation of neural networks, random forest, regression trees and support vector machines. *Ore Geol. Rev.*, 71, 804–818, 2015.

72. Zhang, C. and Ma, Y. (Eds.), *Ensemble machine learning: methods and applications*, Springer Science & Business Media, Springer, 35–86, 2012.

73. Qi, Y., Random forest for bioinformatics, in: *Ensemble machine learning*, pp. 307–323, Springer, Boston, MA, 2012.

74. Mascaro, J., Asner, G.P., Knapp, D.E., Kennedy-Bowdoin, T., Martin, R.E., Anderson, C., Higgins, M., Dana Chadwick, K., A tale of two "forests": Random Forest machine learning aids tropical forest carbon mapping. *PloS One*, 9, 1, e85993, 2014.

75. Konkar, A., Madhukar, A., Chen, P., Creating three-dimensionally confined nanoscale strained structures via substrate encoded size-reducing epitaxy and the enhancement of critical thickness for island formation. *MRS Online Proceedings Library Archive*, vol. 380, 1995.

76. Duplančić, G. and Nižić, B., Reduction method for dimensionally regulatedone-loop N-point Feynman integrals. *Eur. Phys. J. C-Part. Fields*, 35, 1, 105–118, 2004.

77. Konkar, A., Rajkumar, K.C., Xie, Q., Chen, P., Madhukar, A., Lin, H.T., Rich, D.H., *In-Situ* Fabrication of Three-Dimensionally Confined GaAs and InAs Volumes via Growth on Nonplanar Patterned GaAs (OOl) Substrates. *J. Cryst. Growth*, 150, 311, 1995.

78. Gadde, A. and Yan, W., Reducing the 4d index to the S 3 partition function. *J. High Energy Phys.*, 2012, 12, 3, 2012.

79. Shin, E.-C., Craft, B.D., Pegg, R.B., Phillips, R.D., Eitenmiller, R.R., Chemometric approach to fatty acid profiles in Runner-type peanut cultivars by principal component analysis (PCA). *Food Chem.*, 119, 3, 1262–1270, 2010.

80. Reich, D., Price, A.L., Patterson, N., Principal component analysis of genetic data. *Nat. Genet.*, 40, 5, 491–492, 2008.

81. Song, F., Guo, Z., Mei, D., Feature selection using principal component analysis, in: *2010 international conference on system science, engineering design and manufacturing informatization*, vol. 1, IEEE, pp. 27–30, 2010.

82. Yu, P., Applications of hierarchical cluster analysis (CLA) and principal component analysis (PCA) in feed structure and feed molecular chemistry research, using synchrotron-based Fourier transform infrared (FTIR) microspectroscopy. *J. Agric. Food Chem.*, 53, 18, 7115–7127, 2005.

83. Lasaponara, R., On the use of principal component analysis (PCA) for evaluating interannual vegetation anomalies from SPOT/VEGETATION NDVI temporal series. *Ecol. Modell.*, 194, 4, 429–434, 2006.

84. Schmidt, M., Rajagopal, S., Ren, Z., Moffat, K., Application of singular value decomposition to the analysis of time-resolved macromolecular X-ray data. *Biophys. J.*, 84, 3, 2112–2129, 2003.

85. Shen, H. and Huang, J.Z., Analysis of call centre arrival data using singular value decomposition. *Appl. Stochastic Models Bus. Ind.*, 21, 3, 251–263, 2005.

86. Van Der Veen, A.-J., Deprettere, E.D.F., Lee Swindlehurst, A., Subspace-based signal analysis using singular value decomposition. *Proc. IEEE*, 81, 9, 1277–1308, 1993.

87. Kakarala, R. and Ogunbona, P.O., Signal analysis using a multiresolution form of the singular value decomposition. *IEEE Trans. Image Process.*, 10, 5, 724–735, 2001.

88. Oviatt, S., Cohen, A., Weibel, N., Hang, K., Thompson, K., Multimodal learning analytics data resources: Description of math data corpus and coded documents, in: *Proceedings of the Third International Data-Driven Grand Challenge Workshop on Multimodal Learning Analytics*, vol. 414, 2014.

89. Sriramulu, A., Lin, J., Oviatt, S., Dynamic Adaptive Gesturing Predicts Domain Expertise in Mathematics, in: *2019 International Conference on Multimodal Interaction*, pp. 105–113, 2019.

90. Samimi, A., Zarinabadi, S., Kootenaei, A.H.S., Azimi, A., Mirzaei, M., Optimization of Naphtha Hydro-Threating Unit with Continuous Resuscitation Due to the Optimum Temperature of Octanizer Unit Reactors. *Adv. J. Chem., Section A: Theor. Eng. Appl. Chem.*, 3, 2, 111–236, 2020. 165–180.

91. Oviatt, S., Cohen, A., Weibel, N., Hang, K., Thompson, K., Multimodal learning analytics data resources: Description of math data corpus and coded documents, in: *Proceedings of the Third International Data-Driven Grand Challenge Workshop on Multimodal Learning Analytics*, vol. 414, 2014.

92. Musco, C. and Musco, C., Randomized block krylov methods for stronger and faster approximate singular value decomposition, in: *Advances in Neural Information Processing Systems*, pp. 1396–1404, 2015.

93. Jackson, G.M., Mason, I.M., Greenhalgh, S.A., Principal component transforms of triaxial recordings by singular value decomposition. *Geophysics*, 56, 4, 528–533, 1991.

94. Zhu, P., Hu, Q., Zhang, C., Zuo, W., Coupled dictionary learning for unsupervised feature selection, in: *Thirtieth AAAI Conference on Artificial Intelligence*, 2016.

95. Gangeh, M.J., Ghodsi, A., Kamel, M.S., Kernelized supervised dictionary learning. *IEEE Trans. Signal Process.*, 61, 19, 4753–4767, 2013.

96. Jing, X.-Y., Hu, R.-M., Wu, F., Chen, X.-L., Liu, Q., Yao, Y.-F., Uncorrelated multi-view discrimination dictionary learning for recognition, in: *Twenty-Eighth AAAI Conference on Artificial Intelligence*, 2014.

97. Han, T., Jiang, D., Sun, Y., Wang, N., Yang, Y., Intelligent fault diagnosis method for rotating machinery via dictionary learning and sparse representation-based classification. *Measurement*, 118, 181–1935, 2018.

98. Pu, J. and Zhang, J.-P., Super-resolution through dictionary learning and sparse representation. *Pattern Recognit. Artif. Intell.*, 23, 3, 335–340, 2010.

99. Wu, F., Jing, X.-Y., You, X., Yue, D., Hu, R., Yang, J.-Y., Multi-view low-rank dictionary learning for image classification. *Pattern Recognit.*, 50, 143–1545, 2016.

100. Mairal, J., Bach, F., Ponce, J., Task-driven dictionary learning. *IEEE Trans. Pattern Anal. Mach. Intell.*, 34, 4, 791–804, 2011.

101. Zhang, J., Shum, H.P., Han, J., Shao, L., Action recognition from arbitrary views using transferable dictionary learning. *IEEE Trans. Image Process.*, 27, 10, 4709–4723, 2018.

102. Mogha, M., Machine Learning with IOT. *CYBERNOMICS*, 2, 1, 29–32, 2020.

103. Sharma, R., SCM: An approach to Data Warehousing With Machine Learning. *CYBERNOMICS*, 2, 1, 15–19, 2020.

104. Koehn, P., Hoang, H., Birch, A., Callison-Burch, C., Federico, M., Bertoldi, N., Cowan, B. *et al.*, Moses: Open source toolkit for statistical machine translation, in: *Proceedings of the 45th annual meeting of the ACL on interactive poster and demonstration sessions*, Association for Computational Linguistics, pp. 177–180, 2007.

105. Smilkov, D., Thorat, N., Assogba, Y., Yuan, A., Kreeger, N., Yu, P., Zhang, K. *et al.*, Tensorflow. js: Machine learning for the web and beyond. *arXiv preprint arXiv:1901.05350*, 2019.

106. Hope, T., Resheff, Y.S., Lieder, I., *Learning tensorflow: A guide to building deep learning systems*, O'Reilly Media, Inc, 113–150, 2017.

107. Awan, A.A., Bédorf, J., Chu, C.-H., Subramoni, H., Panda, D.K., Scalable distributed dnn training using tensorflow and cuda-aware mpi: Characterization, designs, and performance evaluation, in: *2019 19th IEEE/ACM International Symposium on Cluster, Cloud and Grid Computing (CCGRID)*, IEEE, pp. 498–507, 2019.

108. Ramasubramanian, K. and Singh, A., Deep learning using keras and tensorflow, in: *Machine Learning Using R*, pp. 667–688, Apress, Berkeley, CA, 2019.

109. Gharibi, G., Tripathi, R., Lee, Y., Code2graph: automatic generation of static call graphs for python source code, in: *Proceedings of the 33rd ACM/IEEE International Conference on Automated Software Engineering*, pp. 880–883, 2018.

110. Vasilev, I., Slater, D., Spacagna, G., Roelants, P., Zocca, V., *Python Deep Learning: Exploring deep learning techniques and neural network architectures with Pytorch, Keras, and TensorFlow*, Packt Publishing Ltd, 68–77, 2019.

111. Khan, A., II and Al-Badi, A., Open Source Machine Learning Frameworks for Industrial Internet of Things. *Proc. Comput. Sci.*, 170, 571–5775, 2020.

112. Xiong, W., Wu, L., Alleva, F., Droppo, J., Huang, X., Stolcke, A., The Microsoft 2017 conversational speech recognition system, in: *2018 IEEE international conference on acoustics, speech and signal processing (ICASSP)*, 8, April, IEEE, pp. 5934–5938, 201.

113. Komar, M., Yakobchuk, P., Golovko, V., Dorosh, V., Sachenko, A., Deep neural network for image recognition based on the caffe framework, in: *2018 IEEE Second International Conference on Data Stream Mining & Processing (DSMP)*, IEEE, pp. 102–106, 2018.

114. Gelichi, S. and Sabbionesi, L., *Bere e fumare ai confini dell'impero. Caffè e tabacco a Stari Bar nel periodo ottomano*, vol. 6, All'Insegna del Giglio, 43–57, 2014.

115. Ji, Z., Hg-caffe: Mobile and embedded neural network gpu (opencl) inference engine with fp16 supporting. *arXiv preprint arXiv:1901.00858*, 2019.

116. Yamamoto, M. and Murayama, S., UHF torch discharge as an excitation source. *Spectrochim. Acta Part A: Mol. Spectrosc.*, 23, 4, 773–776, 1967.

117. Collobert, R., Bengio, S., Mariéthoz, J., *Torch: a modular machine learning software library*. No. REP_WORK. Idiap, 2002.

118. Saifutdinov, A., II and Fadeev, S.A., The effect of the external acoustic waves on the plasma torch jet. *J. Phys.: Conf. Ser.*, 1328, 1, 012067, 2019. IOP Publishing.

119. Lötsch, J., Lerch, F., Djaldetti, R., Tegder, I., Ultsch, A., Identification of disease-distinct complex biomarker patterns by means of unsupervised machine-learning using an interactive R toolbox (Umatrix). *Big Data Anal.*, 3, 1, 1–17, 2018.

120. Zhou, C., Ieritano, C., Hopkins, W.S., Augmenting Basin-Hopping With Techniques From Unsupervised Machine Learning: Applications in Spectroscopy and Ion Mobility. *Front. Chem.*, 7, 5195, 2019.

121. Simeone, O., A very brief introduction to machine learning with applications to communication systems. *IEEE Trans. Cognit. Commun. Networking*, 4, 4, 648–664, 2018.

122. Davis II, R.L., Greene, J.K., Dou, F., Jo, Y.-K., Chappell, T.M., A Practical Application of Unsupervised Machine Learning for Analyzing Plant Image Data Collected Using Unmanned Aircraft Systems. *Agronomy*, 10, 5, 633, 2020.

123. Hocking, A., Beach, J.E., Sun, Y., Davey, N., An automatic taxonomy of galaxy morphology using unsupervised machine learning. *Mon. Not. R. Astron. Soc.*, 473, 1, 1108–1129, 2018.

124. Jaeger, S., Fula, S., Turk, S., Mol2vec: unsupervised machine learning approach with chemical intuition. *J. Chem. Inf. Model.*, 58, 1, 27–35, 2018.

125. Jadrich, R.B., Lindquist, B.A., Piñeros, W.D., Banerjee, D., Truskett, T.M., Unsupervised machine learning for detection of phase transitions in off-lattice systems. II. Applications. *J. Chem. Phys.*, 149, 19, 194110, 2018.

126. Chen, Y., Zhang, M., Bai, M., Chen, W., Improving the Signal-to-Noise Ratio of Seismological Datasets by Unsupervised Machine Learning. *Seismol. Res. Lett.*, 90, 4, 1552–1564, 2019.

127. Christopher, M., Belghith, A., Weinreb, R.N., Bowd, C., Goldbaum, M.H., Saunders, L.J., Medeiros, F.A., Zangwill, L.M., Retinal nerve fiber layer features identified by unsupervised machine learning on optical coherence tomography scans predict glaucoma progression. *Invest. Ophthalmol. Visual Sci.*, 59, 7, 2748–2756, 2018.

128. Yeung, K., Algorithmic regulation: a critical interrogation. *Regul. Gov.*, 12, 4, 505–523, 2018.

129. Liu, Q., Zhu, H., Liu, C., Jean, D., Huang, S.-M., Khair ElZarrad, M., Blumenthal, G., Wang, Y., Application of machine learning in drug development and regulation: current status and future potential. *Clin. Pharmacol. Ther.*, 107, 4, 726–729, 2020.

130. Liu, Q., Zhu, H., Liu, C., Jean, D., Huang, S.-M., Khair ElZarrad, M., Blumenthal, G., Wang, Y., Application of machine learning in drug development and regulation: current status and future potential. *Clin. Pharmacol. Ther.*, 107, 4, 726–729, 2020.

131. Nasirian, F., Ahmadian, M., Lee, O.-K.D., AI-based voice assistant systems: Evaluating from the interaction and trust perspectives, 2017.

132. Sokol, K. and Flach, P.A., Glass-Box: Explaining AI Decisions With Counterfactual Statements Through Conversation With a Voice-enabled Virtual Assistant, in: *IJCAI*, pp. 5868–5870, 2018.

133. Hoy, M.B., Alexa, S., Cortana, and more: an introduction to voice assistants. *Med. Ref. Serv. Q.*, 37, 1, 81–88, 2018.

134. Morel, B., Artificial intelligence and the future of cybersecurity, in: *Proceedings of the 4th ACM workshop on Security and artificial intelligence*, pp. 93–98, 2011.

135. Wirkuttis, N. and Klein, H., Artificial intelligence in cybersecurity. *Cyber Intell. Secur. J.*, 1, 1, 21–23, 2017.

136. Thrall, J.H., Li, X., Li, Q., Cruz, C., Do, S., Dreyer, K., Brink, J., Artificial intelligence and machine learning in radiology: opportunities, challenges, pitfalls, and criteria for success. *J. Am. Coll. Radiol.*, 15, 3, 504–508, 2018.

137. Rosten, E., Porter, R., Drummond, T., Faster and better: A machine learning approach to corner detection. *IEEE Trans. Pattern Anal. Mach. Intell.*, 32, 1, 105–119, 2008.

138. Ravì, D., Wong, C., Deligianni, F., Berthelot, M., Andreu-Perez, J., Lo, B., Yang, G.-Z., Deep learning for health informatics. *IEEE J. Biomed. Health Inf.*, 21, 1, 4–21, 2016.

139. Mathieu, M., Henaff, M., LeCun, Y., Fast training of convolutional networks through ffts. *arXiv preprint arXiv:1312.5851*, 2013.

140. Frie, T.-T., Cristianini, N., Campbell, C., The kernel-adatron algorithm: a fast and simple learning procedure for support vector machines, in: *Machine learning: proceedings of the fifteenth international conference (ICML'98)*, pp. 188–196, 1998.

141. Klein, A., Falkner, S., Bartels, S., Hennig, P., Hutter, F., Fast bayesian optimization of machine learning hyperparameters on large datasets, in: *Artificial Intelligence and Statistics*, pp. 528–536, PMLR, 2017.

142. Biamonte, J., Wittek, P., Pancotti, N., Rebentrost, P., Wiebe, N., Lloyd, S., Quantum machine learning. *Nature*, 549, 7671, 195–202, 2017.

143. Kohl, N. and Stone, P., Machine learning for fast quadrupedal locomotion, in: *AAAI*, vol. 4, pp. 611–616, 2004.

144. Caulfield, A.M., Grupp, L.M., Swanson, S., Gordon: using flash memory to build fast, power-efficient clusters for data-intensive applications. *ACM Sigplan Notices*, 44, 3, 217–228, 2009.

145. Hinton, G.E., Osindero, S., Teh, Y.-W., A fast learning algorithm for deep belief nets. *Neural Comput.*, 18, 7, 1527–1554, 2006.

146. Rodríguez, A.C., Kacprzak, T., Lucchi, A., Amara, A., Sgier, R., Fluri, J., Hofmann, T., Réfrégier, A., Fast cosmic web simulations with generative adversarial networks. *Comput. Astrophys. Cosmol.*, 5, 1, 4, 2018.

147. Huang, X. and Pan, W., Linear regression and two-class classification with gene expression data. *Bioinformatics*, 19, 16, 2072–2078, 2003.

148. Papadopoulos, B., Tsagarakis, K.P., Yannopoulos, A., Cost and land functions for wastewater treatment projects: Typical simple linear regression versus fuzzy linear regression. *J. Environ. Eng.*, 133, 6, 581–586, 2007.

149. Leiva Fernández, A.J. and O'Valle Barragán, J.L., Decision tree-based algorithms for implementing bot AI in UT2004, in: *International Work-Conference on the Interplay Between Natural and Artificial Computation*, Springer, Berlin, Heidelberg, pp. 383–392, 2011.

150. Farid, D., Harbi, N., Rahman, M.Z., Combining naive bayes and decision tree for adaptive intrusion detection. *arXiv preprint arXiv:1005.4496*, 2010.

151. Stone, P. and Veloso, M., Using decision tree confidence factors for multi-agent control, in: *Proceedings of the second international conference on Autonomous agents*, pp. 86–91, 1998.

152. Takahashi, F. and Abe, S., Decision-tree-based multiclass support vector machines, in: *Proceedings of the 9th International Conference on Neural Information Processing, 2002. ICONIP'02*, vol. 3, IEEE, pp. 1418–1422, 2002.

153. Roth, A.M., Topin, N., Jamshidi, P., Veloso, M., Conservative Q-Improvement: Reinforcement Learning for an Interpretable Decision-Tree Policy. *arXiv preprint arXiv:1907.01180*, 2019.

154. Zhang, M.-L. and Zhou, Z.-H., A k-nearest neighbor based algorithm for multi-label classification, in: *2005 IEEE international conference on granular computing*, vol. 2, IEEE, pp. 718–721, 2005.

155. Tan, S., Neighbor-weighted k-nearest neighbor for unbalanced text corpus. *Expert Syst. Appl.*, 28, 4, 667–671, 2005.

156. Sun, S. and Huang, R., An adaptive k-nearest neighbor algorithm, in: *2010 seventh international conference on fuzzy systems and knowledge discovery*, vol. 1, IEEE, pp. 91–94, 2010.

157. Raikwal, J.S. and Saxena, K., Performance evaluation of SVM and k-nearest neighbor algorithm over medical data set. *Int. J. Comput. Appl.*, 50, 14, 447, 2012.

158. Li, B., Yu, S., Lu, Q., An improved k-nearest neighbor algorithm for text categorization. *arXiv preprint cs/0306099*, 2003.

159. Li, C., Zhang, S., Zhang, H., Pang, L., Lam, K., Hui, C., Zhang, S., Using the K-nearest neighbor algorithm for the classification of lymph node metastasis in gastric cancer. *Comput. Math. Methods Med.*, 2012, 447, 2012.

160. Farshad, M. and Sadeh, J., Accurate single-phase fault-location method for transmission lines based on k-nearest neighbor algorithm using one-end voltage. *IEEE Trans. Power Delivery*, 27, 4, 2360–2367, 2012.

161. Wang, A.-P., Wan, G.-W., Cheng, Z.-Q., Li, S.-K., Incremental learning extremely random forest classifier for online learning. *Ruanjian Xuebao/J. Software*, 22, 9, 2059–2074, 2011.

162. Yoo, S., Kim, S., Kim, S., Kang, B.B., AI-HydRa: Advanced Hybrid Approach using Random Forest and Deep Learning for Malware Classification. *Inf. Sci.*, 546, 420–435, 2021.

163. Burges, C.J.C., Geometric methods for feature extraction and dimensional reduction-a guided tour, in: *Data mining and knowledge discovery handbook*, pp. 53–82, Springer, Boston, MA, 2009.

164. McInnes, L., Healy, J., Melville, J., Umap: Uniform manifold approximation and projection for dimension reduction. *arXiv preprint arXiv:1802.03426*, 2018.

165. Zhang, T., Tao, D., Li, X., Yang, J., Patch alignment for dimensionality reduction. *IEEE Trans. Knowl. Data Eng.*, 21, 9, 1299–1313, 2008.

166. Ye, J., Janardan, R., Li, Q., Park, H., Feature reduction via generalized uncorrelated linear discriminant analysis. *IEEE Trans. Knowl. Data Eng.*, 18, 10, 1312–1322, 2006.

167. https://twitter.com/hashtag/supervisedmachinelearning

168. https://data-flair.training/blogs/machine-learning-tutorial/

18

Predictive Modeling of Anthropomorphic Gamifying Blockchain-Enabled Transitional Healthcare System

Deepa Kumari*, B.S.A.S. Rajita, Medindrao Raja Sekhar, Ritika Garg and Subhrakanta Panda

Dept. of CSIS, BITS-PILANI, Hyderabad Campus, Hyderabad, Telangana, India

Abstract

The research objective is to explore more about anthropomorphic gamifying elements, mostly on how it can be implemented in a Blockchain-enabled transitional healthcare system in a more lucrative manner. Transitional healthcare services belong to that person who is suffering from lifelong conditions such as asthma, cancer, diabetes, and/or renal transplant. It is necessary to have organized systems, and on the same side, we need resources in place to assure that all needy experience a lucrative healthcare transition.

Anthropomorphic interfaces completely recognized as applying game elements or logistics into non-gaming contexts such as healthcare, by offering a fun and exciting environment. It is observed that there are very few games or web-based applications suitable to patients practically. Then, there is an interface with Blockchain architecture so that we can have health data security as well as motivation for staying healthy via reward mechanism (i.e., by tokenization of activities).

The conceptual framework is expected to come up with the integration of gamification, anthropomorphism, and Blockchain applications into the transitional healthcare system. Further, the output (reward points) from the organized system will help in predicting the health conditions of the patients.

Keywords: Anthropomorphism, gamification, blockchain, transitional healthcare, predictive model, ethereum, smart contract

*Corresponding author: p20190020@hyderabad.bits-pilani.ac.in

Sachi Nandan Mohanty, Jyotir Moy Chatterjee, Monika Mangla, Suneeta Satpathy and Sirisha Potluri (eds.) Machine Learning Approach for Cloud Data Analytics in IoT, (461–490) © 2021 Scrivener Publishing LLC

18.1   Introduction

The overall provision of healthcare facilities helps in utilizing and achieving good health and is a sign of a developed country. Since independence, we achieved very little or limited progress in the healthcare facilities in India. Even though public health centers like hospitals and dispensaries are present, they are not capable to cater to the increasing demands of India's tremendous population day by day. In India, the main shortcoming of healthcare access depends on three factors such as supply, utility, and fulfillment. But, the presence of large gaps among these factors drives it to an unused system with unavailable facilities. So, there is an immense requirement for healthcare systems to be designed by integrating emerged technological innovations to whirl around new models for patient care. Hence, this chapter introduces to the readers a new level of understanding and practices that offer a distinct improvement in healthcare services by acquiring, integrating, analyzing, securing, and exchanging medical data at different levels of the healthcare system.

18.1.1   Transitional Healthcare Services and Their Challenges

Recently, transitional healthcare services have emerged to improve the quality and minimize the costs under the Affordable Care Act of 2010. Transitional healthcare, also called care transition [16], is defined as the systematization and continuousness of healthcare during the progress either from one healthcare setting to another or home. Care transition exists between healthcare specialists and healthcare facilities as their action and care demands change during the continuous period of incurable or acute illness.

In other words, transitional healthcare refers to the service which manages one's health condition, well-acquainted with appropriate knowledge to self-reliance, and then shifts them from hospital care to self-care [28]. This phenomenon belongs to that person who is suffering from some life-long conditions such as asthma, cancer, diabetes, and/or renal transplants. Such prolonged treatment sometimes requires people to transit from one healthcare environment to another such as pediatric treatment to adult healthcare [42]. Thus, it may be burdensome for such people to sustain their engagement in the transition process. For example, an individual suffering from an acute disease at an early age initially needs clinical care, and as time passes, the treatment paradigm shifts to the family members.

In due course of time, this mostly gets shifted to self-care. Certainly, such a prolonged duration of treatment causes a negative impact on the psychological health of the individual and other members of the family. It may happen even due to various factors such as psychological changes, change in the healthcare personnel, and their expertise. Thus, there is a requirement for a targeted process that considers the physical and mental status of the individuals to deal with the transitional healthcare system.

18.2   Gamification in Transitional Healthcare: A New Model

Technology through gamified applications can play a vital role, particularly in transitional healthcare service, through the availability of favorable games for patient care, preferably to stimulate mental and physical health. Most of all, gamification is always proved to be a powerful tool that engages its users at a very high level [47]. Many developers and companies are now investing in gamified healthcare systems [40]. Gamification has been popular in non-game sectors such as business, health, institutions, and trade [49]. It positively inspires an individual to a healthy lifestyle through regular exercise and a healthy diet. Likewise, Fitbit, Jawbone UP, Nike Training Club, etc., use gadgets to keep track of the health activities and sleep score which links to online portals where the game players can track their activities and manage their lifestyle timely. It focuses on the improvement of the patient's engagement, motivation, and performance while executing a certain assigned work by incorporating simulator games, to achieve the goal in a more lucrative manner [45]. It utilizes game elements and dynamics to regulate the way of playing the game and to make routine activities more enjoyable and delightful. It also helps in promoting knowledge, learning, and behavioral aspects of self-management skills.

In game dynamic progression, we have certain game mechanics like achievements, levels, points, badges, trophies, and leaderboards. With the intense use of the internet and its applications, the mechanisms for delivering healthcare program help in encouraging people to record their daily activities in their blogs, uploading photos and videos on social media as well as participating in online surveys. There are three game dynamics: progression, feedback, and behavior. Thus, it is high time to add extra features like newly emerged Avatar concept into gamification to increase health, players' fun, and excitement.

18.2.1   Anthropomorphic Interface With Gamification

In some of the recent studies, it is evident that interfacing anthropomorphic with gamification gives a positive impact on the health of the players [41]. A human-like representation, similar to Avatar, designed with the human traits but is not human in actual, is called *Anthropomorphism*. Anthropomorphic interfaces are popular for applying game elements or logistics into non-gaming contexts such as healthcare or education, by offering a fun and exciting environment [2]. The avatar, human-like representation, is believed to have a positive impact and also provides a trustworthy interface to communicate with. Such mechanisms greatly motivate and encourage users to sustain their engagement. The usage of anthropomorphic agents fulfills dual purposes [7]. Firstly, we can converse (interact) with a virtual agent, and secondly, we can subtly increase the automation of tasks. The term "agent" usually refers to a software agent that performs a number of activities without any human intervention, i.e., highly independent. These agents are in different forms so as to develop the look and feel. They are 3D human representation, 3D non-human representation (with human-like characteristics), 2D human representation, and 2D cartoon-like non-human representation (with human-like characteristics).

There are certain advantages of implying an avatar in any research work. Firstly, it is much convenient for novice users to understand the functioning of the Avatar. Secondly, it is also helpful to grab the user's attention as it is found that people who interacted face to face can give more time on an online questionnaire survey and make fewer mistakes, unlike text questionnaires. Thirdly, it is also more efficient for us to speak questions rather than type them. Fourthly, we, the users do not have to go through painful codes and complex functions as these things are handled by the agent themselves. Somehow, it is evident that people with disabilities are using avatars as online characters while playing online games and the virtual world so as to preserve their anonymity [14]. This helps in overcoming the feelings of being different, social isolation, stigma, and can survive with long-term medical conditions. Certainly, we have already observed and analyzed that the use of gamification is now getting popularity by increasing the process of learning and routine-based healthy lifestyle. The addition of Blockchain for distributing reward points on the basis of routine-based health activities will be more attractive toward self-care.

18.2.2   Gamification in Blockchain

Blockchain is defined as a group of blocks that are connected by cryptographic links and contain distinct information in a secured decentralized manner [34]. Technically, it stores records in a tampered proof architecture. In 2008, Santoshi Nakamoto invented the Bitcoin protocol that remarked the revolution of shifting networking systems from centralized to decentralized systems worldwide. In fact, the achievements in this field have attracted the attention of academia, as the humanistic issues in health and social care are given more priority for further research in the Blockchain system and its ecosystem. After the advent of Bitcoin technology, Blockchain has influenced the interest of investigators to work on a generic technological platform by deploying different kinds of contracts [34].

Unlike Bitcoin, Ethereum has the additional functionality of smart contracts and, thus, helps in building and deploying decentralized applications. Smart contracts impose contractual agreement in the software and hardware so that the code that runs on Ethereum can control valuable digital assets or ETH [25]. It also performs transactions without the involvement of stakeholders and, thus, very complicated or expensive for the infringer involvement. Ethereum usually runs the smart contract codes after depositing transactional fees. Then, EVM executes smart contracts written in bytecode (solidity) on every node. After deployment, no one can alter the code which not only helps in decreasing transactional fees and also handles major risks in case of any faults. Ethereum works on some basic understanding of its underlying functionality and its interaction can be made by the use of Ethereum wallets, Mist as browsers, and Metamask as plugins. However, this platform has not gained wide acceptance among users and providers because of which it is difficult to predict the potential future applications.

The Blockchain ecosystem handles the humanistic and remunerative issues for the users, leading to unforeseen results in decentralized networks. It builds the bond of trust and integrity without any threat of security breaches. It is a recent trend to add features such as reward points to game apps and websites. Likewise, Metal Token [39], HoToKen[1], Sandblock[2], STORM[3], and POINToken[4] are systems to handle tokens and incentive on

---

[1] https://www.hotoken.io/
[2] https://medium.com/sandblock
[3] https://stormx.io/loyalty-program/
[4] https://medium.com/@point_token/the-point-token-systemgamification-and-achievements-for-the-Blockchain-bc368978e36

the Blockchain. These systems are capable to provide the benefits of the Blockchain such as security of data records, transparency, immutability, and transactions by the use of crypto tokens. This ledger will store Blockchain's assets (in the form of rewards and points) across multiple users.

Thus, the emergence of Blockchain leads to unprecedented heights for the potential of gamification when it comes to online engagement. It is therefore valuable to include gamification for healthcare issues in Blockchain technology. This integration helps in providing an incentive mechanism for earning reward points by the health player and also explores the performance of gamifying in a Blockchain system. In the coming years, Blockchain technology would be an indispensable environment for healthcare provisioning [1, 37]. Currently, we are lagging behind in the proper utilization of Blockchain technology as a gamified solution due to the lesser availability of cryptocurrencies and loyalty programs. Actually, it is a very tedious work to keep a patient engaged and motivated. The combined effort of gamification and Blockchain technology will make it possible to overcome the problem of patient engagement. The later section will explain the factors affecting the motivation of patients intrinsically or extrinsically.

18.2.3   Anthropomorphic Gamification in Blockchain: Motivational Factors

Anthropomorphic interfaces in the form of Avatars along with gamification helps a health player to increase the motivation or continue the engagement while interacting with the application [46]. Integration with Blockchain helps in the tokenization of healthcare activities for additional enjoyment and fun for the patients. According to the expert's views, a health player can develop a connection with his Avatar role when he foresees his real self in a virtual environment. It is expected that when people are motivated, their will power makes them follow their routine-based lifestyle or help them to change their behavior or habit at a point of need [43, 44]. So, we expect a similar transformation that may happen in the transitional healthcare people where their involvement toward their health can be improved [48]. To understand the effect of games on motivation [46, 47], we need to have a look at motivational theories.

There are several motivational theories that influence health player's behavior to encourage them for self-care. They are categorized as Maslow's hierarchy of needs, ARCS model of motivational design, and self-determination theory.

Maslow's hierarchy of needs theory [45] states that people's needs generally motivate them to perform actions. It is depicted by a hierarchical pyramid consisting of five levels. The physiological level is at the lower level and self-actualization is at the top level. Whenever the lower-level needs (called as deficiency needs) are satisfied before the top-level needs (called as growth needs), it may influence the behavior of the person. There are some intrinsic motivators (autonomy, mastery, and purpose), and they can be influenced by more or fewer satisfaction levels of Maslow's hierarchy of needs [45]. Basically, these intrinsic motivators aim to shape our lives (autonomy) by learning and creating new things (mastery) by taking care of ourselves (purpose).

In the ARCS (Attention, Relevance, Confidence, Satisfaction) motivational model [47], these four factors are utilized as a guideline for developing health player motivation through learning activities. It is important because patients should be well-acquainted with their health conditions so that they can take care of themselves. Overall, it acts as a problem-solving construct where we can recognize and work out those motivational problems associated with provided instructions. Firstly, Attention is defined to capture the interest of patients, stimulate a behavior of queries, and thus maintain the patient's attention. Secondly, Relevance signifies the process of achieving the patient's needs and also their positive attitude toward their goals. Thirdly, Confidence refers to build a positive expectation for achievement, build up patients' motivation in their competence, and acknowledge them about their real efforts and abilities to achieve success. Fourthly, Satisfaction defines by reinforcing achievement with reward points and also by providing valuable opportunities to patients to use their innovative knowledge or skills.

Self-Determination Theory (SDT) was given by Deci [48] and Ryan [49] where they discussed the challenges faced in lieu to the psychological need of being competent, valid, and autonomous and also to acquire the skill to master newly developed things. It is concerned with supporting the inherent potential of human behavior in simple healthy ways. This theory of motivation comprises intrinsic tendencies like Competence, Relatedness, and Autonomy. Competence can be described as the need to control the aftereffect and being a master. Relatedness refers to interaction, connection, and experience care for others. Autonomy specifies the art of being content and integrated with self. Motivation can be classified into extrinsic motivation and intrinsic motivation. In extrinsic motivation, patients carry out tasks or activities in favor of yielding rewards or benefits upon the execution of activities. But, in intrinsic motivation, patients are actually enjoying while doing activities due to their deeper engagement and higher persistence.

18.3 Existing Related Work

As we are all aware of advancements in electronic health data, patient data protection regulations lead to the opening of new opportunities for the revolution of health data as well as easier for accessibility and shareability of patient health data. Besides this, serious issues of protection of sensitive health-related data can be solved using Blockchain technology that ensures data security and transactions and handles smooth integration with the healthcare organization. Many researchers have put forth their valuable research findings in the area of anthropomorphism, gamification, and Blockchain technology in the transitional healthcare system. We have presented related researchers work in the above areas in tabular format for exploring preliminary designs ideas quickly and efficiently.

Authors	Title of the Paper	Contribution
P. Zhang *et al.* [1]	*FHIRChain: Applying Blockchain to securely and scalably share clinical data*	They first discussed about the Office of the National Health Information Technology (ONC) requirements and then to override all those challenges by building a Blockchain-based decentralized app called FHIRChain (Fast Healthcare Interoperability Resources) for sharing medical data at remote scale.
Banks *et al.* [2]	*Emotion, anthropomorphism, realism, control: Validation of a merged metric for player–avatar interaction (PAX)*	They proposed a PAX (player-avatar interaction) system that works as a correlation between MMO player and game avatar and performs on psychological divergent perspectives. They focused on different psychological factors like paying sensibility and anthropomorphic use in autonomy.

Baranaowski et al. [3]	*Playing for Real. Video Games and Stories for Health-Related Behavior Change*	They demonstrated the positive impacts on health-related behavior by playing video games. They also considered the game elements and measures for employing them systematically into game outcomes.
Barata et al. [4]	*Improving student creativity with gamification and virtual worlds*	They focused on how student autonomy and creativity can be better improvised by combining Avatar into gamification. For this, they also presented a gamified course that performs in a virtual environment by the student and increases their grading performance.
Bartnect et al. [5]	*Measurement Instruments for the Anthropomorphism, Animacy, Likeability, Perceived Intelligence, and Perceived Safety of Robots*	They surveyed the computation of HRI by taking certain elements. They performed questionnaires and distilled their results on semantic different scales. This method helped them in analysing the requirement of standardized measurement tools for HRI.
Bickmore et al. [6]	*Taking the time to care: empowering low health literacy hospital patients with virtual nurse agents*	They illustrated on virtual nurse agent for educating and counselling hospital patients. These patients are mostly having low health literacy but by interacting with a virtual nurse, it is easier for them to follow directions in taking care of their health.

Birk *et al.* [7]	*Fostering Intrinsic Motivation through Avatar Identification in Digital Games*	They discussed the use of an avatar game for increasing the intrinsic motivation of the player. They performed an analysis on 126 participants for playing a customized game and identified that there is a sudden increment of autonomy, immersion, enjoyment, and thus a positive impact on their health and behavior, too.
Bogost *et al.* [8]	*Why Gamification is Bullshit*	They argued that gamification is good or bad for making it useful in our virtual environment. They considered that the use of gamification is nothing to do with the truth, it is just to impress or to conceal and in terms of this, they take out benefit from them.
Brewer *et al.* [9]	*Using Gamification to Motivate Children to Complete Empirical Studies in Lab Environments*	They implemented one solution toward the challenges encountered in small children while their mobile interaction (by touch or gesture interaction). They also conducted with young children and identified different challenges form empirical studies. They proposed validated techniques for the use of gamification to increase their engagement.

JH BrockMyer et al. [10]	*The development of the Game Engagement Questionnaire: A measure of engagement in video game-playing*	They discussed deep engagement while playing with video games and also considered that, presently, there are no measures to compute this subjective experience. For this analysis purpose, they surveyed by developing Game Engagement Questionnaire (GEQ).
CM Fox et al. [11]	*The development of the game Engagement Questionnaire: A measure of engagement in video game playing: Response to reviews*	They arrived with an argument that there are few tools to measure development in human attributes and fall short while calculating meaningful dimensions. For this, they also performed an analysis of ordinal level data and discussed the requirement of converting them into equal time intervals for both qualitative and quantitative data necessarily.
Akrolu et al. [12]	*Gamifying an ICT Course: Influences on Engagement and Academic Performance*	They demonstrated by implementing gamification for observing the effect of positive behavior like engagement and motivation in the field of education. They presented evidence by observing the association of commitment made by students in their studies.

Catrambone et al. [13]	*Quick Quiz: A Gamified Approach for Enhancing Learning*	They performed research on anthropomorphic agents and found that we can utilize an anthropomorphic agent to systematize the research. They discussed important key factors for the influence in the perception of agent-based interfaces.
Cheon et al. [14]	*Avatar: A Virtual Face for the Elderly*	They studied HCI interaction in the view of a user's interaction with avatars in a virtual environment and also discussed their behaviors with an aging population.
Dahl et al. [15]	*Measuring how game feel is influenced by the player avatar's acceleration and deceleration*	They also discussed about the game feel like sensation toward game control which is important for game designers understanding player's experience while playing games.
Daneman et al. [16]	*Moving on: transition of teen with type 1 diabetes to adult care*	They discussed the transfer from an early age to the adolescent medical care where they face certain difficulties in doing self-care within different environments. They also illustrated the purposeful, planned movement of the transition healthcare system for their physical and mental improvement.
Mull et al. [17]	*An exploratory study of using 3D avatars as online salespeople*	They examined the experiences of consumers while using 3D animated avatars despite salesperson. They surveyed 120 participants while interacting with a virtual salesperson in an online retailer

Seaborn *et al.* [18]	*Gamification in theory and action: A survey*	They described the gamification application in the field of the academy, business, information studies, education, HCI, and health. They discussed the standard guidelines required for the underdeveloped theoretical applications and academic experiences.
Barbieri *et al.* [19]	*Optimal predictive model selection*	They discussed the model selection based on accuracy and squared error loss so that it would give a better future prediction. They analyzed their model by Bayesian approach for their optimal results.
Laud PW *et al.* [20]	*Predictive model selection*	They described the problem of choosing the best model out of existing possible models. They described it in the view of predictive Bayesian to ignore the prior details of the given models and detailed interpretation of parameters in each model.
Tsung-Ting Kuo *et al.* [21]	*ModelChain: Decentralized privacy-preserving healthcare predictive modeling framework on private Blockchain networks*	They described a new framework named ModelChain in which they integrate Blockchain technology into their health model. They also described that the additional features of privacy maintaining the health data on the Ethereum network. They designed a new algorithm named as proof-of-information to evaluate online learning to increase interoperability between institutions.

Tsung-Ting Kuo et al. [22]	*Blockchain distributed ledger technologies for biomedical and healthcare applications*	They discussed Bitcoin and its underlying Blockchain technology. They also provided an overview of the latest Blockchain healthcare applications by focusing on improved record management and advanced medical research process.
R. Deng et al. [23]	*CrowdBC: A Blockchain-based Decentralized Framework for Crowdsourcing*	They developed Proof of Weak Hands (PoWH 3D) on the Ethereum platform where users buy tokens to deal with a charge of 10% commission fee and similarly for seller side. Usually, this fee would be distributed among the token holders based on the average rate. Similar to this, many new games developed such as PoWL, PoWD, and PoWC.
Slomiany SD et al. [24]	*Multi-stage multi-bet dice game, gaming device, and method*	They designed BetDice (a roll-a-dice game) where the decision of game players that is win or loss made by rolling a dice. Here is one advantage that the smart contract chooses any target number from 1 to 100 and, thus, ensures fairness to the player. It is one of the famous DApps because of working on the EOS chain; there is no need to go for a gas fee or time delay.

Kharif O [25]	CryptoKitties mania overwhelms Ethereum network's processing	He designed Cryptokitties that is a simulation game developed on the Ethereum platform where the different functions implemented on kitties. The record was made in 2017 by creating massive active users that lead to a great sensation and jammed the Ethereum network.
Lee J *et al.* [26]	*Is a Blockchain-Based Game a Game for Fun, or Is It a Tool for Speculation? An Empirical Analysis of Player Behavior in Crypokitties*	They discussed about Etheremon which is also simulated on Ethereum and also a better version of Pokémon in the view of playability. Other than this, monster types and skill systems are an extended feature in Etheremon so that game would become more interesting. As such, players can capture and train Etheremon so that they can fight to play with each other.
Min T *et al.* [27]	*Blockchain games: A survey*	They developed EOS Knights which is simulated on EOS platform and players in their chosen characters can be used to combat with the monsters in the game but if virtual player loses the game, then they have to deal with their earned items in game play. The strategy of playing game is like if there are more armaments furnished on the virtual player in the game play, then they will earn more rewards, and hence, they are more powerful in the play.

Gordon and Catalini [28]	*Blockchain technology for healthcare: Facilitating the transition to patient-driven interoperability*	They discussed the capability of the Blockchain healthcare system by giving digital access rights, patient privacy in the network, and data invariability and also by managing an excessive amount of health data.
Daisuke *et al.* [29]	*Tamper-resistant mobile health using Blockchain technology*	They performed an experimental analysis of registering health data to the Hyperledger fabric Blockchain platform and for this; they have taken medical records through smartphones.
Anuraag *et al.* [30]	*Implementing Blockchains for Efficient Health Care: Systematic Review*	They discussed the management of healthcare in the Blockchain. They have studied in managing the security and privacy of health records on the cloud system by the use of Blockchain. They have presented the potential benefits as well as limitations of Blockchain in healthcare without any practical implementation and evaluation of the system.
Rouhani *et al.* [31]	*MediChainTM: A Secure Decentralized Medical Data Asset Management System*	They derived an approach to point out the limitations of types of Blockchain and also discussed the utility of the Hyperledger Blockchain platform for the health data managing system.

Wu and Tsai [32]	*Toward Blockchains for health-care systems: Applying the bilinear pairing technology to ensure privacy protection and accuracy in data sharing*	They proposed two network security–based algorithms and also for distributed health data systems. They discussed developing rules and regulations for the healthcare system for security purposes.
Shen *et al.* [33]	*MedChain: Efficient Healthcare Data Sharing via Blockchain*	They designed a system named MedChain for incorporating health data into Blockchain technology through the P2P network. MedChain generates health data through medical services that can be accessed from different sources on the cloud system.
Khezr *et al.* [34]	*Blockchain technology in healthcare: A comprehensive review and directions for future research*	They studied different challenges while managing health data and their respective solution using Blockchain technology. They discussed the latest research going on distributed ledger technology by presenting different possible use cases revolving around Blockchain technology.
Litchfield *et al.* [35]	*A Review of Issues in Healthcare Information Management Systems and Blockchain Solutions*	They presented some challenges faced in the security and privacy of health data. They also discussed the solution to these issues through the use of Blockchain technology.

Vora *et al.* [36]	*BHEEM: A Blockchain-Based Framework for Securing Electronic Health Records*	They presented a Blockchain technology to secure EHR against breaching of patient details and health data. Their framework was analyzed to observe the performance in terms of the demands of a patient, healthcare professionals, and stakeholders.
Zhang *et al.* [37]	*Blockchain Technology Use Cases in Healthcare*	They presented different use cases of healthcare Blockchain. They have also illustrated on potential benefits of the Blockchain healthcare system by providing effective healthcare design.
Siyal *et al.* [38]	*Applications of Blockchain Technology in Medicine and Healthcare: Challenges and Future Perspectives*	They studied the importance of smart contracts for healthcare units by rationalizing the whole process. They discussed the sensitivity of health data and the potentiality of Blockchain in reducing the data loss and preventing data fabrication by the use of secured ledger technology.

18.4   The Framework

Here, we come up with a conceptual framework (refer Figure 18.1). This model consists of two modules. First module explains the working principle behind the anthropomorphic gamification interface with Blockchain technology where generation of tokens (rewards) for every health player takes place with the help of smart contracts based on Ethereum platform. The anthropomorphic interface with layers of gamification in the architecture of underlying decentralized applications is the Blockchain's proof-of-work (POW) implied on game elements. Second module explains the

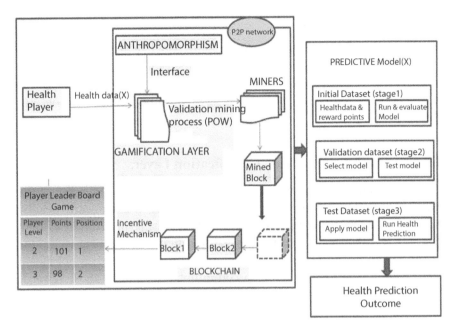

Figure 18.1 Framework of predictive modeling of anthropomorphic predictive modeling of anthropomorphic gamifying Blockchain-enabled transitional healthcare system.

predictive model for the health outcomes where reward points are taken as an input to evaluate it. By this framework, health players need not have to be familiar with the mind wrecking mining process as we are encapsulating the technical details to create a more appealing fun environment (Ganache GUI). With the help of this gamified mining, health players can earn reward points while doing health-related activities and compare them with other health players in the sense of competition among them. These reward points are going to decide the health of every player by the use of a predictive model, and thus, their focus on attaining better health can be achieved. Let us look at the functionalities of the components of the proposed framework.

18.4.1   Health Player

A health player is a patient with some chronic health issues. A sample size of 200 patients' health data was taken for the analysis of reward points and health prediction. We have taken those children and young people who suffered from some chronic diseases like, diabetes, asthma, cerebral palsy, and cancer.

18.4.2   Data Collection

The data comprises patient demographic details like age, weight, height, and also a record of daily activities like kilometer walked, heart rate, exercises, blood pressure, sleep score, and medicines intake. The age of the groups varied from the childhood stage, adulthood stage, and old-age stage.

18.4.3   Anthropomorphic Gamification Layers

The goal of anthropomorphic gamification is to make users aware of the implications of their healthy lifestyle, promoting them toward healthy behavior change, fostering resilience, and increasing motivation to fight diseases [6]. As we believe that in gamification, the popular technique using game progression rewards, trophies, badges, and points is not meant for engaging health players within communities as long as those rewards had no authentic assessment values [4]. Rather, it looks like an artificial form of achievement. Thus, there is a great requirement for adding authentic value (digital currency) to the points by using tokens. For this, we need to create an open standard where tokens are stored on the Blockchain so that a group of health players can easily store earned tokens in their Ethereum wallets. These tokens can be redeemed in the web store as payment for access to the health players which helps in creating a sustainable token economy and community. But, we know that medical data is always considered to be sensitive information and it needs to be protected from unapproved access. So, the main challenges of gamification in healthcare are patient privacy protection and medical data security. From all points of view, we propose Blockchain technology where we use smart contracts based on the Ethereum platform for creating unchangeable and safer utilization in the layer. Smart contracts are the building blocks of code that execute automatically applying the conditions of the agreement and commercial purpose like the game play in a secured fashion.

18.4.4   Ethereum

Ethereum is an open-source network and nowadays it is popular among active users for its Decentralization application (DApp) repository. The evolution of Blockchain technology always offers something new to our list of needs. This is possible due to consensus algorithms that make the Blockchain consensus sequence from each other. These algorithms are helping in making the majority group decision to include or support a new individual to join in that particular group by the voting mechanism. Presently, the Ethereum platform makes use of POW consensus algorithm. POW is important for security which prevents fraud and enables trust. But, it requires all nodes to participate in the transaction for the validation of new nodes on the network. Also, there are certain issues with it like greater computation power is required, and pure decentralization is not achieved. Ideally, the decentralization application tends to recognize insertion anomalies, update anomalies, and missing attributes on the ledger records. It is done by the main elements of the smart contract that are written in Solidity. For the deployment of the smart contracts, we go for the Remix network (or Kovan network), and to deploy on testnet ethers, we need to pay with gas. Paying with gas is required to reduce the usage of computation power and also time to execute the transactions. Sometimes, malicious operators and complex contracts may lead to an infinite loop on the server-side. These payable transaction fees are usually decided by the willingness of the users for each unit of gas.

18.4.4.1 Ethereum-Based Smart Contracts for Healthcare

Smart contracts based on Ethereum platform was coined by "Nick Szabo" in 1993. It is a state machine and needs transactions to change the state through the mining process. It can do logical operations as well. In a general term, it is used for protecting information written in Solidity which is in a high-level programming language, and then, it is compiled into "bytecode", known as Ethereum Virtual Machine (EVM). Then, this contract is executed by all participating nodes by the use of their Ethereum Virtual Machines. Thus, every node holds a copy of the transaction along with its history on the peer-to-peer network. It also maintains the track of the current "state" so that every activity performed by the health player can be utilized to earn reward points. Hence, the EVM finishes the execution of a contract with its regulations that are introduced by the developer.

18.4.4.2 Installation of Ethereum Smart Contract

The following are the steps to install Private Blockchain Network:

1. First of all, we install NodeJS for providing javascript environment that is web3.
2. Then, we install Geth terminal where we write entire command in Go Language.

3. After that we install Git terminal window just like Linux.
4. Further, we install Ethereum Wallet (stores and manages Ethereum accounts and transactions) or Metamask wallet (an extension where to transfer and deposit ethers).

18.4.5   Reward Model

The reward model is used to buffer the reward points that are evaluated on the basis of daily healthcare activities. It works on the basis of the push-based flow method to distribute rewards to all the health players accordingly. This method computes rewards per hour spent in performing activities and operating on-chain computational overhead to a significant extent. It can handle more number of health players at a given instant t, where active health players are engaged in doing healthcare activities, let us say for doing exercises and taking medicines, create distribute events in a given timeline T. For every health player,

$$totalreward_j = sum_t reward_{jt} = activities_j * sum_t \frac{reward}{T_t}$$

that is, total reward for every health patient is calculated on the basis of their routine-based healthcare activities in given timeline order and these rewards are stored in a table in chronological order which is further used in the predictive model.

18.4.6   Predictive Models

There exist many efficient and affordable predictive models because of the increase in the running capacity of thousands of models on multiple cores. What matters is the suitability of the predictive model for a given input dataset. So, it totally depends on the desirable nature of the predictive target. We have taken different machine learning algorithms to design a model. They are linear regression, logistic regression, support vector machine (SVM), artificial neural networks, etc.; the different machine algorithms work on different nature of data. Linear regression is used when we want to predict continuous values. Logistic regression is considered to be a more powerful statistical way of modeling a binomial result with one or more descriptive variables. It estimates the relationship between the categorical dependent variable by the use of the logistic function. Next is the SVM that can be used for binary classification and also for multi-class classification indirectly. It can be used for both linear and non-linear decision boundaries. The last one is an artificial neural network that can be used for multi-class classification and non-linear decision boundaries. The implementation of our chosen model depends on the best accuracy provider for the prediction of the health of the patients.

18.5   Implementation

This section gives a clear picture of our research tasks and of the processes through which our conceptual framework validates the goal of our research work. It explains the purpose of our research and the methodology behind it and, finally, assesses the reliability of our findings in the result analysis section.

18.5.1   Methodology

Initially, a health player with his avatar role participates in the game app and gives challenges by doing healthcare activities and then updates the records by the use of a tracker. The health player is initially given variable tokens. Then, the smart contracts based on the Ethereum platform compute rewards points (token) by the application of logical operations. Every activity performed results in the creation of tokens that is regarded as reward points. These reward points are computed based on the aforementioned formula in the reward model (refer Section 18.4.5). Those health players who are sincerely participate in the game play and perform every activity thoroughly gather the maximum reward points. These stored reward points of respective health players are further used for the analysis of health predictions.

Generally, predictive model comprised of different stages that include preparation of data, quality of data, reduction, simulation, prediction, and result analysis. At the first stage, we apply Principal component analysis (PCA) technique on our dataset. PCA method is an unsupervised machine learning algorithm which is used to reduce the number of features describing our dataset. Apart from this, the PCA method reduces the dimensionality with the motive of retaining information as much as possible. Next, at the second stage, we perform the transformation, center, and scaling feature on the test set as well. We compare logistic regression and SVM models based on their better accuracy. Thereafter, in the third stage, we select the appropriate ML model with the best accuracy for the health prediction of the patients.

18.5.2   Result Analysis

Before we begin with our health dataset, firstly, we need to think about the environment to deploy our smart contracts. We would like to use a local Blockchain that runs on our machine, requires no internet access, and most importantly provides all the Ethers that we need and mines block instantly. Hence, we have opted for Ganache as a local Blockchain. Here, we can see a list of accounts with their respective address, Ether balance, and other relative information (refer Figure 18.2). Accounts with their addresses are actually used for interacting with this Blockchain, and also, we have the list of transactions done in the local network (refer Figure 18.3).

We can have a visualization of the transaction in the Ganache GUI. Then, Web3JS is used to send the data block to the chain after the validation of the transaction is done. The stored reward table is then used by a predictive model. PCA (refer Figure 18.4) is used for feature reduction by extracting the important ones from a large pool. We have graphically represented a heat map of the correlation of features. Figure 18.5 shows the performance of different ML algorithms like logistic regression and SVM.

The performance of the logistic and SVM models is evaluated based on four factors: F1-score, recall, precision, and accuracy that are represented in the below figure (refer Figures 18.5A and B). F1-score is even more suitable for imbalanced class distribution and is more preferable than accuracy to evaluate the models. Next is precision which tells about the relevant output and recall shows whether the output is correctly classified. Thus,

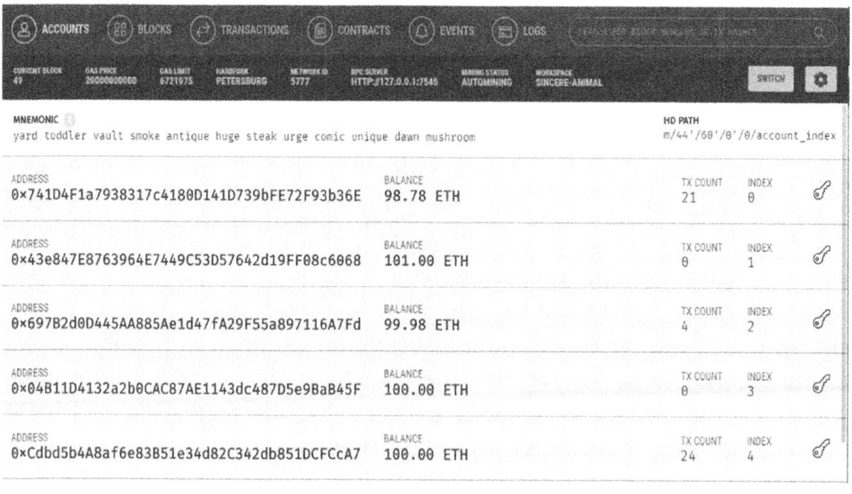

Figure 18.2 Accounts used in making transaction.

Figure 18.3 List of transactions on the network.

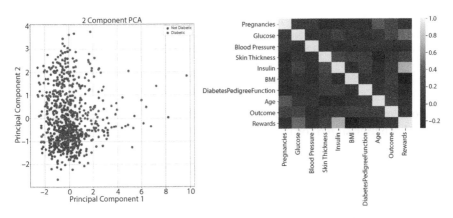

Figure 18.4 Principal component analysis on diabetes patient data and heat map of correlation of features of diabetes patient with their respective earned reward datasets.

logistic regression performs better than SVM in terms of four factors (refer Figures 18.5A and B).

The ROC curve (refer Figure 18.5C) for logistic regression helps in determining the best cutoff value for predicting whether a new observation is a "failure" or a success. As given in the figure, an AUC of 0.83 suggests excellent ability to predict patient health status. Logistic regression is considered to be better because of its 79% accuracy which is quite considerable

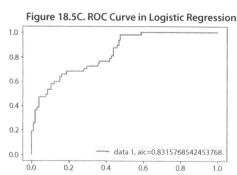

Figure 18.5A. Logistic Regression

	Precision	Recall	F1-Score	Support
0	0.82	0.90	0.86	107
1	0.70	0.55	0.62	47
Accuracy			0.79	154
Macro Avg.	0.76	0.73	0.74	154
Weighted Avg.	0.78	0.79	0.78	154

Figure 18.5B. Support Vector Machine

	Precision	Recall	F1-Score	Support
0	0.77	0.94	0.85	107
1	0.73	0.34	0.46	47
Accuracy			0.76	154
Macro Avg.	0.75	0.64	0.65	154
Weighted Avg.	0.75	0.76	0.73	154

Figure 18.5C. ROC Curve in Logistic Regression

data 1, aic=0.8315768542453768

Figure 18.5 Different ML algorithms' output for computing best predictive model. (A) Logistic regression. (B) Support vector machine. (C) ROC curve in logistic regression.

for our proposed model. It can be concluded that the logistic regression model is better suited for the prediction of the health status of the patient.

18.5.3   Threats to the Validity

Just as every coin has two sides; the proposed framework has also its limitations. One of the major issues with Ethereum is scalability; each smart contract and transaction has to regulate every node to be processed in the network before being validated. In terms of speed also, Ethereum limits 15 transactions per second and 1 million transactions per day as its full capacity, which clearly shows its limit.

Because of the scalability issue in Ethereum, researchers are working on EOS which can scale to millions of transactions per second. This would make it possible to raise the bar in handling the real-world application. Thus, EOS can help to revolutionize the healthcare industry into the most scalable Blockchain network.

18.6 Conclusion

This chapter introduced the fundamental of anthropomorphism that can be interfaced with gamification for better help to transitional healthcare patients. An implementation of the Ethereum Blockchain gamification with incentive mechanism is shown that engages and motivates health players to take care of their health in a lucrative manner. We have shown experimental results of the transaction of nodes while computing rewards to healthcare players. Further, we have shown the performance of selective predictive models in the prediction of the health outcome of any patient.

References

1. Zhang, P., White, J., Schmidt, D.C., Lenz, G., Rosenbloom, S.T., FHIRChain: applying Blockchain to securely and scalably share clinical data. *Comput. Struct. Biotechnol. J.*, 16, 267–278, 2018.
2. Banks, J. and Bowman, N.D., Emotion, anthropomorphism, realism, control: Validation of amerged metric for player–avatar interaction (PAX). *Comput. Hum. Behav.*, 54, 215–223, 2016.
3. Baranowski, T., Buday, R., Thompson, D.I., Baranowski, J., Playing for Real. Video Games and Stories for Health-Related Behavior Change. *Am. J. Prev. Med.*, 34, 1, 74–82, 2008.
4. Barata, G., Gama, S., Fonseca, M.J., Gonçalves, D., Jorge, J., Improving student creativity with gamification and virtual worlds, in: *Proceedings of the First International Conference on Gameful Design, Research, and Applications - Gamification '13 (ACM)*, pp. 95–98, 2013.
5. Bartneck, C., Kulić, D., Croft, E., Zoghbi, S., Measurement Instruments for the Anthropomorphism, Animacy, Likeability, Perceived Intelligence, and Perceived Safety of Robots. *Int. J. Soc. Rob.*, 1, 1, 71–81, 2009.
6. Bickmore, T.W., Pfeifer, L., Jack, B., Taking the time to care: empowering low health literacy hospital patients with virtual nurse agents, in: *Proceedings of the SIGCHI Conference on Human Factors in Computing Systems (ACM)*, pp. 1265–1274, 2009.
7. Birk, M.V., Atkins, C., Bowey, J.T., Mandryk, R.L., Fostering Intrinsic Motivation through Avatar Identification in Digital Games, in: *Proceedings of the 2016 CHI Conference on Human Factors in Computing Systems - CHI '16*, pp. 2982–2995, 2016.
8. Bogost, I., Why Gamification is Bullshit, in: *The Gameful World. Approaches, Issues, Applications*, S.P. Walz and S. Deterding (Eds.), pp. 65–80, The MIT Press, Cambridge, 2015.
9. Brewer, R., Anthony, L., Brown, Q., Irwin, G., Nias, J., Tate, B., Using Gamification to Motivate Children to Complete Empirical Studies in Lab

Environments, in: *Proceedings of the 12th International Conference on Interaction Design and Children (ACM)*, pp. 388–391, 2013.

10. Brockmyer, J.H., Fox, C.M., Curtiss, K.A., McBroom, E., Burkhart, K.M., Pidruzny, J.N., The development of the Game Engagement Questionnaire: A measure of engagement in video game-playing. *J. Exp. Soc. Psychol.*, 45, 4, 624–634, 2009.

11. Fox, C.M. and Brockmyer, J.H., The development of the game Engagement Questionnaire: A measure of engagement in video game playing: Response to reviews. *Interact. Comput.*, 25, 4, 290–3, 2013.

12. Çakiroğlu, Ü., Başibüyük, B., Güler, M., Atabay, M., Memiş, B.Y., Gamifying an ICT Course: Influences on Engagement and Academic Performance. *Comput. Hum. Behav.*, 12, 10, 98–107, 2016.

13. Cheong, C., Cheong, F., Filippou, J., Quick Quiz: A Gamified Approach for Enhancing Learning, in: *Proceedings of the 17th Pacific Asia Conference on Information Systems (PACIS 2013)*, pp. 1–14, 2013.

14. Cheong, Jung, Y., Theng, Y., Avatar: A Virtual Face for the Elderly, in: *Proceedings of the 10th International Conference on Virtual Reality Continuum and Its Applications in Industry (VRCAI '11)*, ACM, New York, NY, USA, pp. 491–498, 2011.

15. Dahl, G. and Kraus, M., Measuring how game feel is influenced by the player avatar's acceleration and deceleration, in: *Proceedings of the 19th International Academic Mindtrek Conference on - AcademicMindTrek '15*, pp. 41–46, 2015.

16. Daneman, D. and Nakhla, M., Moving on: transition of teen with type 1 diabetes to adult care. *Diabetes Spectr.*, 24, 1, 14–18, 2011.

17. Mull, I., Jamie, W., Moon, E., Lee, S.-E., An exploratory study of using 3D avatars as online salespeople. *J. Fash. Mark. Manage.*, 19, 2, 154–168, 2015.

18. Seaborn, K. and Fels, D.I., Gamification in theory and action: A survey. *Int. J. Hum.-Comput. Stud.*, 74, 14–31, 2015.

19. Barbieri, M.M. and Berger, J.O., Optimal predictive model selection. *Ann. Stat.*, 32, 3, 870–97, 2004.

20. Laud, P.W. and Ibrahim, J.G., Predictive model selection. *J. R. Stat. Soc.: Ser. B (Methodol.)*, 57, 1, 247–62, 1995.

21. Kuo, T.T. and Ohno-Machado, L., Modelchain: Decentralized privacy-preserving healthcare predictive modeling framework on private Blockchain networks. *arXiv preprint arXiv:1802.01746*, 28, 3, 340–456, 2017.

22. Kuo, T.T., Kim, H.E., Ohno-Machado, L., Blockchain distributed ledger technologies for biomedical and health care applications. *J. Am. Med. Inf. Assoc.*, 24, 6, 1211–20, 2017.

23. Deng, R., Liu, J.-N., Zhang, Y., Xiang, Y., Yang, A., Li, M., Hou, L., Weng, J., Lu, W., CrowdBC: A Blockchain-based Decentralized Framework for Crowdsourcing. *IEEE Trans. Parallel Distrib. Syst.*, 11, 1–8, 2018.

24. S.D. Slomiany, L.E. Demar, D.F. Brown, Inventors, Multi-stage multi-bet dice game, gaming device, and method. United States patent US 7,811,165. Patent, 2010.

25. Kharif, O., CryptoKitties mania overwhelms Ethereum network's processing, in: *Bloomberg*, vol. 4, pp. 34–42, 2017.

26. Lee, J., Yoo, B., Jang, M., Is a Blockchain-Based Game a Game for Fun, or Is It a Tool for Speculation? An Empirical Analysis of Player Behavior in Crypokitties, in: *Workshop on E-Business*, Springer, Cham, pp. 141–148, 2018.

27. Min, T., Wang, H., Guo, Y., Cai, W., Blockchain games: A survey, in: *2019 IEEE Conference on Games (CoG)*, vol. 6, pp. 1–8, 2019.

28. Gordon, W.J. and Catalini, C., Blockchain technology for healthcare: Facilitating the transition to patient-driven interoperability. *Comput. Struct. Biotechnol. J.*, 16, 224–230, 2018.

29. Daisuke, I., Kashiyama, M., Ueno, T., Tamper-resistant mobile health using Blockchain technology. *JMIR Mhealth Uhealth*, 5, 111–121, 2017.

30. Vazirani, A.A., O'Donoghue, O., Brindley, D., Meinert, E., Implementing Blockchains for Efficient Health Care: Systematic Review. *J. Med. Internet Res.*, 21, 439–451, 2019.

31. Rouhani, S., Butterworth, L., Simmons, A.D., Humphery, D.G., Deters, R., MediChainTM: A Secure Decentralized Medical Data Asset Management System, in: *Proceedings of the 2018 IEEE International Conference on Internet of Things*, vol. 3, pp. 332–340, 2018.

32. Wu, H.T. and Tsai, C.W., Toward Blockchains for health-care systems: Applying the bilinear pairing technology to ensure privacy protection and accuracy in data sharing. *IEEE Consum. Electron.*, 8, 65–71, 2018.

33. Shen, B., Guo, J., Yang, Y., MedChain: Efficient Healthcare Data Sharing via Blockchain. *Appl. Sci.*, 9, 1207–1215, 2019.

34. Khezr, S., Moniruzzaman, M., Yassine, A., Benlamri, R., Blockchain technology in healthcare: A comprehensive review and directions for future research. *Appl. Sci.*, 19, 9, 1736–1742, 2019.

35. Litchfield, A.T. and Khan, A., A Review of Issues in Healthcare Information Management Systems and Blockchain Solutions, in: *CONF-IRM*, vol. 454, pp. 3452–3460, 2019.

36. Vora, J., Nayyar, A., Tanwar, S., Tyagi, S., Kumar, N., Obaidat, M.S., Rodrigues, J.J., BHEEM: A Blockchain-Based Framework for Securing Electronic Health Records, in: *Proceedings of the 2018 IEEE Globecom Workshops (GC Wkshps)*, Abu Dhabi, UAE, vol. 1, pp. 10–18, 2018.

37. Zhang, P., Schmidt, D.C., White, J., Lenz, G., Blockchain Technology Use Cases in Healthcare, in: *Advances in Computers*, vol. 111, pp. 1–41, Elsevier, Amsterdam, The Netherlands, 2018.

38. Siyal, A., Junejo, A., Zawish, M., Ahmed, K., Khalil, A., Soursou, G., Applications of Blockchain Technologyin Medicine and Healthcare: Challenges and Future Perspectives. *Cryptography*, 3, 3–11, 2019.

39. D.J. McCauley and inventor, RZ Management Inc, assignee. Process for making a decorative metal slot machine token. United States patent US 6,616,983, 2003 Sep 9.

40. Kuramoto, I., Ishibashi, T., Yamamoto, K., Tsujino, Y., Stand up, heroes! Gamification for standing people on crowded public transportation, in: *The series of Lecture Notes in Computer Science*, vol. 8013, pp. 538–547, Springer, Berlin, Heidelberg, 2013.

41. Otake, K., Sumita, R., Oka, M., Shinozawa, Y., Uetake, T., Sakurai, A., A Proposal of a Support System for Motivation Improvement Using Gamification. *Lect. Notes Comput. Sci.*, 8531, 571–580, 2014.

42. Wilson, A.S. and McDonagh, J.E., A gamification model to encourage positive healthcare behaviours in young people with long term conditions, in: *EAI Endorsed Transactions on Game-Based Learning*, vol. 14(2), pp. 303–311, 2014.

43. Johnson, D., Deterding, S., Kuhn, K.A., Staneva, A., Stoyanov, S., Hides, L., Gamification: designing for motivation. In Google scholar Digital Library. *Internet interventions*, 19, 4, 14–21, 2012.

44. Hamari, J., Koivisto, J., Sarsa, H., Does gamification work? –a literature review of empirical studies on gamification, in: *47th Hawaii international conference on system sciences (IEEE)*, vol. 43, pp. 3025–3034, 2014.

45. Maslow, A.H., A Theory of Human Motivation. *Psychol. Rev.*, 50, 370–380, 1943.

46. Pink, D., *The Surprising Truth about What Motivates Us*, vol. 5, pp. 445–460, Riverhead, New York, 2009.

47. Keller, J., *Motivational Design for Learning and Performance: The ARCS Model Approach*, First Ed, vol. 1(1), pp. 54–64, Springer, New York, 2010.

48. Deci, E. and Ryan, R., *Intrinsic Motivation and Self-Determination in Human Behavior*, vol. 1(1), pp. 34–42, Plenum Press, New York, 1985.

49. Ryan, R. and Deci, E., Self-Determination Theory and the Facilitation of Intrinsic Motivation, Social Development, and Well-Being. *Am. Psychol.*, 55, 68–78, 2000.

Index

3-way, 126
5G networks, 398
  communication, 403
  content caching, 405
  data collection and sharing, 403
  device-to-device communication,
    403
  energy trading, 405
  federation learning, 403
  heterogeneity, 416
  interpretability, 418
  network virtualization management,
    403
  resource utilization, 417
  spectrum management, 404

Aadhar, 375
Accuracy, 464
AdaBoost, 63
Adani power, 347, 353, 357, 363, 366,
    369, 371
Advanced encryption standard, 110
AES, 124, 126, 157
AI (artificial intelligence), 1–3, 7, 11,
    16, 22, 54
AIaaS, 83
Alluring, 330
Amazon AWS, 145
Analytics,
Anthropomorphism, 465–467
Apache Hadoop, 378
APIs, 120, 128
Applications, 253

blood pressure monitoring, 260
body temperature monitoring, 261
electrocardiogram monitoring, 260
glucose level detection, 260
healthcare, 259, 260
oxygen saturation monitoring, 261
smart city, 256
smart energy and smart grid, 258
smart factory and industry 4.0, 256
smart farming, 254
smart home and smart metering,
  257
video surveillance, 258
weather forecasting, 258
Applications of ML,
  rules, 434
  terminology, 432
  unsupervised vs supervised, 434
Applications of unsupervised learning,
  advancements, 444
  effective marketing, 444
  faster computing, 444
  ML in voice assistance, 443
  regulation, 443
  the end note, 445
Applications using ML algos,
  decision tree, 446
  dimensionality reduction, 448
  gradient boosting, 448
  k-means, 447
  k-nearest, 447
  linear regression, 445
  logistics regression, 446

naïve byes, 446
random forest, 447
SVM, 446
ARCS model, 465, 480–481
Artificial intelligence, 41
As late as possible (ALAP) algorithm, 213–215
Association rule learning, 10
Asymmetric key cryptography, 149
Automobile, 347, 353, 357, 368
Autonomic protection, 138
Autonomic security, 137
Autonomic self-healing, 138
Autonomic systems, 137
Avatar, 463, 465–466
Average resource utilization (ARU), 201

Bacterial folio blight, 336
Bagging, 63
Banking, 347, 353, 357, 359
BDA, 54
Big data, 54
Biometrics, 135
BLE, 182
Block cipher, 124–127
Blockchain, 397, 479, 482–483
    consensus protocols, 415
    distributed ledger technology, 397
    resource management, 402
Blowfish, 112, 126, 158
Bootstrap, 63
BPaaS, 82
Brown folio spot, 336
Bull market, 348, 349
Business intelligence (BI), 168

CaaS, 82
Cardiac and atrial fibrillation, 173
Certificate authority (CA), 132
Challenges and issues, 234
    challenges for data management, 239

interoperability and standardization, 235
machine-machine communication, 238
personalization and adaptation, 236
virtualization and entity identification, 237
Chronic diseases or persistent disorders, 174
CIA, 151–152
Cipla limited, 353, 357–358, 371
Citizenship Amendment Act (CAA), 376
Classical cryptography, 147–149
Classification, 63
Cloud, 36
Cloud computing, 7, 26, 27, 38, 39, 144, 167, 196–197, 230
    feature of cloud computing, 231
Cloud computing over on-premises IT operation, 73–74
Cloud data, 37
Cloud deployment model, 77–79
Cloud provider, 103
Cloud security, 38
Cloud service model, 79–83
Cloud storage, 37
Cloud storage service, 38
Cloud-based data analysis techniques and models, 243
    directed acyclic graph (DAG), 245, 248
    Hadoop, 245–247
    MapReduce for data analysis, 243
    MapReduce, 243–245
    NoSQL, 243, 247, 248, 262
Cluster evolution, 282
Communication technologies, 241
    bluetooth low energy (BLE), 242
    digital enhanced cordless telecommunications ultra low, 242
    energy (DECT-ULE), 242

IEEE 802.11 (Wi-Fi), 242
IEEE802.15.4, 243
ITU-T G.9959, 243
narrowband IoT (NB-IoT), 243
near-field communication (NFC), 243
Sigfox, 242
Community cloud, 101
Confidential information, 122
Convolution neural network (CNN),
    181, 323, 329, 331, 342
Core attributes of cloud computing,
    75–77
Core components of cloud computing
    architecture, 83–84
Coronavirus, 349, 374
Cost, 201
Covert channels, 121
COVID-19, 349, 350, 369–371
Critical-path-on-a-processor (CPOP)
    algorithm, 208–210
Cross-site scripting (XSS) attack, 108
Cryptography, 119, 120, 123, 124
Cryptography algorithm, 123
Cryptoware, 33
CSP (cloud service provider), 119, 120
CSP accountability, 106
Curse of dimensionality, 12
Cyber attack, 31
Cyber crime, 26, 27, 33
Cyber security, 26, 30, 43, 45
Cyber threats, 31
Cyber warfare, 117
Cyber-fusion, 178

DaaS, 81
Data acquisition, 12
Data analysis, 1–4, 7, 13–17, 19
Data analytics, 167, 347–350, 352, 354,
    356, 358, 360, 362, 364, 366, 368,
    370, 372
Data archival, 103
Data breach, 108

Data cleaning, 14, 63
Data destruction, 104, 107
Data encryption standard (DES), 110
Data formats, 13
Data integration, 63
Data life cycle, 103, 104
Data loss, 108
Data mining, 55, 248, 250
    BIRCH (balanced iterative reducing
        and clustering using hierarchies),
        250
    clustering, 249, 250, 254, 255
    K-means clustering algorithm, 250
Data outsourcing, 108
Data persistence, 106
Data relocation, 108
Data representation, 16
Data security, 30
Data visualization, 15
DDoS, 153
DDoS attack, 45
Decision trees, 9, 56
Deep learning,
Demand prediction, 59
DES, 124, 126, 158
Descriptive analysis, 56
Desert locust (Schistocerca gregaria),
    324
Diffie-Hellman key exchange, 111
Digital certificates, 132
Digital network 5G, 175
Digital security, 26, 29
Directed acyclic graph (DAG), 197,
    201, 220
Distributed computing, 7
Distributed denial-of-service (DDoS),
    44
Domain name server (DNS) attack,
    109
DRaaS, 82
DRL, 399
    resource management, 401

DSA (digital signature algorithm), 112
Dual sink, 274

E-business, 53
Economy, 347–349
Edge computing, 6
Efficiency, 200–201
Elliptic curve cryptography (ECC), 113
Embedded sensors, 169
Environmental monitoring, 232
Error rate, 60
Estimated computation time (ECT), 199–200
Ethereum, 465, 480–481
Ethers, 462–463
Evaluating cloud infrastructure, 84–85
Evaluating cloud provider, 85–86
Evaluating cloud security, 86
Evaluating cloud service level agreements (SLA), 87
Evaluating cloud services, 86–87
Extrinsic motivation, 463

F1-score, 464, 466
Facial recognition, 60
Factors need to consider for cloud adoption, 84
Fast-moving consumer goods, 347, 362
FHE, 150
Financial prediction systems, 352–353, 355–357
Fog computing, 6

Game elements, 466
Gamification, 482
GBM, 57
GLM, 57
GOST, 125
Gradient boost algorithm, 56
Green cloud computing (GCC), 308
Green protection, 173
GUI processing, 179

Hadoop, 7, 20
Hadoop distributed file system (HDFS), 378–379
Hash cryptography, 148
HE, 149
Health player, 466–467
Heterogeneous earliest finish time (HEFT) algorithm, 202–203, 207–208
Heuristic algorithms, 201
Heuristics of task scheduling algorithms, 195–224
  heuristic task scheduling algorithms, 201–203, 207–215, 217–220
  major objective of scheduling, 198
  performance analysis and results, 220
  performance metrics, 200–201
  system computing model, 198
  task computational attributes for scheduling, 198–200
  workflow model, 197
Hindustan Unilever Limited, 363, 365
Histogram, 383
Hybrid cloud, 101
Hypothesis testing, 18

IaaS, 79
IAM (identity and access management), 114
ICICI bank, 347, 353, 357, 359–361, 371
Identity management, 133, 134
Imbalanced datasets, 11
Incentive, 467
Information and communication technologies (ICTs), 307
Information concealment engine (ICE), 126
Infrastructure as a service (IaaS), 102
Intellectual property (IP) rights, 121
Intelligent homes, 170

Internet, 348, 373
Internet security, 29
Intrinsic motivation, 467
Investors, 347–351, 353, 371
IoT (Internet of Things), 3–5, 7, 11, 27,
    40, 54, 167, 228–230, 234, 398
  clustering and data aggregation, 409
  content caching, 407
  D2D communication, 409
  heterogeneous networks, 411
  inference management, 408
  MIMO, 411
  mobility patterns, 411
  NOMA, 412
  power allocation, 408
  resource allocation for QoS, 408
  resource and cell selection, 410
  resource management, 402
  resource management in vehicular
      networks, 407
  security & privacy, 416
  spectrum sharing, 407
  traffic scheduling, 407
IoT cyber security, 35
IoT devices, 28
IoT service, 29
IP address, 36
ITC, 347, 353, 357, 363–364, 369, 371,
    374
ITU-T G.9959 (Z-Wave), 183

KASUMI, 127
Keras (neural network API), 330
Key distribution, 132
Key emerging trends in cloud
    computing, 89–94
Key management, 132
K-means, 57

Learning analysis, 20
Least square regression, 56
Limitations of cloud computing, 74

Limitations to cloud adoption, 87–88
Linear regression (LR), 350
Lockdown, 349, 373
Locust, 324
Locust Warning Organization (LWO),
    324
Logistic regression, 467
LOKI97, 125
Long-short term memory (LSTM),
    347, 352, 356, 371
LoRaWAN, 183

M2M, 54
Machine isolation, 107
Machine learning, 26, 27, 41, 43, 53,
    251, 253, 255, 256, 258, 259,
    347–375, 399
  artificial neural network (ANN),
      251
  support vector machines (SVMs),
      251
Machine learning techniques, 47, 49
Mahindra & Mahindra Limited,
    368–371
Malware, 32
Man-in-the-middle attack (MITM),
    109
MapReduce, 378
Market-based analysis, 21
Maruti Suzuki India Limited, 368,
    370–371
Maslow hierarchy of needs, 467
Mean-squared error (MSE), 354
Memory cards, 135
ML (machine learning), 1–3, 11, 12
ML model, 467
Motivation, 466, 479–480
MS/TP, 183
Multiple keys, 133

National population register (NPR), 375
NB-IoT, 183

Network security, 116
Network to network VPNs, 129
NFC, 183
NIST (National Institute of Standards and Technology), 112
NVIDIA deep learning accelerator (NVDLA), 182

Open source platform,
    caffe, 442
    keras, 441
    microsoft cognitive toolkit, 442
    scikit learn, 441
    tensor flow, 441
    theano, 442
    torch, 442
Outlier, 57
Overfitting, 12

PaaS, 80
Paillier cryptography, 159
Pandemic, 349, 369, 371
PARC model, 114
Passwords, 134
Performance effective task scheduling (PETS) algorithm, 217–220
Pharmaceutical, 347, 350, 353, 357
PHE, 149
Phishing, 32
Phishing attacks, 109
Platform as a service (PaaS), 102
PLC, 183
POCaaS, 83
Power, 353, 357, 363–369, 371
Power Grid Corporation of India Limited, 364–365, 367, 371
Precision, 481
Predictive data analytics, 53, 55
Predictive model, 482
Prescriptive analysis, 54
Private cloud, 101
Private data, 122
Probability, 61
Public cloud, 101

Public information, 122
Public key infrastructure (PKI), 132
Python, 352–353

R language, 61
Random forest, 63
Ransomware, 33
RC 2, 125
RC 5, 125
RC 6, 126
RC5 (rivest cipher ver.5) algorithm, 113
Recall, 484–485
Regression, 56
Regression analysis, 18
Reinforcement learning, 8, 10
Remote access VPNs, 129
Resource pooling, 100
Resource utilization, 201
Retail industry, 53
Rewards, 484–485
RFID, 5
RFID technologies, 177
RGB to HIS (hue, saturation, intensity), 332
ROC curve, 485
RSA, 157
RSA (Rivest, Shamir, and Adleman) algorithm, 111
RSA homomorphic, 160

SaaS, 80
Sales analytics, 59
Scale-processing, 168
Scheduling length ratio (SLR), 200
SECsaS, 81
Secure computation, 107
Security management, 122
Self determination theory, 484
Sensitive data, 122
Sensor alert service (SAS), 180
Sensor observation device (SOS), 180
Serialized global trade object (SGTIN-96), 177
Sigfox, 183

Smart cities, 167
Smart contract, 484
Smart environments, 169
Social distancing, 349, 370
Social engineering, 117
Software as a service (SaaS), 102
Solutions,
    closer look, 437, 438
    dictionary learning, 439
    insufficiency, 436
    overfitting, 437
    SVM, 439
    the latent, 440
    using ml, 436
Spear phishing, 33
Speedup, 200
Spyware, 33
STaaS, 81
State Bank of India, 359, 362
Stock market, 347–373
Supervised learning, 8, 41
Supply chain, 59
SVM, 484
SWHE, 150
Symmetric encryption, 112
Symmetric key cryptography, 124, 148
Syntactic assortments, 18

Technologies used for designing
    cloud-based data, 240
Tensor processing unit (TPU), 181
TensorFlow (software library by
    Google), 330
Three fish, 127
Time series, 57

Times-slotted channel humping
    (TSCH) modes, 182
Tokenization, 18
Tokens, 135
Torrent Pharmaceuticals Limited,
    359–360, 369, 371
Traffic analysis, 121
Transforming business through cloud,
    88–89
Transitional healthcare, 484
Triple data encryption system (3DES),
    110

Ubiquitious computing, 28
Ubiquitous network arrangement, 100
UIDAI, 377
Unet, 279
Unsupervised learning, 8, 10, 42

Verifiable computing, 107
Verticillium wilt of cotton, 336
Virtualization, 84
Visualization, 352, 355–357
VPN (virtual private network), 35,
    128–131, 308
VPN tunneling, 130

Wireless body area network, 273
Wireless technologies, 167
WLAN, 177
Wrapping attacks, 109

XaaS, 81

Yahoo finance, 352–353, 355–357